Conceptualizing International Practices

This book brings together the key scholars in the international practice debate to demonstrate its strengths as an innovative research perspective. The contributions show the benefit of practice theories in the study of phenomena in international security, international political economy and international organisation, by directing attention to concrete and observable everyday practices that shape international outcomes. The chapters exemplify the crossovers and relations to other theoretical approaches, and thereby establish practice theories as a distinct IR perspective. Each chapter investigates a key concept that plays an important role in international relations theory, such as power, norms, knowledge, change or cognition. Taken together, the authors make a strong case that practice theories allow to ask new questions, direct attention to uncommon empirical material, and reach different conclusions about international relations phenomena. The book is a must-read for anyone interested in recent international relations theory and the actual practices of doing global politics.

Alena Drieschova is Assistant Professor in International Relations at the University of Cambridge. She is currently working on her book manuscript, which provides a macro-historical analysis of international order stability and change based on changes in material culture.

Christian Bueger is Professor of International Relations at the University of Copenhagen, Honorary Professor at the University of Seychelles and a research fellow at the University of Stellenbosch. He is the author of *International Practice Theory* (2018, with Frank Gadinger).

Ted Hopf is a Research Fellow at the Helsinki Collegium of Advanced Studies. His main fields of interest are international relations theory, qualitative research methods, and identity. His article, 'Change in International Practices,' published in the *European Journal of International Relations*, received the European International Studies Association Award for Best Article in EJIR, in 2017.

Conceptualizing International Practices

Directions for the Practice Turn
in International Relations

Edited by

Alena Drieschova
University of Cambridge

Christian Bueger
University of Copenhagen

Ted Hopf
University of Helsinki

CAMBRIDGE
UNIVERSITY PRESS

CAMBRIDGE
UNIVERSITY PRESS

Shaftesbury Road, Cambridge CB2 8EA, United Kingdom

One Liberty Plaza, 20th Floor, New York, NY 10006, USA

477 Williamstown Road, Port Melbourne, VIC 3207, Australia

314–321, 3rd Floor, Plot 3, Splendor Forum, Jasola District Centre, New Delhi – 110025, India

103 Penang Road, #05–06/07, Visioncrest Commercial, Singapore 238467

Cambridge University Press is part of Cambridge University Press & Assessment, a department of the University of Cambridge.

We share the University's mission to contribute to society through the pursuit of education, learning and research at the highest international levels of excellence.

www.cambridge.org
Information on this title: www.cambridge.org/9781009055604

DOI: 10.1017/9781009052504

First published 2022
First paperback edition 2024

A catalogue record for this publication is available from the British Library

Library of Congress Cataloging-in-Publication data
Names: Drieschova, Alena, 1982– editor. |
Bueger, Christian, 1975– editor. | Hopf, Ted, 1959– editor.
Title: Conceptualizing international practices / edited by
Alena Drieschova, Christian Bueger, Ted Hopf.
Description: Cambridge, United Kingdom ; New York, NY : Cambridge
University Press, 2022. | Includes bibliographical references and index.
Identifiers: LCCN 2021059206 | ISBN 9781316511398 (hardback) |
ISBN 9781009052504 (ebook)
Subjects: LCSH: International relations – Philosophy. |
BISAC: POLITICAL SCIENCE / International Relations / General
Classification: LCC JZ1305 .C578 2022 | DDC 327.101–dc23/eng/20220125
LC record available at https://lccn.loc.gov/2021059206

ISBN   978-1-316-51139-8   Hardback
ISBN   978-1-009-05560-4   Paperback

Contents

Figures

Table

Contributors

EMANUEL ADLER is Professor Emeritus in the Department of Political Science at the University of Toronto and Bronfman Chair of Israeli Studies Emeritus at the Munk School of Global Affairs and Public Policy, Toronto.

JONATHAN LUKE AUSTIN is Assistant Professor of International Relations at the University of Copenhagen.

STEVEN BERNSTEIN is Distinguished Professor of Global Environmental and Sustainability Governance in the Department of Political Science at the University of Toronto and Co-Director of the Environmental Governance Lab at the Munk School of Global Affairs and Public Policy, Toronto.

CHRISTIAN BUEGER is Professor of International Relations in the Department of Political Science at the University of Copenhagen.

ALENA DRIESCHOVA University Assistant Professor in the Department of Politics and International Studies at the University of Cambridge and Postdoctoral Research Fellow at the Centre for Global Cooperation Research at the University of Duisburg-Essen.

JOELLE DUMOUCHEL is an independent researcher based in Montreal.

MICHAEL FAUBERT is a PhD candidate in the Department of Political Science at the University of Toronto.

FRANK GADINGER is Senior Researcher and Research Group Leader in the Centre for Global Cooperation Research at the University of Duisburg-Essen.

TED HOPF Research Fellow in the Helsinki Collegium for Advanced Studies at the University of Helsinki.

FRIEDRICH KRATOCHWIL is Professor Emeritus at the European University Institute in Florence.

MARION LAURENCE is Assistant Professor in the Department of Defence Studies at the Royal Military College of Canada, Kingston.

ANNA LEANDER is Professor of International Relations and Political Science at the Graduate Institute, Geneva, and at the Pontifical Catholic University of Rio de Janeiro (Pontifícia Universidade Católica do Rio de Janeiro [PUC-Rio]).

VINCENT POULIOT is James McGill Professor in the Department of Political Science of McGill University, Montreal.

HILMAR SCHÄFER is Visiting Professor in the Department of Social Sciences at the Humboldt University, Berlin.

WILLIAM WALTERS is Public Affairs Research Excellence Chair in the Department of Political Science and in the Department of Sociology and Anthropology at Carleton University in Ottawa.

Acknowledgements

Practice theorizing is a vibrant mode of analysis in International Relations (IR). Scholars have provided major alternative understandings of order, power and change by paying close attention to mundane activities, relations, tacit forms of knowledge and material objects. Over the years the debates have become richer not only in empirical terms, but also by relying on more diverse theoretical frameworks gathered from social theory and taking inspiration from science studies, psychology and anthropology, among other disciplines. Some practice scholars even develop new innovative approaches that are original to IR and might be exported from IR to other cognate disciplines.

Recognizing that the core strength of practice theorizing is its plurality and diversity was the starting point for this book. If this is the case, how could the debate be productively organized and steered into new directions? How could the conversation among practice theorizers and proponents of other cultural approaches be strengthened?

The answers we develop in this book take concepts as focal points around which conversations between various practice scholars and scholars from cognate approaches can develop. Concepts are major building blocks of any theory. Since many practice theorizers do not aim to work with rigid frameworks or advance general theory that can be tested, the status of concepts is even more important. Concepts provide intellectual anchors and sensitizing frameworks for the empirical work of practice scholars. The focus on concepts also allows us to re-tell the history of the concept of practice in interesting ways, as we show in the Introduction. The other chapters highlight how concepts form the grounds for conversations with practice theory's intellectual neighbours, such as institutionalism, norm constructivism and discourse theory. The concepts discussed moreover lay out new challenges and set a forward-looking course for the practice theorizing agenda.

Like other agenda-setting contributions, this book is the outcome of a collective effort that required many helping hands and support from different sources.

The dedication of all chapter authors to advance the practice debate through this concerted effort needs appraisal. The chapters went through various debates and rounds of revisions over the course of which the conversation between the chapters and their authors intensified, and we were able to identify a number of unforeseen links between debates and approaches. We are also grateful for the chapter authors' patience and responsiveness to editorial interventions.

The first author workshop titled 'Mapping Practices' was held at the School of Law and Politics at Cardiff University in October 2016, with generous funding from the Economic and Social Research Council's grant (ES/K008358/1) for the project 'Counter-Piracy Governance: A Praxiographic Analysis'.

Subsequently we are grateful to the International Studies Association which provided a grant for the 'Catalytic Research Workshop' scheme. This allowed us to continue our discussion. We met for a one-day workshop, under the new title 'Conceptualizing International Practices', at the International Studies Association Annual Convention in Baltimore in February 2017.

In September 2017, we also met at the European International Studies Association (EISA) Conference in Barcelona, as part of the section 'international practices'. In the section, the drafts of the book chapters were presented for the first time to a wider audience, and we also held a roundtable on the current challenges and future directions of practice theorizing. The section, co-founded by Christian Bueger and Alena Drieschova, has since been turned into a standing section of the EISA and has become the major annual hub for the discussion of international practice theorizing.

For their creative inputs and suggestions, we are grateful to Rebecca Adler-Nissen, Merje Kuus, Morten Andersen, Iver Neumann and Ole Jacob Sending, who participated in the first two workshops and provided great support and intellectual guidance afterwards.

Several other colleagues participated in some of the events and provided their time to act as chairs or discussants. We would like to thank Sara Dezalay, Hannes Hansen Magnusson, Hannah Hughes, and Peter Sutch who participated in the Cardiff Workshop.

A number of colleagues involved in the EISA section commented on drafts at different stages or provided support or suggestions in other ways. We thank Niklas Bremberg, Niels Byrjalsen, Jeremie Cornut, Scott Edwards, Kristin Annabel Eggeling, Alejandro Esguerra, Nina Graeger, Thomas Henökl, Gunther Hellmann, Jorg Kustermans, Max Lesch, Deepak Nair, Jon Harald Sande Lie, Dylan Loh, Sebastian Schindler, Øyvind Svendsen, Ole Waever, Antje Wiener and Tobias Wille.

Amaha Senu, Rupert Alcock and Jan Stockbruegger provided invaluable logistical and editing support. Organizing the workshops and panels and editing the book would not have been possible without their dedication.

A first draft of the full book was submitted to Cambridge University Press in 2019. We thank John Haslam for his support in this process as well as the two anonymous reviewers for their insightful comments on the first draft of the manuscript.

For institutional support Christian Bueger wishes to thank Cardiff University, the University of Stellenbosch, the Asia Research Center of the National University of Singapore and the Department of Political Science, University of Copenhagen, all of which provided the space and time to work on this manuscript at various stages. He also acknowledges the support from the Economic and Social Research Council of the UK (ES/K008358/1; ES/S008810/1), the British Academy (GF16007) and the Danish Ministry of Foreign Affairs (DANIDA/AMARIS).

Alena Drieschova is grateful to Cardiff University for providing institutional and financial support to carry out the bulk of the research related to this project. She also wants to thank the Centre of Global Cooperation Research/Käthe Hamburger Kolleg of the University of Duisburg-Essen for a research fellowship that permitted her to finalize the last steps of this book manuscript.

Ted Hopf thanks the National University of Singapore for its institutional support as well as Deepak Nair and Srdjan Vucetic.

Part I

Introduction: Conversations and the Evolution of Practice Theorizing

1 Conceptualizing International Practices
Establishing a Research Agenda in Conversations

Alena Drieschova and Christian Bueger

The practice turn arrived in International Relations (IR) because it had become obvious to many that what goes on in international politics every day was largely ignored by IR theory. While many scholars were focused on what elites said and wrote, not many were paying attention to what they, let alone people in general, actually did. Notably, practice scholarship highlights a significant gap between IR scholars' theoretical endeavours and how practitioners of international politics themselves understand what they are doing. It thus allows scholars to shed light on phenomena that have hitherto been at the margins of IR scholarship. When we examine in microscopic detail how state representatives actually conduct negotiations, how international organizations operate or how wars are being fought, we find a series of puzzling phenomena that shape IR. For example, by zooming in on how the permanent representatives of member states negotiate in the European Union, Adler-Nissen and Drieschova (2019) found that, contrary to bargaining theory and rational choice approaches, diplomats reach compromises by editing text. When there are many parties to negotiations that operate at high speed, diplomats can occasionally lose track of the circulation of texts and even agree to something that none of the negotiating parties intended. Such practical activities tend to be overlooked by the more macroscopic generalization-driven scopes that IR scholarship often adopts, be it in the form of large N-studies, grand theory development, causal hypothesis testing or theoretical modelling.

The often unconscious and habitual doings and sayings of people make a difference to international political outcomes. Random coincidences and encounters with technologies matter, whether it is struggling with a bureaucratic form, or the glitches of a social media account. Everyone may potentially be involved in politics, be it interpreters who work in the UN General Assembly or farmers who help to smuggle migrants across their territory. As Walters observes (Chapter 6), everyday practices of farmers in southern France can operate as resistance against the state's migration policies. Farmers smuggle migrants across borders, not for profit, but out of a sense of moral obligation. Only a practice perspective allows us to identify these activities as part of the making of world politics, as it is the practices of not-for-profit smuggling that give meaning to the farmers' resistance. Austin and Leander (Chapter 10), in turn, show how aesthetic practices of making torture invisible, and the more or less competent performances of these practices of rendering invisibility, lead world public opinion to perceive some state regimes, such as the Syrian one, as crueller than others, for example the United States.

Several scholars, each from a slightly different theoretical angle, have introduced into IR scholarship practices as an ontological phenomenon and analytical framework, and they have spelled out the spectrum and consequences of the practice turn for the field (Adler and Pouliot, 2011a, 2011b; Bueger and Gadinger, 2015, 2018; Hopf, 2010; Neumann, 2002; Pouliot, 2010). Other works have explored the internal theoretical diversity of practice theories (Frost and Lechner, 2016b). And still others have advocated for a distinct version of practice theory to analyse and interpret specific phenomena in IR with the help of the work of Luc Boltanski (Gadinger, 2016), Pierre Bourdieu (Eagleton-Pierce, 2013; Mérand, 2008; Pouliot, 2010), Michel DeCerteau (Neumann, 2002), Michel Foucault (Neumann and Sending, 2010; Walters, 2012), Gilles Deleuze (Acuto and Curtis, 2013), Erving Goffman (Adler-Nissen, 2014), Karin Knorr Cetina (Bueger, 2015), Bruno Latour (Bueger and Gadinger, 2007; Walters, 2002), Theodore Schatzki (Bially Mattern, 2011; Navari, 2011), Etienne Wenger (Adler, 2005, 2019) and Ludwig Wittgenstein (Frost and Lechner, 2016a; Grimmel and Hellmann, 2019), among others.

These theoretical approaches have informed the study of a wide range of empirical phenomena, ranging from the workings of international organizations (Bueger, 2015; Pouliot, 2016a) and global governance (Best and Gheciu, 2014a; Neumann and Sending, 2010) to processes of European integration (Adler-Nissen, 2016; McNamara, 2015), international law (Brunnée and Toope, 2010), the international political economy (Eagleton-Pierce, 2013; Seabrooke, 2012), peace-building (Autesserre, 2014), diplomacy (Neumann, 2002; Sending et al., 2015), security (Abrahamsen and Williams, 2011; Adler-Nissen and Pouliot, 2014; Mérand, 2008; Villumsen, 2015) and war (Sylvester, 2012).

With so much theoretical and empirical work already in place, it seems to be the right time to reflect and clarify in what ways the community of practice scholars shares a common agenda that is broad enough to allow for disagreements and controversies but is also recognizable as a dedicated form of IR scholarship. This implies further elaborating what forms the convergence among practice scholars, but also invites discussion of the boundary zones to other forms of IR theorizing, in particular constructivism. To date no explicit collective discussion has taken shape about the contours that define the practice turn in IR as a distinct set of theoretical approaches, or about the added value of practice theories in general compared with other IR approaches. The purpose of this edited volume is to do precisely that. It provides a clearly laid out understanding of practice theories as an analytical vocabulary with a history anchored in IR theory that can grasp the diversity of practice scholarship on the one hand but also provide a shared direction on the other.

In IR, theoretical approaches have sometimes coalesced around a single monograph, such as Waltz's (1979) *Theory of International Politics* or Wendt's (1999) *Social Theory of International Politics,* which have provided the core to neorealism and constructivism, respectively. In many ways, these texts established an authoritative, quite complete and closed statement around which other texts of the given theoretical approach have grouped. While a *Practical Theory of International Politics* might be in the making, scholars engaged in the practice turn do not consider practice approaches to lend themselves to grand theory-making. Practice theories differ. In the words of Nicolini (2013: 9), 'while [practice-theoretical approaches] can be compared to the tributaries of a lake (the "grand lake" of practice-based approaches) they do not contribute to a "grand" theory of practice and form; instead, they comprise a complicated network of similarities and dissimilarities'. Practice approaches do not appear to lend themselves to a definitive canonical and internally complete text that provides a firm foundation on which others can build. Perhaps this is so because of the ways in which practice scholarship has developed in the discipline of IR, with one of its most authoritative texts so far being an edited volume (Adler and Pouliot, 2011c), followed by an emerging plurality of practice voices. Another reason could be the world view that emerges once we direct our attention to practices as the fundamental ontological entities.

Instead of a canonical text this volume proposes a new way for setting out the intellectual identity of practice scholarship and how it relates to other forms of IR research. Concepts, rather than generalized systems of assertions (theory), provide the building blocks of international practice theorizing and allow for unity in diversity (see Chapter 12). Concepts also allow for more ready comparison with existing streams of IR thought, hence highlighting precisely what the contributions of practice theories are to broader debates. How scholars agree and diverge over the meaning and use of concepts, and how they are shared with other approaches in IR, provides the contours of international practice theorizing. The volume thus structures its discussion around concepts. This helps to open up collective, dynamic and necessarily open-ended conversations to explain different practice-theoretical approaches. The contributions to the volume look at practices through the prism of a key concept in IR (such as power, norms or change) and engage with their interlocutors through that prism. Each chapter showcases how a practice-theoretical understanding sheds new light on familiar IR concepts or introduces an underexplored one. This allows scholars to ask different kinds of questions, direct attention to uncommon empirical material and reach new conclusions about IR phenomena. Each chapter has an empirical illustration that showcases how practice theories provide a gateway to new empirical insights. A focus on key concepts allows for conversations with other IR theoretical approaches and enables conversations and debates within practice theorizing. Each chapter engages in cross-linkages and conversations with other concepts developed in the volume. The outcome is an intellectual clarification of the promises, contours and challenges of practice theorizing and associated research. On the basis of collective conversations rather than canonical texts, the volume situates practice research as a distinct set of theoretical perspectives in the discipline and outlines the agenda for their further advancement.

In this Introduction, we first identify the value-added of practice theorizing for IR scholarship. Next, we provide a narrative of the evolution of practice-theoretical thinking in IR. This is to demonstrate that such research in many ways advances earlier thoughts expressed in the discipline, but also to argue that practice-driven research breaks with existing ideas in significant ways. With this narrative we respond to some allegations and misunderstandings within the discipline that the practice talk is plainly a reinvigoration of old ideas, that there is little new about practice approaches or that they present us with a new version of constructivism (McCourt, 2016; Ringmar, 2014). Third, we proceed in discussing the scope and contours of practice-driven research by discussing how the practice debate might be ordered. Arguing against pitching discrete practice approaches against each other, we draw attention to a number of fault lines that run through the practice debate. We then showcase how each chapter in this volume engages with broader IR scholarship, and how it provides a new practice-driven vista on relevant IR questions.

The Value-Added of Practice Theorizing in IR

For practice scholars, quotidian and more aggregated practices matter. Central banking is, for example, an aggregated practice composed of many individual practices. As an aggregated practice, central banking had a specific historical starting point and went through an evolution with important consequences for international political economy (see Dumouchel, Chapter 7). Yet even seemingly mundane practices can make a difference. The outcomes of international negotiations are not only influenced by calculations of the national interest, material capabilities, and norms, but also by small practical details. Quotidian details have an effect, such as at what point in the process negotiators are served a drink, have a smoke, when a light lunch or big meals are provided, how the chairman of the negotiation is dressed, or what degree of language proficiency participants possess (Adler-Nissen and Drieschova, 2019). When alcohol starts rolling in the Council of Ministers of the European Union, the diplomats may become each other's best friends. They frequently pat each other on the shoulder, the negotiations become more amicable and agreeable. A hungry stomach (as well as sleep deprivation), in turn, can lead negotiators to more easily accept an agreement to be able to break for lunch (or finally get some rest). It might not be a coincidence that many multilateral agreements are reached in the early hours of the morning. If diplomats lack adequate language proficiency, and so perform incompetently, their interlocutors might not understand their negotiating position appropriately, and the misunderstood diplomats will not be able to adequately defend their national interest.

Rather than focusing on the motivations in people's heads, or structures of power and meaning, practice scholars direct attention to concrete and observable processes and patterns of activities that shape international outcomes, or to the norms that underlie such activities. They start from a conception of human nature that accentuates the entanglement of conscious and unconscious processes and focuses on situated and embodied action in concrete places, or that highlights the dispersion of global practices. They hence oppose Cartesian assumptions of human beings as disembodied minds wandering in a stylized world. Practical reasoning emerges as an analytical category that is distinct from instrumentalist calculations or technical rule following (Adler, 2019; Bourdieu, 1990; Pouliot, 2008; Kratochwil, Chapter 11). The goal is not to derive abstract theoretical models with universal generalizability. Experience-near research methodologies, such as participant observation and ethnography, lead many practice scholars to favour more inductive or abductive research designs through which they develop empirically grounded, and spatially and temporally specified theoretical perspectives.[1] In the process, practice scholars often uncover and demonstrate the surprising effects of

---

[1] An abductive approach moves back and forth between deduction and induction, between theoretical generalities and empirical specificity.

actors, things and processes that might be deemed trivial from the outset in formalized models of theory. Some scholars adopt a more macroscopic lens and historicize practices to get a better understanding of change over time (Go, 2008; Nexon and Neumann, 2018). For instance, Lechner and Frost (2018: 3) conceive of practices as 'an institution which constitutes a meaningful framework for interaction' and focus on global practices, such as non-intervention. Adler (2019) develops a perspective of cognitive evolution to understand how social orders remain meta-stable or change over time through changes and adaptations in practices. Or scholars study anchoring practices and analyse how specific key practices hold societies together by creating a foundational scaffold on which other practices depend (Sending and Neumann, 2011; Swidler, 2001).

Given that a focus on practices has the potential to shed light on the phenomena conventional IR scholarship was at pains to explain, a quite significant number of scholars turned to developing practice-based research and theories. After a series of prolific publications introduced the notion of practices as a distinct ontological phenomenon to the discipline (Adler and Pouliot, 2011a, 2011b; Neumann, 2002), International Practice Theories (IPT) have become a strong voice in the repertoire of IR theory over the last decade. Practice-driven research remains a set of very young, elastic and dynamic theoretical approaches to the study of IR.

Several promises are associated with practice as an analytical lens. Most importantly perhaps, the focus on practice promises empirical insights into the working of IR that have gone unnoticed so far (Pouliot, 2008). It is also seen as opening up avenues for cross-paradigmatic debates (Adler and Pouliot, 2011a). 'It offers a way out of Procrustean yet seemingly inescapable categories, such as subject and object, representation and represented, conceptual scheme and content, belief and desire, structure and action, rules and their application, micro and macro, individual and totality' (Stern, 2003: 185). It promises research that is more perceptive to short-term change and the transformation of order and power relations (Adler, 2019; Neumann, 2002). And lastly, it creates possibilities for engaging in forms of knowledge production that have practical value and are carried out through different forms of collaboration with practitioners (Eikeland and Nicolini, 2011; Tickner, 2014). An expanding community of scholars has seized the opportunity practice theories provide for understanding world politics, developing new kinds of theory and engaging in new forms of empirical analysis. Indeed, the practice turn appears to be one of the most productive theoretical and empirical endeavours of IR scholarship in the present decade.

Border Zones: The Evolution of Practice Thinking in IR

Practice theorizing has not developed from nowhere. Practice-theoretical thinking has seen quite an evolution, and in consequence the list of ancestors is long. It makes little sense to draw out a fully fledged history of the concept of practice (or practice as it relates to the international). Let us point to some of the ways in which the concept of practice has emerged in the discipline before the phrase 'practice turn' was introduced. This brief historical narrative, like any other, is incomplete and highlights certain developments, while underplaying others. If we cannot offer a 'representative' narrative (whatever this may mean), we have two goals. First, revisiting the history of practice thinking in IR allows us to understand where some of the divergences within practice thought come from. Second, it provides us an understanding of the 'border zones' that exist between practice theories and other research programmes in IR.

Historical sketches of practice thinking written in other disciplinary contexts have alluded to the importance of a range of theoretical predecessors (see Freeman et al., 2011; Guzman, 2013; Hillebrandt, 2014; Miettinen et al., 2009). Aristotelian philosophy, Francis Bacon's relational understanding of science and Karl Marx's Feuerbach Theses are emphasized. These thoughts find continuation in the work of Antonio Gramsci, American pragmatists such as John Dewey and George Herbert Mead, the later works of Ludwig Wittgenstein, and the philosophy of Martin Heidegger. More contemporary thinkers, who have been influential for practice scholarship include Hannah Arendt, Pierre Bourdieu, Michel de Certeau, Gilles Deleuze, Jacques Derrida, Harold Garfinkel, Erwin Goffmann, Michel Foucault, Anthony Giddens, Jürgen Habermas, Thomas Kuhn, Richard Rorty and William Sewell – a list which could without doubt be extended substantially. As Hillebrandt (2014) observed, in particular in two emerging disciplines – science studies and cultural studies – these ideas were taken forward to form a sort of collective movement that speaks about a 'practice turn' (see Schatzki et al., 2001).[2] Following these leads, a number of other empirically oriented social science disciplines picked up these ideas. Especially in organization studies, educational sociology and policy studies, the idea of turning to practice gained a strong foothold from the late 1990s. Indeed, in organization studies, a quite extensive series of collective

---

[2] It is revealing that the majority of contributors to the edited volume which is hailed as kick-starting the talk about a practice turn are situated in science studies.

publications, even including a handbook devoted to the practice turn (Golsorkhi et al., 2010), documents the strength of the field. IR is therefore to be seen as a relative latecomer to practice theorizing.

For understanding the trajectory of practice thinking in IR, some of the ancestors important in other disciplines, such as the work of Kurt Lewin or of Chris Argyris and Donald Schon in the 1970s, are largely irrelevant. Each of the social sciences has developed its own trajectory towards practices. In IR, prior to the practice turn, practice thought emerged in several different strands of scholarship. Many of these strands present versions of what is conventionally described in the discipline as 'constructivism'.[3] Practice theorizing is rooted in post-positivism and closely related to the interpretive, hermeneutic, phenomenological or post-structuralist traditions to knowledge production. These have often in the discipline been equated to constructivism. As such, the history of practice theorizing, at least in methodological terms, is closely tied to the rise of constructivist thought in IR.

All of the strands presented in the following sections of this Introduction have contributed to shaping the practice turn in IR, and they continue to be close 'neighbours' to practice theorizing, with which they share substantial 'border zones'.

Practice Thinking in IR: A Short History

The first strand of IR scholarship that theorized practices was *pragmatism*. Although hardly recognized by the writers of disciplinary history, pragmatism is a sort of hidden paradigm in IR. Its authors have focused on questions of knowledge and action. A line of thought, influenced by American pragmatism, stretching from the work of David Mitrany and Karl Deutsch to Ernst Haas, John Ruggie and Emanuel Adler, argued that the foundation of IR is epistemic. Approaches such as the epistemic community framework relied, for instance, on ideas presented by Thomas Kuhn and acknowledged the importance of the practical conditions of knowledge production. The core focus of this pragmatist research has been to understand how knowledge is produced and relates to (international) action. Although emphasizing key categories of importance in practice thinking, these scholars did not focus their work on the concept of practice. With the arrival of culturalist theorizing and the reception of the linguistic turn in the discipline in the late 1980s and early 1990s (Ashley, 1989; Ashley and Walker, 1990;

---

[3] As many authors have pointed out, the term 'constructivism' is ambiguous and has served to cluster together various forms of theorizing. For a recent re-construction, see Kessler (2016).

Lapid, 1989; Lapid and Kratochwil, 1996), a first generation of practice theorizing emerged. As the concept of practice started to be used substantially, pragmatism saw a renaissance. Indeed, Neumann's (2002) influential introduction of practice theorizing was published as part of a special issue on pragmatism.

Constructivists, influenced by Wittgensteinian thought, constitute the second line of reasoning. This was particularly evident in the work of Kratochwil (1989) and Onuf (1989). Two ideas were central. First, the concept of 'rule following' implied that rules do not contain the rules of their application and are hence dependent on practical knowledge and practical reasoning. Second, the concept of 'speech acts' drew attention not only to the importance of 'speaking' – a vital component of widespread definitions of practice – but also led to the recognition that language is not only, or primarily, descriptive, but productive or performative of realities. In these works, practice is used considerably as an important concept. For instance, Koslowski and Kratochwil (1994: 216) foreshadowed the practice-theoretical argument when they suggested that 'any given international system does not exist because of immutable structures, but rather the very structures are dependent for their reproduction on the practices of the actors'. Transformations occur 'when actors, through their practices, change the rules and norms constitutive of international interaction' (Koslowski and Kratochwil, 1994: 216). If many important practice-theoretical ideas started to be expressed in these works, their major theoretical focus was a different one.

Third, the work of Anthony Giddens visibly influenced the discipline. This was largely the result of Wendt's (1987) translation work, which soon – despite the protests of the Wittgensteinians (Kratochwil, 2000; Onuf, 2002) – became recognized as the authoritative voice of constructivism. For Wendt, the work of Giddens was of particular importance to make the discipline aware of the 'agency-structure' problematique. Giddens not only provided the foundations for a meticulous reconstruction of the dilemma (see Wendt, 1987: 356ff),[4] he also provided an innovative solution in that he proposed the concept of practice. Following Giddens, practices negotiate between structure and agency[5] – an insight that shaped the discussion in IR's agency and structure debate, but did not lead to substantial interest in

[4] Wendt used the broader term structuration theory to refer to his work and also included Roy Bashkar and Pierre Bourdieu in this category.
[5] For a detailed reconstruction and critique of the practice theory of Giddens, see Nicolini (2013).

further conceptualizing the notion of practices, as Doty (1997) noted. Nonetheless, Wendt introduced an important practice-theoretical thinker to IR, whose insights for practice theorizing remain to this date underdeveloped in the discipline.

Fourth, neo-institutionalist theory, arriving in the discipline from sociology, provided another line of reasoning. In particular, in March and Olson's (1998) foundational text, practice is an important category. Indeed, institutions were defined in neo-institutional theory as 'settled practices'. Although, in the majority of studies, practice remains an abstract concept rarely filled with empirical content, since the concept of institution does all the work, scholars such as Michael Barnett and Martha Finnemore who develop neo-institutionalism stress the significance of institutional culture as action (e.g. in Barnett and Finnemore, 2004). Recent scholarship within neo-institutionalism is concerned with the concept of 'routine', which has many affinities with the concept of practice.[6]

Fifth, post-structuralist thoughts gained traction with the turn to culturalist theories in the discipline in the late 1980s and early 1990s. Indeed, the first article we could identify in a major IR journal that extensively draws on the concept of practice develops a post-structuralist perspective. In a 1988 article in *International Studies Quarterly*, Shapiro, Bonham and Heradstveit (1988) argued for the importance of what they called 'discursive practices'. The emphasis on practices here highlights the contingency of structures of meaning. It points to the need that such structures require to be constantly enacted to have constitutive effects on the identity construction of subjects and on policy practices (Doty, 1993; Hansen, 2006; Milliken, 1999). Practices became the concept to study how discourses are contested and how in these processes of contestation some become hegemonic, while others turn into subjugated knowledges (Ashley, 1989; Doty, 1996; Milliken, 1999). While a focus on discursive practices primarily directed attention to the constitutive dimension of linguistic practices, the notion of speech acts – acting through speaking – already vital in the work of the Wittgensteinian-influenced constructivists, added an emphasis on the material context in which words are uttered and on their direct material consequences. The focus is on speech as a performance in the world, which leaves a felt impact (Buzan and Waever, 2003; Waever, 1995).

---

[6] See, in particular, the development within organizational sociology, where much of the neo-institutionalist theorizing is driven forward. See e.g. Miettinen and Virkkunen (2005) for a summary and discussion.

Sixth, for feminists, gendered practices of discrimination have formed a key object of their study. While postmodern feminists focused on how gendered roles are created in language (Zalewski, 2000), many others looked at the micro-level political practices that have an impact on women. Among the different research programmes in IR, feminism was perhaps the one which took the embodied nature of practices the most seriously. Simultaneously, with their emancipatory focus, feminists have highlighted the contingency of practices, but also their structural effects on creating gendered forms of discrimination (Goldstein, 2001; Tickner, 1997). Feminist scholars have conducted deep ethnographic research to develop experiential knowledge of everyday IR practices and highlight the often hidden, yet key, role that women perform in international politics. They analysed such phenomena as the gendered practices of conflict resolution (Tickner, 2014), practices of social mobilization (True, 2003), international business practices (Hooper, 2001), practices of prostitution around military bases as forms of diplomacy (Moon, 1997) and practices of rape as a weapon of war (Enloe, 2000). The goal of this research has been to develop 'practical knowledge' (Tickner, 2014: 22), that is, not only knowledge about micro-level practices but also applicable knowledge which can contribute to the emancipation of women (True, 2008). To achieve this goal, already in 2005, feminist IR scholars advocated innovative research strategies, such as participatory action research, which are now gaining more widespread traction in IR (Tickner, 2005). In sum, feminist scholarship has developed a rich understanding of practices on which the current turn to practice could perhaps rely more than it has done hitherto. Feminists, in turn, could gain new theoretical insights from practice theorizing in IR but have so far been reluctant to fully engage with the approach. The reason for this may be that they have been studying practices for a long time now and feel that they might not have much to gain from the turn to practices, and, moreover, their engagement with practices has not been fully acknowledged.

Seventh, a range of other theoretical perspectives needs to be taken into account. These perspectives have influenced the practice debate, albeit often more implicitly. Like feminist thought, Marxist scholarship has an emancipatory dimension and is interested in the practical activities that can lead to change in social reality. The objective for Marxists is to develop theories that inform practices, which will then render the theories obsolete, because they will lead to a change in social reality (Kilminster, 1982). Rather than studying practices per se then, Marxists have focused on developing theories with practical value.

Approaches that have not primarily studied the social constitution of reality have also paid attention to the role of practices. Classical realism, for example, deemed 'practical reasoning' a key element for good state-craft (Brown, 2012). Classical realists have emphasized the importance of statesmen's prudence and practical wisdom for conducting sound foreign policies. Practical experience in the real world is key, and theo-retical knowledge derived from studies only plays a supporting role. These kinds of practical experience come with age, and older statesmen appear to be more adept in conducting sound foreign policies. Classical realist scholarship differs from current practice theory work, however, in that it focuses on the intellect and entirely omits one of the key foci of international practice theories, namely embodied habitual action.

Moreover, in English School scholarship, practice serves a role, albeit subordinate to norms and rules. Thus, in his study of interna-tional order, Bull highlights 'rules of general application, like the rules of coexistence, arise out of custom and established practice, and are in some cases confirmed by multilateral conventions' (Bull, 2012: 68). For Bull, international order is maintained by institutions such as diplo-macy, war, international law and the balance of power. These insti-tutions can easily be studied from a practice perspective if the focus shifts slightly from the normative dimension to practical doings. Other English school scholars have similarly concentrated their attention on the normative side of practices – for example, Wight (1966) and Watson (1982) in their work on diplomacy. Bain (2003) and Jackson (2000) have made use of the notion of practices to get a better understand-ing of prevailing norms, but in doing so they often failed to study the actual material manifestations of practices; rather, they concentrated on the analyses of texts about practices (Navari, 2011). In their work, they were inspired by Oakshott's conception of 'practical activity' that is 'rule-governed' (Navari, 2011: 615).

These approaches all gave the concept of practice some prominence in IR. They hence allowed for core ideas that shape today's practice thinking to gradually influence the discipline's theory debates and opened up the intellectual space in which practice theories could thrive. Foregrounding the importance of episteme, of practical knowledge and reasoning, of the performativity of speaking, the interest in overcom-ing dichotomies between structure and agency, or questions of how activities become routinized and form institutions, how structures of meaning condition actions and how knowledge becomes embodied, are all relevant to practice thinking. In this sense, Ringmar (2014) was right, when he argued that 'practices of one kind or another are what scholars of IR always have studied'. In contrast to these discourses, contemporary international practice theorizing promotes 'the concept of practice from a supporting to a leading role' (Bueger and Gadinger, 2015: 450).

The Status and Contours of Contemporary Practice Theorizing in IR

It is noteworthy that the notions of 'practice theory' and 'practice turn' were introduced in the discipline by relating them to these earlier works. In particular, Neumann (2002) argued that post-structuralists had underplayed the importance of practice, and Pouliot (2008) discussed practice thinking in relation to earlier constructivisms and neo-institutionalist theorizing. On the surface, it appears that Neumann and Pouliot presented opposing arguments. For Neumann, practice theorizing was to be seen largely as a continuation of established research, an argument that then later became presented in different cloths by Ringmar (2014) and McCourt (2016). In this perspective, practice theories are a continuation of, complement to or advancement of existing theorizing. It was a reminder to constructivists that discursive formations are made by both sayings and doings; texts needed to be supplemented with practices. By contrast, Pouliot (2008) argued that we should think about practice theorizing as a break from earlier theorizing. For him, it had to be seen as a novel alternative to established constructivist theorizing, which he called a 'logic of practicality'. Most practice work in IR has embraced this latter position. The argument is that practice theorizing provides new tools and reveals phenomena that are fundamental for the working of IR, and which have been neglected in prior research.

The positions can be reconciled by drawing on Reckwitz's (2002) categories that were introduced by Bueger and Gadinger (2015). Reckwitz argued that practice theories should be seen as part of culturalist theorizing. He convincingly showed that cultural theorizing fundamentally differs from works that adopt a logic of consequences and appropriateness and focus on interests and norms, respectively. While the difference to the rational actor model of the logic of consequences is obvious, the crucial difference between norm-oriented research and culturalist theorizing has been best demonstrated in IR by Sending (2002). As Sending showed, the logic of appropriateness fails to account for the collective patterns of action and for changes in ideational structures that are vital in culturalist theorizing. Reckwitz (2002) demonstrated that practice theory is a unique perspective within culturalist theorizing, which substantively differs from the other culturalist approaches that centre on discourses and structures of meaning on the one hand and cognition on the other. If we adopt Reckwitz's distinction, we recognize a fundamental difference within constructivism, namely between those that adopt a culturalist perspective and those that rely on a logic of appropriateness.[7] It then becomes clear that many of the voices that see practice theorizing as standing for a break argue against the constructivism that draws on the logic of appropriateness. By contrast, those that emphasize the continuity of practice thought foreground the shared assumptions of the different strands of culturalist theorizing and point to the many relations that connect practice thought to the pragmatist or post-structuralist works, discussed earlier. Without doubt, this does not solve the question as to what practice theory brings to the table and what it allows us to do, see and say differently. A debate over whether practice theory represents a Kuhnian revolution and a paradigm shift in IR is, however, unnecessary. Instead, we have to appreciate the variety within practice theorizing and the various links these diverse approaches establish to earlier research. We now turn to the question of how to grasp the complexity and plurality of practice theorizing.

Fault Lines: Categorizing Practice Theorizing in IR

In the recent turn to practice, IR scholars have taken inspiration from a whole series of sociological and theoretical approaches outside of IR when developing their theoretical perspectives on practices, from which different notions of practice have resulted. Bueger and Gadinger (2018) distinguish seven approaches, namely those inspired by (1) Pierre Bourdieu, (2) Michel Foucault, (3) Etienne Wenger, (4) Theodore Schatzki and (5) Luc Boltanski, as well as the looser research programmes of (6) Actor-Network Theory (ANT) and (7) Narrative Theory. The Bourdieusian notion of practice understands practices as embodied, and often subconsciously executed activities that perpetuate existing power dynamics and thus stabilize established social orders. Foucault's highly prolific and disparate scholarship has generated a variety of concepts that made inroads into practice theorizing. One of those avenues focuses on discursive practices in interaction with bodily disciplines and highlights the contingency of established power dynamics (rather than order), married with historicity, which combine in the method of genealogy. By contrast, a Wengerian approach to practices

---

[7] Several commentators, among them Guzzini (2000), Hopf (1998) and Fierke (2010), have noted a major divide within constructivism.

emphasizes the communitarian dimension of practices and how they integrate individuals and groups into larger collective wholes. It focuses on processes of social learning, but does not pay as much attention to materiality, historicity and power. Practice approaches inspired by Schatzki conceive of practices as 'nexuses of doings and sayings' (Schatzki, 1996: 89) that are amalgamated into larger wholes, such as the practice of central banking. Rules ensure societal consistency. Practices are open-ended and evolving; they create social orders by fluidly establishing relations between their parts. A practice understanding from a Boltanskian perspective focuses on the normative dimension underpinning practices, by directing attention to the everyday practices of justification through which actors adjudicate between different normative orders. The focus is on contestations and the fragility of orders. Narrative approaches focus on linguistic practices. They conceive of storytelling as a social practice which consists of a set of different linguistic practices and helps to create communities and social identity. Narratives have a stabilizing effect on practices and order the world into coherent configurations. Lastly, ANT studies material objects and social practices as parts of contingent actor-networks that can break down at any moment. The focus is on everyday, micro-level practices in their material and discursive dimensions, with little attention paid to power dynamics and longer-term historical processes.

This list of different conceptions of practices merits further expansion in light of new publications. American pragmatism, and notably the work of John Dewey with his notions of practical learning, deserve a mention (see Adler, 2019). But IR scholars keep discovering new theoretical inspirations to study practices, and they also develop new theorizations from their empirical discoveries – a testimony to the vibrancy of practice theorizing in IR. Only one contribution to this volume can be adequately described as neatly falling into the categories listed above. Adler and Faubert substantially draw on Wenger's concept of communities of practice. Walters borrows Foucault's notion of counter-conduct, but considerably expands on it and takes it into new theoretical dimensions in the light of Walters's empirical observations. Gadinger combines three of the approaches listed above to analyse the normativity of practices. The other contributors work with more heterogeneous and diverse resources and hence raise questions about how well international practice theorizing can be grasped through a set number of discrete approaches.

Identifying a precise set of theoretical approaches that inspire practice theorizing in IR only impedes understanding of the emerging and plural nature of the current practice debate. Equating approaches with a single theorist risks contradicting an understanding of theorizing as a practice, that is, as a process of continuous revisions and readjustments. It invites a focus on interpreting canonical texts instead of explaining and understanding real-world phenomena, of putting theory before practice. Yet most of the branches of practice theorizing in IR are not so much about introspections of the grand writings of particular theorists as they are evolving approaches. Bourdieu's work, for instance, has inspired broader thinking on fields and field theory on the one hand, while work on the concept of habits, on the other hand, significantly departs from the author's original understanding and intentions. Work on communities of practice has evolved in a way that Wenger is hardly more than one reference point among others, and so on. Identifying such approaches also raises questions in terms of the approaches that are not mentioned. For example, to the list above inspired by Bueger and Gadinger (2018) one could add assemblage thinking, which is closely related to ANT but should not be equated with it, symbolic interactionist perspectives or feminist approaches of practices, for instance developed in conversation with Judith Butler's understanding of performativity. This raises the question of whether organizing the debate in such a way is the right way forward.

Thinking with Fault Lines

Instead, we put forward an alternative pathway to group the different conceptions of practice that exist in IR and the ones that are still to emerge. We propose to think in terms of 'fault lines' when delineating the different notions of practice in the discipline. To think in this way is productive as it brings difference and diversity to the fore. Unfortunately, it also carries the risk of reproducing rather problematic dichotomies that practice theories have set out to transcend. We can think of fault lines as rifts or cracks in theorization, where a particular piece of research lies either on one side of the crack or on the other, and it can be very close to the edge, or quite far removed from it. Some scholars, of course, have succeeded and others will succeed to build bridges across the cracks. Bridge-building, however, often requires considerable efforts. Several commentators on practices have already alluded to some of these fault lines (e.g. Bueger and Gadinger, 2015, 2018; Frost and Lechner, 2018; Kustermans, 2016; Wille and Schindler, 2019). We propose to divide the conception of practices along five fault lines, those of (1) stability and change, (2) materiality and consciousness, (3) the everyday and the aggregate, (4) power and communities and (5) theory and practice.

The first fault line concerns the question whether scholars think of practices as primarily stabilizing features or as ways for conceptualizing change. Accounts differ in terms of whether they see practice thinking as implying a continuous process of change (e.g. through the principle of indexicality) and, hence, the puzzle becomes a question of whether and how the social achieves any form of stability, or whether the core challenge is to study and understand change, taking stability as the normal state. For example, Bernstein and Laurence oppose the continuous variation of day-to-day practices with a certain normative stability. Pouliot's answer is that, while practices perpetually vary at the micro-level, only a few of these variations actually get retained and lead to macro-level change.

Second, the question of materiality and consciousness largely concerns the importance scholars attribute to the embodied nature of practices versus the role of discourses, consciousness and normativity. While all practice theorizing agrees on the material and practical effects of practices, some practice scholarship puts more weight on studying discursive practices, the underlying norms inherent in practices, and primarily focuses on the immaterial side of practices as the key explanans. Others insist that bodies and material objects are the primary carrier of practice and hence contend that research needs to be initiated from there. In Chapter 10, Austin and Leander propose an approach that highlights the material dimensions of practices and various tools that, for example, render specific forms of torture invisible, and how this influences the emotionality of the observer. By contrast, Gadinger emphasizes the linguistic justification practices that enter the discussions of the ethicality of particular practices. He thus focuses on the reflective and conscious dimension of practices.

A third fault line concerns the question of the scale of practice theorizing. Here one can usefully distinguish between those studies that are concerned with larger aggregates in terms of time, space, agency and practices, and those scholars who focus on the everyday actions of individuals in concrete settings. The former study, for example, the aggregated practices of warfare over centuries or highlight the profiteering practices companies engage in. In the latter understanding, any larger aggregates are dependent on enactments in concrete situations. In Chapter 9, Schäfer documents how specific micro-practices of drafting documents define the world heritage programme. Kratochwil stresses that taking praxis seriously will imply investigating the choices that actors make in distinct situations. Others, such as Adler and Faubert, Dumouchel and Pouliot, argue for operating at a larger scale.

For Pouliot, evolution operates at the structural level. He believes that it is necessary to consider the structure of different practices to understand which micro-level variations are retained.

The fourth fault line opposes those perspectives that see practices as naturalizing inherent power dimensions in societies, and those approaches that focus on the integrative, communitarian and/or relational dimension of practices. In the latter case, scholars highlight the community-building effects of practices, how they create shared understandings and provide for societal cohesion, or how they contribute to the formation of networks and assemblages. By contrast, others suggest that this community-building dimension of practices actually camouflages inherent power dynamics. The contrast is the most marked between a Bourdieusian and Foucaultian approach to practices versus a Wengerian community of practice approach or narrative perspectives, but these differences run through all practice theorizing. In Chapter 5, Gadinger, with his focus on learning shared social values, emphasizes the communitarian dimension of practices. By contrast, Walters highlights the power dimensions that are inherent in practices and how ordinary individuals can seize those opportunities to mount large-scale challenges against the state and beyond.

A fifth fault line concerns the relations between 'theory' and 'practice' that scholars rely on. Lechner and Frost (2018) have phrased it as a question about whether theorizing evolves from the *outside* or from *within* a practice – an argument that follows from Kratochwil's plea to start thinking from the midst, give up the search for coherence and an overarching logic of practice and instead attend to the messiness of practical activities. To start from the outside is to construct general categories of practice, which are then used to identify what qualifies as a practice and to study its composition. This leads one to start out from theory rather than practice and to continue to entertain the hope for a more general theory of practice. Those arguing for initiating from the midst of practice abandon such hope. As called for paradigmatically by Kratochwil (2011), there is nothing general about a practice and, in this sense, theorizing cannot strive for universality. Identifying a practice then implies to search for patterns that reveal themselves through empirical research and to search for those normative understandings and actor descriptions that give a practice coherence. In Chapter 8, Pouliot develops a more general theory of how practices change at the macro-level with the help of an evolutionary vocabulary, whereas Walters highlights the situated dimension of counter-conduct as a form of power that is not timeless but needs to be adapted to specific circumstances.

This fault line can also be rendered as a methodological question, as a question from where to initiate the empirical study of practice. Studying from within implies a certain degree of immersion and participating in a practice, which allows one to identify patterns and the understandings and descriptions of actors. Those prioritizing theory over practice are less dependent on immersion and the more elaborate conceptual apparatuses allow them to produce insights through more distant research techniques and spectator positions.

These fault lines offer a productive way of introducing order and a sense of debate to what often appears to be the 'mess' of practice theorizing. The chapters in this volume first of all tease out why and how practice-driven research has already lived up to its promises, and then show what practice thought adds to the table. They draw out the relations of practice thinking to other IR theories, in particular constructivism, and detail how practice theories provide new conceptualizations and new empirical observations. In offering various answers as to how to address the fault lines, they also establish new directions for further developing the practice-theoretical project.

Structure and Contributions of the Volume

We have divided the volume into four parts. In the first part, following this Introduction, Ted Hopf investigates the criticisms articulated against practice theories in the discipline thus far, and demonstrates how the chapters in this edited volume address some of those shortcomings. Part II consists of chapters that explore key concepts in the discipline of IR. They demonstrate how a focus on practices allows for a new take on these concepts that leads to original theoretical insights and unfamiliar empirical lenses. The chapters in this part discuss the concepts of knowledge, norms, normativity, power, authority and change. Part III introduces concepts that are at the margins of IR theory but are key for practice-theoretical thinking. Part of the value-added of practice theorizing in IR is that it permits scholars to shed light on phenomena that the broader IR discipline has so far not paid much attention to. Repetition and visuality are two concepts for which practice theorizing is uniquely positioned to elaborate upon. These concepts allow practice scholars to establish important links to other turns discussed in the discipline, in particular the post-structuralist debate and the visual and performative turns. Part IV offers two concluding reflections. The first represents a conceptual critique of practice approaches. The second highlights how concepts form the primary building blocks of international practice theories and how conversations around concepts form a semiotic web that characterizes the practice approach in IR, as highlighted by the conversations between the chapters in this volume.

Part II starts with Emanuel Adler and Michael Faubert's chapter, which revisits the concept of knowledge by engaging with IR approaches to the study of knowledge, primarily, but not exclusively, the epistemic community framework. The chapter suggests focusing on epistemic communities of practice, a concept which highlights that knowledge and power play a ubiquitous role in international politics. The theoretical framework of epistemic communities of practice broadens the epistemic communities research agenda. Practices are pervasive in international politics, and knowledge is always inherent in those practices, because practices can be performed more or less competently. The actors, who perform well, automatically obtain more power. The chapter illustrates the role of epistemic communities of practice by focusing on the establishment of a nuclear arms control verification practice, particularly regarding test-ban treaties, during the Cold War, and the recent spread of a populist 'post-truth' community of practice and its capacity to disrupt international order.

In the following chapter, Steven Bernstein and Marion Laurence investigate the possible disjunctures that can occur between norms and practices and which scholars can only notice if they focus on practices as a separate ontological category. The authors argue that a practice approach allows us to discern these disjunctures, and that these disjunctures can lead to changes in international norms in the long term. The chapter thus illustrates how practice-theoretical scholarship can complement constructivism, and it provides a new theoretical model to explain international norm change. Empirically the chapter stresses how a whole series of everyday practices in United Nations peace-keeping operations seem – at first glance – to undermine impartiality, a core legitimating norm of those operations. The authors study such practices as the use of force and taking sides in targeted offensive operations, collaboration with host governments in conflict zones, and post-conflict peace-building, including such activities as the drafting of constitutions, the organization of elections and the training of police officers. Interestingly, staff do not see these practices as transgressing existing norms or as establishing new norms, but rather as practical tools that serve to accomplish their mission. The practices do not represent a deliberate challenge to the norm of impartiality, but rather a shift in standards of competent performance, all the while the norm of impartiality remains in place. Over time, however, the practical imperatives on the ground and resulting changes in practices may lead to norm change. This process highlights not just change from below, change that comes from the daily practices of actual local actors, but also the unintentionality of it all, from bottom to top.

In opposition to Bernstein and Laurence, Frank Gadinger develops the argument that practices always contain a normative dimension, and he suggests that studying norms from a practice perspective would provide value-added to norm constructivism. Normativity is the normative dimension of practices, which also highlights the fluidity of norms. Gadinger introduces three key advantages of normativity in the chapter: normativity includes a power dimension into the study of norms, as norms draw lines between legitimate and illegitimate practitioners. A communities of practice perspective furthermore highlights how newcomers do not just learn how to perform competently within a given community, but simultaneously, and typically unconsciously, learn the moral standards of appropriate behaviour. Third, a practice focus draws attention to the practices of justification and contestation, based on which the normative standards of appropriate behaviour are disputed, and thus highlights the contingent and unstable nature of norms. Gadinger illustrates these advantages of putting practices first in normative scholarship with a few examples. For instance, directing attention to practices of justification in the Abu Ghraib prison controversy permits one to identify the controversy between proponents of two normative perspectives, on the one hand the prohibition of torture, and on the other hand a technocratic perspective about the alleged necessity for efficiency in a context of war. A practice perspective demonstrates the complex and layered nature of the normative environment, whereas a norms perspective might lead one to conclude that the norm of the prohibition of torture has come to an end.

In his chapter, William Walters studies the actions of the French farmer Cédric Herrou, who, with the support of friends, smuggles migrants across the border with Italy, because he feels that the state is not responding adequately to the migrant crisis. In this activity, Herrou makes use of his practices and skills as a farmer in rough mountainous terrain and readapts those practices to new objectives. He purposefully publicizes his activities and voluntarily undergoes trial to raise awareness about the inadequate response of the state to the migrant crisis. He creates a scene – he infuses everyday practices with emotions to generate affect and obtain a public response. Herrou engages in counter-conduct. Foucault developed the concept of counter-conduct to define practices of resistance to power that are based on ethical grounds and envisage a different, normatively superior form of governing. Counter-conduct is a unique practice-oriented approach to power. It falls in line with Foucault's tendency to offer, not a fixed typology of power, as is common in IR scholarship, but rather to analyse the historically contingent, case-focused, localized and situated forms of power that emerge. Counter-conduct allows us to think about the way that individual actors – dissidents, conscientious objectors and so forth – can make a difference in contentious politics. This goes against the grain of a certain social bias in IR, which tends to focus on major social movements and social forces. IR tends to consider a focus on individuals as old-style history. Yet, as recent cases such as 'Snowden' imply,[8] there is a need for new tools to make sense of situations in which individuals emerge as key figures and nodal points of resistance. In addition, Walters foregrounds the often neglected and perhaps even rejected method of 'description'. Detailed contextualized reconstruction of a meaningful 'doing' is perfectly consistent with the promise of practice in IR, as it reveals precisely how meaning is being made in the most 'de-theorized' site a scholar can create.

Joelle Dumouchel's chapter argues for a contribution that practice scholarship can make to the concept of authority as a form of power that is distinct from violence on the one hand and persuasion on the other hand. She claims that practice scholarship adds a dynamic dimension to constructivist and interactionist accounts of authority that permits scholars to theorize how the intersubjective context under which authoritative relations are considered as legitimate emerges, changes and disappears. Practice scholars focus on two distinct processes, on the one hand on the practices of claiming and recognizing authority, and on the other hand on the practices that produce an object of authority, over which authority can then be claimed. Empirically, Dumouchel studies the emergence of central bankers' authority, which has been an interactive process between the production of central banking as an independent object of governance, the creation of the distinct political and social role of the central banker and the recognition of central bankers' expertise.

Against historical institutionalism, and the more prevalent assumption across the social sciences that self-contained individuals change the social world through reflection and calculation, Vincent Pouliot encourages the reader to consider the messiness and incoherence in the evolution of social orders. Social orders evolve gradually over time

---

[8] Edward Snowden was a subcontractor of the CIA, who leaked information about the American National Security Agency's surveillance programs. Following his revelations populations and governments across the world were shocked about the extent of the NSA's surveillance of ordinary citizens, diplomats, and governments, even of 'friendly' nations. Snowden is sought in the United States for violations of the Espionage Act, but he escaped to Russia. While some treat him as a traitor, others see him as a whistleblower.

and emerge from agents' struggles over competent practices, and improvisations in the form of various slippages from standard ways of doing things. Individual practices vary considerably, but whether these individual micro-level variations amount to more than minor adjustments to the prevailing social order depends upon the environment of surrounding practices, and three types of practices in particular: (1) demonstratory practices, which permit new practices to be displayed publicly; (2) cross-cutting practices, which allow new practices to travel to other issues areas, and therefore also multiply audiences; and (3) codification practices, which serve to codify and therefore stabilize newly emerged practices. Pouliot illustrates his approach on UN Security Council practices and their variation during the Libya crisis. He finds that giving the dissenting Libyan delegation the floor at the UN Security Council had to be justified as falling within the realm of competent performances, although it was an alteration of standing practices. He concludes, however, that this variation is one of the many instances that is unlikely to be selected and retained.

Part III starts with Hilmar Schäfer's chapter, which analyses the practices of drafting final documents in the UNESCO world heritage programme – one of the most widely ratified treaties, currently with 193 signatories. Schäfer observes the continuity in drafting practices despite frequent changes in committee membership and diplomatic representation. He suggests that the notion of routine is insufficient to capture this phenomenon, and argues that we need to focus on the concept of repetition to grasp the co-occurrence of continuity and change. To do so, he enriches practice-theoretical scholarship with post-structuralist insights. The notion of repetition involves doing almost the same thing as has been done before, as exact replication is impossible. Furthermore, the context in which the doing occurs differs every time, which means that the practices and the meaning they contain will also slightly vary each time. The repetition of practices thus always introduces the possible instability of those practices, and therefore the possibility of change at the micro-level. The chapter complements Pouliot's discussion of change, in that while Pouliot focuses primarily on the role of selective retention, in the evolutionary vocabulary, Schäfer focuses on one mechanism of creative variation.

Jonathan Luke Austin and Anna Leander's chapter develops a new mode of power. Who or what is seen or, inversely, remains unseen is essential for socio-political hierarchies. Regimes of visibility endow actants with greater or lesser (in)visibility 'capital', generating important political consequences: regimes of visibility carve up what can be seen, heard and felt about the world. Politics is about vision, and the anti-political is about attempting to make invisible; crime remains best unseen if one wants to remain unaccused of it. The chapter illustrates the effects of regimes of visibility in a comparative analysis of extraordinary rendition (and torture) in the case of the United States and the Syrian Arab Republic. When the United States transports prisoners of war, they bind them to the floor by mesh cables, have them wear heavy-duty earmuffs, and make them wear hoods. The equipment ensures total sensory deprivation, and immovability. Soldiers appear relaxed while transporting their 'cargo'. By contrast, Syrian soldiers do not have the same kind of equipment to ensure the docility of their prisoners and have to beat and whip them. They appear to be involved in torture. Regimes of visibility have hidden the US torture programme, which was just as brutal, albeit smaller in scale than the Syrian one. It is important that practice scholars sensitize themselves to the concept of regimes of visibility, because the study of any other set of practices is filtered through regimes of visibility: practices of visibility translate the way we see all practices.

The final part of the book, Part IV, starts with Friedrich Kratochwil's chapter, which provides a conceptual critique of contemporary practice theorizing in IR, arguing that the current debate is destined to fall into the same traps as earlier waves of constructivist theorizing. Taking practices seriously, the author argues, entails a much more fundamental change in the research orientation than just having a new formal object, such as focusing on practices rather than on 'power' or 'systems'. It requires giving up on the idea that theorizing, that is, the universal application of abstract logical principles to concrete situations, is a practically useful endeavour. Kratochwil cautions practice scholars in particular against importing concepts from other disciplines without accounting for the semiotic context into which they are embedded. Instead, he encourages scholars to focus on practical judgement in concrete, temporally and contextually specified situations. This entails identifying a particular situation, the relevant facts and the appropriate, and potentially contradictory, norms and principles that apply to the case. The practical imperatives of the situation require a quick diagnostic, a criterion of completeness in assessing the situation, experience and imagination in applying analogical reasoning and a flexible heuristics.

The final chapter, by Alena Drieschova and Christian Bueger, concludes by showcasing in which sense and to what extent this edited volume has laid out the foundations for conceiving of practice theories as a distinct set of approaches to IR. The volume proposes a new way for setting out the intellectual identity of practice scholarship and how it relates to other forms of IR research. Concepts, rather than generalized systems of assertions (theory), provide the building blocks of international practice theories and allow for unity in diversity. The conclusion of the volume provides a rationale for the focus on concepts, rather than intellectual figures, theoretical approaches or vocabularies. This approach helps to provide a shared direction while remaining committed to the heterogeneity and plurality of practice thinking. The volume has thus structured its discussion around concepts. This has opened up collective, dynamic and necessarily open-ended conversations to define the theoretical approach and to delimit it towards other approaches. Each of the contributions to the volume looks at practices through the prism of a key concept in IR and engages with their interlocutors through that prism. The conclusion sketches out the semiotic web of interrelated concepts that emerges from these conversations. It investigates the links between concepts and reflects on the epistemological and methodological importance of understanding the flexibility of the vocabulary of international practice theories.

2 Critiques of the Practice Turn in IR Theory
Some Responses

Ted Hopf

In this chapter, I analyse how the practice turn in IR (PTIR) has been criticized over the last ten years, offer some suggestions of my own on how to address them and then elaborate on the responses the authors of this volume have offered to those critiques. I of course have my own criticisms, and have made them in various places (Hopf, 2010, 2018), but I do not reiterate them here.

I start out by identifying what critiques already exist. I then classify, or order them, in some fashion, pointing out the primary weak spots in the PTIR programme thus far. We should bear in mind that PTIR is a very young research programme indeed. I wanted to make visible the kinds of responses PTIR scholars make to the critiques that have surfaced over the last five to ten years. I hasten to caution that I, initially at least, take no position on the validity of these critiques; I merely present them. I offer some possible ways of addressing them, and conclude with an elaboration of how authors of this volume have responded to them.

A caveat is called for before beginning. Adler and Pouliot figure most prominently as targets of the already-existing critiques, both as co-authors and Pouliot as sole author. There are a number of plausible reasons for this, but not because their scholarship is any more or less critique-worthy. The most important reason is that they are far and away the most-cited PTIR scholars; their work, along with Iver Neumann's opening salvo, *Millennium* (2002), have garnered the most attention. Adler and Pouliot's edited volume, *International Practices* (Cambridge, 2011), has garnered over 1,100 citations; Pouliot's *International Organization* article, 'Logic of Practicality' (2008), has 700 and his first book, *International Security in Practice* (2010), has 600. Neumann's (2002) 'Returning Practice to the Linguistic Turn' has 700 citations but has attracted no visible critique at all, at least that I could find. Why Neumann's immunity from critique?

The obvious answer is that everyone has more or less agreed that the linguistic turn as played out in constructivism and in social theory and IR in general had forgotten that discourses are made of both sayings and doings, not just sayings. Moreover, in that article Neumann did not go much beyond calling for scholars to turn their gaze towards practices; while he proposed a model of order and change, he did not recommend any particular theoretical approach or offer methodological desiderata.

This changes with Adler and Pouliot's scholarship. Perhaps this is because Adler and Pouliot issued a kind of field-defining manifesto, attracting the attention of every practice theory scholar in IR, each of whom has a different idea of what a practice is, how it should be theorized, how it should be studied and how its implications should be understood. Moreover, Pouliot is the only author, so far, to have written two book-length monographs, as deeply theoretical as they are empirical, providing perhaps the only substantial target available to critics from within or outside PTIR. Bueger and Gadinger (2014, 2015), on the other hand, have co-authored important books and articles, not in the field-defining vein, but rather in the manner of 'let 1,000 flowers bloom', inviting scholars interested in practice to choose from a multifarious tasting menu of social theories of practice: from Bourdieu to Dewey, from Foucault to Latour, from Wenger to Reckwitz, from Boltanski to Schatzki – and many others.

Just because Adler and Pouliot have been the immediate cause of most critiques, it does not mean that many of the criticisms made are irrelevant to PTIR in general and specific scholars within it. The authors of this volume are certainly not primarily motivated to critique Adler and Pouliot, but rather are intent on developing PTIR in their own ways, following theorists other than Bourdieu or Goffman, and handling critiques against PTIR in general and specific theoretical streams in particular.

A Sample of Critiques

Critical work on PTIR originates from both inside and outside it. The former overwhelmingly dominates, perhaps 90 per cent or more of the written critiques I could find.[1] As one might expect, the insiders have

---

[1] I must thank George May for his research assistance on recovering these critiques. We started with the usual suspects: journal articles that used the practice turn in their work. The journals surveyed were *European Journal of IR*, *Millennium*, *International Theory*, *Journal of International Relations and Development*, *International Studies Quarterly*, *Review of International Studies* and *International Political Sociology*. We also tracked down works that were cited by scholars in these journals. In addition, we looked for book review articles on Vincent Pouliot's *International Security in Practice* and *International Pecking Orders*; Emanuel Adler and Pouliot's *International Practices* edited volume; Christian Bueger and Frank Gadinger's *International Practice Theory*; and Rebecca Adler-Nissen's *Opting out of the European Union* and her edited volume *Bourdieu in International Relations*.

a completely different set of critical observations than the outsiders: they do not share the same criteria of evaluation. One important issue this chapter raises is whether PTIR scholars should care about outsider critiques at all; or, contrariwise, should they be very concerned about them, since ignoring or dismissing them probably consigns PTIR to a narrow subfield within broader IR, having conversations exclusively with itself?

Classifying Critiques

Criticizing Social Theories of Practice Themselves, but Primarily Bourdieu There is much criticism of the social theories of practice themselves, their intrinsic inadequacies, inconsistencies, incompatibilities and lack of utility in animating PTIR. To the extent that PTIR relies on Bourdieu for its theorization of practice, it is a lightning rod for critiques of the 'structuralist' Bourdieu who has no adequate account of change Adams (2006), Hopf (2010) and Joseph and Kurki (2018: 85–8). This is a charge, despite repeated rejections by Pouliot and Adler-Nissen in particular, that will not go away. It is as if Bourdieu himself is a fundamentally contested concept. Erik Ringmar, for example, takes PTIR to task for trying to claim that Bourdieu has somehow resolved the tension between meaning and materialism. He claims that Bourdieu has not, and instead that 'he is a materialist, "in the last instance," if not before' (Ringmar, 2014: 9). In general, Ringmar (2014: 9) asserts, PTIR scholars cherry-pick Bourdieu for what they wish to demonstrate, while 'characteristically shy[ing] away from his rump Marxism'.[2] Many critics have puzzled over how PTIR can take any theorization of change from Bourdieu. Even those PTIR scholars who use Bourdieu write that 'Bourdieu's thought is at core a theory of domination'.[3] Bueger and Gadinger (2014: 29, 60–2) write that Bourdieu's thought does not provide a starting point for 'a theory of social change'.[4] They later write that 'the emphasis of Bourdieu's praxeology is on stability, regularity, and reproduction of practices and less on subversion and renewal' and recommend that PTIR 'should focus less on Bourdieu and reproduction and hierarchies and more on pragmatism and contingency and change' (2015: 449–55). The problem with Bourdieu's concept of hysteresis, as used by Pouliot in his

---

[2] Ringmar charges Adler, Pouliot, Adler-Nissen, Williams and Abrahamsen with this misuse of Bourdieu.
[3] For example, Pouliot and Mérand (2013: 36).
[4] See also Hopf (2010, 2018).

work on NATO–Russia relations after the Cold War, is that the origins of change are not within practice itself, but rather in the misalignment of dispositions within the social field, a mismatch between a habitus acquired in one field and now maladapted to a new, or changing, field (Schindler and Wille, 2015: 336–8).[5] As we will see in the section on change, Duvall and Chowdhury trace Adler and Pouliot's inadequate theorization of change in their version of practice directly to their reliance on Bourdieu, whose theorization of habitus 'privileges a stable and iterable foundation to practice that is univocal within a particular community' (2011: 349).

Anna Leander, perhaps frustrated and hoping just to get on with the PTIR's work, responds by asking for a ceasefire: 'I think that Bourdieu-inspired scholars would be well-advised to cease chastising people who use Bourdieu ... if they fail to use it fully or if they do not engage all its aspects and to distance themselves from an all-or-nothing approach to theoretical endeavours' (2011: 309).

Criticizing How PTIR Uses Theories of Practice   Beyond criticizing the social theories of practice themselves, critics of PTIR question how other PTIR scholars have used these theories, accusing them of inaccuracy, incompleteness and misunderstanding the theories they use. Scholars are also accused of using the 'wrong' social theories of practice; instead they should be using other theories, usually those favoured by the critic.

For example, Martin-Maze (2017: 203) criticizes Adler and Pouliot for removing struggles from Bourdieu's structural constructivism in order to frame practices as 'the smallest unit of analysis'. Instead, they should be giving more prominence to Luc Boltanski's sociological theory of practice. Martin-Maze faults Bueger and Gadinger for 'obfuscating these differences', and wants to 'mount a challenge to the translation of Bourdieu's work by Pouliot and that of Boltanski's by Gadinger'. He accuses Pouliot of 'conflating the concepts of community and field', important because communities are not characterized by differences and struggles, while fields are (2017: 204–10). In fact, Martin-Maze argues, 'Bourdieu forged the concept of field precisely to break away from the irenic vision of the social world conveyed by the notion of community' (2017: 209).

Some critics object to the ontological priority given to practice and its logic of practicality or habit over the alternative logics of

---

[5] Others reject Bourdieu's hysteresis in general as a fruitful concept; see for instance Jackson (2011: 21).

consequentialism and appropriateness. For other scholars, 'practice is not the element constituting all aspects of our social world, but an element of it' (Bourbeau, 2017: 3–4).[6] Ringmar goes further, arguing that if meaning really has priority, then PTIR has an implicitly post-structuralist ontology and should adhere to it more faithfully. If practices are truly responsible for the production of both agents and structures, as Adler and Pouliot claim, then they should be in agreement with Cynthia Weber (cited in Ringmar, 2014: 17), who has argued that 'sovereign nation-states are not pre-given subjects but in process and that all subjects in process (be they individual or collective) are the ontological effects of practices which are performatively enacted'.

Joseph and Kurki, criticizing those in PTIR who reject the structuralism obvious in Bourdieu, while distancing themselves from Bourdieu's lack of relationalism in conceptualizing social structures, argue that such practice scholarship 'is unable to conceptualize things beyond what is observable in practice and is thus trapped in an insider view of the "field" that is remarkably unreflective about how the field itself might be constituted by anything other than the agents directly involved' (2018: 91).[7] In a similar vein, Ringmar observes that Adler and Pouliot 'make the mistake of treating practices as though they were "raw data" – data which is given before any theorization – yet there is no such thing as a practice apart from the theories and research questions which identify it' (2014: 6).[8]

Holmes and Traven (2015) claim that Hopf and Pouliot have their psychological micro-foundations wrong, and offer the idea of 'rational intuitionism' as an alternative. To be fair, their criticism is far better aimed at Hopf than Pouliot, who have vast differences on the place of experimental psychology and neuroscience in the practice turn in general.

Holmes and Traven also point out the absence of any theorization of affect or emotions in PTIR. They argue that 'emotions such as fear, anger, joy, and disgust, as well as emotional contagion' can 'inform practices without being reducible to them' (2015: 423).[9] Even if we do not credit the very idea of discrete emotions, we can probably agree that 'circulations of affect', as elaborated by Andrew Ross (2013), are part of practice and should be part of PTIR's theoretical agenda.

---

[6] Bourbeau goes on to cite Severine Autesserre's work in particular in this regard. See also Hopf (2010), and Watson (2011: 533–4). One should also look at Bernstein and Laurence in this volume (Chapter 4).

[7] For a similar critique see Nair (2020).

[8] See also Andersen and Neumann (2012: 467–8) for a similar critique.

[9] For the exception that perhaps proves the rule see Bially Mattern (2011).

Criticizing the PTIR's Contribution to IR Theory More Generally
Erik Ringmar has probably offered the most comprehensive criticism of PTIR heretofore, especially of the contributions of Adler and Pouliot. He claims that practices are hardly a new concept, and are easily to be found in classical realism, neorealism, functionalism, neoliberal institutionalism, constructivism and post-structuralism, so PTIR is hardly offering anything necessarily innovative (2014: 2). He also takes issue with the foundational conceptualization offered in Adler and Pouliot (2011b) that practices are always 'competent performances' judged by members of a community of practice for their accuracy and effectiveness. He notes that in the 2011 edited volume there are many different conceptualizations of practice in evidence in the contributed chapters that are not consistent with Adler and Pouliot's more restrictive definition.[10]

Perhaps the most frequent criticism of PTIR is its inability to provide a convincing account of change in world politics. In Duvall and Chowdhury's critical concluding chapter to Adler and Pouliot's *International Practices* volume, they observe that changes in practices cannot be theorized properly without taking seriously 'incompetent practices' and those actors who 'are resisting or transgressing the existing rules'. Moreover, they observe, none of the chapters in the volume 'shed light on fundamental changes' in world politics, and instead at best deal with only 'incremental changes', or how exogenous factors lead to changes in practices (2011: 343–8).[11] They ground this critique of Adler and Pouliot in the two scholars' 'assumption that practices are to be understood as expressing and conveying a univocal meaning for the practitioner and the broader community of practice' (2011: 337). Adler and Pouliot, in Duvall and Chowdhury's view, obscure 'the inherent instability of practices themselves' (2011: 337). Duvall and Chowdhury instead argue, drawing on Butler and Foucault, that at least 'the possibility of polysemy is a structural necessity of practices' because signifiers within a discourse only gain their meaning through their differences from other signifiers (2011: 345). Within any community of practice then, separate communities of meaning can form around any number of signifiers or practices, hence opening the door to contestation and change.

---

[10] For a similar observation on the 'moving target' that is practice, see Kustermans (2016: 175), and Onuf (2010: 116).
[11] See also Bourbeau (2017: 15), Hopf (2018), and Svendsen (2020). For a more sympathetic view, see Kustermans (2016: 181–83), although even he points out PTIR often conflates process with change.

Martin-Maze argues, for example, that a proper appreciation of Bourdieu, in particular his theorization of fields as arenas of symbolic struggles, would find real change as 'actors successfully do battle over the cognitive categories that are used to construct the world, they change how the world is perceived and practiced' (2017: 217). Schindler and Wille also take PTIR to task for not theorizing change adequately. In their case, they criticize Pouliot's use of Bourdieu in explaining change in relations between NATO and Russia after the Cold War. They claim he fails to grasp in Bourdieu the 'inherent instability of practice', inevitable because of 'uncertainty about the meaning of the past destabilizes present practices and thus makes sudden and drastic change possible' (2015: 330). They argue that it was because NATO and Russia never agreed on the meaning of the end of the Cold War that diplomatic practices between them were inherently subject to endogenous change. Ringmar puts it starkly: 'Practices cannot simultaneously be the origin of one thing – stability – and its opposite – change' (2014: 18). As Adler and Pouliot acknowledge, it is an open question 'what other determinants to add on to practices in explaining transformations'. Indeed, it may be necessary to invoke 'a plethora of other factors ... in combination with practice – intersubjective structures, material forces, etc' (2011: 19–21).[12]

Craig Parsons argues that until PTIR scholarship starts to seriously engage with alternative theoretical accounts of the same phenomena, we will never know whether PTIR is making any contribution beyond already-existing approaches. He observes that PTIR scholars in general 'counsel against competing alternatives of all sorts' (2015: 503).[13] One of the problems for Pouliot's work on NATO–Russia relations in particular is that he cannot convincingly argue that his practice-based account is better or more credible than alternative accounts.[14] It is difficult to distinguish between what Pouliot calls practices and what others would perhaps call decisions. For example, Pouliot observes that the NATO enlargement decision of December 1994 was an event that was followed by changes in Russian 'practices'. But what were these practices? Russia's decision to elaborate a new national security doctrine that identified external threats

---

[12] See also Hopf (2018) for an effort to establish conditions under which change occurs through practice and exogenous conditions that render more likely changes of practice. See also Pouliot's contribution to this volume (Chapter 8).

[13] Here he cites Guzzini (2000), Pouliot (2008, 2010), Mérand (2010), Adler and Pouliot (2011b) and Adler-Nissen (2012, 2014a).

[14] See, for example, the critiques on these grounds by Hopf (2011: 773), Ringmar (2014: 9), Marshall (2010: 1418), Watson (2011: 533), Jervis (2011) and Forsberg (2012: 171), who suggests 'more familiar concepts of worldviews, strategic culture, perceptions, belief systems, and identities' could plausibly explain what Pouliot attributes to practices.

for the first time since 1992 as more important than internal weaknesses; Russia's decision to increase its military forces in the West; and more resistant negotiating positions within the NATO council. It is hard here to distinguish practices from policies, and Pouliot provides no guidance. In fact, one could argue that adopting a new policy entails new practices, so the practices of resistant diplomacy in Brussels are a consequence of a new Russian policy towards the West in the face of NATO enlargement. Nor is it easy to distinguish between a habitus and an identity. Pouliot, for example, argues that Western decisions such as NATO enlargement, abrogation of the Anti-Ballistic Missile Treaty and launching the Iraq War in 2003 evoked a 'Russian great power habitus' (Pouliot, 2010: 179). How to know if a habitus, or at least its predispositions, was invoked, or instead a particular discourse of Russian national identity was empowered? Both are intersubjective structures and both imply a different set of practices once instantiated. Perhaps we could devise an empirical test. Pouliot's argument implies that practices themselves constitute identity; I might claim that this is true, but identities also imply practices. So, in the face of NATO expansion, what happened in Russia–NATO relations? Did Russia begin to change diplomatic, foreign policy and security practices in response to NATO expansion, which was accompanied by the construction of a new Great Power habitus? Or, alternatively, did NATO expansion evoke a Great Power discourse of Russian national identity accompanied/followed by new practices? These processes should be empirically distinguishable, although it might not be the case that Pouliot would agree to the derived hypotheses as a fair test. At the very least, we would have to agree in some detail as to what the observable empirical markers of habitus and identity are, and how to differentiate them from each other.

Robert Jervis notes as well that sometimes in Pouliot's book it is hard to know if Pouliot is writing about practices rather than policies. He observes that while some of Pouliot's interviews deal with the practices of diplomacy, most of them and 'all the history treat practice in a more conventional way as the policies of the states and the interactions among them' (2011: 23).

Robert Jervis begins his review of Pouliot's work on NATO–Russia relations with a summary view:

'Pouliot shows that some insights can be derived from Bourdieu, but I believe that the main lines of the narrative re-describe in different language what close observers of the interaction of Russia and the West had previously understood. (For a related account of Western policy in the Bosnian crisis that like Pouliot's book is valuable for deeply engaging with empirical material but similarly subject to the criticism of being largely a redescription in less traditional language, see Hansen, 2006; a study that is more successful is Autesserre, 2014)' (2011: 22).

I reproduce this quote in full because it shows how Jervis puts Pouliot and Hansen in the same box: old wine in new bottles. In essence, he is saying there's nothing new here. But, importantly, he distinguishes those two works from that of Autesserre's work on peacemaking in Congo. I will return to a comparison of these two works.

Once again, this is a call for PTIR scholarship to make a better effort to differentiate their analyses from those that are already out there. Why should we prefer PTIR interpretations of events and phenomena in world politics to alternative accounts? What criteria should we use to make such comparative evaluations? Shouldn't PTIR scholars start providing such criteria? Shouldn't they start entertaining alternative accounts alongside their own accounts, as Parsons suggests? Isn't this a way to get PTIR beyond a conversation with itself to a conversation with IR scholarship more generally?

Jervis goes on to point out that Pouliot's explanation for the turn in post–Cold War NATO–Russia relations was brought about by the 'double-enlargement' of NATO beginning with its expansion to new members in Eastern Europe in December 1994, followed by new missions in Bosnia in 1995 and Kosovo in 1999: 'Pouliot describes this in terms of hysteresis, the clash of habitus and field. The crucial question is whether these concepts carry us deeper into the interactions and the actors' worldviews and conceptions of their interests than do more familiar conceptions' (2011: 23). Jervis acknowledges that Pouliot, in his concluding chapter, circles back to argue the superiority of practice theory in accounting for these events, but what Jervis suggests is that Pouliot (and I would say PTIR scholarship in general) make his Bourdieusian analysis clear in his historical chapters. In not doing this himself, Jervis indicates that Pouliot's historical analysis is 'not closely related to Bourdieu's framework, and for the rest Bourdieu does not take us into new territory' (Jervis, 2011: 23). Outside readers such as Jervis, and perhaps even readers inside PTIR, should expect to see the practice turn in action during the empirical analysis, continually pointing out along the way the unique insights that practice is bringing to the table. This is not a 'gladiatorial model' of scholarship, as Pouliot (2016b: 15) puts it in his most recent book, but rather an opportunity to show how the theoretical approach is working in practice. It is not a question of setting up a test of competing theories at the outset and then gathering empirical evidence that counts for and against them, as in a typical *International Security* article, but rather revealing to readers along the way the constant contributions PTIR is making to a unique analysis of whatever phenomena are being investigated.

Some authors in PTIR are lauded for their methodological rigour and/or self-consciousness. Bourbeau (2017: 180–1), for example, singles out Pouliot's work on NATO, Autesserre's work on peacekeeping and Bueger and Gadinger's methodological suggestions in *International Practice Theory*. As previously noted, Parsons encourages PTIR scholars to explicitly compare their practice-based accounts with competing alternatives. According to Bourbeau (2017: 181), Adler-Nissen does so in her contribution to the Sending, Pouliot and Neumann edited volume *Diplomacy and the Making of World Politics*. She concludes that Robert Putnam's view of foreign policy as two-level games is not accurate as diplomats don't think in terms of 'win-sets', but rather in terms of relations and 'being within the target'. These findings would indeed disconfirm Putnam's theory, but Bourbeau points out that Adler-Nissen only relied on 'two anecdotes' as empirical evidence, so was not as convincing a refutation of Putnam as it could have been.

Critiques of PTIR – So Far

There are several pretty constant critiques that PTIR attracts: the mis/use of social theories of practice, especially, but not exclusively of Bourdieu; the unwillingness to engage seriously with alternative explanations; the inability to provide an adequate account of non-trivial change; the unsatisfying quality of non-ethnographic methods to get at practices; and the contested ontological priority of practice. Before turning to how some of the authors in this volume have addressed these concerns, I suggest how one might go about responding to them.

First, it is perhaps desirable to agree with Leander's plea (2011) that we stop arguing about who has Bourdieu right or wrong and just get on with our work. I would associate myself with those sentiments, as after all the pay-off from theorizing practice in any particular way is in the quality of the interpretations it allows of phenomena in world politics. So long as the scholar makes explicit and crystal-clear her particular reading of Bourdieu or Wittgenstein or Latour, and points out that there are alternative readings that if adopted would contradict her own subsequent work, I see no reason to turn all PTIR scholars into social or political theory scholars. In fact, I doubt many PTIR scholars have ever published in a political theory journal; I doubt any of us would pose as authorities on Bourdieu in the way, say, Herbert Dreyfus could be identified as such on Heidegger or Foucault. I think this goes for all the other social theoretical traditions identified and limned by Bueger and Gadinger in their work. Indeed, let's argue about Boltanski's privileging of creative agency, and whether we find it convincing, and let's argue about whether the use of Boltanski by PTIR scholars is illuminating or not. But let's also keep our eye on whether or not, whatever our social theoretical choices, we actually produce work that offers an understanding or explanation that is convincing.

This brings us, secondly, to the issue of entertaining alternative explanations; or, perhaps more simply, making a practice theoretical account distinguishable from alternative accounts. That would be the very first step, and I don't mean in the abstract. By now, it is obvious that social theories of practice provide unique understandings for how the social world works, how order is maintained and how orders change. The question is how do these theories differ from, and indeed how they are better or worse than other theories that claim to do the same (Wallmeier, 2018). There is no reason of course to require all PTIR scholars to make their work legible to those not immersed in social theories of practice. But there are reasons to make the effort. Intellectually speaking, there is rarely a better opportunity for clarification of one's own theory than having to explain it to those who are unfamiliar with that literature (think about teaching undergraduate students, for example). It forces us to make explicit what would otherwise remain implicit, and to put into everyday language concepts that would otherwise remain in obscurantist jargon. It forces us to translate ourselves, always a good and edifying, process, both for ourselves and for our readers. In addition, if PTIR wants to be read beyond itself, it must make itself intelligible to others. One way of accomplishing that goal is to compare a practice theoretical account of some issue to alternative IR theoretical accounts of the same. I offered one possibility earlier in distinguishing between habitus and identity in Pouliot's work.

Third, on the question of change, my experience at least, in conversations with PTIR scholars on this question, is exasperated frustration at the ignorance of the one making the enquiry. They retreat to the ontological position of processualism, such that change is of course ubiquitous and constant. But when pressed to indicate the conditions under which such constant change actually produces change we can see and appreciate as change, there is usually little there in response. (Pouliot's contribution to this volume is a welcome departure.) This is a pity, as social theories of practice include conditions for change, both endogenously, through practice, and exogenously, when practices are interrupted by conscious reflection (Hopf, 2018). Moreover, given all the critical scholarship I have cited that finds practice theory wanting in theorizing change, it is quite obvious that the message is not getting through. Most of the time in PTIR literature, the assumption of constant change is baldly asserted, with a citation to some social theorist or another, or increasingly, and worse, to an IR scholar of practice. It is never elaborated or defended. We should be able to justify all our assumptions beyond just citing literature that declares them to be true. Sometimes one can be ontologically accurate but effectively trivial. What I mean is that just because we agree everything in the world is constantly changing (I as a subject am not the same subject as I was when I started writing this sentence) doesn't mean it is more than trivially true. That is, it is true, but not meaningfully enough to account for the kind of change we all care about, even if, as I tried to show in Hopf (2018), this post-structuralist, processual, Scottian, Butlerian account of micro-practices can lead to change we appreciate.

Fourth, is ethnography necessary to get at practice – especially given agreement that one of the single most important contributions of practice theory is a renewed focus on non-representational knowledge; the knowing how, rather than knowing that? If this is the case, as Jervis has already intimated in his citation of experimental psychology on the subject, interviews will not reveal unarticulable know-how, but rather will reveal post facto articulable know-that.[15] If practice theory is correct, the only way to observe the unobservable taken-for-granted substratum of common-sense, or background knowledge, is through the observation of practices themselves, not what people say about what they are, or were, doing. Wittgenstein, a prominent source for practice theory, repeatedly argued in *Philosophical Investigations* that one could *never* articulate why one actually followed a rule, because why one followed it was something that could only be made manifest 'in use'; that is, while implementing the rule that cannot be specified.

This appears to be one of the fundamental contributions of the practice turn to social theory. So, what is the status of interviews in practice turn methodology? A second-best method, at best, and it should be acknowledged as such; it is perhaps at the same level as textual analysis. Reading private correspondence between a foreign minister and her husband during a negotiation over a treaty with a foreign power surely shouldn't have less epistemic value than interviewing her about what she is doing. On the other hand, being present while she is negotiating, preparing for the negotiations, relaxing after them and ordering subordinates to do things for her certainly has to be the gold standard for finding what is taken for granted and assumed, and yet unarticulated.

What is interesting is that we arrive at the need for ethnography through social theories of practice, such as Wittgenstein and Heidegger, for example,

---

[15] See also Lechner and Frost (2018: 42–63), for a critique of 'externalist' approaches to practice that do not approximate ethnographic recovery of practices as understood by those doing the practising.

and through experimental cognitive psychology and neuroscience. Jervis makes the point for the latter in his review of Pouliot: 'Indeed, psychologists have discovered that even the most honest self-reports about why people form their impressions and beliefs are often quite incorrect – so much psychological processing is unconscious and inaccessible to us that we often understand ourselves no better than we do others' (2011: 25).[16]

Given the extraordinary difficulty in gaining access to sites where foreign relations are made, PTIR scholars have understandably resorted to interviews. But that does not mean they should ignore the epistemic costs of the choices they have made. They should not only acknowledge that interviews are second best, but also elaborate in some detail just what is likely to be lost by relying on interviews. And of course they should report interview responses with far greater care, circumspection and contextualization than is currently the practice. While we can only speculate about why Jervis wrote he was more convinced by Autesserre's empirics than Pouliot's, it could be because she spent year/s on the ground participating in and observing peacekeeping practices, and so was able to report not just the sayings but also the doings, and contemporaneous doings at that, not retrospective remembered sayings.[17]

Finally, what are the stakes in insisting on the ontological priority of the logic of practice or habit over the logics of consequentialism and appropriateness? First of all, it makes no sense from a commonsensical point of view. As I hope I have demonstrated elsewhere (Hopf, 2010, 2018), social theorists of practice themselves not only don't insist on such a priority, but also argue that which logic takes priority is a matter of context, not ontological givenness. Moreover, few believe that non-reflective practices alone produce social reality, the strong argument being that people do things without thinking, and then they figure out that they are in their instrumental interest or are normatively appropriate for the occasion. This is just silly. Learning isn't only mimetic or an apprenticeship. Parents teach their children through explicit injunctions and teachers through textbooks and car mechanics through factory manuals, as well as saying 'see here what I'm doing...'. Finally, why not just agree that ontological priority is an empirical question to be answered in context. In other words, there is no such thing as ontological priority, only a hunch

---

[16] Jervis cites Timothy Wilson (2002). For a summary of the experimental findings, see Jackson (2011), who made a similar point about the incompatibility of interviews with the practice turn's evidentiary demands.

[17] It could also be the problem of separating policies from practices when interviewing policy practitioners. Are they describing what they do in making policy or describing how or why they made the policies they did?

that one's ontology, whatever it is, is more important than others, but one is perfectly happy to be shown to be wrong (Wallmeier, 2018: 12).[18]

Responses to Prevailing Critiques from Our Authors

While none of the authors for this volume were asked to specifically respond to any of the critiques of the practice turn, I have elaborated here, they managed to deal with quite a number of them in different ways. Let me single out how they addressed the issue of alternative explanations, change and the ontological priority of practice.

Considering Alternatives, or Not

Adler and Faubert (Chapter 3) offer a 'community of practice' perspective to explain international cooperation, in the case described here among Soviet/Russian and US nuclear weapons scientists during and after the Cold War. They explicitly distinguish their approach from the earlier work, in which Adler was of course central, on epistemic communities. They argue that, unlike the latter, which is interested in how communities of knowledge get empowered in a particular policy field, communities of practice focus on 'understanding how epistemic practical authority is created and maintained in and through practice'. International cooperation, to Adler and Faubert, occurs when practices spread across borders, or when 'communities of practice expand in space'. This is quite different from the transfer of beliefs from one community to a target community; instead, it is expansion through common practice, not through inculcation or norm entrepreneurship.

Bernstein and Laurence (Chapter 4) untangle the relationship between norms and practices by comparing the conventional constructivist account of norms as implying practices with practice theory's expectation that norms themselves are the products of daily practices. In looking at the practice of United Nations (UN) peace operations, the authors find that the norm of 'impartiality' has become decoupled from how it is implemented on the ground. So, while originally, peacekeeping practices were consistent with the general understanding of being impartial, over time practices have become far removed from that original conceptualization. In this sense, practices are constituting the

---

[18] Wallmeier has a Wittgensteinian take on this that supports Pouliot's position on the ontological priority of 'forms of life' over 'knowing our way around in them' that bears considering more seriously.

effective meaning of the norm of impartiality, but without any explicit contestation of the norm's meaning.

Dumouchel (Chapter 7) compares her account of how authority emerges in international affairs from rationalist accounts that argue authoritative relations emerge and last through rational decisions. So, for example, traditional international political economy scholars have attributed the international authority of central bankers to the institutions they represent and to their expertise, but have ignored the processes and practices that have led to such authority being recognized. Both constructivist and neoliberal institutionalist scholarship, in Dumouchel's view, have fixed authority in specific institutions, rather than treating authority as a process that is always becoming and may be reversed.

Schäfer (Chapter 9) also finds the constructivist literature wanting because of its 'interactionist' ontology, which assumes in his telling that the identity of practices, subjects or material things is determined in contexts. But these contexts are treated by constructivists as too rigidly bounded and self-contained, while a proper practice theoretical approach would expect these contexts to 'transcend any given situation and constitute identity in relation to other elements of the social such as other practices, the past, and different sites'. Schäfer explores this translocality in his ethnographic studies of UNESCO meetings on the designation of world heritage sites.

While the previous authors compare their own approaches with alternatives, two authors, Gadinger (Chapter 5) and Walters (Chapter 6), caution against such a practice. In direct conversation with, and in contradistinction to, the work of Bernstein and Laurence in this volume, Gadinger argues that from a practice-oriented perspective, it is not possible to differentiate between practices and norms in ontological terms, and so one cannot, even for analytical purposes, separate them. Since norms, from the practice approach, are unstable, they cannot perform the function of a 'core analytical category'. Gadinger also criticizes norm-centric constructivism for treating norm contestation as a problem to be solved, rather than as a normal occurrence. Moreover, such normal contestation need not threaten the validity of existing norms, but might even strengthen them. Gadinger, in contrasting his approach with Adler's treatment of socialization within security communities, argues we should start our analysis not with fixed norms, but rather use 'disputes and the practice of justification to understand the competing and changing moral claims' in any community of practice.

Walters, in his discussion of the Foucaultian practice of 'counter-conduct', takes issue with the advice to practice theorists to compare their accounts with others. He argues that Foucault's epistemological stance of 'historical nominalism' would be vitiated if we leap to compare before we even establish the meaning of a practice in context. Moreover, since Foucault argues that 'there is no such thing as power or resistance *in general*', there is no general theory against which to compare the deeply situated practices of counter-conduct. We must approach such practices in terms of 'singularities' in particular contexts. Instead, Walters suggests that if 'we are to fully register the diversity of practices', we must develop a new respect for 'description, of a new relation, a new practice, a new space that confounds the lines and logic of [any] typology'. Otherwise, any comparisons will be more than misleading, as they will also prevent us from uncovering all the variations in any given practice we choose to label as an instance of some general phenomenon, including counter-conduct.[19]

The Ontological Priority of Practice, or Not

Directly related to the differences over the advisability of treating practice as one alternative explanation against others between Bernstein and Laurence (Chapter 4) and Gadinger (Chapter 5), or perhaps even the very basis of them, is their positions on whether or not practices should be considered ontologically prior to all else, including norms, of course. Bernstein and Laurence explicitly contrast their own views with those of Gadinger in this volume on the question of ontological prioritization. The former treat norms and practices as analytically separable, and in their empirical evaluation of the norm of impartiality and its instantiation by practitioners on the ground keeping and making peace, show that the practices become unmoored from the original, explicit and authorized meaning of impartiality. In other words, whether norms and the practices that follow from them, or reflect them, are distinguishable from each other is, and should remain, an empirical question in each case. Gadinger maintains that 'it is ontologically not possible to distinguish practices from norms', and this 'implies that theoretical primacy is reserved for practice, and analysis always starts with practice, not norms'.

Change in Practices

Pouliot (Chapter 8) theorizes change from the perspective of practice. He offers an evolutionary model of change in practices. He builds on,

---

[19] Lechner and Frost (2018: 42) also recommend that practice turn scholars pay more attention to description, invoking Peter Winch's 'descriptivism' as an appropriate practice.

and transcends, my recent contribution (Hopf, 2018), which offered scope conditions for reflective sources of changes in practices, as well as a list of mechanisms for how changes in practice through practice might occur. Pouliot effectively proposes scope conditions for change in practice through practices themselves. He points out that the myriad micro-deviations or performances of a practice might amount to nothing, or even strengthen a particular practice, unless the following three conditions hold: survival beyond first occurrence; accumulation over time and space; and the formation of new, unintended, patterns. These three conditions are most likely to occur if the new practices are public, cross over into other relations and are codified or institutionalized within a community of practice.

In Chapter 9, Schäfer zeroes in on the 'logic of iterability' to ground his argument that changes in practice are continuous and unavoidable. While he grounds this insight in the work of Derrida, one could as well adopt a Wittgensteinian approach, or myriad others, that recognize it is logically impossible to do the same thing with the exact same meaning over time, let alone across places and contexts. Nor does what one says have the exact same meaning the second or third time one says it. The progression of time, let alone changes in audience and situation, ensures that one gets repeated routines without replication.

Adler and Faubert argue in Chapter 3 that change is inherent in any community of practice since 'contestation is necessary for learning taking place'. Practices have to be defined and must adapt to environmental challenges. In Chapter 4, Bernstein and Laurence identify changes in practices emerging from how practitioners on the ground in peacekeeping and peacemaking communities perform their roles. They find that the norm of impartiality becomes unrecognizable from its previous explicit meaning in New York at the UN as practitioners themselves perform new, previously unprescribed, tasks in the field.

In Chapter 6, Walters understands counter-conduct itself as a source of change in practices. As a form of contestation, in his case that of a single French farmer defying the law to assist illegal migrants across the French border, it 'creates new patterns of governance'. Moreover, as noted above, deep and thick empirical descriptions of instances of counter-conduct enrich our understanding of how change may occur in practice.

In sum, many of the authors of this volume have offered responses to the critiques that have been raised against PTIR scholarship over the last ten years. These are just a spur to conversations of the future, however, and hardly a last word.

Part II

Key Concepts of IR Scholarship

3   Epistemic Communities of Practice

Emanuel Adler and Michael Faubert

Introduction

The epistemic community research programme, which in the last generation helped frame IR understandings of the relationship between knowledge/expertise and power, has so far been overwhelmingly conceptually driven, focused on policymaking and theoretically restrained. Its main focus has been on whether, how and why epistemic communities help affect, cause or constitute international politics in fields where scientific and technical expertise are required. A mostly overlooked alternative path is conceptually pluralistic, driven to explain international politics more broadly, and thus theoretically expansive. This alternative may conceive of epistemic communities, most likely together with other concepts, as part of mechanisms aimed at explaining international politics more generally. This chapter argues that both paths stand to gain from opening their respective research programmes to explaining knowledge and power in and by practice. With this goal in mind, we introduce the concept of communities of practice. Because practices are at the core of what epistemic communities are, do and aim to achieve, the concept of community of practice helps to understand conceptually epistemic communities from a practice perspective. By identifying epistemic communities as a special and heuristically important case of communities of practice, we will open new and exciting avenues of theory-making and empirical research. To this end, the implications for adopting this heuristic regarding the establishment of a nuclear arms control verification practice during the Cold War and the recent spread of a populist 'post-truth' epistemic community of practice will serve to illustrate its potential.[1] Regardless of the epistemic community research path we choose to take, from now on we should talk about 'knowledge, power and practice'.

---

[1] Pointing to the domination purpose involved in post-truth, Adler and Drieschova (forthcoming) call the phenomenon 'truth subversion'.

Epistemic Communities and Their Discontents

The implications of this approach are far from being strictly theoretical. First, by changing our understanding of how knowledge helps to construct social reality, it promises to change the focus from scientific and non-scientific 'ideas' that people 'possess' in their minds to knowledge that is practised. The epistemic community literature equates knowledge with intersubjectively held beliefs. Initially defined as 'the communicable mapping of some aspects of experienced reality by an observer in symbolic terms' (Haas, 1992: 21), knowledge amounts to a set of consensually held propositions (i.e. causal and normative beliefs) about a particular domain of reality. It takes knowledge as a product of epistemic communities, which amount to 'cognitive baggage handlers as well as gatekeepers governing the entry of new ideas into institutions' (Haas, 1992: 27). Despite Davis Cross' (2013) expansion of the kinds of knowledge that can be transferred to non-scientific communities and Dunlop's (2009) more nuanced and elaborated modelling of the learning mechanisms at play between decision-makers and epistemic community members, the knowledge transferred still amounts to a set of beliefs. From a pragmatist perspective, however, which we will follow, knowing requires active participation in social communities and knowledge is not a product but is bound with action (Wenger, 1998b). The focus shifts away from the transfer of beliefs, as in the epistemic communities' research programme, towards the ongoing practical activities of interpretation, deliberation and judgement, as in communities of practice.

Second, returning to epistemic communities' roots (Foucault, 1971; Ruggie, 1975), a practice-oriented programme on epistemic communities will explore practices not only as enacted by agency but also as being intertwined with social structures or 'epistemes' (Ruggie, 1975). What distinguishes epistemic communities from other groups is not solely a consensus surrounding a particular set of scientific beliefs, but also their claim to be socially relevant and have recognized expertise, which confer them with authority (Adler and Haas, 1992; on authority see Dumouchel, Chapter 7). Epistemic community scholars have made attempts to account for how this authority arises, either from internal dynamics (Davis Cross, 2013) or as a result of their interaction with broader sources of what constitutes legitimate knowledge (Adler and Bernstein, 2005; Antoniades, 2003). By using an epistemic community of practice approach, it is possible to incorporate Ruggie's initial insights with recent articulations of how broader epistemological approaches construct epistemic communities' authority.

Third, a focus on epistemic communities as a subset of communities of practice will change how we think about political diffusion and the institutionalization of knowledge.[2] Departing from classic constructivism's concepts, such as persuasion and socialization, a practice-oriented approach will help explain the adoption of knowledge-generated practices by the very nature of practising and joining communities of practice (Adler, 2005, 2008, 2019; Wenger, 1998b). Importantly, this follows from rearticulating knowledge not only as a product that is packaged or framed, but also and particularly as knowledge-making and knowledge-carrying practices that highlight participation, learning and contestation within and between communities of practice.

Finally, our practice-oriented approach will encourage researchers to study epistemic communities not only as explaining policymaking and policy coordination, but also as developing IR theories that, rather than assuming a dichotomy between change and stability, such as this volume's editors do, explain international politics as simultaneously involving the change and stability of social orders (Adler, 2019). An epistemic community of practice approach also allows the analyst to shift the 'seat of action' to a wider array of sites that are relevant to understanding international political phenomena in a much broader sense. As will be evident in the illustrative sections, international arms control agreements crucially depend upon ongoing verification practices and performances. For example, the concern with post-truth is not primarily focused on altering particular policy decisions (although it inevitably entails shifts in these outputs), but on the implications of post-truth practices and knowledge for liberal democratic regimes and the epistemic foundations of a post–Second World War liberal international order.

While the adopted interpretation of epistemic communities (Adler and Haas, 1992; Haas, 1992) did catch aspects of what goes on, it was ultimately insufficient because it failed to place a larger emphasis on the social construction of knowledge (Adler, 1997; Guzzini, 2000), and its ontology was relatively narrow. Thus, to understand the epistemic foundations of international political life we need to go beyond strands of social theory that place culture solely in people's minds (psychological approaches), intersubjectivity-building interactions (classic constructivism) and discourse (critical theory and post-structuralism), and focus instead primarily on practices, which are culture in motion

---

[2] Our chapter builds on and contributes to the literature of epistemic communities. There are, however, other rich approaches to the role of knowledge in IR that deserve scholars' attention from a practice perspective. See, for example, Bueger (2014), Sending (2015) and Allan (2018).

(Reckwitz, 2002). Culture is not only in people's minds (it is there), about discourse (it is) and interaction (it plays a crucial role), but also in the very performance of practices. Practice rests on intersubjective background knowledge (Searle, 1995; Adler and Pouliot, 2011a, 2011b), which it embodies, enacts and reifies all at once; it is bound up in performances and can only be expressed as such.

Pragmatism, Practices and Communities of Practice

Next, we ground the concept of social practices on philosophical pragmatism's arguments, and define and describe the concepts of social practices and communities of practice.[3]

One of pragmatism's most important conceptions is the primacy of practice (Hellmann, 2009; Putnam, 1995: 52). We know and understand through action and practice (Amin and Cohendet, 2004: 64; Dewey, 1922). Knowledge means active involvement in the world, not just communicating something but producing a physical change in the world. On one hand, knowledge is a by-product of activity (Menand, 2001: 322), while on the other, it is an instrument of successful action (Dewey, 1988: 180; see also Menand, 2001: 361). Dewey (1916: 334) considered practices as helping to turn thinking into knowledge.[4] William James concurred: 'It is far too little recognized ... how entirely the intellect is built up of practical interests ... Cognition, in short, is incomplete until discharged in act' (cited in Richards, 1987: 447).

Second, we owe to pragmatism the view that both dispositional and reflexive knowledge does not precede but is bound up in the execution of practices. Scientific and social reasoning, therefore, are not 'causal' forces antecedent to practice, but rather are its 'laborious achievement' (Dewey, 1922: 198). Contrary to the classic view, therefore, that individual mind and intersubjective collective understanding form social groups' habits, customs and most importantly practices, it is rather habits, customs and practices that form and nurture minds and collective understandings (Dewey, 1922: 63).

---

[3] It is imprecise to interpret the 'practice turn' in IR as being influenced by two opposing orientations, one critical and Bourdieu-oriented and the other pragmatist oriented (Bueger, 2015). Bourdieu's concept of 'habitus' is essentially pragmatist. The literature is extensive. Important overviews of pragmatism include: Bernstein (1985); Haak (2006); Menand (1997, 2001); Misak (1999); and Putnam (1995).

[4] 'Knowledge as an act is bringing some of our dispositions to consciousness with a view to strengthening out a perplexity, by conceiving the connection between ourselves and the world in which we live' (Dewey, 1916: 400).

Third, according to pragmatism, thinking, deliberation, judgement and interpretation can only be understood as taking place within and by communities whose members learn from each other by and through practice; the fixation of belief results from a limited local convergence by a particular community at a particular time (Hausman, 1993: 216). Dewey and George Herbert Mead (in Gronow, 2011: 68) thought that 'sociality does not crush individuality and is not restricted to particular "topics"'. Dewey argued that 'individuals grow to a sense of self-consciousness *through* the communities in which they live, not simply *in* them' (in Gronow, 2011: 68).

Pragmatism's fourth legacy is taking social learning as a communal and practical endeavour. Practitioners learn by becoming a community of practice's active participants in which 'newcomers', by learning the community's practice from 'old-timers', adopt the background knowledge that constitutes such practice (Wenger, 1998b). Within communities, practitioners not only learn competent skills but also adopt identities, artefacts and related practices, and immerse themselves in a type of rational persuasion that must aspire, but cannot always be assimilated, to models of deductive proof or inductive generalization (Bernstein, 1985). Communities, 'characterized by conventions of meaning and communication and the cultures of action and interpretation ... act as learning environments in their own right' (Amin and Cohendet, 2004: 66).

Finally, pragmatism takes individuals' habits, as well as patterned and structural social customs and practices, as what is being transmitted within and between communities (Adler, 2019), sometimes unimpaired and most often with an increment of meaning that becomes the baseline for the next step in the process of constructing social worlds (Dewey, 1922). As such, communities, as vehicles of practice and of the background knowledge on which they nurture, account simultaneously for the social world's stability and transformation (but see Drieschova, Bueger and Hopf, Chapters 1 and 2). On one hand, social action relies on habitual dispositional knowledge and expectations that are embedded in social practices. On the other hand, endogenous and exogenous factors awaken and stir human reflexive creativity, which lead to the transformation of practices and the knowledge bound with them (Joas, 1996).

Moving to practices, it is in and through these that the key dimensions of social and political life take shape: structures, agency and subjectivity, material resources and meaning, stability and change, rationality and rules, morality and interests, and more. Practices are socially meaningful patterns of action that, in being performed more or less competently, simultaneously embody, act out and possibly reify background knowledge and discourse in and on the material world (Adler and Pouliot, 2011a: 6). Specifically, practices are patterned actions embedded in organized contexts and, as such, are articulated into specific types of action and socially developed through learning and training. Practices not only organize the social world but are the raw materials that comprise it.

The relationship between practices and the social world is constitutive. Institutions, systems of governance and social orders are constituted not only by material power and organized violence, or exclusively by ideas, norms, values and discourses, but primarily in and by practices. Practices, in turn, are contained in and carried by communities of practice. The communities in which practices become embedded, however, dissipate their collective understandings beyond their original boundaries and, via social and political processes, lead to their selective retention and institutionalization (Adler, 2019). This last statement needs to be unpacked.

A practice approach prioritizes knowledge, as much as the epistemic community does, but it puts knowledge where it belongs, as practices' background knowledge, which includes the knowledge required to execute certain practices and the knowledge that emerges from the execution of practices. Background knowledge, including scientific knowledge, which consists mainly of intersubjective expectations and dispositions, is not only located behind practice, as in ideas, beliefs and reasons, but is also bound up in the very execution of the practice. Background knowledge, however, is far from being tacit. Rather, it depends on individuals' reflexive, normative and instrumental judgements to remain effectively institutionalized.

The attributes of practice acquire concrete and workable theoretical and empirical meaning in the concept of communities of practice (Brown and Duguid, 1991; Coe and Brunell, 2003; Lave and Wenger, 1991; Wenger, 1998b; in IR see Adler, 2005, 2008; Adler and Pouliot, 2011a). Practices develop, diffuse and become institutionalized in such collectives. According to Etienne Wenger, who together with Jean Lave first developed the concept, a community of practice is a configuration of a domain of knowledge that constitutes like-mindedness, a community of people that 'creates the social fabric of learning', and a shared practice that embodies 'the knowledge the community develops, shares, and maintains' (Wenger et al., 2002: 28–9). The knowledge domain endows practitioners with a sense of joint enterprise, which 'brings the community together through the collective development of a shared practice' and is constantly being renegotiated by its members (Wenger, 1998a: 2). People function as a community through relationships of mutual engagement that bind 'members together into a social entity'. Shared practices, in turn, are sustained by a repertoire of communal resources, such as routines, sensibilities and discourse (Wenger, 1998b: 75–85, 209). Interaction between practitioners in communities of practice gives rise to emergent properties, which means that we cannot reduce communities of practices' properties to those of their individual and corporate practitioners.

Communities of practice are learning communities, where learning means participation in and engagement with the meanings, identities and language of communities of practice and their members (Wenger, 1998b: 55). As a source of social structure, learning is 'what changes our ability to engage in practice, the understanding of why we engage in it and the resources we have at our disposal to do so' (Wenger, 1998b: 95–6). Communities of practice thus consist of people informally as well as contextually bound by a shared interest in learning and applying a common practice.

Membership in communities of practice entails a shared identity, which is constituted through the forms of competence it entails. Thus, communities of practice are not about 'habits mechanically reproducing themselves' but are 'a matter of investment of one's identity and thus of negotiating enough continuity to sustain an identity. From this perspective, practice is different from a physical system, because people do not merely act individually or mechanically, but by negotiating their engagement with one another with respect to their shared practice and their interlocked identities' (Wenger, 1998b: 97).[5] Moreover, the community of practice concept encompasses the conscious and discursive dimensions and the actual doing of social change. Communities of practice are intersubjective social structures that constitute the normative and epistemic grounds for action, but they are also agents, made up of real people, who – working via network channels, often across national borders and organizational divides, and in the halls of government – affect political, economic and social events (Adler, 2008; Adler and Pouliot, 2011a).

We can grasp communities of practice primarily analytically and relationally, as social spaces that are organized around practices and 'are known only in one very limited respect and ... may *never* be encountered face to face' (Urry, 2004: 116). Still, communities of practice are grounded in places and represented in the material world (Sassen, 2000). They differ from the oft-used concept of 'network'

---

[5] Pragmatists, such as Dewey, while referring mainly to individuals' habits, considered them as social, rather than merely individual attributes.

(Castells, 1996) mainly because they involve not only the functional interpersonal, inter-group and inter-organizational transmission of information as networks do, but also processes of social communication and identity formation through which practitioners bargain over and fix meanings, learn practices and exercise political control. Akin to field theory (Bourdieu, 1977; Fligstein and McAdam, 2011) and network theory (Castells, 1996), relational factors play a major role in the way communities of practice structure social order change and stability. But while Bourdieu's (1977) and Fligstein and McAdam's (2011: 17) relational factors are subservient to power relations as hierarchies, in the case of communities of practice, material and social power is subservient to relational processes both within and between communities of practice. In this case, power also means 'horizontal accountability', which is 'associated with engagement in joint activities, negotiation of mutual relevance, standards of practice, peer recognition, identity and replication, and commitment to collective learning' (Wenger, 2010: 13).

It is important to underscore, however, that practitioners may have different interests, authority, institutional resources, innovation and interpretive capabilities. But 'the power that institutions ... or individuals have over the practice of a community is always mediated by the community's creation of its practice' (Wenger, 1998b: 80). Crucially, one should take contestation as one of the most important attributes of communities of practice. This is necessary for learning to take place in communities of practice; it is a process through which practitioners dynamically define their practice, adapt to environmental challenges and adopt a common identity.

Because the boundaries of communities of practice are determined by people's knowledge and identity and by the discourse associated with a specific practice, communities of practice are not necessarily 'congruent with the reified structures of institutional affiliations, divisions and boundaries' (Wenger, 1998b: 118–19). As boundaries form in and around practice, communities of practice link up with their social environments and with other communities of practice to form community-of-practice constellations (Wenger, 1998b: 129); examples are diplomats, security analysts and financial consultants. Several communities may share objects and meanings; Wenger (1998b: 106–8) calls these 'boundary objects'. While communities of practice are not international actors in any formal sense; they coexist and overlap with them. What states do versus other states, the moves they make, the signals they give and the language they speak, are constituted by the practices they share.

Epistemic Communities as Communities of Practice

Peter Haas's (1992) widely accepted definition correctly captures the knowledge and power components of epistemic communities. However, a practice interpretation of epistemic communities may conceive them as consisting of:

(1) A domain of background knowledge that, bound-up in the performance of practices, is validated in and through practice.
(2) An emergent community of practitioners where learning takes place and practices are created.
(3) Shared practices that embody the consensual knowledge the community develops, shares and maintains. Epistemic communities have a sense of shared enterprise, which results not only from abstract shared knowledge, but also primarily from the practical application of their knowledge for solving problems in the world. Their shared practices are sustained not only by collective knowledge, but also by material and organizational resources, and by shared routines and discourses.

From a community of practice perspective, therefore, what explains how practical epistemic authority takes hold is not just scientific consensus and not merely bureaucratic politics, persuasion, lobbying, imitation and agenda-setting, but primarily the adoption of the competence of doing and practising something by a growing number of practitioners across space and time (Adler, 2019). International cooperation takes place, in turn, when state and non-state actors adopt the same practices across functional and geographical borders, namely, when communities of practice expand in space. When practices are learned and adopted by future practitioners, communities of practice also expand in time, thus keeping social order institutionalized (Adler, 2019). Also important in making knowledge authoritative is – using Mary Douglas's (1986) apt term with regard to institutions – the naturalization of practices, at which time alternative knowledge, identities and power relations are set aside, both collectively in communities of practice and in individuals' minds.

At the micro-level, communities of practice acquire their influence when practices stabilize changing social structures and fix subjectivities in people's minds (or determine the dominant ideas that corporate actors focus on at a given point in time), thus constructing agents and agency. Practices structure and congeal thought and language into regular patterns of performance and turn contexts or structures into (individual and corporate) agents' dispositions and expectations.

As vehicles of individual and collective practices, communities of practice play a role not only in what practices are adopted by nation-states and societies, but also in the preferential evolution of some practices over others (Adler, 2019; see also Pouliot, Chapter 8). As such, they are a source of social order, though not the only one. At the micro-level, they constitute international social order when their practices socially empower individuals, as well as corporate actors and their elites and leaders, to act in one way rather than another. At the macro-level, however, international social order emerges from configurations of practices, which become routine and taken for granted. According to this account, an epistemic community of practice may consist of scientists and technical experts, whose practices and the knowledge they produce expand across functional and geographical boundaries.

Recently, the authority of and trust in scientific expertise has been undermined. Moreover, scientific expertise must compete with other kinds of knowledge and epistemic communities of practice, which may consist of configurations of domains of social knowledge, law, ethical understandings and religion (Sandal, 2011). As Hajer (2003: 185) writes, 'a positive way to understand this is to see that it is essentially a democratization of knowledge that has created the *social explosiveness* of many contemporary practices'. This raises the question, as we begin exploring post-truth in this chapter, what difference does it make to political and social reality, and the evolution of international practices, that background knowledge that constitutes epistemic communities of practice is scientific and enjoys people's legitimacy?

Science, Practice and Communities of Practice

The recent emphasis in Science and Technology Studies on science as a practice opens another window through which we can observe knowledge as inseparable from action (Dewey, [1929] 1984). An approach to science that focuses not just on abstract scientific theories, but primarily on science as a set of practices (Kuhn, 1962) enriches the ontology of the social construction of knowledge and our understanding of the construction of social and political realities. Such an approach is less an alternative to social-constructivist interpretations of scientific knowledge, as it is sometimes viewed in science studies (Rouse, 2003), than a means of strengthening and enriching social constructivism. From the perspective of science as activity or practice we want to know how epistemic communities, as 'factories of practice', motivate certain political moves through the adoption of new practices. We also want to know how scientific practices help to at least partly construct not only what experts consider to be 'consensual knowledge', but also what political actors consider to be most politically viable.

A practice-based science should thus be understood not simply as 'an intimate encounter between a research problem and a problem solver' (Friedrichs and Kratochwil, 2009: 710–11), but more as a socially collaborative and communal activity (Hagstrom, 1965; Latour, 1987; Knorr Cetina, 1981b), 'taking place in communities of practice' (Friedrichs and Kratochwil, 2009: 710–11). The lesson drawn from Cultural Studies of Scientific Knowledge – that there is a constant 'traffic between the establishment of knowledge and those cultural practices and formations which philosophers of science have often regarded as "external" to knowledge' (Rouse, 1993: 4, 1996) – also suggests the notion that scientists and experts move within and between communities of practice:

Our ability to know is shaped in ... landscapes of practice. For instance, the body of knowledge of a profession is not merely a curriculum. It is a whole landscape of practices – involved not only in practicing the profession, but also in research, teaching, management, regulation, professional associations, and many other contexts ... The composition of such landscape is dynamic as communities emerge, merge, split, compete, complement each other, and disappear (Wenger, 2010: 183).

Focusing, as Wenger proposes, on scientists' and experts' knowledge as emergent social structures, which are sustained and transformed by means of practice rather than merely as ideas scientists and experts carry in their heads, suggests treating epistemic communities as domains of background knowledge that constitute the like-mindedness of their members, a community of people that creates the social fabric of learning, and a repository of shared practices that embodies the knowledge the epistemic community develops, shares and maintains.

Epistemic Communities in Combination with, or Instead of, Communities of Practice

Since Lave and Wenger (1991) suggested the concept of communities of practice, it has generated a vast literature. A quick search with Google Scholar shows 694 million entries (8 March 2020). The product of collaboration between a Xerox computer scientist (Wenger) and an anthropologist (Lave), communities of practice was first and foremost conceived as referring to local small communities at the level of organization, firm, school and the workplace, where in most cases practitioners know and are in contact with each other. In his 1998 book,

Wenger used the example of insurance claim processors. Soon enough, organizations such as the World Bank deliberately began setting up communities of practice (Adler, 2005). From a disciplinary perspective, the concept was mainly adopted in management science, business administration, education and economics, and soon took a prescriptive direction that aimed to improve learning in educational settings, organizations and firms. It also became related to the efficiencies and strength of communication between organizations and firms (Bueger, 2011). Wenger (1998a) was careful to argue, however, that nothing prevents application of the concept on a larger, perhaps even global, level, and that there is nothing intrinsically progressive or regressive about communities of practice.

During the last twenty years, an interdisciplinary literature began comparing communities of practice with other knowledge-based communities, including epistemic communities. Usually strongly reifying the epistemic communities and communities of practice concepts, scholars began arguing not only about which concept best helps to explain policymaking in a variety of fields, learning in the workplace, good management and communication across communities, but also whether these communities coexist and co-evolve within organizations, firms, laboratories and universities. We cannot cover this genre's large quantity of publications here. To illustrate, however, based on ethnographic fieldwork among quantum information physicists, Hansen (2015) identifies scientific communities of practice and argues that in science and education they 'have existed in various forms for more than a century, but have only recently been formalized into practice'. By comparison, however, Créplet et al. (2003: 1–2) consider that epistemic communities are truly oriented towards new knowledge creation, whereas communities of practice are oriented towards the achievement of an activity; nonetheless, these communities 'might populate diverse organizational contexts'. Håkanson (2010: 1809) also distinguishes between the two communities and argues that epistemic communities bear strong resemblance to communities of practice, but prefers to study firms as epistemic communities. Writing about medical knowledge, Akrich (2010: 13) argues that collectives emerging from communities of practice came to form an epistemic community. Meyer and Molyneux-Hodgson (2010: 4), in turn, argue that 'the notion of epistemic community proves most fruitful when combined with other concepts, such as communities of practice'. Cohendet et al. (2001: 9) add that the core of the formation of organizational learning resides in interaction between epistemic communities and communities of practice. Amin and Cohendet (2004: 77) reach a similar conclusion, arguing that while 'epistemic communities may be established explicitly as knowledge communities, the sociology of their knowledge practices is not radically different from that of communities of practice'. And Meyer (2010: 2) argues that 'scientists move in communities of practice ... that very often don't have clear boundaries'. He shows how amateur and professional scientists meet through a journal or conference, thus building an epistemic collective through weak ties.

Regardless of the type of arguments cited here, their authors refer to epistemic communities and communities of practice mostly as reified entities, which exist and work in organizational contexts, side by side, sometimes overlapping in either symbiotic, hybrid, parallel or subordinated relationships, and to which some organizational, economic or political benefit can be attributed. These and other studies neglect, however, perhaps with some outstanding exceptions, such as Amin and Cohendet (2004), to use these concepts analytically and heuristically with the goal of understanding broader social phenomena. To this end, we turn now to illustrations of nuclear arms control verification practices and the recent phenomenon of post-truth's wider implications for liberal democracy and post-war international institutions.

Verification: Epistemic Communities of Practice and Nuclear Arms Control

For any arms control agreement to effectively limit the testing, use or reduction of nuclear weapons requires establishing the techniques and procedures necessary to monitor and verify compliance with negotiated conditions. Monitoring capabilities (e.g. the use of satellite, aircraft, mobile and stationary sites) are necessary but alone insufficient; they must provide a precision and accuracy of data such that each party can confidently verify whether a violation has occurred (Hafemeister, 2016: 137–8). Early attempts to establish verification practices to complement the first nuclear arms control agreements between the United States (US) and the Soviet Union (USSR) – the Threshold Test Ban Treaty (TTBT) and the Peaceful Nuclear Explosion Treaty (PNET) – were important for arriving at a consensus not only over their implementation, but also their very possibility. Thus, they played a decisive role in initially inhibiting and subsequently allowing for the treaties' ratification. When we focus on epistemic communities as communities of practice, the construction of the nuclear testing verification regime was more than the innovation, diffusion and adoption of a set of ideas by the rival superpowers (Adler, 1992). Rather, it hinged on the active participation by a group of transnational physicists and seismologists in the production of new technologies and practices in and through which the knowledge required to sustain the arms control treaties could be maintained. By first examining the initial failure to establish an effective nuclear testing ban, the practices necessary for the ongoing stability of the arms control regime are put into higher relief, and suggest why there may be cause for concern regarding the future of US–Russia nuclear cooperation.

Establishing a Ban on Nuclear Testing: 'Trust, but Verify'

Shortly after the end of the Second World War and the devastating effects of using nuclear weapons on Hiroshima and Nagasaki, calls emerged from within the US and the USSR to limit their use while also recognizing the immense civilian potential that nuclear power afforded. While President Eisenhower's Atoms for Peace speech at the UN on 8 December 1953 signalled to the world that nuclear energy could be harnessed for non-violent purposes, it was not a foregone conclusion that the control, or even the limiting and reduction, of nuclear weapons would emerge as a constitutive feature of Cold War international relations (Miller, 2006). Indeed, there were those advocating nuclear superiority, against which an arms control epistemic community had to compete both intellectually and politically (Adler, 2005: 154). Even throughout the process of establishing the logic of US–Soviet nuclear cooperation, any suggestion of arms control eventually confronts the problem of verification.

As early as 1946, with the Soviets advocating a ban on nuclear weapons, the US was adamant that an effective mechanism to verify violations would be a prerequisite for any nuclear arms control agreement. Despite initial opposition from the Department of Defence, the Atomic Energy Commission and various physicists, the US began diplomatic talks to create a means of monitoring secret weapons testing. Insisting that technical meetings were required to establish the basis on which the verification of violations could be achieved, experts from the US and the USSR met in Geneva in 1958 to discuss their various proposals for recording acoustic and seismic waves, radioactive debris and radio signals, which could detect detonations in the air, land, sea and space. While recognizing the difficulty of definitively establishing the potential to detect underground explosions (the only data available was the seismic measurements from a single US underground explosion test, Rainier, with a small yield of only 1.7 kilotons), it was a sufficient basis on which to begin diplomatic negotiations for a test ban on 31 October 1958. During the second technical meeting in late 1959, however, controversy arose between US and Soviet experts. The American delegation argued that in light of new data from recent tests and of the RAND

Corporation's publication of a theory suggesting underground explosions could be concealed (namely that detonating explosives within a cavity could render yields twenty times the size of that dropped on Hiroshima undetectable), it was significantly more difficult than previously thought to differentiate an underground nuclear test from the thousands of small earthquakes that occurred annually. The Soviet experts responded that no renegotiation of detection capabilities was required, dismissed the new US data as irrelevant, challenged the hydrodynamic assumptions underlying RAND's theory, and rejected the US use of Benioff seismographs on the grounds that they did not meet the criteria previously agreed upon. While the US position was that verification would be a lot more difficult than they had previously anticipated and required further theoretical and technical development, the Soviets insisted that their previous agreement was enough to allow diplomatic negotiations to continue. The technical controversy went unresolved and remained an ongoing diplomatic point of contention. A lack of expert consensus deadlocked future negotiations (Barth, 1998).

Eventually, a Limited Nuclear Test Ban Treaty (LTBT) was signed by President John F. Kennedy and Premier Khrushchev in 1963, no doubt partially resulting from a renewed sense of urgency triggered by the Cuban Missile Crisis (Fischer, 1997: 94). However, LTBT only limited testing in the atmosphere, outer space and under water. When the TTBT and PNET were signed to regulate underground testing, in 1974 and 1976 respectively, establishing some means of verification was still required. While agreements were signed, which in itself was a significant feat given the stakes involved, performing nuclear arms control involved much more than the emergence of an ideational consensus. We will argue that through mutual learning and contestation an epistemic community of practice consisting of US and Soviet scientists designed the practice of effective verification (a necessary but insufficient condition) that made the 1988 Joint Verification Experiments (JVE) agreement feasible. Rather than looking at how an epistemic community achieved scientific consensus on arms control verification and persuaded decision-makers to adopt it, we explore how the epistemic community of practice made the practice of arms control verification possible. The latter helped to constitute a social order that became key for stabilizing US–Soviet relations at the end of the Cold War, survived the collapse of the USSR and may still play a role in future arms control verification treaties.[6]

---

[6] Here we are referring to constitution as creating conditions of possibility (Adler, 2019: 43).

The Joint Verification Experiments

Considerably delaying the ratification of TTBT and PNET were problems that plague almost all international agreements between states: mutual distrust and the potential for cheating (Keohane, 1984). Particular concern surrounded the testing of underground nuclear devices above the 150 kiloton limit (Hafemeister, 2016: 139). The verification techniques and procedures necessary to assuage the superpowers' suspicions arose from an unprecedented international scientific collaboration between American and Soviet experts, wherein US monitoring stations were setup in Semipalatinsk, Kazakhstan, and Soviet monitoring systems were installed around the Nevada nuclear test site in 1986 (Barth, 2006: 182). The test results from these experiments built the confidence necessary for the treaties' ratification in 1990 (Hecker, 2016: 32). However, it was the extensive coordination and joint learning that led up to the JVE, the practices that emerged and were established during the JVE and the subsequent Lab-to-Lab collaboration, which sustained nuclear arms control cooperation into the post–Cold War period.

A short methodological note is necessary here. Since a focus on epistemic practices attempts to move beyond equating knowledge with mere intersubjective belief, looking into the situated activities of knowledge-making requires an examination of the sites where practices are performed (Latour, 1987). When discussing international scientific collaboration, conferences are often one of these important locations, whether they serve as locations for innovation, as with the Pugwash Conferences and the initial formulation of arms control (Rotblat, 1967), or controversy, as illustrated by the deadlock over underground testing at the 1958/9 Geneva conferences described earlier. When the verification practice succeeded, the relevant sites were the US and Soviet nuclear laboratories and monitoring stations. With this methodological consideration in mind, the following analysis relies heavily on a recently published series of interviews with both Soviet and American experts who were actively involved and present at the JVE sites and laboratories involved in the subsequent Lab-to-Lab collaborations (Hecker, 2016).

As mentioned previously, significant distrust persisted between the superpowers following the signing of both TTBT and PNET; when coupled with the Soviet invasion of Afghanistan, along with the US deployment of the Pershing II missiles in Western Europe, official diplomatic communication ceased entirely between 1983 and 1986 (Barth, 2006: 187). Notably, despite ongoing negotiations over a potential Comprehensive Test Ban Treaty prior to these events, President Ronald

Reagan withdrew from the talks in 1982 citing the need for more nuclear testing and reiterating the lack of verification measures (Barth, 2006: 188). More agreements were signed, but with Cold War tensions now at their strongest, their implementation hinged on the verification issue.

Despite this breakdown of official diplomatic channels, cooperation over nuclear arms control and non-proliferation continued between various non-government organizations, the most noteworthy being the Federation of American Scientists, the US National Academy of Sciences, the Carnegie Corporation, the National Resources Defence Council (NRDC) and the Soviet Academy of Sciences (Hecker, 2016: 79). To overcome the problem of verification, Thomas Cochran and the NRDC published the Nuclear Weapons Databooks that contained information on all previous US nuclear tests. However, the data on smaller underground explosions remained difficult to collect; seismic waves caused by the nuclear devices were virtually indistinguishable from the earthquakes common in the Nevada test site locality (Barth, 2006: 191). The notion of setting up seismic monitoring stations to verify whether future secret tests were being conducted was soon explored by Soviet and US officials (Barth, 2006: 192). In response to Reagan's 'Star Wars' speech in 1983, Yevgeny Velikhov and other Soviet scientists founded the Committee of Soviet Scientists against the Nuclear Threat, using the term *politicheskaya fiska* (political physics) to describe their activities (Barth, 2006: 193). After developing a working relationship with the Federation for American Scientists before becoming part of Premier Gorbachev's inner circle in 1985, Velikhov was instrumental in warming the USSR to the idea of joint verification sites and promoting it at the Moscow Workshop in 1986 (Barth, 2006: 196). During these talks and others in Geneva, JVE came to involve each side bringing their own equipment to each other's site, and as the physicist at the head of the US delegation, Siegfried Hecker, recalls, 'the principle of complete reciprocity was to be preeminent throughout the process' (Hecker, 2016: 87). Security interests were accommodated at every step in the process, accuracy of measurement being balanced with the degree of intrusiveness of the technique in order to protect any secret design information that might be gleaned in collecting the necessary data. At the fourth Washington Summit on 8 December 1987, Reagan and Gorbachev established a formal commitment to JVE (Hecker, 2016: 88).

JVE was unprecedented in more than one sense: it was the largest privately funded scientific exchange with the USSR, a completely novel approach to developing nuclear verification practices, and the first time US scientists had been behind the Iron Curtain at the secret Soviet nuclear test sites (Hecker, 2016: 90). In 1986 Thomas Cochran and James Brune flew to Karkaralinsk, Kazakhstan, to set up three seismic stations roughly 120 miles from the Soviet test site, and soon after began recording earthquake signals to calibrate the seismometers to the region's geology (Barth, 2006: 200). Importantly, this produced completely new data for the Americans and revealed a significant geologic difference between Semipalatink and the Nevada test site. Keith Priestley from the University of Nevada notes that '[i]f two tests, one at Nevada and one at Semipalatinsk, are identical in size, the amplitude of the Kazakhstan test will show up twice as large' (cited in Barth, 2006: 201). This stands as a clear illustration of how important joint participation was when developing verification practices for arms control. While the US had previously accused the Soviets of violating threshold yields, those accusations depended on the assumption of a similar geology; working collaboratively through various technical problems that arose through joint learning allowed the two groups of scientists to ameliorate these concerns. Two examples are particularly noteworthy.

First, by measuring yields using the hydrodynamic method, they recognized the potential for sensitive information about the weapon's technology to be transmitted between the sensors and registers. Nikolai Voloshin notes that to ameliorate such security concerns an anti-intrusion device was jointly developed, autonomously fabricated and then submitted to cross-testing (Hecker, 2016: 106). Second, debates arose several times during the Soviet trip to the Nevada site concerning the interpretation of data, potentially threatening a controversy similar to that experienced in 1959. After finding marked differences between Soviet and American analyses of some initial tests and working together to find the source of discrepancy, it was found that several factors had not been taken into account when the Americans created the data processing programme. Both the US automated and the Soviet 'pen and paper' methods were used jointly in order to read accurately when false pulses were recorded, or when sensors failed to respond during the actual testing (Hecker, 2016: 114–16). Two nuclear weapons explosions were conducted, one at the Nevada test site on 17 August 1988 and one at the Semipalatinsk test site on 14 September 1988. The verification protocols that had been developed gave each side the right to choose from a menu of agreed verification means when an explosion was planned, all of which had been devised and tested during the JVE (Hecker, 2016: 92). On 25 September 1990 the US Senate unanimously agreed to ratify the TTBT and PNET, while the USSR ratified them on 9 October 1990, with the CIS adopting the same agreements when the USSR broke apart (Hecker, 2016).

For the various scientists who were part of the US and Soviet delegations, the process of closely working together to develop the verification practices had significant implications for their interpersonal relationships, as well as for the superpowers' wider diplomatic relations. Cooperatively constructing and jointly manning the three seismic stations, the twenty-six American experts and a larger group from the USSR that travelled together during the JVE consistently noted their change in attitudes, recognizing their international colleagues as scientists with similar ambitions and capabilities. Stephen Younger was surprised to realize that: '[o]ur Russian counterparts were as dedicated to the security of their nation as we were to ours. They were committed to technical excellence and were proud of their achievements. While the physical surroundings were different, there were times when the Americans thought that they were looking at themselves in a mirror as they stared across the conference table' (Hecker, 2016: 118). The JVEs helped constitute an epistemic community of practice that enabled further collaboration between Soviet, now Russian, and American nuclear scientists even as the Berlin Wall fell.

Post-Soviet Nuclear Arms Control: Lab-to-Lab and Emerging Challenges

The Nunn-Lugar Cooperative Threat Reduction programme and Lab-to-Lab followed from the JVE. The US's major concern after the collapse of the USSR was 'loose nukes' – 39,000 were spread across eleven time zones of the Soviet republics – with the worry that nuclear weapons, materials and experts would be exported through various channels (Hecker, 2016: 35). Soviet scientists recognized that the end of the Cold War would require collaboration rather than confrontation. Discussions immediately began regarding how the US scientists could support their Russian peers. The Carnegie Corporation funded a Belfer Centre study on the impact of the USSR's breakup on nuclear arms control, which recommended joint action by the US and Russia to provide financial and technical support for the former superpower's nuclear material and facilities (Hamburg, 2015: 109–11). Supported by Senators Sam Nunn and Richard Lugar, the Soviet Nuclear Threat Reduction Act of 1991 passed into law on 12 December 1991, giving the Department of Defence the authority to transfer US$400 million towards the joint efforts. This involved the dismantling and disposition of nuclear weapons in Ukraine, Kazakhstan and Belarus, but also the US airlifting of 600 kg of highly enriched uranium from the city of Ust-Kamenogorsk to the US (Hecker, 2016: 41). The execution of post–Cold War security initiatives required a considerable amount of expert participation with shared practices.

Specifically, these types of joint arms control measures required close collaboration between several US and Russian nuclear laboratories. The Warhead Safety and Security Exchange and the International Science and Technology Centre (ISTC) were subsequently launched by the US State Department in order to enlist technical support from three nuclear laboratories and provide the funds necessary to prevent a 'brain drain' of nuclear scientists from Russia (Hecker, 2016: 42). Crucially, it was the epistemic community of practice that JVE fostered that allowed for the lab director exchanges in 1992, which began the Lab-to-Lab collaborations that provided not only financial assistance to Russian scientists, but also genuine research partnerships on joint projects. Hecker, who along with John Nuckolls (Director of the Lawrence Livermore National Laboratory) travelled to Sarov (a previously secret Russian city where the Soviet nuclear bomb had been created) to initiate Lab-to-Lab, recalls the effects of joint research:

Scientists and engineers want to create new knowledge, develop new technologies, and build things. Doing so together in early lab-to-lab projects built professional respect, which, in turn, made it easier to establish trust ... We treated each other as equals, not as donors or recipients of US aid, as was often the case in government circles ... Creating things together through scientific cooperation became the hallmark of our relationship. (Hecker, 2016: 42)

Two main principles emerged to guide Lab-to-Lab: side by side as equals and step by step. The former implied that the Los Alamos National Laboratory scientists were not at the Russian lab simply to pick up technology on the cheap. Rather, the US scientists were there to jointly pursue scientific advances. The latter simultaneously sought to recognize the sensitive security status of their cooperation, working quickly but always being deliberately transparent by keeping both of their governments informed (Hecker, 2016: 45). Lev Dmitrievich Ryabev, who was involved through the ISTC's existence, notes that the funds were provided for travel, publication and attending conferences, but also crucially for upgrading storage facilities and jointly solving various problems associated with weapons, material transports and stockpile stewardship (Hecker, 2016: 58). This type of relationship did not apply across the board, with little cooperation relating to civilian nuclear energy, for example, but JVE experience was a crucial precedent when cooperation over warheads began (Hecker, 2016: 59). Joint participation in arms control monitoring and verification during and immediately following the Cold War suggests that the development of this epistemic community of practice was crucial for establishing the implementation and stability of international nuclear agreements. However, when looking to the future of nuclear weapons reduction, regulation and non-proliferation, this recognition provides cause for concern.

Since the early 1990s both Russia and the US have continued to develop and modernize their nuclear arsenals, while simultaneously attempting to reduce overall stockpiles and negotiate new arms control agreements. The Strategic Arms Reduction Treaty (START) signed by President Bill Clinton and Premier Boris Yeltsin in 1991 was followed by START II in 1993, which never entered into force, and the ratification of the 2002 Moscow Treaty (a shorter and simpler version of START I/II) and New START in 2010 (Hafemeister, 2016: 140–1). Despite the optimism these agreements might have produced, several observers have touched upon their common concern with verification. There has been a 50 per cent reduction in the number of facilities to be inspected (Hafemeister, 2016: 141), while inspection practices themselves have been drastically altered.

Moreover, owing to ongoing technological improvements, verification procedures need to evolve and require more intrusive measures than are currently available (Arbatov, 2016; Pifre, 2017). Yet, while extensive and intimate scientific collaboration enabled the establishment of verification practices in the recent past, the ending of the Nunn-Lugar Cooperative Threat Reduction Program in 2013, Russia's withdrawal from the ISTC in 2010 and the closure of its Moscow office in 2015 (Kassianova, 2016), along with Moscow's refusal to participate for the first time in the Fourth Nuclear Security Summit in early 2016 (Arbatov, 2016), all indicate a contraction of the epistemic community of practice outlined here. These developments, coupled with the supply-side limitations for nuclear proliferation as a result of overall increases in global technological capacity, access to technical information and lower costs of industrial requirements (Kemp, 2014), as well as domestic political developments in both Russia and the US, continue to constrain and challenge future nuclear arms control efforts. At the same time, these developments also illustrate the importance of further research on international arms control epistemic communities of practice.

In sum, the concept of epistemic communities of practice improves on the concept of epistemic community in various ways. First, the concept of epistemic communities of practice shows how the knowledge necessary to control nuclear testing did not precede action but was generated in and by joint action. Second, verification practices, as the practitioners themselves admitted, constituted the conditions of possibility for nuclear testing to take place. Third, while the concept of epistemic communities reduces the notion of experts' efficacy to their individual, albeit intersubjective, beliefs, our short case study shows that epistemic communities of practice give rise to emergent properties, which become institutionalized in laboratories, instruments and working habits. Fourth, rather than focusing on how experts persuade decision-makers, we show how mutual trust was generated in and by practice. Finally, one of the most important advantages of our approach is analytically integrating the knowers and the doers as part of the same community.

Post-Truth

In order to demonstrate the scaling potential of the epistemic community of practice concept, we now take a broader approach by outlining the relationship between the recent phenomenon of post-truth, the current rise of populism and its potential to disrupt aspects of a liberal international order. Since the Oxford Dictionary's induction of 'post-truth' into its lexicon, many definitions and formulations have been developed. This not only signifies the relativism of 'truth' in the public sphere, however, but also the rise of alternative epistemic authorities. Specifically, these include populist epistemologies that valorize individual experience over traditional academic and scientifically generated claims. This type of background knowledge lies at the heart of the renewal of post-truth practices performed by populist leaders across the globe, which are most visible in their challenges to, and successful removal of, independent media and constitutional legal authorities.

Sergio Sismondo (2017: 588) finds five major characteristics of post-truth: (1) emotional resonance trumps the factual basis of claims; (2) self-confirming opinions are more significant than facts; (3) public figures make statements without regard to their factual basis, coupled with the public's inability to make a fact/fiction distinction; (4) loss of public trust in traditional media; and (5) dishonesty and demagoguery, seen as distinct from merely lying, are accepted as part of public life. While most of these themes are arguably unsurprising in the context of politics, it is their increasing frequency and deliberate use as means of domination that characterize the qualitative shift in the relationship between various institutional authorities and democratic governance worldwide.[7]

As Hannah Arendt (2006: 257) argued, 'the result of a consistent and total substitution of lies for factual truth is not that the lies will

---

[7] For an important distinction between belief and truth from a philosophical perspective, see Kratochwil, Chapter 11.

now be accepted as truth, and the truth be defamed as lies, but that the sense by which we take our bearings in the real world ... is being destroyed'. The rule of law, democracy, education, markets, trade and peace – to mention some salient practices, all of which rely on tacit and/ or explicit social epistemic agreement – break under the weight of post-truth, resulting in enhanced possibilities for violence, economic failure, surprises, physical harm, human insecurity, human-rights violations and a growing poverty of imagination (Adler, 2019).

From an epistemic community of practice perspective, traditional epistemic authorities erode through post-truth practices with trust shifting from 'experts' to populist leaders and individuals' alternative facts, opinions and emotional reactions. In contemporary liberal democracies, epistemic authority is disaggregated and distributed across a range of institutions such as legal courts, journalism, universities, civil services and public opinion. When post-truth challenges this disaggregation of authority and mutual contestation, democracy's stability and flexibility can falter. Rather than inter-institutional conflicts occurring within a broadly shared epistemic standard (e.g. debating the best policy prescriptions from a shared set of facts), challenges threaten the very basis of institutional authority. The most recent illustration of this is the practice of accusing media outlets of propagating 'fake news'. Populist leaders and segments of the general public no longer engage in debate over various propositions, but instead dismiss journalistic outlets as incapable of making authoritative claims regarding the very facts of the matter. This practice is by no means a strictly American phenomenon, but an expanding community with leaders across the globe swiftly adopting the technique (Milbank, 2018). In an environment of persistent lies, accusations of fake news and anti-science sentiment, trust in traditional epistemic authorities is eroding and shifting towards new sources of authority. The case study that follows offers insight that complements Dumouchel, Chapter 7, particularly by showing how sources of authority and influence unravel and are substituted by alternatives.

Post-'Truth': A Populist Challenge to the Authority of Expertise

The widely recognized growth of populist movements across the globe is a crucial driver of this erosion. The definition of populism is widely contested and variously defined as an ideology, discourse, strategy or political style (Moffitt, 2016). We define populism as a set of practices that position a country's leader, whether from right or left, as the true moral representative of the people, the only person deemed willing and able to find solutions to people's problems, to the detriment of representative institutions, ruling elites and technocratic and scientific expertise. Therefore, populism is normally conceived as synonymous with democratic illiberalism, at best, and authoritarianism at worst. What links the current wave of populism to post-truth is the nature of epistemic authority that validates both leaders' and people's populist beliefs.

Studies of populist media outlet discourse have given rise to the concept of 'epistemic populism'. This type of epistemic authority takes individual first-hand experiences as more reliable than knowledge produced using theories and other academic methods, views emotional intensity as an indicator of an opinion's reliability and results in the dismissal of all other modes of knowing as elitist and therefore illegitimate (Saurette and Gunster, 2011: 199). Moreover, complexity is stigmatized, as complicated explanations are deemed not only incorrect but also morally corrupt (Saurette and Gunster, 2011: 207). We rightly recognize that these epistemic practices are intimately tied to politics. Epistemic populism calls for political knowledge to be derived from the direct experience of the 'people'. Populist political projects similarly call for the dismantling of all mediating and reflective institutions in liberal democracies that promote public reasoning and maintain a distinction between public and private spheres (Saurette and Gunster, 2011: 212). In sum, privileging post-truth practices implies a demand for the reconfiguration of knowledge and authority, wherein the latter is directly tied to the lived experiences of the people, to their emotions, and to the rejection of current sources of expertise.

The hollowing out of traditional epistemic authorities, which creates space for populist leaders to arise, is exacerbated by the speed and scope of communication made possible by the internet (Adler and Drieschova, 2021). In a recent meta-analysis of the political communications literature, Aelst et al. (2017: 15) found that while there does not appear to be a significant increase in the relative amount or quality of political news available, there is some evidence that fragmentation and polarization is occurring, and the sheer volume of information and misinformation has created a 'crisis of verification'. There is increasing relativism towards 'facts, evidence and empirical knowledge', whereby previously established facts become open issues of public debate (Aelst et al., 2017: 14). Part of what enables this crisis are that (1) this influx of information renders personal preferences more salient (Aelst et al., 2017: 7); and (2) algorithmic filtering coupled with confirmation biases serve to reinforce prior beliefs based on these preferences (Aelst et al., 2017: 15–18). There has been a general narrowing of the types of information one is exposed to through the internet, with a decline in the power of general interest intermediaries to create a wide range of chance encounters and a diversity of shared experiences (Sunstein, 2008).

Leaders such as US President Donald Trump appeal to people's populist 'alternative facts' in their own home base, in constituencies that are willing to believe their leader's deliberate and manipulative lies, or do not care whether s/he is lying, as long as s/he fights for the 'right' causes (e.g. claiming that the number of attendees at Trump's inauguration was larger than Obama's) (Wallace et al., 2017). In so doing, populist leaders and their followers, by expanding this community of post-truth practices, sow the seeds of destruction for reasoned common-sense reality, liberal social orders and democracy, according to which rule is distributed horizontally across many individuals and institutions. When reasoned common-sense reality is challenged by a mixture of populism and post-truth practices, it erodes what Adler (2019, see also Adler and Drieschova, 2021) elsewhere calls 'epistemological security', namely individuals' and communities' experience of orderliness, safety and lack of threat to their physical integrity and identities, resulting from justified beliefs and trust in the knowledge on which their 'common-sense reality' (Ezrahi, 2012: 106) is based. In other words, 'epistemological security' is based on the 'socio-epistemological ground for determination of a public and commonsensical world of facts' (Ezrahi, 2012: 106), or on reality as a condition of intelligibility (Adler, 2019).

Populism thus reflects a unique epistemic attitude, a shared background knowledge within both mobilized mass movements and their leaders. Important here is that the appeal to the 'people' involves the denigration of expertise as 'elitist', and heightens the appeal of populist alternative fact opinions relative to bureaucratic and technocratic knowledge. Populist leaders appeal to the notion that they are the pre-eminent epistemic authority. In opposition to socialist movements that sought to liberate people from 'false consciousness' through re-education, populist practices appeal to people's 'common wisdom' as the basis for and necessary condition of all good politics (Mudde, 2004: 560; Oliver and Rahn, 2016).

Post-Truth Practices: A New Ghost in the Democratic Machine

As indicated, one of the most recent and visible practices accompanying post-truth is the vocal attack on what is rhetorically called the 'mainstream media'. Charges of fake news and accusations of using alternative facts in the US context are instances of a more widely shared practice among populist leaders, as conventional media outlets are considered part of the elite against which the 'people' is contrasted

(Kramer, 2017). Moreover, mass media becomes a process of mediation that inhibits a direct link between the people's will and political authority. Despite the fact that direct access is nevertheless an ideal that can never be achieved in practice, the internet and in particular Web 2.0 communications technology has been the platform of choice for populist leaders to engage with their supporters under the presumption of speaking face to face with the 'people' (Moffitt, 2016: 70–94).

This epistemic challenge in the media environment has not gone unnoticed. Commonly held as a skill that pervades all journalistic communities, fact-checking has emerged in the world of alternative facts as an independent practice that is quickly spreading. While journalists have always attempted to be objective observers, until the last decade this has implied restraint from taking a strong stance on either side of a dispute. Whereas previously the 'facts of the matter' would be considered sufficient, these new practices explicitly demarcate the boundary between what is true and what is false (Gieryn, 1999; Sismondo, 2010: 32). Post-truth is a prominent case of contestation between two competing communities of practice involved in the social controversy over epistemic authority: one that carries and promotes post-truth practices, the other that protects a liberal democratic order with the adoption and promotion of fact-checking practices.

What Kim Scheppele (2014, 2016; Pech and Scheppele, 2017) has variously described as 'rule of law backsliding' or 'constitutional coups' resulting in 'democratorships' is the proverbial populist epistemic ghost in the democratic machine. These hybrid regimes, which have features of both democracy and autocracy, result from populist movements that simultaneously skirt and then remove the institutions of legal and political expertise that mediate between the 'people' and political authority: Russia, Hungary, Poland, Venezuela, Ecuador and Turkey have all experienced this process. We briefly discuss Hungary and Poland. Their relationship to the European Union (EU) is particularly useful to show how the spreading of the populist post-truth epistemic community of practice, bound with alternative facts background knowledge, might challenge the international liberal order and the communities of practice that sustain it. Poland's and Hungary's drift to illiberal democracy, however, have potentially wider implications for current international institutions and for liberal international order more generally. This drift was explicitly promoted by Prime Minister Victor Orbán's vision of Hungary as an illiberal democracy (Toth, 2014).

Immediately after Orbán's Fidesz party won 54 per cent of the vote in 2010, the constitution was changed. Couching these amendments in the name of a popular mandate, it gave the government control over constitutional judicial appointments and concentrated power in the executive (Scheppele, 2016). It is crucial to emphasize that these actions are not illegal. While formally in line with what a democratic system permits, by rejecting traditional epistemic authorities in favour of people's populist alternative fact opinions and fomenting a reliance on a single authority to champion this background knowledge, the nature of these activities is fundamentally altered, ultimately serving to change the configuration of practices that uphold a liberal democratic order.

Like Orbán, Jaroslav Kaczynski came to power in 2015 through a campaign employing post-truth practices that derided globalizing elites and emphasized restoring political institutions based on the will of the people (Scheppele, 2016: 14). More brazen than Orbán, however, the Law and Justice party of Poland has been passing unconstitutional legislation and then simply refusing to publish the decisions of the constitutional courts (Scheppele, 2016: 31). With Orbán proclaiming Hungary's solidarity with Poland against an alliance that 'includes the bureaucrats and we may call it the [George] Soros empire' (Byrne, 2017), the EU is under challenge. Far from suggesting that the project of European integration is coming to an end, the challenges represented by Hungary and Poland, coupled with Brexit, are indications that the spread of practices predicated upon a background knowledge that eschews expertise in favour of people's alternative fact opinions presents unique challenges to the sustainability of EU-based expertise and science's epistemic authority. The latter, after all, enabled the verification practices and the type of knowledge transfer previous epistemic community scholarship has identified more generally. Thus, while post-truth practices challenge the expertise on which the post–Second World War global order is based, the epistemic communities research programme is short of tools to study it. It can study the role of science for policymaking, but less what happens when science is delegitimized, which is another reason why we need to establish a broader communities of practice approach.[8]

Epistemic Communities' Two Research Programmes

Embedding theory and research on epistemic communities in a pragmatist framework that links knowledge and power to practices suggests at least two kinds of programmes on epistemic communities as communities of practice. The 'specific research programme' follows, but can

[8] We thank Alena Drieschova for this insight.

also improve, past studies of epistemic communities. As mentioned in the introduction, it is likely to be theoretically restrained and concerned with whether, how and why epistemic communities, understood as a special case of communities of practice, help affect, cause or constitute international politics in fields where scientific, technical and other types of social knowledge and practices are required. The short case study on verification arms control treaties has briefly illustrated this specific research programme.

Alternatively, the 'expanding research programme' is conceptually pluralistic, driven to explain international politics more broadly, and therefore theoretically expansive. This approach may conceive of epistemic communities, most likely together with other concepts, as part of a mechanism or mechanisms aimed at explaining international politics more generally. The post-truth illustration briefly shows the benefits of an expanding research programme. The two programmes are equally useful and important; pursuing one or the other depends on scholars' research interests. Both programmes, however, benefit from an epistemic community of practice perspective because they widen the ontology and stretch our understanding of how knowledge, practice and political power and authority interact.

Perhaps the most important pay-off of an expanding programme of epistemic communities of practice is the ability to explain world ordering from social epistemological and practical perspectives. Questions concerning the social epistemological foundations of international social orders, how and why they change, and how and why they are kept in a meta-stable condition come to mind. Particularly, we should study the propensity of post-truth practices to undermine the liberal international order – which is already highly contested and challenged by alternative background knowledge understandings, practices, and communities of practice – and the epistemological security of individuals and institutions around the world. A cognitive evolution approach (Adler, 2019; also compare with Pouliot's evolutionary approach to practices, Chapter 8), which focuses on collective learning and contestation within and between communities of practices, can shed light on world ordering processes and their epistemological and practical foundations.

Second, an expanded agenda on epistemic communities of practice may focus on the simultaneous change and meta-stability in global governance. Scholars have already linked epistemic communities to global governance (Davis Cross, 2013; Haas, 2004), showing how problems become global thus requiring global institutional solutions. From this perspective, epistemic communities are the means by which knowledge is translated into power (Davis Cross, 2013). Scholars have

also researched epistemic communities and global governance by looking at the proliferation of non-state actors and the diffusion of political authority, thus opening space for studying the roles of epistemic
communities in the institutionalization of cooperation on global issues
(Haas, 2004). From an expanding programme perspective, however,
epistemic communities of practice would look at the role of practice in
translating knowledge into power, and the role played by institutions
and organizations in global governance. The approach would also look
not only at how scientific, disciplinary and technical, but also social,
legal and religious (Sandal, 2011) habits of action, practices, traditions
and customs may become part of the explanatory mechanisms for the
evolution of global governance at multiple levels (Enderlein et al., 2010;
Hurrell, 2007). Focusing on epistemic communities of practice may
also help us better understand how in and through practice, norms and
legal criteria acquire their normative and legal authority (Brunnée and
Toope, 2010). The emphasis, thus, would be less on how epistemic communities are empowered in a policy field than on understanding how
epistemic practical authority is created and maintained in and through
practice (Adler, 2019).

Third, we should consider expanding the scope of research on epistemic communities and social learning. The subject of learning has
been part and parcel of the epistemic communities research programme from the start (Adler, 1992; Adler and Haas, 1992; Dunlop,
2009; E. Haas, 1997, 2000; P. Haas, 1992). An expanding programme
on epistemic communities that focused on learning, however, would
look beyond how specific actors in specific fields learn from epistemic
communities' frames and prescriptions. Such a programme could take
a couple of directions:

(1) There is the road already paved by Ernst Haas (1997, 2000) on
    the relationship between knowledge, learning and progress in
    international relations. An expanding programme would look at
    how progressive practices aimed at reducing war, human misery,
    environmental degradation and human rights violations are gener-
    ated within and between epistemic communities of practice and
    adopted by ever larger numbers of practitioners across geographical
    and functional borders.
(2) An expanding programme may also focus on learning as commu-
    nities of practice's core mechanism of expansion across space and
    time. This would mean studying learning as something that changes
    practitioners' ability to engage in practice, their understanding of
    why they engage in it, and the resources they have at their disposal

to do so (Wenger, 1998b). Learning in this case means acquiring competence in, and knowledge about, a community of practice's meanings, and how to bargain in order to determine what these are. This would take us in the direction advocated by Davis Cross (2013) of inquiring into the politics within epistemic communities.

(3) Finally, an expanding programme may complement, and in some cases replace the study of interactive networks and fields in IR with the study of epistemic communities as communities of practice. This would require looking at power not only from a hierarchical perspective, but also a horizontal one, as associated with negotiations of mutual relevance and standards of practice, peer recognition, identity and replication, and commitment to collective learning of practices. Such an agenda could also link the study of epistemic communities of practice to democracy, by examining not only how post-truth epistemic communities of practice undermine democratic practices and institutions, but also the epistemic and normative requirements for the promotion of democracy at national and regional levels.

An IR agenda that can explain the epistemic foundation of international relations requires theory that combines knowledge, power, and practice. Pragmatist philosophy is a fertile ground for inspiration regarding how these three concepts combine. We do not need to start from scratch, however. All we really need is to build on the fruitful research programme of epistemic communities that was launched in IR more than twenty years ago. We need to embed this programme's lessons in pragmatist and practice-driven social-theoretical understandings of knowledge as being inseparable from action, taking knowledge and practices as sources of authority for the construction of novel governance systems and international orders, and for the development of better understandings of learning and (albeit limited) human progress (Adler, 2019; Linklater, 2011).

4   Practices and Norms
Relationships, Disjunctures and Change

Steven Bernstein and Marion Laurence

Introduction

The rise of practice-based approaches to the study of international politics has led to questions about the relationship between constructivism and practice theory, and between their main (ontological) objects of study: norms and practices. Like McCourt (2016: 476) we believe it makes sense to assess the contributions of practice-based approaches, at least in part, 'in *relation* to the continued value of constructivist theorising, and not separately'. We also believe the reverse – norm-based approaches would benefit from closer engagement with the practice turn. Yet, as Bourbeau (2017: 3–5, 16) laments in a recent review of influential works by practice scholars, despite the 'similarity' of arguments among many norm and practice theorists in tackling common themes, and the complementary approach employed by some practice theorists (e.g. Autesserre, 2014; Schmidt, 2014), the work of creating dialogue and developing theoretical insights from these relationships has yet to be done. Bueger (2017a: 14) similarly argues that 'links between practice theory and other IR theories need to be better understood'. We take up that challenge.

Specifically, we argue that examining the relationship *between* norms and practices can be fruitful for questions that interest both groups of scholars. Here we focus on two: better understandings of the dynamics of norms and practices; and how studying their interaction can inform a theory of social change by identifying previously obscured patterns and processes. We thus engage in detail with the first fault line outlined by the editors – whether practices are primarily stabilizing or a way to conceptualize change – by identifying four scenarios of change and stability that could be obscured by focusing on only norms or practices in isolation. The 'value added' of a practice lens in addressing these questions is twofold. First, practice theory draws attention to the many situations in which social action flows from tacit knowledge, not conscious reflection and decision-making. Hence, it overcomes the representational bias that characterizes much of the existing research on norms (Pouliot, 2008: 257). This shift, in turn, makes it easier to grapple with empirical puzzles that other theories either ignore or struggle to explain – a key point that Drieschova and Bueger make in Chapter 1. Second, as they also note, practice theory facilitates research that is more attentive to short-term change. For example, we argue below that a practice lens allows us to perceive changes that can easily pass undetected when norms are given analytical precedence over practice. At the same time, processes that could lead to macro-change remain opaque if viewed solely through a practice lens. Such processes can be made visible by focusing on the interaction between norms and practice.

Many first-generation international practice scholars took great care to distinguish practice-based and norm-based approaches to the questions they address. Practices have a material dimension that norms lack and operate via a fundamentally different logic – of practicality, not appropriateness (Pouliot, 2008: 258). Yet practices, understood as 'competent performances', are often tied to norms, which embody shared expectations about appropriate behaviour; in other words, what counts as 'competent' is often implicitly defined by normative commitments (Adler and Pouliot, 2011a: 6). Raymond Duvall and Arjun Chowdhury (2011: 349) go further, asserting that 'competence is always in relation to existing norms and mores'.

The resulting ambiguity in its treatment of the link between norms and practices leaves practice theory, unnecessarily in our view, vulnerable to criticisms of reification and an inability to account for change. For example, Duvall and Chowdhury (2011: 343) argue that practice theory and scholarship reify existing orders by focusing on successful performances, as defined by existing norms, instead of actors that transgress or resist rules. Such assertions challenge the argument of practice theorists that their ontology can accommodate change as well as reproduction. We also find the suggestion in parts of the literature that norms can be subsumed by practices indefensible. This view is inconsistent with the premise of practices as 'competent' or 'incompetent' performances, which require judgements according to some standard that stands in relation to them. Only by recognizing some autonomy of norms and practices, we argue, can practice theory avoid the reification of existing orders and open up space to fully examine how changes in practice, including micro- and incremental changes that may seem inappropriate from a normative perspective, can be transformative. To that end, we address two questions. How closely are norms and practices linked? Do changes in one produce changes in the other, and under what conditions?

While some scholars do not draw sharp distinctions between norms and practices, we argue that it is not only reasonable and helpful to do so but also that the relationship between norms and practices can vary. The connection between a particular norm and associated practices should, therefore, be treated as an empirical question. Norms and practices may be tightly coupled, but disjunctures between them are also possible. In some cases, practices – and the background knowledge on which they are based – clearly tap into extant norms, frames or discourses. In other cases, practices become disconnected from the norms to which they are attributed. In still other situations, norms may evolve away from practices, sometimes through intentional agency when activists may act 'inappropriately' or norm entrepreneurs promote a new norm to push for normative change (Finnemore and Sikkink, 1998: 897–898). A practice-based approach makes it possible to detect and explore these inconsistencies, which might otherwise pass unnoticed over the short term. Over the long term, inconsistent practices can lead to overt contestation and norm change, and vice versa.

This treatment of the relationship between norms and practices stands in contrast to scholars such as Gadinger (Chapter 5), on the one hand, who views norms as either part of background knowledge or as always 'subordinate [to practices] as a fragile, emerging phenomenon', or such as Wiener (2004, 2009) on the other hand, who views norms and practices as so tightly coupled that changes in the latter define changes in the former. Treating them as relatively autonomous is something akin to the methodological move Neumann (2002) makes to model the relationship between discourse and practices to analyse change. As he puts it, 'This question of changing practices may be empirically studied in terms of an analysis of the interplay between discourse and practices' (2002: 651). Even as his model of change views discourse and practice as partially co-constitutive (a view we similarly hold about norms and practices), the move 'places discourse and practice [or, for our purposes, norms and practice] in two different time tracks by letting them emerge in different ways'. Thus, like Neumann, our move is heuristic and methodological, not ontological. It allows for an analysis of the relationship between norms and practices, which, among other analytical benefits, is especially productive for understanding patterns of change in global governance.

To support these arguments, we proceed as follows. First, we review the literature on norms and practices, highlighting ambiguities and disagreements about the relationship between them. Second, we explore that relationship to identify ways in which they can be tightly coupled or temporarily disconnected. Third, we examine the possibility of disjunctures in more detail, drawing on the illustrative case of United Nations (UN) peace operations.[1] Fourth, we discuss the implications of our argument for addressing questions of change. We conclude with a brief discussion of directions for future research.

Defining Norms and Practices

When Iver Neumann first called for a 'turn to practice' in IR, he meant it as a corrective to blind spots in the 'linguistic turn'. Proponents of the linguistic turn had, in his view, lost sight of 'social action itself' (Neumann, 2002: 628). Too many scholars relied on 'armchair analysis' of texts instead of looking at 'how foreign policy and global politics are experienced as lived practices' (Neumann, 2002: 628). This desire to focus on what people actually *do* – on 'practical enactments in concrete situations' (Bueger and Gadinger, 2015: 451) – has become a hallmark of the practice turn. It is also, according to many practice theorists, a key feature that distinguishes their work from norm-based approaches.

Norms define and regulate appropriate behaviour for actors with a given identity (Finnemore and Sikkink, 1998: 291; Katzenstein, 1996: 4), and are publicly or collectively understood as such. They constitute identities and meanings by defining who may act, in what context they may act, and what their actions mean in that particular context. They also regulate by pre/proscribing how actors should behave in defined contexts (Dessler, 1989: 456). In short, norms identify 'notions of what appropriate behaviour ought to be' (Bernstein, 2000: 467). These notions are, to some extent, abstracted and fixed in time. Empirically, they are often most obvious when they are violated – when failures to respect a norm lead actors to engage in justification, denunciation, and contestation (Finnemore, 1996: 158–159). Even when they have not been violated, international and transnational norms may leave 'behavioural traces'. Empirically, these traces include treaty commitments, resolutions, standards, policies, action programmes, and statements of leaders and stakeholders. These traces can include practices, but norms are not the same as action itself (Bernstein, 2013: 128).

---

[1] The article draws on data collected during five focus groups and 39 key informant interviews, most of them conducted during research trips to Sierra Leone, Côte d'Ivoire, and UN Headquarters in New York from 2013 to 2015. The remaining interviews were conducted by phone. Most of the research participants asked to remain anonymous. Participants cited here include UN officials, diplomats, personnel from UN missions, and other stakeholders. Where possible, we have provided more detailed information about their positions and roles.

Practices are 'doings enacted in and on the world' (Adler and Pouliot, 2011c: 13).[2] As such, they have a material dimension that norms lack. Norms may acquire meaning through practice, and practices may make norms visible, but the precise relationship between 'collective expectations' and 'doings' in the world is not always clear. Many scholars believe one cannot exist without the other. Yet it is possible to imagine a norm without corresponding practices. For example, the Outer Space Treaty, which entered into force in 1967, articulates norms for the exploration of the Moon and outer space that – because of technological limitations – did not always have corresponding practices (United Nations, n.d.-b). It is perhaps unusual for a norm to exist without a practice, but it is possible.

Practices also differ from norms insofar as they operate through a different logic – a logic of practicality, not a logic of appropriateness.[3] Most norm-oriented theorizing focuses on the latter – on conscious decisions about how to embrace and follow social rules (Sending, 2002: 444). Actors use these rules – even when they are taken for granted – to make decisions about what constitutes proper or 'appropriate' behaviour in particular situations (March and Olsen, 1989: 160). This means that – in addition to being regulative and constitutive – norms serve a *deontic* function. They express values that create rights and responsibilities (Onuf, 1997; Ruggie, 1998: 21); they are evaluative, embodying 'oughtness' and shared moral assessment in a way that other rules do not. This prescriptive quality does not mean that all norms are necessarily 'good'. As Finnemore and Sikkink (1998: 891–892) point out, even 'bad' norms, such as those invoked to justify imperialism or genocide, are based on claims about 'appropriateness'. What 'good' norms and 'bad' norms have in common is an overt, prescriptive quality that actors routinely use to justify their actions.

Focusing on a logic of appropriateness helps answer certain types of questions, but practice theorists believe it leads scholars to mischaracterize much of what actors do in the world.[4] In their view, social action is often governed by a 'logic of practicality'. It does not flow from conscious reflection or deliberation, but from stocks of 'unspoken know-how'

---

[2] International Practice Theory is diverse. We engage primarily with the version of practice theory presented by Adler and Pouliot (2011b) and Pouliot (2008). See Bueger and Gadinger (2014, 2015) for a broader critical survey of the field.

[3] Pouliot (2008: 258) also contrasts the logic of practicality with the 'logic of arguing', by which actors debate norms of appropriate behaviour.

[4] According to Sending (2002), focusing on a logic of appropriateness (LOA) also makes it difficult to explain change. In his view, the LOA accounts for norm-following behaviour, but it cannot account for the action mechanism through which normative change occurs.

that make what is to be done appear self-evident (Pouliot, 2008: 270). This tacit knowledge – also known as background knowledge or practical knowledge – is 'unreflexive and inarticulate through and through' (Pouliot, 2008: 265). It is also deeply practical; background knowledge is 'oriented toward action', and 'often resembles skill much more than the type of knowledge that can be brandished or represented, such as norms or ideas' (Adler and Pouliot, 2011a: 8). Practices are, therefore, best understood as 'competent performances'. They are 'socially meaningful patterns of action which, in being performed more or less competently, simultaneously embody, act out, and possibly reify background knowledge and discourse in and on the material world' (Adler and Pouliot, 2011b: 6). The key difference here is between representational knowledge or 'knowing-that', which can be verbalized and articulated, and practical knowledge or 'knowing-how', which is automatic, unspoken, and experiential (Pouliot, 2008: 271). Norms involve the former – even the most deeply entrenched or taken-for-granted norm can be consciously invoked if challenged – while practices embody the latter.

These definitions – and the distinctions we have made between norms and practices – are not universally accepted. Some norm scholars effectively subsume practices within categories of norms. For example, Finnemore and Sikkink (1998) argue that once a norm has been thoroughly internalized, deliberate compliance gives way to patterns of action that are taken for granted. Internalized norms are 'hard to discern' precisely because actors 'do not seriously consider or discuss whether to conform' (Finnemore and Sikkink, 1998: 904). In this account, internalized norms bear a striking resemblance to background knowledge. Other scholars treat practices as an extension of norms, conceptualizing them primarily in terms of norm 'implementation'. For instance, Alexander Betts and Phil Orchard (2014: 282) argue that 'puzzles of variation in practice' are best understood in terms of variation in norm implementation. These accounts are problematic for two reasons. First, they exhibit a 'representational bias'; they assume that taken-for-granted knowledge always starts out as representational knowledge, something that should be an open question (Pouliot, 2008: 264). In doing so, they fail to account for the concrete, experiential character of background knowledge. Second, practices are more than just the 'internalization' or 'implementation' of a norm; they are constitutive insofar as they seek to create things they describe (Best and Gheciu, 2014b: 33). Failing to acknowledge their constitutive power obscures the transformative potential of practices.

Some norm scholars are more attentive to the fluidity of norms and to the reciprocal relationship between norms and practices. Antje Wiener, for example, argues that a norm's meaning is always embedded in social practice. She subsumes practices and background knowledge within norms, using the concept of 'meaning-in-use' to explore variation in how norms get interpreted and applied (Wiener, 2009: 179–180). For her, norms and practices are always tightly coupled: 'if a practice changes so will the meaning of the norm' (Wiener, 2004: 192). This account is at odds with our claim that it is useful to treat norms and practices as – at least partly – autonomous. We should not assume that practice change leads immediately and automatically to norm change. To be clear, we do not believe that norms and practices are wholly disconnected and acknowledge that there is active debate about their relative ontological status. Rather, we view the distinction as a useful heuristic device and methodological move that helps us recognize temporary disjunctures between them and analyse change. In doing so, we draw inspiration from Neumann (2002) but also from the strategy of 'bracketing', which figured prominently in early work on the agent-structure debate in IR (Wendt, 1987: 364). This strategy allows for continuous interplay between norms and practices, but it also provides a useful entry point for empirical research. It breaks that interplay down into cycles of interaction over time. Norms and practices are mutually constitutive, but examining them separately – and sequentially – means we can explain change in terms of their interaction over time (Archer, 1988: 76; Carlsnaes, 1992: 258–259).

Many scholars within the practice turn will also take issue with the distinctions we make between norms and practices. As Schatzki (2001: 17) explains, some are open to the idea that practical understandings are 'supplemented by some combination of perception, propositional knowledge, reasons, and goals'. Most, however, insist that other social phenomena can only be analysed via the field of practice (Schatzki, 2001: 12). Norms are no exception. Joseph Rouse (2007b: 2), for example, does not believe it makes sense to treat practices as 'objectively' similar performances, or as performances 'identifiable by their common "presuppositions"'. Drawing on Stephen Turner's work, he rejects these 'regularist' and 'regulist' conceptions, arguing that they lack 'causal efficacy' and 'psychological reality' (Rouse, 2007b: 2; Rouse, 2001: 199). Instead, he favours a 'normative' conception of practices. In this account, actors share a practice if their actions are 'appropriately regarded as answerable to norms of correct or incorrect practice' (Rouse, 2001: 199). This conception of practices depends on a very broad definition of normativity. Rouse (2007b: 3) uses the term to describe 'a whole range of phenomena for which it is appropriate to apply normative concepts, such as correct or incorrect, just or unjust, appropriate or inappropriate, right or wrong, and the like'.

This definition collapses beliefs about competence and appropriateness into a single, all-encompassing category. This is unhelpful given that beliefs about competence may have very little to do with beliefs about justice, for example. Rouse's normative conception of practice is also, to a large extent, unnecessary. As Friedrich Kratochwil (2011: 52) points out, Turner's – and Rouse's – concerns about causality spring from the idea that 'explaining something is tantamount to establishing a "causal link"'. Not all explanations take this form, however. Concerns about psychological reality are also misplaced, according to Kratochwil. They reflect a mistaken belief that social phenomena must always be explained in individual terms (Kratochwil, 2011: 52–53).

If readers accept the distinctions we make between norms and practices, one pay-off will be a more nuanced understanding of social change. Treating them as relatively autonomous opens up avenues for inquiry that would be missed if we assume that one is ontologically primitive or derivative of the other (McCourt, 2016: 479).

Questions remain, though, about the relationship between norms and practices. Specifically, what is the relationship between shared standards for judging 'competence' and the standards for moral assessment that norms provide? What counts as competence may be implicitly defined by normative commitments. Take, for example, the emergence of 'best practices' as a mode of global governance. These practices obtain public authority by reference to lessons learned through shared experience of existing practice, the *appearance* of consensus (i.e. narratives around what is 'best'), and demonstrating 'fitness' with the broader normative environment, including expectations about appropriate behaviour (Bernstein and van der Ven, 2017). Similarly, Brunnée and Toope (2019: 73–74) highlight that even though norms may be subject to ongoing contestation and reconstruction, 'the stabilizing or maintenance of a norm through the dynamics of daily contestation and reconstruction' is also possible. They focus on the specific case of legal norms, which are stabilized through the 'practice of legality'. Drawing on the work of Lon Fuller (1969), cited in Brunnée and Toope, 2019: 75–6), they argue that this practice means legal norms must meet socially embedded (within legal communities of practice) criteria of legality to remain stable, or they risk being replaced or displaced by other norms. These criteria include that legal norms be stated as general rules, public, prospective as opposed to retrospective, non-contradictory, possible, relatively constant, and congruent with 'the actions of officials operating under the law' (Brunnée and Toope, 2019: 75).

This pattern of embeddedness of practices in societal norms is not the case for all practices, however. Beliefs about competence may be more closely tied to notions of effectiveness, efficiency, or skilfulness; their connection to larger norms may be limited. In some cases, practices may even seem at odds with prevailing norms. These situations highlight the transformative potential of practices. Existing scholarship does not fully acknowledge or account for these possibilities. In the sections that follow, we demonstrate the importance of doing so.

Links between Norms and Practices

Avoiding the reification of existing orders that concerns Duvall and Chowdhury (2011) requires recognizing some autonomy of norms and practices. They can be, however, and often are, closely linked: practices – and the background knowledge on which they are based – often tap into extant norms, frames, or discourses. Our argument is that practice theory should pay more attention to the *variation* in that linkage. Doing so opens up space to examine how changes in practice, including micro- and incremental changes that may constitute inappropriate performance from a normative perspective, can produce change.

For example, norms and practices are tightly coupled when beliefs about what constitutes competence reinforce and reproduce existing understandings of what a norm means and what it requires. However, at other times, and in different circumstances, norms and practices can be much more loosely coupled. They may even challenge each other, such as when new norms arise that make justifications for practices incomprehensible or incongruent (thus changing understandings or narratives of competent and incompetent). Conversely, connections weaken when practices are enactments of resistance or transgression. Lack of attention to this variance is the equivalent – though some may bristle at this analogy epistemologically – of selecting on the dependent variable. Thus, while we fall clearly on the 'change' side of the change/stability fault line in the practices literature identified in Chapter 1 – especially in highlighting the variability of practices at the micro-level – we see at least four possibilities of social stability and change depending on the interaction, and enactment, of norms and practices in particular locations and times. We believe studying these interactions can be a productive way of foregrounding processes of change unavailable to analyses that focus solely on practices and must therefore rely on principles such as indexicality (i.e. micro-adjustments or adaptations), repetition and evolution to understand change (see Pouliot, Chapter 8, and Schäfer, Chapter 9).

The first possibility is the condition already described – the default in much of the literature – where norms and practices are tightly coupled.

In this situation, practices are generally performed competently, understood as consistent with some set of standards that resonate with broader normative systems (however defined – and recognizing that there are differences in the literature on this point).

Second, practices may be performed 'incompetently', or incorrectly, either through misunderstanding or errors, without fundamentally challenging the link between practices and the normative commitment (Adler-Nissen and Pouliot, 2014: 903–904). However, ongoing incompetent performances can undermine normativity or gradually erode the sense of obligation to a norm. For example, a legal norm may be entrenched in a treaty, but 'not be supported by sufficient shared understandings, or sufficiently meet the requirements of legality' to remain law (Brunnée and Toope, 2019: 76).

Third, however, one could imagine incompetent performances not as misunderstandings, errors, or neglect, but as resistance or transgression. This would signal the most overt action to challenge prevailing norms and might be best understood through normative as opposed to practice logics, focusing on 'inappropriateness', overt contestation, or new norm promotion. This could include situations where conflicts between opposing norms play out in practice. From a practices perspective, this third scenario encompasses Neumann's (2002: 637) original characterization of change when he first brought the 'practice turn' to IR: that is, the 'possibility ... that people will not act in accordance with a given practice [following the introduction of new narratives], in which case established discourse [or norms] will come under strain'. Similarly, Acharya (2004) has identified a set of practices in the 'localization' of norms that could be considered a subset of this category of change. While not overtly challenging the norm, localization can include practices of 'framing' and 'grafting' to reconstruct international norms to fit with local norms or to reinforce local beliefs or institutions (Acharya, 2004: 243). As Gadinger (Chapter 5) points out, shifting the analytic focus to practices in processes of learning, socialization, and diffusion that have preoccupied norm-theorists can bring actors, agency, and power back into play as they actively attempt to adapt, resist, or reshape norms. We would also place in this category Adler-Nissen's (2014b) arguments about 'norm-violating' and 'transgressive' states. She shows, for example, that Cuba successfully used a strategy of counter-stigmatization – of turning 'vice into virtue' – to resist the United States' attempts to make the country's Communist government an international pariah (Adler-Nissen, 2014: 165). These types of active and strategic attempts to cope with stigma play a part in constructing, and sometimes reshaping, social order. Here the autonomy of norms and practices is most visible. Accepting the possibility of this situation – which, despite exceptions such as Neumann and at least implicitly Alder-Nissen, many practice theorists resist – still requires further development of explanations of the mutual effects of norms and practices under these conditions.

Fourth, perhaps most theoretically challenging and interesting, is a situation in which micro-changes or alterations in practices occur that can be interpreted by external audiences as consistent with norms, but that may require ongoing reinterpretation and justification. This situation has been the focus of most of the practices literature interested in change. While such micro-alterations and reinterpretations may explain change, much more work is needed on how much tension can exist between norms and practices before social change is recognized. The challenge may be especially great since much of the practices and norms literatures suggests reproduction of practices and resilience or robustness of norms are common features of most social orders. In these circumstances, practices and norms may show signs of decoupling, but justifications and reinterpretation of competency occur in ways that reinforce or stabilize normative underpinnings and background knowledge. Under such conditions, performances are not viewed by audiences as incorrect or incompetent, although reinterpretations may be judged and contested. It is also important to note that this interpretation is inconsistent with a 'practices all the way down' – or practices as ontologically prior – argument. Reinterpretations... and justifications under this scenario ultimately must be consistent with the legitimacy of the norm in question, which stands apart from its performance or its reception.

Change under this scenario could take several forms: communities of practice (see Adler and Faubert, Chapter 3) may shift in composition or recognize the evolution of practices; communities of practice may borrow or copy practices from other fields that they view as providing justifications and legitimacy relevant to their activities; new circumstances might arise where existing practices do not work, alterations or borrowing of practices work better, or communities of practice may, as a result, view alternate practices as more relevant; or norms may evolve in wider fields in which the practices are embedded – for example, by changing discourses around rights that intersect with a variety of fields – which put pressure on communities of practice to shift their justifications.

Take the example of new practices to build authority in international standard setting and informal international law more generally, where many of these processes can be observed. Unlike traditional international law, practices have rapidly evolved in informal law-making over the last 20 or so years, with some international lawyers identifying a possible emerging set of 'procedural meta norms related to authority, procedure and substance' (Pauwelyn et al., 2014: 758). They particularly emphasize that procedural norms that involve all stakeholders can generate legitimacy through 'thick stakeholder consensus', while other authors have begun to talk about multi-stakeholderism as an emerging (if inchoate) institutional form (Pauwelyn et al., 2014: 755; Raymond and DeNardis, 2015). These norms emerged from various communities of practice including those engaged in sustainability standard setting (such as for forest, fisheries, and coffee certification), new circumstances such as the need to regulate the internet, and evolving norms around democratic and civil society participation in international forums (Bernstein, 2014; Pauwelyn et al., 2014: 755; Raymond and DeNardis, 2015). However, norms and practices around political authority in informal law or multi-stakeholder institutions do not necessarily move together coherently or even necessarily in the same direction.

Identifying Disjunctures: The Case of UN Peace Operations

While norms and practices are often tightly coupled, too little attention is paid to the disjunctures that can, and frequently do, arise between them. We are particularly interested in our fourth scenario, where there may be no overt resistance or transgression, but where disjunctures nonetheless arise. When we refer to disjunctures, we do not mean to suggest that norms have some pure, 'objective' meaning and that we as external observers can judge whether practices are at odds with that meaning. Norms are dynamic, indeterminate, and always subject to interpretation (Krook and True, 2010: 104–105; Sandholtz, 2008: 103). A given norm invariably 'means different things to different people' (Niemann and Schillinger, 2016: 33). Rather, we use the term 'disjuncture' to describe situations where practitioners' standards for judging competence shift over time. Disjunctures arise between new practices and existing beliefs about what a norm requires, not between new practices and the 'true' meaning of a norm. This temporal aspect is crucial. Standards for judging competence can change dramatically while abstract beliefs about 'appropriateness' remain fairly stable. UN peace operations provide a striking example, as the brief sketch that follows illustrates.

Impartiality is a core legitimating norm for UN peacekeeping missions – part of the 'holy trinity' of guiding norms for UN peace operations (Bellamy et al., 2010: 196). When the UN first began deploying peacekeepers in the 1950s, being impartial was a way of proving the organization's commitment to fairness and non-interference (Paddon Rhoads, 2016: 49–51). Over time, the meaning of impartiality was established through practice. In order to be considered 'competent', peacekeepers were supposed to avoid taking sides, promoting any particular ideology, or involving themselves in the domestic affairs of host states. For example, members of the UN's first peace operation, the United Nations Emergency Force, were expected to 'refrain from any activity of a political character' (Hammarskjöld, 1957: 5). In concrete terms, their activities were mostly limited to observing ceasefires and liaising between parties to a peace agreement (Panel on United Nations Peace Operations, 2000: 3). With few exceptions, the norm of impartiality – and these benchmarks for judging peacekeepers' competence – went unquestioned for close to four decades. During that time, norms and practices were tightly coupled. Traditional peacekeeping practices were understood as consistent with a set of standards that resonated with broader normative systems – especially with norms around state sovereignty, autonomy, and non-interference.

UN peace operations began to change, after the end of the Cold War. Standards for judging competence shifted as the organization came under pressure to protect civilians from harm and address the 'root causes' of civil conflict (International Commission on Intervention and State Sovereignty, 2001: viii; Paris, 2004; Woodward, 2007: 145). UN personnel adopted a range of new practices that were both intrusive and ideologically prescriptive. Militarily, peacekeepers began using force and taking sides in ways that would previously have been considered 'incompetent'. In 2013, for example, UN troops in the Democratic Republic of the Congo (DRC) began launching targeted offensive operations against armed groups in the eastern part of the country. Composed of infantry battalions, special forces, and an artillery company, the mission's Force Intervention Brigade (FIB) has attacked and sought to 'neutralize' armed groups that threaten civilians or challenge the authority of the Congolese state (United Nations Security Council, 2013).[5] More recently, UN troops in Mali began working with the host government to extend state authority and confront armed groups such as Al-Qaida in the Islamic Maghreb (United Nations, n.d.-a). In doing so, they have effectively become involved in counterinsurgency and counter-terrorism operations (Karlsrud, 2015: 45–47).

The UN has also expanded the scope of its activities in conflict zones, and post-conflict peace-building has become an integral part of most

---

[5] See Laurence (2019) for a more detailed discussion of impartiality and the UN's move toward unorthodox peacekeeping practices in the DRC.

missions. International peace-builders rewrite national constitutions; organize and administer elections; draft legislation; train police officers, lawyers, and judges; and formulate economic policies. Sometimes they administer entire territories on a temporary basis. These activities are inevitably prescriptive. In contemporary missions, they are generally rooted in a commitment to political and economic liberalism (Joshi et al., 2014: 368–372; Paris, 2004: 4). In short, the benchmarks for judging competence in UN peace operations have shifted. Personnel in many missions believe they are more than disinterested mediators; they now see themselves as advisors, mentors, lobbyists, and enforcers of rules on behalf of the international community.

It is tempting to view these changes exclusively through the lens of norm change and contestation. Many of these practices clearly tap into new norms, frames, and discourses. Peacekeepers' attempts to protect civilians from large-scale atrocities can, for example, be understood as enactments of the emerging responsibility to protect norm (Welsh, 2013: 388). Some might view the decision to have UN troops exchange fire with an armed group as an act of resistance or transgression – a deliberate act of 'incompetence' aimed at challenging the norm of impartiality.

Evidence from UN peace operations does not support this interpretation, however. In our view, the most interesting thing about the new practices described here is the extent to which they pass unacknowledged. They are not treated as 'incompetent' performances. While some observers worry that new practices violate the norm of impartiality (Lamont and Skeppström, 2013: 27; Rosenthal, 2013), mission personnel tend not to think in those terms. They are more concerned about demonstrating competence than about whether their actions are congruent with abstract norms. In the words of one former peacekeeper, a UN Civil Affairs Officer, 'field staff, down on the ground, they're not really thinking about principles and concepts'; instead, 'they want to know how, what are the actual tools ... [they] can use' to accomplish their day-to-day work (Interview with UN official, 2014). Practices such as organizing elections and using force to protect civilians have become unremarkable – they are just ways of demonstrating competence on a 'practical operational level' (Interview with UN official, 2014). These beliefs about competence among peacekeepers mark a clear departure from the historical meaning of impartiality. Yet practitioners do not seem very aware of this departure. Questions about appropriateness fade away. When asked about new practices – especially those that seem intrusive or prescriptive from an outsider's point of view – mission personnel downplay their novelty. When asked whether new practices are compatible with impartiality, mission personnel are often perplexed by the question. When pressed, many practitioners claim that they are compatible. They describe unorthodox practices as new ways of being 'impartial', usually noting that impartiality is central to the legitimacy of all UN peace operations (Interviews with UN officials, 2013–2015). In the words of one UN peacekeeper in Côte d'Ivoire, mission personnel have 'a duty to remain impartial. We're not there to judge … It's not our business' (Interview with UN official, 2015).

This is not the response one would expect from practitioners seeking to openly challenge a norm through deliberate acts of 'inappropriateness'. Rather, it is an example of the fourth scenario described earlier. Standards for judging competence have shifted, but new practices are still justified in familiar terms. Mateja Peter (2015: 352) reaches a similar conclusion; in her view, there is a 'collective denial of the mismatch between doctrine and practice' in contemporary peace operations.

In some ways, this phenomenon is similar to what Michael Lipson calls 'organized hypocrisy', defined as 'inconsistent rhetoric and action – hypocrisy – resulting from conflicting material and normative pressures' (Lipson, 2007: 6). Lipson uses the concept to explain failures in UN peacekeeping missions. Specifically, he uses the concept of 'counter-coupling' to argue that rhetoric often compensates for a lack of action. In places such as Rwanda and Bosnia, Security Council resolutions and high-level rhetoric around human rights actually 'diffused and deflected pressure to act in response to ethnic cleansing and genocide' (Lipson, 2007: 15).

Like Lipson, we observe that UN peace operations are subject to conflicting normative and material pressures. Peacekeepers, for example, are supposed to respect national sovereignty while also upholding international human rights norms (United Nations Department of Peacekeeping Operations, 2008: 13–15, 37). This helps account for disjunctures between rhetoric and action.[6] We also agree that organized hypocrisy is not necessarily bad – disjunctures between norms and practices may serve a purpose, fostering coexistence, adaptation, and survival within organizations such as the UN (Lipson, 2007: 13).

Our account differs from Lipson's in three ways, however. First, he uses organized hypocrisy to explain situations where practices lag behind

---

[6] More research is needed to determine whether these types of disjunctures are 'normal' in international politics. Lipson argues that organized hypocrisy is common within international organizations (IOs) (Lipson, 2007: 12). Martha Finnemore and Michael Barnett also find that 'normalization of deviance' is common within IOs (Barnett and Finnemore, 1999: 721–722). Our sense is that such disjunctures are fairly common in the realm of global governance, but some disjunctures are more significant than others.

norms, specifically where the UN failed to make good on rhetorical commitments around protection of civilians and peacekeeping reform. We focus here on the inverse: a situation where patterns of action change while norms – and rhetoric around impartiality – remain fairly stable. Some might argue that new ways of practising impartiality *are* products of norm change and contestation – that documents such as the Brahimi report are proof that the meaning of impartiality was deliberately revised after peacekeeping failures in Rwanda and the former Yugoslavia. This argument is plausible up to a point, but many of the practices described earlier – especially the move towards offensive military operations in Mali and the DRC – go far beyond the 'assertive' conception of impartiality that gained currency in the early 2000s (Paddon Rhoads, 2016: 81; Peter, 2015: 352). There is now a 'time gap between practice and policy, with practice preceding policy and doctrine development at UN headquarters' (Karlsrud, 2013: 530). Second, Lipson (2007: 13) frames his discussion in terms of 'conflicting logics of consequences and appropriateness'. In his view, UN peacekeeping is characterized by organized hypocrisy because, when making decisions, the organization must concern itself with both legitimacy and effectiveness. This account assumes a degree of conscious, deliberate decision-making that mischaracterizes the behaviour of many practitioners. In her wide-ranging ethnographic study of 'interveners' in conflict zones, Séverine Autesserre (2014: 33) shows that many peacekeepers and peace-builders 'do not even consider that alternative ways of living and working are possible'. Instead, they rely on established routines and rituals, which allow them to 'circumvent' conscious decision-making much of the time (Autesserre, 2014: 37). Finally, Lipson's expectations around 'counter-coupling' differ from ours. He says disjunctures between rhetoric and action can have paradoxical policy implications. If action is 'insulated' from rhetoric, changes in one are unlikely to produce changes in the other (Lipson, 2007: 23–24). We believe this account is overly static. We discuss ways to introduce dynamism to the relationship between practice change and norm contestation in the next section.

Practice Change and Normative Contestation

Lipson is right to point out that discrepancies between norms and practices can persist over time. Krasner (1999), for example, shows that norms associated with sovereignty have long been decoupled from action. In their work on internet governance, Raymond and DeNardis (2015) find that many governance practices do not match rhetoric about multi-stakeholder engagement. Still, there are good reasons to believe that many disjunctures will be temporary. According to Adler and Pouliot (2011a: 14), a practice 'does something in the world, and thus can change the physical world as well as the ideas that individually and collectively people hold about it'. It should come as no surprise, then, that inconsistent practices can produce normative contestation and change. However, even in drawing attention to the tension between practices and norms, and to our view that in the long run there will be a tendency for those disjunctures to produce change and a pull towards congruence, we recognize there is much work to be done to develop a fuller account of when and how change occurs.[7]

In particular, further theoretical and empirical work is needed on micro-processes, on determining at what point tension will result in significant shifts in practices or justifications, and even how to judge when change is occurring, although one possibility is when new alignments occur following disjunctures.[8] At one extreme, a version of such a theory that took the autonomy of norms and practices very seriously might posit that each has its own, independent, logic of change; widening disjunctures create tension that increases along a continuum, perhaps with a tipping point where the pull towards congruence becomes almost irresistible. Such a theory of change, however, strikes us as partial at best. Even if one accepts the possibility of two independent logics (one of practicality and the other of appropriateness and/or arguing), it would still require a detailed explication of how they interact. At worst, it would satisfy neither the practice nor norms camps, who might have difficulty accepting the independence of these logics. Our hunch is that a middle ground would be to focus on the link between standards for judging competence and ideas about appropriateness, and under what conditions their overlap or disjuncture would create a pull towards congruence. The realm of global governance – since it is norm-governed by definition – seems a promising arena in which to expect such a pull.

We can already see hints of such linkages in both sets of literature, but they are nascent. For example, to date, the response of practice theory has been largely to view change self-referentially, in an ontological universe that ignores the autonomy of norms. Pouliot (Chapter 8) argues that:

---

[7] Our description of a 'pull toward congruence' borrows rhetorically from two sources in legal scholarship:Franck (1990: 24), who argues that, when rules and rule-making institutions are recognized as legitimate, they will exert a 'pull toward compliance'; and Fuller (1969), who, as noted earlier, argues that normative stability, in the form of legality, demands some 'congruence' between a norm and the actions of those operating under the norm.

[8] See, for example, Schäfer's discussion of routine, repetition, and change (Chapter 9).

The adaptive nature of practice is a given, opening up the possibility for incremental change. In that sense, I would argue that the competency of a given performance is inherently dual in nature – in meeting other practitioners' expectations about the practice, on the one hand, as well as in adjusting to changing circumstances, on the other.

The unresolved ambiguity in this position, however, is Pouliot's acknowledgement that it is not just changed circumstances and micro-adaptations that lead to change but also 'social expectations about competent performance', which sounds to us a lot like norms. At a minimum, 'social expectations' reflect normativity even if the expectations are not universally recognized as legitimate or fully institutionalized. While such expectations may always be open to interpretation and reinterpretation, and are often contested, we agree with Onuf (1997: 32) that norms remain 'discrete positivities' independent of the beliefs, intentions, and expectations of individual actors, as well as of practices. As we argued earlier, norms do leave behavioural traces, often being stated or written down (in treaties and other forms of international law, standards and other forms of 'soft' law, statements of leaders and/or large swaths of civil society, and so on), or at least their propositional content is capable of being stated or written down.

Thus, we argue, it cannot simply be that sources of change are inherent in the very logic of practicality, where 'non-finite' social rules leave open changing understandings of competence (Pouliot, Chapter 8). Like Barnes (2001: 29), we are wary of 'an ungrounded prejudice in favor of know-how at the expense of know-that'. Hopf (2018: 688) makes a related argument; he supplements existing theories, which focus on unconscious changes in practice *through* practice, by offering a two-step model of deliberation and practice, and an account of practice change through 'deliberate conscious reflection'. While the two logics may intermix, theoretically and empirically separating norms and practices offers greater leverage to both observe and possibly explain social change as opposed to subsuming all change as change in practices and performance. In other words, 'what works' or competency cannot be entirely reduced to practice, and, indeed, such a position is in tension with the idea that norms and practices have separate logics.[9]

[9] We have difficulty accepting an ontology that acknowledges different logics but views one logic as ontologically prior to the rest, which is the position taken by Pouliot (2008: 276). He states: 'One important implication of this line of argument is that the logic of practicality is ontologically prior to the three other logics of social action often referred to in IR theory (consequences, appropriateness, or arguing). To state it simply, it is thanks to their practical sense that agents feel whether a given social context calls for instrumental rationality, norm compliance, or communicative action'. It seems illogical to us that practices can at once be prior to norms and be judged competent or not based on them.

This view is in tension with Pouliot's more recent account of practice change (Chapter 8), but it is not completely at odds with it. Like him, we are interested in how the 'social environment … may be more or less supportive of particular deviations [in practice]'. Instead of limiting our focus to broader 'webs' of practice, however, we would view norms as part of the social environment within which practice change occurs.

We do not claim to provide a unified theory of social change, nor can we provide an exhaustive discussion of how – and under what conditions – logics of practicality and appropriateness interact. We can, however, suggest an entry point for studying the interplay between them. When discussing disjunctures between new practices and the norm of impartiality in peace operations, we noted that unorthodox practices are not viewed as 'incompetent' performances. We also noted a dearth of overt contestation in UN missions. This evidence highlights a shortcoming in the literature on norm contestation – a tendency to assume that new practices are products of argumentation and debate.[10] Yet a focus on overt contestation may elucidate one process by which a pull towards congruence could play out. Specifically, it might help us understand how practices can exert a pull on norms. Sandholtz (2008: 103) argues that norm change is often a product of 'practical disputes arising out of specific actions'. Being persuasive in these debates depends on whether an actor can invoke past actions as 'pertinent precedents' to support a particular interpretation of a norm (Sandholtz, 2008: 107). In other words, actions themselves can become justifications. In Sandholtz's account, precedents are used to advance a pre-existing interpretation of a norm. Still, we could imagine a situation where interpretations are extrapolated from current practice. Beliefs about appropriateness might shift to reflect existing standards for judging competence. This would be one example of a pull towards congruence.

Preliminary evidence from UN peace operations provides some support for this view. Many of the new practices described here – such as joint military operations and pre-emptive attacks on certain armed groups in the DRC – now figure prominently in disputes about impartiality and the future of UN peace operations. Russia, for example, has expressed concerns that offensive operations will become standard practice in UN missions even though it believes they are at odds with the norm of impartiality (Security Council Report, 2014). Legal experts have also argued that the FIB mandate makes it difficult for UN troops to claim impartiality (Lamont and Skeppström, 2013: 27).

---

[10] Stimmer and Wisken (2019) and others have started to grapple with this problem, introducing the concept of 'behavioural contestation', but the tendency remains in much of the norms literature.

The Security Council has tried to forestall concerns of this nature. The resolution authorizing the FIB claims to do so 'on an exceptional basis' and 'without creating a precedent or any prejudice to the agreed principles of peacekeeping' (United Nations Security Council, 2013). This language is unusual and suggests that other deployments do constitute 'precedents'. It is also at odds with assessments by many diplomats and UN bureaucrats. In the words of one staff person from the Department of Peacekeeping Operations (DPKO), 'everybody's smiling about that [description of the FIB] because of course it's a precedent' (Interview with UN official, 2014). This is significant because, according to another DPKO official, precedents carry rhetorical weight: 'it's interesting to see the logic of ... "well, we did it like this here, so we should do it like that again"' (Interview with UN official, 2014).[11] One Western diplomat confirmed that the FIB has become a 'precedent' insofar as Mali's foreign minister referenced it when requesting a similar UN response in his own country (Interview with Western diplomat, 2015).

It may be too early to judge whether stakeholders' ideas about appropriateness are changing to match new standards for judging competence in UN peace operations. Still, 'precedents' from the field – including new ways of being 'impartial' – may well put pressure on existing norms. We know that the Department of Peacekeeping Operations has invested considerable time and resources in a 'learning infrastructure' to identify and disseminate 'best practices' across missions (Benner and Rotmann, 2008: 43–44). This matters because 'best practices' derive legitimacy in large part from their feasibility. They are 'perceived as legitimate because they are already in-practice' (Bernstein and van der Ven, 2017: 4). The rise of 'best practices' in peace operations may be an intermediate step that illustrates pressure towards congruence between norms and practices. Pouliot (Chapter 8) also notes the 'force of precedent' in the evolving working methods of the Security Council, suggesting that a preoccupation with past practice is not unique to peace operations or the UN Secretariat.

It will be clear from this tentative sketch that we are not articulating a comprehensive, causal theory of change. All change is not reducible to changes in norms or practices. The IR literature has no shortage of hypothesized causes or drivers of change, ranging from external shocks

---

[11] We use the term 'precedent' because it appears repeatedly in official documents and interviews, but given its legal connotations it might make more sense to speak of 'referents'.

and power transitions to new ideas, ideologies and technologies. Rather, the pay-off of focusing on the interaction of norms and practices is to help understand what is going on when social orders change, since social order is frequently described and understood through the language of *norms* (i.e. norms order institutions, expectations of how actors ought to behave, and the appropriate order of things). Meanwhile, what actors actually do to get on with things – to act competently – is described and even understood through the language of *practices*. Thus, a focus on their interaction enables not only the recognition of change, but the identification of processes that create mounting pressure for change. To that end, our main goal has simply been to foster a conversation between these two related sets of literature that sometimes speak past one other.

Summing up, norms structure behaviour, but they are also malleable and acquire meaning through practice. For a scholar who 'locates the norm itself in the practice', the change is immediate (Wiener, 2004: 191). For those, like us, who believe they are related but separate, this is too neat a solution and is inconsistent with what we observe in the play of practices and norms in many settings, and in particular in our peace operations example given here. Indeed, the 'normal' state of affairs is some tension between norms and practices, since both are moving targets. What is less clear, and what we have tried to open up space for investigating by defining scenarios of change, is how long disjunctures can last, how great they can be before the pull to congruence kicks in, or the exact process through which they might be resolved.

Conclusion

We have argued that gaps remain in our understanding of the relationship between norms and practices. While some scholars argue that norms are embedded in practice (Wiener, 2009), others insist that practices are normative in their own right (Rouse, 2001, 2007a). In our view, insisting on the primacy of either concept is unhelpful and forecloses interesting avenues for empirical research. When grappling with puzzles like the one we describe in the case of peacekeeping, it is both reasonable and useful to maintain clear analytical distinctions between norms, practices, and background knowledge. We argue that some autonomy is possible. Following Neumann (2002), this move is heuristic and methodological, not ontological. It makes it possible to detect disjunctures between norms and practices, and it is particularly useful for studying questions of change in global governance and social order.

We further argue that the relationship between a norm and associated practices can vary, and that the nature of this relationship should be treated as an empirical question. We identify four possible scenarios, though these may not be exhaustive. In the first, norms and practices are tightly coupled. This means that practices are generally performed competently and are understood to be consistent with some set of standards that resonates with broader normative systems. In the second scenario, practices are performed 'incompetently', or incorrectly, but without challenging the link between practices and overarching normative commitments. In cases like this, a practitioner's 'incompetence' springs from mistakes or misunderstandings. In the third scenario, incompetent performances are deliberate acts of resistance or transgression, undertaken to challenge prevailing norms. Such actions might be best understood through normative as opposed to practice logics by focusing on 'inappropriateness', overt contestation, reconstitution, or the promotion of new norms. This is the scenario where the autonomy of norms and practices is most visible. In the fourth scenario norms and practices also show signs of decoupling, but new practices are not perceived as 'incompetent' or 'inappropriate', nor do they spring from a conscious desire to challenge a prevailing norm. Instead, practices – and standards for judging competence – shift over time, but they are still justified in familiar terms. UN peace operations provide a striking example. For many years, the norm of impartiality was tightly coupled with practices such as observing ceasefires and liaising between parties to a conflict. After the end of the Cold War, UN peacekeepers and peace-builders adopted a range of intrusive and prescriptive practices. For practitioners, these practices are just new ways of being 'impartial'. In other words, practices have become (at least temporarily) disconnected from pre-existing beliefs about the meaning and requirements of impartiality.

Together, these four scenarios help us identify and make sense of variation in the relationship between norms and practices. Being attentive to this type of variation opens up space to explore how incremental, micro-changes in practice, including those that seem to constitute inappropriate performance from a normative perspective, can produce change. More work is needed to determine when and how disjunctures between norms and practices will lead to overt contestation and change. Moving forward, this will probably mean exploring the link between standards for judging competence and ideas about appropriateness. Under what conditions do overlaps and disjunctures between them create a pull towards congruence? We sketch out one possible mechanism by which the pull towards congruence might play out, showing that practices can serve as 'precedents' or 'referents' that carry normative weight. This research agenda is unlikely to find favour among scholars who reject our argument about the autonomy of norms and practices. Nevertheless, we believe the relationship between norm-based approaches and practice-based approaches should be one of complementarity. Drawing on insights and concepts from both fields can contribute to better understandings and explanations of change in international politics.

5   The Normativity of International Practices

Frank Gadinger

Introduction: From Norms to Normativity in IR

Since the beginning of the practice turn in IR, scholars have dealt with a range of conceptual challenges such as the stability, materiality, and normativity of international practices.[1] Since these challenges are philosophical in character, there are no straightforward answers. The normativity of international practices is one of those key puzzles that provoke further debates on different forms of conceptualization and methodological implications. Adler and Pouliot's widely used definition of practices as 'competent performances' in reference to Barnes (2001) is a good starting point from which to reflect upon the normative dimension of practice. As they rightly argue, 'the structured dimension of practice stems not only from repetition, but also, and in fact primarily, from groups of individuals' tendency to interpret their performance along similar standards', which can be 'done correctly or incorrectly' (Adler and Pouliot, 2011c: 7–8). This implies that social recognition is a fundamental aspect of practice, as its (in)competence is never inherent, but attributed in and through social relations appraisable by a public audience (Adler and Pouliot, 2011c: 7). While such an understanding of practice as competence may also be criticized as foregrounding competent in contrast to incompetent performances (Duvall and Chowdhury, 2011: 351), it reminds us, first, that terms such as competency and correctness are always established within a community and, second, that these terms imply a standard against which practice can be judged (Gross Stein, 2011: 88). Practice theorists, however, emphasize that these standards are primarily implicit, as practices derive from background knowledge that is shared and established within a community.

[1] For comments on this draft and an earlier version, I would like to thank Steven Bernstein, Christian Bueger, Alena Drieschova, Katja Freistein, Petra Gümplova, Gunther Hellmann, Ted Hopf, Jonathan Joseph, Marion Laurence, Max Lesch, Holger Niemann, Elena Simon, Christopher Smith Ochoa, and the participants of the ISA workshop in Baltimore (2017) and the EISA conference in Barcelona (2017).

From such a viewpoint, norms, standards, and rules are not understood as fixed entities independent from activities and situations, as espoused by *homo sociologicus* and the assumption that actors should be treated as 'normative dopes' (Kratochwil, 2011: 50). In practice theory, norms are but one among many interconnected elements. These include practical understandings, situated learning, bodily performances, rules of thumb, and knowledge inscribed in artefacts; importantly, norms cannot exert influence outside of practice (Bueger, 2017b: 128). Therefore, from a practice-oriented perspective, it is not possible to differentiate between practices and norms in ontological terms, similar to the enmeshed nature of acting and knowing (Friedrichs and Kratochwil, 2009).

Practice theorists (e.g. Schatzki, 2002; Rouse, 2007a; Nicolini, 2013) therefore prefer the term 'normativity' to shift the perspective towards a relational understanding of normative issues in social life, and foreground practices as driving forces for rules and meaning.[2] As norms lose their stable nature, their significance as a core analytical category is fundamentally undermined. The widely used term 'community of practice' in IR, for instance, signifies that practices and normativity are brought together as members of a group constitute a forum that deliberates on what is considered acceptable and what oversteps the mark. As Rouse (2007b: 48) argues, we should not think about practices and normativity by reducing them to governing rules or exhibited regularities. Instead, a 'practice is maintained by interactions among its constitutive performances that express their mutual accountability' (Rouse, 2007b: 48). However, the normativity of practice should not be understood in terms of instrumental rationality, as human agents never definitely know if the use of a term or a rule in a situation is right or wrong. A practice-oriented view draws our attention to the untenability of the rationalist programme of 'deciding before acting', and emphasizes the unarticulated nature of the basis of our shared understandings (Nicolini, 2013: 39). Moreover, it reminds IR scholars of the relevance of social philosopher Wittgenstein (2009: §219), who remarked that obeying a rule is a practice that is not rationally chosen, but rather performed blindly and fundamentally embedded in our routinized everyday activities.

Not surprisingly, Wittgenstein's influential reflections on the primacy of practice in social life have had a major impact on recent practice

---

[2] Following Rouse (2007: 48), the notion of normativity can be understood in a broader sense of the whole range of phenomena 'for which it is appropriate to apply normative concepts, such as correct or incorrect, just or unjust, appropriate or inappropriate, right or wrong, and the like'. In this sense, every ethical concept or moral category such as wrongness, virtue, or well-being involves normativity of some kind.

turn debates in social theory (e.g. Bloor, 2001; Schäfer, 2013; Frega, 2014) and IR (Adler and Pouliot, 2011b: 8; Kratochwil, 2014; Frost and Lechner, 2016a, 2016b; Gadinger, 2016; Niemann and Schillinger, 2016; Hopf, 2018; Grimmel and Hellmann, 2019).[3] Both practice turn scholars and many norm research scholars share his core assumption that 'following a rule is a practice' (Wittgenstein, 2009: §202) and understand rules in their constitutive nature as constraining and enabling (Frost and Lechner, 2016a: 339).[4] Rules therefore 'enable people "to go on", and thereby also change the processes of social reproduction' (Kratochwil, 2011: 54). Such an understanding implies that meaning is never fixed but needs to be understood in and through practical enactment. Wittgenstein's notion of practice as language games is therefore highly relevant for current debates on normativity, as it points to some major issues: learning the 'rules of the game' always involves an intersubjective dimension, as establishing a standard cannot be done by a single individual; the relationship between practices and normativity is conflict-driven because it is important for individuals to be recognized as competent members within a community; and mistakes can happen and practices can fail when deemed to be recognizably 'incorrect' acts by other people (Winch, [1958] 2012: 30). This shows the relevance of following a rule as a general concept in social life but also its ambiguity.

While some early constructivists (e.g. Kratochwil, 1989; Onuf, [1989] 2012) similarly theorized norms, normativity, and constitutive rules, the later empirical turn in norm research in the 1990s led to a different research objective by transforming the concept of norm into positivist research designs (e.g. Cortell and Davis, 1996). Scholars of constructivist norm research, however, have recently rekindled these theoretical and conceptual interests and begun to focus less on the effects of norms and more on the processes, practices, and actions in international politics in which norms are negotiated, contested, and embedded. By using different concepts such as contestation (Wiener, 2014), ambiguity (Engelkamp and Glaab, 2015), translation (Zimmermann, 2016), erosion (Panke and Petersohn, 2012), resistance (Epstein, 2012), multiplicity (Winston,

---

[3] See Fierke (2002) for an early consideration of Wittgenstein in IR theory.
[4] Following Frost and Lechner (2016a: 344), a general feature of rules is 'that they are "action-guiding" (normative) considerations'. While social action implies shared meanings, it also implies the presence of meaningful social standards – rules – that govern the actions of several individuals, and transform these individuals into participants in a shared practice. A practice (Wittgenstein's language game) is a rule-based framework that enables each participant to act on a particular occasion, which depends on the need to know the constitutive rules of the practice in order to perform the requisite action in a competent way (Frost and Lechner, 2016a: 344).

2017), agency (Jabri, 2014), and change (Sandholtz and Stiles, 2009), these scholars are more interested in a processual perspective aiming to overcome simple explanations built on the agency–structure dichotomy and the separation between the local and the global. This is also one of the major concerns of practice theory (Adler and Pouliot, 2011b: 15; Bueger and Gadinger, 2015: 456).

In this chapter, I first argue that the budding conversation between practice theorists and norm researchers is analytically fruitful, as both are concerned with similar research challenges around norms and normativity: the consideration of power and agency, a social understanding of learning and a relational notion of identity, and the contestation and multiplicity of norms/normative orders. However, such a conversation does not aim to simply synthesize both research perspectives, but can rather be understood as a mutual task of 'language learning' (Hellmann, 2017: 298) in conceptual and methodological terms. In this sense, the argument differs from Bernstein and Laurence's suggestion (Chapter 4) to explore the relationship between practices and norms by combining both perspectives. Second, I argue that practice approaches contribute to this conversation by providing innovative conceptual vocabulary and methodological tools. Third, however, there remains a difference between norm research and practice theory. For practice-oriented scholars (following Wittgenstein), it is not ontologically possible to separate practice and norms. This differs from Bernstein and Laurence's view that we need to recognize some autonomy between both concepts (i.e. norms and practices). They claim that we must be wary of subsuming norms under practices to explain how social change remains possible. Although it is analytically legitimate to argue along these lines, I claim that a practice-oriented perspective is equally equipped to explain social reproduction and changes in normative and moral issues. Unlike norm research, theoretical and analytical primacy is here reserved for practice rather than norms. Interpreting practice as the core unit of analysis does not imply treating practices like 'things' (Kratochwil, 2011: 55) or 'atom-like units' (Frost and Lechner, 2016b: 303), but follows the methodological dictum of starting with empirical phenomena (Bueger and Gadinger, 2018: 131). Theory and empirical research are closely connected, and both realms are methodologically reassessed in their mutual entanglement (Schmidt, 2017: 5). Such a practice-oriented perspective on normativity speaks to many of the 'fault lines' identified by Drieschova and Bueger in Chapter 1. A focus on the normativity of practices rather emphasizes change and contestation than stability. As norms and rules are inherent, the conscious and reflective dimension of practices is foregrounded, particularly in pragmatist accounts. Finally, the integrative dimension of practices is underscored in community conceptions of social learning, which involve shared moral values.

I demonstrate the added value of such a practice-oriented perspective by presenting three research examples in IR that study normativity from different angles. Based on the case of the anti-whaling norm, Epstein (2013) shows that normativity and power are closely related in a field where political actors struggle for hierarchical positions. Using the Bourdieusian concept of *nomos*, she foregrounds power relations of structuring normative orders. Adler (2008) demonstrates in his research on NATO as a learning security community that rule following involves a strong interactional dimension and reveals questions of identity in terms of belonging to a community as a competent member. Normativity lies in the practice of social learning, which includes active participation and the absorption of moral standards. Cooperative security and self-restraint is understood as a conflict-driven learning process and not as a functionalist process of norm implementation. Finally, I show by reference to my own research (Gadinger, 2016) that the Abu Ghraib torture scandal is less about the erosion of norms, but instead highlights the normative contestation between different orders of worth as evaluating moral narratives. Inspired by pragmatic sociology I study normativity in disputes by taking actors' critical capacities and competing moral claims seriously. The notion of 'test' provides a methodological entry point to studying normativity in practices of justification and critique, such as public hearings.

Norm Research and International Practice Theory: An Introductory Conversation

Constructivist norm research is often equated with much empirical scholarship from the 1990s (e.g. Finnemore and Sikkink, 1998) that demonstrated that, in many cases, norms matter in international politics. Although these scholars based their work on a constructivist ontology that gives equal weight to agency and structure, it is fair to say that these perspectives were more interested in the structural side of norms and their effects. As Bucher (2014: 742) has since argued, this 'eclipse of agency' is, on the one hand, a result of structural metaphors (diffusion, cascade, life cycle) that point to mechanistic and automatized processes; on the other hand, norms are often placed in the subject position in sentences, leading to narrative structures that create an illusion of agency 'without accounting for the processes through which norms are articulated, propagated, contested, adapted, or rejected'. Bucher's

(2014: 745, 755) suggestion of focusing on norm politics, underlying power relations, and the role of 'agency within social arrangements' is an exemplarily critical call in recent debates on norm research to change the research agenda by following the objectives of early constructivism.[5] Onuf ([1989] 2012: 52, emphasis in original), for instance, centred his account on the notion of rules, and emphasized that 'all rules in a socially constructed reality are related to *practice*'. His emphasis on rules as constitutive and regulative (Onuf [1989] 2012: 51–52) is also a major topic in Kratochwil's (1989) work, in which the author argues that the interpretation of meaning depends upon situations, context, and conditions of practical reasoning, and cannot be explained by simple rule following in terms of methodological individualism. As Kratochwil (1989: 61) argued early on, 'actors are not only programmed by rules and norms, but they produce and change by their practice the normative structures by which they are able to act, share meanings, communicate intentions, criticize claims, and justify choices'.

Such a view implies that practices always entail a dynamic dimension of 'play' and indeterminacy between agency and structure (Doty, 1997: 377). The normativity is produced in and through practice by actors, who use many means of social action (communicate intentions, criticize claims, justify choices) to deal with problematic situations in the everyday world, and thereby, as Kratochwil describes, create 'the normative structures' around them. That is, the 'programming' or learning of the 'rules of the game' is not based on a single action, but rather is embedded in social activity. It does not follow a two-step process of learning a rule and then applying it; instead, rule following encompasses a variety of means such as imitations, corrections, and tips that we get from parents, friends, and teachers (Kratochwil, 2011: 53). For Wittgenstein, to make sense of why we act, we must look around us, not within us. In Wittgenstein's (2009: §54) language, 'one learns the game by watching how others play it'. Diplomats, for instance, mostly learn relevant practices in and through trial and error and are oriented towards the behaviour of established agents (Pouliot, 2016a: 18). A practice-oriented view on normativity is therefore primarily interested in the interplay between agency and structure and the dynamic, often contested production of normativity in political contexts. As I argue in the following pages, norm researchers are not only discovering the concept of practice, but have also begun to tackle research challenges shared by practice theorists in IR.

---

[5] There is a recent tendency among norm researchers to use the term 'critical' instead of 'constructivist' to underline this new research agenda.

Research Challenge I: Power and the Role of Agency

Bucher's description of norm politics and the missing power dimension in conventional norm research is a widely mentioned critique on the need to consider the dynamics of power around normative phenomena. Kersbergen and Verbeek (2007: 217) argued more than a decade ago that norm implementation is not only a matter of internalization and compliance but also of redefinition, which points to the 'recurrent battles for and over norms in international politics'. Epstein (2012), for instance, criticizes the functionalist notion of socialization as a linear and unproblematically liberal one that tends to exclude the perspective of the socializee and, furthermore, infantilizes them. Such perspectives criticize the concealing stance of conventional norm research as neglecting their own normative origins and simply assuming global norms as progressing and positively featured in terms of cooperation and mutual understanding. In doing so, they 'purport to cast as universal what is always necessarily a localized and historically specific set of values' (Epstein, 2012: 136). Critical perspectives on norm research therefore put more emphasis on the underlying power relations in social dynamics of seemingly neutral processes of 'diffusion', 'implementation' and 'normalization'. They consider the unequal nature of the international system between the global and the local and take into account forms of resistance such as postcolonial agency (Jabri, 2014), which also constitute the normative construction of the international order.

The power dimension and the role of agency are also major challenges in practice theory. Owing to their relational ontologies, power is often not explicated as a major concern. In that sense, all practices and relations are of power. In Actor-Network Theory approaches, for instance, power emerges through successful translation and performativity. Following the influential suggestion by Barnett and Duvall of employing different facets of power, Sending and Neumann (2011: 235) argue that a 'turn to practices allows us to explore how different forms of power can be at work simultaneously'. Foucault's notions of productive power and governmentality were therefore used in practice approaches to study power relations in global governance in their diffuse ways, for instance when states use international organizations to enforce social order and increase their power position (Neumann and Sending, 2010). Foucault's work offers even more opportunities to map and study different forms and modalities of power such as counter-conduct as a particular kind of resistance (see Walters, Chapter 6). Bourdieu's work has also had a major impact on practice turn debates as it enables IR researchers to study power relations with a rich vocabulary by analysing practices in distinct fields (Adler-Nissen, 2013b).

A practice-oriented understanding of power overcomes static notions of authority and is therefore better equipped to account for change. Authority in a practice-based conception is understood as a process that can account for the dynamics of authoritative relations (see Dumouchel, Chapter 7). As the work of Adler-Nissen and Pouliot (2014) shows, their notion of 'power in practice' around the international intervention in Libya at the United Nations Security Council is primarily interested in such a sociological analysis of power. They reveal the inner workings of power in the Council between member states by showing how the struggle for competence in everyday performances led to different claims of authority and distinct hierarchies in the field. Such a 'neutral' stance of describing power games has been criticized (Ralph and Gifkins, 2017), however, for shying away from the effects of these struggles and downplaying the normativity of practices and their contested nature. Discussions around agency are less based on the local-global divide, and centre instead on the blurring distinction between humans and non-humans. For practice theorists, many artefacts such as documents and material objects (e.g. surveillance technology) are also capable of producing normativity in practice.

Norm researchers and practice theorists have both tended to downplay the effects of power. Contemporary norm research operates with a stronger emphasis on agency; a critical view on norms therefore asks what role do which actors play in agential norm politics (Lesch, 2017a). This implies reflecting upon the often-assumed passive role of 'local' actors as norm recipients. Such a view reassesses the impact of (Western) norms as the main driver for power struggles, and claims that local agency needs to be taken seriously to shed light on hierarchies and inequalities. From a practice-oriented perspective, power is an effect of practice and is produced within it. The notion of competence without considering normative positions in Adler-Nissen and Pouliot's Libya intervention case shows that the normativity of practice can be a controversial issue. For Ralph and Gifkins (2017), the uncritical acceptance of pre-reflexive practices such as 'penholding' as markers of competence ignores the notion of ethical competence and the linkage between practice theory and normative theory. Such controversial empirical cases are useful for further examining the normative dimension of practices.

Research Challenge II: Learning and Identity

A closely related challenge is finding ways to overcome a functionalist notion of learning in conventional norm research. Processes of norm diffusion and implementation follow a (mostly implicit) understanding of learning as a mechanistic two-step process of explaining and applying, by conceptualizing the intersubjective dimension as a simple master–pupil relationship. The reproduction of global hierarchies within the master–pupil perspective has been problematized by Acharya (2004: 242), for instance, as a 'moral cosmopolitanist' perspective that assumes 'good' transnational and 'bad' local norms. He thus states that 'studies of norm dynamics should account for a range of responses to new norms, from constitutive compliance to outright rejection, and evolutionary and path-dependent forms of acceptance that fall in between' (Acharya, 2004: 242). Acharya (2004: 269) dismisses the perspective of 'norm-taker' as a passive learner, and instead shows how local actors are 'actively borrowing and modifying transnational norms in accordance with their preconstructed normative beliefs and practices'. This more intersubjective view on learning as a common mutual process is closely related to new perspectives on identity and norms. Epstein (2011) deconstructs the essentializing notion of identity often found within constructivism in general and norm research in particular. She problematizes that the reliance on social-psychological concepts such as self-scheme and self-esteem in norm research gives way to a tendency in which 'behavioural change is appraised as the passage from one stable state to another along the trajectory of internalization of a new norm' (Epstein 2011: 334). In this perspective, (un-)successful learning depends upon an identity that is stable and 'given'. Further problems arise where these assumptions are applied to collective actors, such as the state, to theorize their agency. Epstein (2011: 344) instead proposes a Lacanian perspective, which focuses on the ways in which actors 'define themselves by stepping into a particular subject-position carved out by the discourse'.

In practice theory, scholars similarly aim to overcome functionalist notions of learning and identity (see Adler and Faubert, Chapter 3). The community of practice approach used by Wenger, and introduced by Adler (2005, 2008), has had a major impact on understanding learning as social practice. This implies that learning is less a cognitive process, but rather socially grounded by 'belonging, engagement, inclusiveness, and developing identities' (Nicolini 2013: 80). Until now, practice-oriented research on community-building has often focused on 'success stories' insofar as new members are willing to be part of the community and are accepted by the existing members. But as Nicolini (2013:82) rightly argues, such a perspective on learning 'makes clear that handing-down process is not a smooth or friendly affair'. Hofius (2016), for instance, considers this aspect of community-building in the case of the boundaries of the European Union (EU) with its neighbour Ukraine, and highlights the exclusive practices of demarcation as the opposite side of inclusive practices of membership, an issue that is often not taken into account. She demonstrates that the EU field diplomats function as 'boundary workers', as they are engaged in practices on a day-to-day basis, which reveals a more complex understanding of community and identity as an emergent structure of possibilities and experienced as borderland. Such rare perspectives shed light on 'the normative background that is located in the relationships among those people who mutually engage in a specific set of practices and establish a shared repertoire of communal resources', which can be conceived 'as the principal source of the EU's coherence' (Hofius, 2016: 941).

Norm research and practice theory have both changed earlier static notions of learning in IR. However, the dimension of identity is – in comparison to post-structuralism – a rather neglected issue in practice-based and norm research. Scholars seem to be hesitant to take a closer look at the 'dark side' of membership in terms of belonging, exclusion and power. Relational accounts such as those of Epstein and Hofius are rare exceptions. Moreover, the challenge of translating social processes such as learning into methodological frameworks and empirical research remains. One reason for this might be that practice theory shies away from a closer link to the tradition of intersubjectivism. By drawing on Goffman, Adler-Nissen's (2014b) work on stigma management in international relations is a rare example of an intersubjectivist and practice-based framework. In contrast to conventional notions of norm diffusion, she shows that states are not passive objects of socialization, but active agents that cope strategically with their stigma and are even able to transform a moral discourse.

Research Challenge III: Contestation and Multiplicity

There is a growing consensus in critical norm research that the meaning of norms is contested, or, at the very least, ambiguous. Wiener's reflexive approach of norm contestation represents a major reference point in the debate, and distances itself from behaviourist understandings by focusing on 'the meaning of norms that is embedded in social practices' (Wiener, 2008: 30). By assuming a dual quality of norms, such a view implies the ontological rejection of stable norms, and instead privileges a major interest in their contested nature, their practices of interpretation, and cultural contexts. For Wiener (2007: 6), norms are 'contested by default', which reveals the intersubjective, contingent, and invisible dimension of this 'duality' as 'actors operate within a context that is structured by the inter-play between structures of meaning-in-use and individuals' enact-ing of that meaning' (Wiener, 2009: 178). Although the conceptual challenges of how to combine stability and change in norm contes-tation and how to fulfil the dual quality of norms on the level of encounters remain (Niemann and Schillinger, 2016), the overall aim of developing conceptual and methodological frameworks to anal-yse contestation as political practice in different forms such as arbi-tration, deliberation, justification, and contention (Wiener, 2014) has provided novel insights on how norms function. Zimmermann, Deitelhoff, and Lesch (2018) even argue for transcending the distinc-tion between the local and global by taking practices of contestation as constitutive for normative agency. Such a perspective shifts the focus of analysis from norms to different types of contestatory prac-tices and shows how they affect norms.

Practice theorists are generally sceptical of universals and fixed enti-ties, owing to their preference for relational ontologies used, for exam-ple, in Actor-Network Theory and assemblage approaches. Such a relational view obviously implies a different notion of contestation and multiplicity (Frankel Pratt, 2020). For practice theory, there are no single, universal, or essential wholes. Instead, the world is seen as com-posed of multiple and overlapping orders that are changing and emerg-ing (Schatzki, 2002). From a Bourdieusian point of view, however, change in international practices is a rather structural phenomenon that takes place over time in social transformation (see Pouliot, Chapter 8). Practice-oriented works in IR inspired by pragmatic sociology are by contrast intrigued by the fragility, uncertainty, and disorder of the social and the material, as well as by the way actors are nevertheless often able to coordinate their lives and reach agreements in a complex world. Boltanski and Thévenot's (2006) concept of orders of worth,[6] or 'repertoires of evaluation consisting of moral narratives and objects that enable tests of worth' (Hanrieder, 2016: 8), puts strong emphasis on the irreducible plurality of moral standards in political life. Many moral conceptions of global politics, such as health, development, and aid are ambiguous and contested. Hanrieder (2016), for instance, shows in the case of global health that four different orders of worth (survival,

---

[6] The term worth refers to higher normative principles regarding a common good in a respective society. It also relates to a more Bourdieu-inspired understanding (capital) of people that often submits that often the 'same people pass all or most tests' (Boltanski, 2011: 38). By using criteria of equivalence, disputing actors assess the relative value – 'greatness' in Boltanski's vocabulary – of beings engaged in a specific dispute in terms of worth. However, the result of a test is never fixed in advance.

fairness, production, spirit) are used in political controversies, thereby revealing the plurality of differing, but equally acceptable, moral evaluation schemes dependent upon the situation and context.

By prioritizing norms, norm researchers are challenged to understand contestation not as a disruptive force in empirical terms, but rather productively as a routine occurrence in politics. The recent turn to resistance and protest as legitimate practices of contestation points to such a new direction of norm research (Zimmermann, 2016). The same can be said for the multiplicity of norms, a rather new topic that goes beyond the usual empirical research focus on the effects of single norms. Recent attempts (e.g. Winston, 2017) to conceptualize norms as clusters in different structural components allowing for multiple combinations of distinct values and behaviours transcend the assumption of stable norms. They do not adopt a relational ontology, however. For practice theorists, in contrast, contestation is not understood as a major problem to be solved, but as a normal occurrence in social interaction that does not affect the validity of rules, and is rather perceived as a turning point in how things ought to be done after a conflict is solved (Nicolini, 2013: 177). By accepting that questioning and disruption are inherently part of social ordering in everyday life and not an external threat to it, a practice-oriented perspective highlights the fragility and instability of the relationship between norm and deviation. If rules are not static, external entities that determine distinct behaviour, then the possibility of failure, deviation, breach, and mistakes exists in every situation (Schäfer, 2013: 32) and allows for agency.

As this and the other two research challenges show, there is a process of rapprochement between norm researchers and practice turn scholars, particularly in terms of crucial concepts such as agency, learning, and contestation. One major difference remains, however. Despite their stronger consideration of practice and hesitant relational thinking, norm researchers still prioritize the concept of the norm and shy away from taking an explicit practice-oriented view on normativity. Wiener's research around contestation illustrates this dilemma for norm researchers. Although she sympathizes with practice-oriented research and understands contestation as political practice, the prioritization of norms as units of analysis is taken for granted. Owing to the research agenda, the methodological starting point is always the norm, as they 'represent the legitimating core of global governance' (Wiener, 2014: 4). The cause of this dilemma seems to be that it is easier for practice-oriented scholars to accept relational notions such as contestation than it is for norm researchers who touch the 'hard core' of their concept of the norm (Niemann and Schillinger, 2016: 48).

Studying the Normativity of Practices: Power, Learning, and Disputes

The following examples of practice-oriented research in IR demonstrate that there are different ways to study the normativity of international practices. Although none of these accounts claim to adopt an explicit Wittgensteinian notion of practice as language games, some aspects of his work are touched upon. Moreover, the examples also show that the usage of different concepts (power, learning, disputes) imply different methodological ways of studying practices.

The Shift from Whaling to Anti-Whaling: The Power of Line-Drawing Categories

The normative change from whaling to anti-whaling is a phenomenon, similar to the banning of slavery, that is often used in norm research to demonstrate the power of emerging norms over rationalist assumptions of economic interest and strategic calculation. However, as Epstein (2013) shows in her study of whaling, practices and power relations are relevant in explaining the political dynamics behind such normative changes, but not in terms of simple actor models. She uses Bourdieu's vocabulary (field, *doxa*) and his less known concept of *nomos* as a promising way to analyse the underlying normative order structuring a field of interactions, which concretizes fundamental assumptions on normative grounds. For Epstein (2013: 165), the major advantage of this concept is that it foregrounds power relations front and centre, whereas constructivist analyses of given norms in an issue area of international politics tend to downplay the dynamics of power running through it. For Epstein (2013: 169–170), the *nomos* is first and foremost 'a principle of inclusion and exclusion that sets the boundaries of a field' and provides a 'principle of vision and division'.

Using whaling, Epstein shows how the concept of *nomos* can be used to illuminate the line-drawing practices of inclusion and exclusion within a distinct field, in this case comprising the consumptive and non-consumptive utilizations of the whale across different countries. The whaling field regularly materializes at the annual meetings of the International Whaling Commission (IWC), where its practices and power dynamics can be studied. From such a view, the 'actors are more or less powerful according, not merely to the size of their purse, but to the lay of the *nomos*', and where they stand within it (Epstein, 2013: 172). This perspective explains how, in the field marked by an anti-whaling *nomos*, a non-governmental actor such as Greenpeace can be a more powerful actor than a state actor such as Japan; 'simply because that actor stands on the "right" side of where the lines have been drawn' (Epstein, 2013: 172–173). Until the mid-1960s, the global whaling order was clearly based on the single purpose of enabling whaling, even after the disappearance of whales endangered both the whalers' livelihoods and the IWC scientists' professional *raison d'être*. The emergence of the anti-whaling order can be explained by the fundamental reordering of the field and a new way of categorizing whaling practices. This turn was not reached on the basis of improved knowledge and new scientific classificatory schemes, but was brought about by a 're-drawing of lines through the types of whaling that led to separating out "commercial" from "aboriginal subsistence"' (Epstein, 2013: 174). This new categorization led to the shift in the field's *nomos* from whaling to anti-whaling, changed the entire field of whale-related discourses, practices, and policies, and laid the grounds for the global moratorium passed in 1982 that outlaws commercial whaling to this day. Moreover, this categorization establishes criteria of practices, as commercial whaling is normatively grounded as 'bad', whereas aboriginal subsistence whaling is grounded as acceptable in terms of exotic, different, or cultural practice (Epstein, 2013: 174).

The controversial point is that while the powerful categorization may describe Alaskan whaling, it does not reflect the realities of whaling in small coastal villages in Japan or Norway. Although whaling peoples around the world have rejected this distinction, they have little to say in terms of changing the established categories. As Epstein (2013: 174) argues, the symbolic power to decide what whaling qualifies as good/ aboriginal or bad/commercial is thus not in the hands of those who have material interests in the practice, owing to their exclusion from the field. This force of the anti-whaling *nomos* explains the puzzling role of Japan, the nation harbouring the largest whaling fleet, which sends the largest delegation to the IWC and has largely underwritten the activities of the IWC's scientific committee, but has not been successful in establishing either a third category enabling whaling (i.e. on a small-scale coastal basis), or in using its economic power to change the rules (Epstein, 2013: 174–175). Japan's case demonstrates that the struggle for recognition is not a struggle to be able to continue whaling, but rather to be reincluded on the side of those who draw the lines.

Epstein's Bourdieu-inspired perspective on norms as laden with power comes closer to the analytics of power by Foucault, as both critical theorists understand the normative order not as an ethically neutral space within which actors can deliberately argue. Bourdieu's notion of *nomos* is therefore quite similar to Foucault's distinction between 'normation' and 'normalization' as primordial organizing principles in bringing deviant behaviour back within the range of acceptable boundaries. The point is that the notification of deviance requires an initial line-drawing to demarcate the 'normal' from the 'abnormal', which implies that 'normation' is historically prior to 'normalization', as it first takes knowing where 'the normal' actually lies before any process of normalization can start to occur (Epstein, 2013: 171). Thus, the *nomos* 'is the underlying matrix of norms regulating the practices, or ways of doing and seeing, pertaining to a particular field. It is founded upon an original process of exclusion and line-drawing which established, first, what lies within the field and what does not, and, second, where the standards of normality lie within it' (Epstein, 2013: 171). Such a perspective sheds light on practices such as categorizations, by which normative claims are negotiated and established with all their material consequences for the political actors. For Epstein (2013: 175), a further promise is that the relationship between norms and identity is revealed in a new way, as actors such as Japan, though paying high costs, still belong to the community, whereas others including Canada withdrew directly from the IWC. Furthermore, the researcher takes a clearly critical perspective on a distinct field of international politics, and brings diffuse power relations to light. Finally, it broadens the scope from single norms to an organized ensemble of normative grounds, and the field serves as a useful analytical entry-point for research.

Learning Moral Standards through Participation: The Case of Security Communities

Adler's (2005, 2008) idea of understanding the expansion of security communities such as NATO by using the concept of community of practice in the tradition of Wenger (1998a; see also Lave and Wenger, 1991) is not only useful for the introduction of a key approach in international practice theory (IPT); it also reinvigorates the stagnating IR research on learning by interpreting it first and foremost as a social practice. Such a perspective is therefore highly relevant for studying the normativity of practice, as it sheds light on the notion of learning as a socially structured process by which one absorbs the practical knowledge necessary to be accepted as a competent member in a community. In Adler's (2008) work on security communities, it becomes clear that such a practice-oriented perspective goes beyond IR's norm-oriented approaches, as the spread of self-restraint and peaceful change in NATO's transformation process is explained by a shared interest in learning and applying a common practice such as cooperative security. Such a notion of learning therefore involves the (mainly implicit) adaptation of moral standards. As Adler (2008: 198) argues, it might not be prudent to treat liberal democracy and self-restraint norms and practices as separate normative categories. Instead, self-restraint (the abstention from the use of force) is 'not to be found *exclusively* in cost-benefit analyses, socialization and persuasion-based normative diffusion, or in the moral directives of a particular ideological doctrine, such as Kantian liberalism, but also in particular security-community *practices*' (Adler, 2008: 204–205). What Adler (2008: 210) demonstrates in his study is that self-restraint and cooperative security among established NATO agents and new partners are learned and performed through practical activities (joint training, planning), common initiatives such as the Partnership for Peace, and mutual exchanges carried out on an everyday basis. The interesting question is therefore not whether Polish or Czech officials were deeply persuaded by Western values, as Adler (2008: 215–216) further argues, but how the background knowledge of European security and NATO's practices evolved, thus making security partnerships and a common 'we-feeling' among military elites and other practitioners, whose experience was formerly based on using violence against other states, learnable and possible. Adler's research demonstrates that the spread of security communities is difficult to explain using norm diffusion and individualist methodological approaches based on persuasion and socialization. Rather, his work suggests that if liberal norms of peaceful change and cooperation are adopted by new participants in a community, it is much more revealing to focus on learning as a social activity with others in order to understand how cooperative security practices and the normative notion of self-restraint evolve, and how these are related to meaningful social standards (i.e. rules) of the community.

Such a perspective puts emphasis on the notion of learning as Wittgenstein understands it. New members of a community not only acquire the necessary knowledge to perform the activity but also 'absorb a moral way of being; that is, a model of excellence specific to that practice that determines at once an ethic, a set of values, and the sense of virtues associated with the achievement of the high standard of conduct implicit in the practice' (Nicolini, 2013: 84). To be absorbed in a practice is to accept the authority of those standards held by a distinct community, which can evoke conflicts. As Adler (2008: 205) further argues, the spread of social structure in liberal security communities occurs through an identity/power mechanism that depends not only on liberal recognition but also on disciplined subjectivity. Learning is therefore not a straightforward and purely deliberate process, because new and old members decide through mutual exchange what counts as relevant and legitimate knowledge, and play distinct powerful roles. Wittgenstein (2009: §206) similarly states that 'following a rule is analogous to obeying an order' which involves training, drills and education (Wittgenstein uses the stronger German term *Abrichtung* in relation to education). The establishment of joint military forums as part of the Partnership for Peace, 'where thousands of partner officers learned about civil-military relations, the separation of powers, accountability of the armed forces, and the practice of inter-institutional and international cooperation' (Adler, 2008: 214) can be interpreted in Wittgenstein's notion of practice as language games. However, the expanding community of practice between old and new NATO members cannot be described as a simple master–pupil relationship. NATO leaders had limited experience with cooperative security as an alternative to balance-of-power politics between alliances, and had to renew the moral expectations and dispositions of self-restraint by acquiring experience in new partnerships (Adler, 2008: 213).

Locating normativity in the process of learning as active participation in communities implies a completely different research perspective than technical notions of norm implementation and socialization suggest. Such a perspective highlights the active engagement of newcomers as learners within a community whereby they gain the competence to participate and become a member. This notion of learning also points to marginalized aspects in IR research such as the criteria of belonging in groups and communities. The further suggestion by Wenger (1998b: 72–85) that a community of practice entails a set of relations in three dimensions by which practice is the source of coherence (mutual engagement, joint enterprise, shared repertoire) is a useful conceptual refinement of combining learning and identity issues. As Adler and Greve (2009) demonstrate in a different account on security communities, practices such as 'joint enterprise' and 'shared repertoire' are more than statements of purposes or strategic tools; they are negotiated in relations of mutual accountability (see also Brunnée and Toope (2011) for an application in international law). The regime of accountability in community-building becomes an integral part of the practice, but it 'may not be something that everyone can articulate very readily, because it is not primarily being reified that it pervades a community' (Wenger, 1998b: 81). This nicely underlines Wittgenstein's premise that we obey rules rather blindly, and emphasizes the normativity of practice.

The Dispute on Torture: Justification and Critique as Practice

The US war on terror and the torture scandal surrounding the Abu Ghraib prison is often used in IR as a textbook case demonstrating the erosion of norms (e.g. McKeown, 2009). However, as I (Gadinger, 2016) and a few others argue (e.g. Lesch, 2017b), the case is much more illuminating not in supporting the either/or logic of the presumed clear premise of erosion, but for shedding light on the normative contestation and moral ambiguity in political controversies. The methodological starting point is therefore not the norm (prohibition of torture), but the dispute surrounding it. By analysing the interplay between justification and critique in public hearings before the Senate Armed Services Committee in the United States (US) Congress (2005), it becomes clear that the disputing actors fundamentally disagreed on the limits of the war on terror in its moral grounds. While the critics' main argument was that the war on terror undermined core democratic principles and contradicted the objective of defending the national security of the US in the long term (in terms of a loss of credibility), justifications by members of the Bush administration and the US military were primarily based on rationalist and technocratic orders of worth by using short-term objectives (a state of emergency, 'we are at war', etc.). A detailed reconstruction of the dispute, for instance between Senator Dayton and General Myers/Secretary Rumsfeld, shows that the political actors fundamentally disagreed on the question of the most significant common good for the American people. The interplay between justification and critique reveals the different normative points of reference in competing orders of worth. While Senator Dayton employed orders of worth of the civic world and interpreted the behaviour of the Department of Defense as 'antithetical to a democracy' and 'against our principles', General Myers and Secretary Rumsfeld, as members of the US military, were more strongly bound to practices of justification by using moral claims of effectiveness, control, and security (Gadinger, 2016: 199–200). This constitutes a typical 'reality test' (in Boltanski's vocabulary), as actors disagree on reality as it is ('[i]t's a misunderstanding of the situation', in the words of Rumsfeld).

At that point in time, the normative contestation could not be resolved, as different rationalities in modern democratic governance were revealed. The critics' moral concern with the breach of the torture norm and the undermining of civil liberties contradicted the overall emphasis on national security measures whereby democratic and legal standards needed to be downplayed during wartime to guarantee the safety of 'our troops' (Gadinger, 2016: 200). The case also demonstrates how disputing actors use distinct principles of equivalence, that is, differing criteria of judgement on definitions about the good, the just, or the morally right thing to do, which include distinct moral narratives and objects that enable tests of worth. Actors therefore use different measuring instruments, proofs, and objects established in each order of worth. Critics, for instance, used the external authority of non-governmental organizations and their expertise as evidence for the systematic nature of prisoner abuse, while military officials used historical comparisons of earlier war experiences and statistics to strengthen their moral claims, when, for instance, the number of 'seven bad apples' in Abu Ghraib was compared by justifying actors with the total number of American troops to relativize the scandal as an 'isolated incident' (Gadinger, 2016: 200).

The pragmatist notion of 'test' is therefore a useful methodological entry point when shedding light on how actors resolve uncertainty expressed in disputes, and the way in which normative backgrounds are revealed through the imperative of justification. According to Boltanski (2011: 25, emphasis in original), the social world becomes fragmented in such disputes and should therefore be described *'as the scene of trial,* in the course of which actors in a situation of *uncertainty* proceed to *investigations,* record their *interpretations* of what happens in *reports,* establish *qualifications* and submit to *tests'.* A key feature of such tests is their inherent character of contention (Boltanski and Thévenot, 2006: 133), as disagreeing actors are often uncertain of the worth of people in a given situation.

Furthermore, the notion of test as critical moments of dispute in social life comes close to Wittgenstein's understanding of practice as language games. The analysis of the public hearings shows the implicit moral standards and shared values within the 'official investigation' practice in the US context. Although the repetitive, routinized statements made by nearly all senators lauding the merits of the US military could be interpreted as empty phrases, they reveal the practical understanding and implicit rule of safeguarding the US military as a credible institution that has guaranteed national security throughout its long history. While this tendency of the established practice can be criticized as support of militarization, it sheds light on the criteria of how political actors follow rules, which implies narrow limits in formulating critique in this case. Finally, while convicting seven low-level 'bad apples' in the military may have been acceptable, it seems that risking the general credibility of the institution by bringing top-level decision-makers such as former defence secretary Donald Rumsfeld to court was not. Reconstructing the 'official investigation' practice from within the language game reveals the military culture and normative context as enabling structures of such prisoner abuse scandals, and how it became possible to breach the torture norm. Such a pragmatic perspective provides a different way to study norm contestation by starting the analysis not with fixed norms, but instead by using disputes and the practice of justification to understand the competing and changing moral claims in complex societies.

The major interest of pragmatic sociology lies therefore not in the mere identification of different normative orders or orders of worth. Instead, the core aim is to analyse how actors coordinate their differing claims and find mutual agreements, which nevertheless remain fragile. The pragmatic approach is therefore able to deal with the plurality and multiplicity of normative orders as overlapping moral narratives; this is regarded as the rule rather than the exception. From a practice-oriented perspective, the deviation of a norm and its ongoing negotiation, such as the prohibition of torture, can be seen as a normal if not necessary aspect of both social and legal norms that are interpreted as positively marked possibilities (Lesch, 2017b). Thus, a plurality of repertoires in the everyday is emphasized, as is contestation as the regular mode of 'testing' reality. Finally, a pragmatic perspective on moral disputes provides the analytical possibility of recognizing emerging orders of worth. The permanent justification of torture in recent decades in terms of 'exceptional necessity' and a 'state of emergency' across many Western countries (Liese, 2009) in the context of rising counter-terrorism activities could point to such a new order of worth as a legitimate and enduring future moral narrative.

Conclusion

The normativity of practice remains one of the major research challenges in current debates on the practice turn but also provides an excellent way to demonstrate the promise of IPT for a wider IR audience. This chapter shows that the budding conversation between norm researchers and practice-oriented scholars is analytically fruitful thanks to their similar research concerns around power and agency, learning and identity, as well as the multiplicity and contestation of norms/normative orders. Norm researchers share one of the core premises of the practice turn by overcoming simple explanations built on the agency–structure dichotomy and addressing processual perspectives on phenomena in world politics. Despite further conceptual and methodological potential from this conversation, the chapter also demonstrates a remaining difference between norm research and IPT. Practice-oriented scholars (following Wittgenstein) do not distinguish practices from norms, thereby reserving theoretical primacy for practice. Consequently, empirical analysis always begins with practice, not norms. Most norm researchers do not completely subscribe to this Wittgensteinian premise and, as a result of a new-found identity through constructivist research since the 1990s, still prioritize the concept of norm as a core unit of analysis. Many norm researchers welcome the practice turn, but nevertheless hesitate to blur the analytical separation between practices and norms in favour of relational ontology. As a more newly established stream of research, practice-oriented scholars working on normative research issues operate with very different conceptual backgrounds and are not as connected as a community. The chosen examples of research by Epstein, Adler, and Gadinger, for instance, deal with the normativity of practices from different angles and shed light on different aspects such as power, learning and contestation. However, they have yet to form part of a coherent debate. Although I identified some aspects of Wittgenstein's notions of language games and rule following in the three research accounts, it would be misleading to claim that there is a clear Wittgensteinian approach in IPT and an equally deliberate choice to study the normativity of practice. As some have recently begun, the ideas of social philosophers such as Wittgenstein, MacIntyre, and Rouse must be translated into the IPT research programme.

A promising way to further develop these conceptual thoughts can be found in discussions on controversial empirical cases. The above-mentioned debate between Adler-Nissen/Pouliot and Ralph/Gifkins around the practices of the Security Council in the Libya intervention could serve as an exemplary case for further conceptual and method-ological discussions. The case demonstrates that actors use the notion of competence in situations of normative contestation to legitimate their position. The Bourdieu-inspired view that interprets domination as a crucial marker of competence obviously ignores the ethical dimension of practices, as Ralph and Gifkins (2017) rightly argue. They contend for a stronger linkage between practice theory and normative theory, as other scholars have done (Frost and Lechner, 2016a). Despite obvi-ous common research interests, this missing link can also be observed between practice theory and legitimacy research (e.g. Reus-Smit, 2007). The debate on the normativity of practice underlines that there are not only different ways to study practices but also different ways to criti-cize them (Schindler and Wille, 2017), thus provoking important questions on reflexivity when doing practice-oriented research. However, the aim of more strongly linking practice theory and normative theory also involves a potential risk. The major strength of IPT as a productive research programme lies in its potential to break new ground in empiri-cal research through innovative research techniques (e.g. ethnography) and by introducing a stronger sociological perspective. Most politi-cal theorists and philosophers are less interested in doing empirical research. Frost and Lechner's (2016a: 349) plea for Wittgenstein, for instance, remains quite abstract, particularly when suggesting studying the practices of international society through specific practice-defining rules such as the rules of war and diplomacy. The 'success' of relevant practice-oriented research lies in finding a good balance between philosophical and normative reflection while engaging in interesting empirical research beyond disciplinary reservations.

6   Resistance as Practice
Counter-Conduct after Foucault

William Walters

Introduction

In an impressive critical assessment of recent practice-theoretical research in IR, Bueger and Gadinger (2015: 454) note that one intellectual figure in particular has dominated understandings of practice: 'A vast majority of current practice theoretical work takes Bourdieu's approach as a starting point to the degree that "Bourdieusianism" dominates the discussion on practice in IR'. While Bourdieu's work lends much to the study of domination within world politics, this over-reliance on his version of practice, they argue, has occluded the potential for other thinkers and perspectives to illuminate international practices. In this chapter, I take up Bueger and Gadinger's call for a theoretical broadening in practice-oriented approaches to world politics. I do this by bringing certain themes from the work of Michel Foucault into a conversation with practice-oriented approaches to power. In particular, I explore Foucault's contribution to the study of resistance as practice.[1]

Whereas Foucault's voice is very prominent in the wider practical turn at play in the social sciences, with certain notable exceptions (e.g. Neumann, 2002), he has surprisingly not been regarded as a key thinker of practices in IR. The fact that Foucault has been somewhat marginal to IR's practice turn is rather curious, given the epistemological and methodological orientation of much of his work. One need look no further than the commentary of one of Foucault's friends and colleagues, the eminent historian Paul Veyne, to find an appreciation of Foucault

---

[1] Bourdieu is quite explicit about the place of practice in his work, for example *Outline of a Theory of Practice*. This is surely one reason why he has become a standard reference in IR practice debates. By contrast, Foucault was highly provisional and tactical in his use of concepts. He identifies very few key concepts that knit his entire work together. Instead, he chops and changes, quite avowedly refusing to settle on anything that might resemble a unified theoretical system or continuous conceptual vocabulary. While he does speak in many places of practices, he also uses a variety of neighbouring terms including technologies, techniques, mechanisms, instruments, procedures, apparatuses, and modalities.

as an innovative scholar of practices. Veyne goes as far as to aver that Foucault 'revolutionizes history' precisely through his insistence that our histories – the stories we tell about what we once were and what we are becoming – should centre on practices. Foucault's 'revolution' is to invert the relationship we assumed to prevail between objects and practices: 'Objects seem to determine our behavior, but our practice determines its own objects in the first place' (Veyne, 1997: 155).

In this chapter, I argue that Foucault does offer original and practice-oriented tools to study resistance. While Foucault's famous remark that 'where there is power, there is resistance' (Foucault, 1990: 95) is widely cited in IR circles, his is perhaps not the first name scholars would look to when conceptualizing resistance. Overwhelmingly, I argue, Foucault has been read in IR as a theorist of social *order*, a major thinker who engages power at the level of its discourses, mechanisms, tactics, and technologies. Less often have IR scholars viewed Foucault as a scholar who might illuminate practices of insubordination, civil disobedience, recalcitrance, and insurrection (Death, 2010). While these were arguably never central preoccupations in his historical research, there are nevertheless places where Foucault brings his distinctive methods to bear upon these modes of behaviour. I examine one such Foucauldian encounter: I look at his elaboration of the idea of 'counter-conduct'. Foucault's analysis of counter-conduct arises primarily in his 1978–9 lecture series on *Security, Territory, Population* (Foucault, 2007). The theme of governmentality – which he first formulates in those lectures – has been widely debated and extended in IR, whereas the theme of counter-conduct has only very recently been engaged (Cadman, 2010; Death, 2010; Davidson, 2011; Odysseos et al., 2016; Tazzioli, 2016). Lending support to these engagements, this chapter argues that counter-conduct illustrates how Foucault speaks not just to questions of power, but to politics as well, and not just to themes of discipline and regulation but also to their contestation.

A focus on counter-conduct can make an important contribution to the study of international practices. Counter-conduct offers a nuanced view of the relationship between *practices of politics and resistance* and *practices of the self*. International practice theorists have paid very little attention to practices of the self. They have tended to treat practices as particular forms of action undertaken *by* groups of individuals. They have not examined at length the way in which individuality and self-hood might themselves be the constituted effects of regimes of practice, and how such regimes relate to the practices of governing states, societies, international issues, and so on. This is, of course, precisely the move Foucault and like-minded scholars make, canvassing a broad history of practices through which subjects and subjectivities are constituted. These range from confession – whether grounded in religion or the secular forms of the psy-sciences (Foucault, 1990) – to such everyday operations on the self as diary-keeping (Joyce, 1994), self-esteem, and self-help (Cruikshank, 1996). With his reflections on counter-conduct, Foucault examines how certain forms and experiences of the self are constituted in and through practices of contestation. However, it should be stressed that not all forms of resistance are at the same time forms of counter-conduct. Resistance can be fleeting, spontaneous, faceless, anonymous, and almost a reflex action. But when resistance is tied to and embedded within practices that enact a sense of, say, conscience in the subject, when it entails the enunciation of ethical principles, and an alternative conception of how one wishes to be governed, not to mention the elaboration of alternative practices of living, then we can speak of counter-conduct. In this way, we can study how individuals and groups are not merely preconstituted agents, but emergent subjects or becoming-subjects within particular forms of resistance.

The chapter is organized into four sections. First, I offer some brief reflections on the way in which Foucault thinks about power in his later studies of government. I stress that Foucault is a *historical nominalist* when studying power, and that greater appreciation for the diverse modes of power and resistance which his work traverses could advance the dialogue between Foucault and IR on this question. One contribution this chapter makes is therefore to refine IR's mode of engaging with Foucault. Whereas many IR scholars associate Foucault with categories such as 'constructivism' or 'poststructuralism', and often for good reasons, I suggest the connection with historical nominalism is a fruitful line to explore. Second, I discuss counter-conduct, situating it within this wider field of forms of power and resistance. I highlight some of its distinctive features, including the immanence and constructive qualities of resistance, and the novel perspective on the relationship between ethics and politics that counter-conduct implies. Amongst the most valuable insights Foucault's writing on counter-conduct offers IR scholars is an account of political change in terms of immanence and recombination (Collier, 2009). Foucault stresses that in counter-conducts resistance accomplishes change not by bringing entirely novel structures and logics into the world but by recombining and rearticulating existing elements to produce new assemblages. Third, I ask what a perspective of counter-conduct might bring to our understanding of contemporary struggles. Here I stress that Foucault always develops his concepts in context. He is a very 'site-specific' thinker (Valverde, 2007: 160), a feature that ought to form a bridge to practice theory which Adler-Nissen (2016: 99) nicely describes as 'methodologically situationalist'. Foucault's primary model for counter-conduct is derived from the religious movements of the Middle Ages, which both contest and extend pastoral power and contribute to the fracture of the Church. Rather than directly transpose Foucault's historically contextualized account of counter-conduct onto the present, I argue that counter conduct needs additional concepts and considerations if it is to be useful in analysing contemporary practices of resistance. The one theme I emphasize is a concern with the politics of visibility. And here I emphasize that counter-conduct is valuable because it offers a way to theorize the difference which particular *individuals* and not just groups can make in struggles. Yet it does so without romanticizing or essentializing the individual. Finally, I illustrate and deepen this reading of counter-conduct by playing it through a contemporary case: the ongoing controversy regarding practices of citizen solidarity and support towards migrants, and resistance towards the rebordering of Europe. Deploying counter-conduct in this way I shift it from the historical contexts within which Foucault developed the term, to very current and salient issues of the making and unmaking of international borders, and the politics of migration and anti-migration. Cases should do more than illustrate: I use this case to develop a concept of *scene* that can bridge between questions of resistance and themes of political communication. In foregrounding a concern with scene I hope to extend the conversation about the politics of visibility which Austin and Leander (Chapter 10) have identified as a useful direction for a practice-oriented approach to IR.

Foucault, Power, and IR

Before we can grasp what Foucault means by counter-conduct, and properly assess its contribution to broadening practice-theoretical approaches to power in world politics, we need to briefly consider the wider field of Foucault's understanding of power. As recent surveys have shown, Foucault's work has made a major impact on understandings of power within IR scholarship (Guzzini, 2005; Selby, 2007; Merlingen, 2006; Bonditti et al., 2017). Yet it's probably fair to say that readings of Foucault have tended to be highly selective in terms of *which* Foucault they mobilize. For certain scholars in International Political Economy, Foucault is a theorist of disciplinary power, and more recently liberal governmentality, who offers an important complement to structuralist conceptions of international political order (Joseph, 2010; Jessop, 2011). For others, he is exemplary as a theorist of power/knowledge who emphasizes the interplay of expert knowledge and practice in the regulation of global processes (Neumann, 2002), or the role of discourse in constituting modern subjects (Barnett and Duvall, 2005; Lukes, 2005). Meanwhile a prominent line of scholarship has flourished which takes up Foucault's rather brief reference to biopower, and connects this idea to theories of sovereignty (Agamben, 1998) and empire (Hardt and Negri, 2000). The grand-theoretical ambitions of this latter line of inquiry may be somewhat at odds with the decidedly empirical and site-specific way in which Foucault studies power relations. Yet this discrepancy seems not to have lessened the impact it has made within IR.

All of these interpretations are well founded, and many have employed Foucauldian ideas to good effect in advancing understandings of power and world politics. Furthermore, there is nothing wrong or unusual about reading major thinkers selectively and tactically. Nevertheless, these somewhat selective readings of Foucault are now in need of revision. They are in need of adjustment in light of the publication and translation of Foucault's previously unpublished lectures, delivered largely at the Collège de France, between 1976 and 1984. Apart from the extraordinary historical breadth of Foucault's scholarship, what these lectures underscore is the way in which Foucault practises a version of *historical nominalism* (Foucault, 1990: 93; Rabinow, 2003: 66–8; Lemke, 2007; Valverde, 2007; Collier, 2009; Veyne, 2010: 10). The lectures make good on Foucault's claim that there is no such thing as power or resistance *in general*. In place of a general theory of power, or theory of the state, Foucault approaches power in terms of 'singularities' (Foucault, 2008: 49n, 130, 165): he writes genealogies of particular figurations of power/knowledge, examines how subjects have been constituted in terms of practices and technologies in various contexts, and traces the lines by which particular games of power come into existence, combine, transform, and break up. He presents us with a remarkably varied landscape of forms of power which includes reflections on forms of sovereignty and early modern *raison d'état* (Foucault, 2007), the rise and transformation of pastoral power (the 'shepherd-flock game') (Foucault, 2007), race struggles and state racism (Foucault, 2003), the *polizeiwissenschaft* of cities and provinces, the contrast between disciplinary and security logics of governing, and, of course, the birth and mutation of a liberal government of subjects and populations (Foucault, 2008). It is out of these and other elements that Foucault sketches not a theory but a genealogy of modern European states (Valverde, 2007), while also offering some indications of a non-reductive, nominalist approach to international government (Dean, 2010). Drieschova and Bueger (Chapter 1) observe that many practice theorists are cautious about theoretical models that claim universal applicability, preferring to develop concepts out of inductive and abductive research processes. It is a point that Foucault shares and is reflected in his commitment to a genealogy of governmental knowledges and practices rather than a theory of political power.

The fact that Foucault's eminently practice-oriented approach to power covered a far greater spectrum of forms, contexts, and logics than has often been appreciated by IR scholars, and that this work is now widely accessible, is significant. It means the prospect now exists for a fuller dialogue between Foucault scholarship and the analysis of power in world politics. This point can be elaborated by considering the impressive and insightful analysis of power in contemporary IR which Barnett and Duvall (2005) offer us. In their 2 × 2 typology of power, Barnett and Duvall (2005: 20) quite reasonably locate Foucault's contribution in the quadrant they call 'productive power', highlighting the 'production of subjects through diffuse social relations'. In making this move they reflect the wider perception that a broad distinction can be made within IR between approaches that take what Lukes (2005: 485) has called a 'general strategic agents-interacting-within-structures explanatory approach', and approaches whose privileged theoretical image is not 'agents' pursuing 'interests' but rather 'subjects' and the relations and practices that constitute those subjects.[2]

Bearing in mind what we have just said about the diversity of power relations that Foucault sketches in his genealogy of modern government one response to Barnett and Duvall's (2005) typology would go as follows. It would question whether Foucault should be neatly placed in just one quadrant. As we will see, counter-conducts are by no means merely 'discursive' or 'diffuse' in their focus. They are not just a matter of challenging identities and subjectivities, though they are that as well. There is also a very direct and proximate aspect to counter-conduct, a fact that places it close to Barnett and Duvall's 'compulsory power'. It is an aspect which also connects counter-conduct to a point the editors of this volume make: that a practice approach is often attuned to 'quite embodied and physical activities' (Drieschova et al., Chapter 1). When certain religious groups or political dissidents invoke conscience as their grounds for defying Church or state authority, when they endure imprisonment or even death as the punishment for such acts of defiance, and when they rally others through the moral and symbolic force of

---

[2] It could be argued that constructivism within IR straddles this divide between strategic agents and constituted subjects: as Guzzini (2005: 508) notes, it tends to 'add Foucault (or Bourdieu) to Lukes' three dimensions of power'.

their actions, one is dealing with a power struggle that in key respects could not be more direct or compulsory in its nature. In short, a focus on counter-conduct will show that equating Foucault *only* with discursive power risks missing the many other dimensions and types of power relations his work invokes.

A second response to Barnett and Duvall's typology is also conceivable. This one would query what it is we do when we develop typologies of power. Any typology runs the risk of positing false limits to its field of analysis. Of course, typologies are helpful for clarifying the stakes in a debate where different participants mean different things by power. But if we are to better appreciate the diversity of practices then we need to realize a new found respect for *description* (Orford, 2012): the description of a new relation, a new practice, a new space that confounds the lines and logic of the typology. Long treated by political science as the poor cousin of *explanation*, there is much that renewed respect and commitment to the work of description can still bring to the practice turn. In this way can we better register the manifold forms of power at work, and capture their endless capacity for variation. Deleuze (1988) once described Foucault as a cartographer of power. This epithet nicely captures the sense in which power is never a fully known quantity: there are always unmapped territories whose discovery throws into question what we thought we knew.

This is not the place to explore the broad range of forms of political power that Foucault's later work sketches, nor to venture on a search for undiscovered practices of power. Instead, I shall confine my remarks to one particular theme that Foucault examines within this incomplete and discontinuous genealogy of the modern state. It is the theme of counter-conduct. But to understand counter-conduct we first have to grasp what Foucault understands by conduct. Foucault reflects at some length on the theme of conduct in *Security, Territory, Population*. If his reflections on prisons and disciplines had foregrounded relations of power that are geared to taming, moulding, and domesticating subjects, forging them as useful and productive individuals, in this turn to conduct Foucault scrutinizes not so much a disciplined as an *ethicalized* subject. Now some have equated Foucault with an 'ultra-radical' view that 'strips the subject of both freedom and reason' (Lukes, 2005: 492). However, this charge is not true of Foucault's turn to conduct and counter-conduct; here it is precisely the ways in which '[a]t the heart of the power relationship, and constantly provoking it, are the recalcitrance of the will and the intransigence of freedom' (Foucault, 2000: 342).

To begin, we should note there is something very significant about the way Foucault approaches ethics. He approaches ethics like everything else: not a universal or transcendental realm of our existence, but a field of practices – and in this case practices of the self (Dean, 1994). A key theme in his studies of governmentality is the central role which the self – understood simultaneously as a target, a vehicle and an effect of power relations – will play in forms of rule and their contestation in the modern West. Conduct is for Foucault a zone of *indirect* power relations since it involves action on the action of others, and always presupposes a certain element of freedom on the part of the subject of power (Gordon, 1991; Foucault, 2000).

As with all the power relations Foucault examines, conduct is not regarded as a universal attribute of social relations. Rather, conduct itself needs to be historicized. To clarify this point, let us consider one way in which Foucault perhaps parts company with much practice-oriented scholarship. One of the distinctive and important contributions of practice theory has been to move analysis from a *substantialist* to a *relational* view of the social. Whereas substantialists presume fixed essences and things as their units of analysis (e.g. the state), relationalists pan out, as it were, to focus on the relations and practices that forge the essences (or the semblance of essences) in the first place (Adler-Nissen, 2016; Dumouchel, Chapter 7). Foucault makes a similar move: rather than ontologizing the social, he engages with the practices that have objects, subjects and boundaries as their effects (Mitchell, 1991; Veyne, 1997). Yet when it comes to their use of action concepts, practice theorists seem not to pan out and speak instead of action in somewhat fixed terms. Practice theorists often mobilize terms such as 'action' and 'behaviour' as though they were general features of human relations (e.g. Adler and Pouliot, 2011c: 6). This move tends to neglect the historical and socio-material matrices within which human *being*, as such, has been forged. By contrast, very few of Foucault's concepts exist outside specifiable processes of historical formation and emergence.[3] Hence, conduct is not something universal but has as its correlate specific practices, institutions, and authorities. In the governmentality

---

[3] What we think of as stable features or social, psychological, and emotional faculties of humans always bear some co-constitutive relationship with socio-technical systems. We can see this in a very contemporary way. What it means to *like* something or someone is being transformed before our eyes by Facebook, and myriad other digital platforms, which systematically enjoin us to 'like' or to 'share' a variety of digital objects and experiences. At last we can see that liking and sharing are not universal dispositions so much as distributed actions that have technological circuits of desire as their socio-material infrastructures. Of course, some would say these digitally-mediated operations are not 'genuine' friendships and acts of appreciation. Yet I suspect our modes of relating to ourselves and others have never been entirely free of prosthetics and technical enhancements. What is a bunch of flowers, after all?

lectures the milieu of practices, institutions, and authorities in terms of which Foucault identifies conduct is often the Christian pastorate. What Foucault sometimes calls confessional technology is exemplary in this regard, since it presents us with a set of practices in and through which the self is produced as a target and an effect of power relations.

To speak of confession, or of other technologies of the self, in this way will raise an immediate objection. It will invite the suspicion that Foucault is simply pushing his mesh of power relations even further: now they are inside the soul of the individual! If even the self is an effect of power, traversed by power relations, then there can surely be no freedom (Lukes, 2005). Yet this is a very selective reading of Foucault. Power may be pervasive, but his is not a gloomy picture in which our lives are fully determined by power relations. Certainly we are all implicated in games of power. Yet neither the outcomes nor the rules of these games are permanently fixed, and new experiences of freedom can always arise out of these games. This should be clear as we turn to examine counter-conduct more fully.

What Is *Counter*-Conduct?

Counter-conduct is not a general theory of resistance for Foucault. Just as he eschews a general theory of power in favour of more contextualized, situated, and historicized mappings of specific practices, regimes, and modalities of governing, then so too does he reject talk of resistance as a generic phenomenon. Instead, Foucault seeks to identify particular modalities by which power is challenged, reversed, questioned, refused, recognizing these modalities have immanent relations to that which they oppose. The socio-historical field in which he theorizes counter-conducts is, as we noted, the Christian pastorate. If the pastorate introduced into society new instruments of governing people in their daily lives, if it made dimensions of our conduct into something knowable and actionable, counter-conduct is Foucault's name for a dispersed yet overlapping play of revolts, dissidences, and refusals, which, beginning in the Middle Ages, will challenge this pastoral power at multiple points and from many angles. 'They are movements whose objective is a different form of conduct, that is to say wanting to be conducted differently, by other leaders (*conducteurs*) and other shepherds, towards other objectives and forms of salvation, and through other procedures and methods' (Foucault, 2007: 194–5). Foucault cites many religious groups, sects, orders, and movements as exemplars in this respect, including the Hussites, the followers of Luther, the Anabaptists, and the Waldenasians. It is important to recognize, then, that these are not rebellions against authority per se, but against *this* practice or *this* figure of authority; not resistance against any power that governs us, but against *this* one.

The advent of these movements will contribute to a fracturing of the Church. But note that these counter-conducts are in no way confined to the religious sphere. A core theme in Foucault's lectures is that more secularized forms of pastoral power emerge by the eighteenth century, the more that political and not just religious government becomes focused upon the regulation of people's conduct. But as pastoral power diffuses itself beyond the Church, so does counter-conduct. Hence Foucault cites conscientious refusals against military conscription, revolts against certain medical programmes such as vaccination, and political secret societies, as modern forms of counter-conduct.

There are three features of Foucault's treatment of counter-conduct I want to elaborate: the immanence of this particular form of contestation, the constructiveness of counter-conduct, and finally its relationship to what I call ethical forms. Each theme offers lessons for practice-theoretical understandings of power and resistance.

Counter-Conduct Is Immanent and Not Exterior

Counter-conduct offers us a particularly subtle way to understand how contestation and practices combine to create new patterns of governance. This is one of its genuine analytical strengths and a useful lesson for practice-oriented approaches to IR. This point can be underscored if we look closely at Foucault's account of what dissidents and other religious splinter groups actually do when they challenge the Church.

Foucault identifies five fundamental elements that recur within the movements of counter-conduct that break out within and around the Christian pastorate in the Middle Ages. They are eschatology, scripture, mysticism, the community, and *ascesis*. He states that 'these themes that have been fundamental elements in these counter-conducts are clearly not absolutely external to Christianity, but are actually border-elements, if you like, which have been continually re-utilized, re-implanted, and taken up again in one or another dimension or another direction, and these elements ... have been continually taken up by the Church itself' (Foucault, 2007: 215). The struggle around the Church in the fifteenth and sixteenth centuries 'was not conducted in the form of absolute exteriority, but rather in the form of the permanent use of tactical elements that are pertinent in the anti-pastoral struggle, insofar as they fall within, in a marginal way, the general horizon of Christianity' (Foucault, 2007: 215).

So his discussion of counter-conduct illustrates a view of power relations in which actors are continually appropriating and repurposing practices, remaking themselves in the process through a play of practice and identity. These dissenting sects reach into Christianity's past, reviving marginalized elements and practices, giving them a new centrality and significance, in ways that pose a challenge for the dominant, institutionalized form of power. In contrast, authorities, in their confrontations with these insurgencies and dissidences, might appropriate some of their practices, taking them over as their own. This seems to me a highly significant insight. At a time when some theorists of international practice are seeking a more robust and complex analysis of change (see Pouliot, Chapter 8), it offers us a more variegated understanding of change that is neither linear nor dialectical, but recombinatory and topological (Collier, 2009).[4]

Counter-Conduct Is Constructive and Not Merely Reactive

Given that movements of counter-conduct call into question and oppose themselves to established ways of governing, it could be argued that they radiate what Adler-Nissen (2016) has called 'disordering practices', in contrast with the 'ordering practices' of the established, dominant Church. This point is valid in an immediate sense, in that a great deal of what we call resistance entails actors engaging in the disruption of a given regime of power. Yet even here we should not overlook the fact that disruption is never self-evident, but has a strong component of practical knowledge. Practices of disruption and protest do not fall from the heavens: they have to be invented. There is substantial creativity to opposition; indeed, there must be, given the asymmetrical nature of power relations that typically pertain between the dominant and the marginal.

But when we look at counter-conducts specifically, something more can be said. What counts as ordering and disordering is usually highly contextual and relative. From the perspective of dominant religious or civil authorities, these acts of dissidence might well be perceived as bringing disorder. But then from the perspective of the dissident groups themselves,

---

[4] Think of the way in which internet-based file-sharing became in the 1990s more than merely a form of resistance to practices of copyright and corporate ownership in digital domains. For file-sharing acquired elements of a counter-conduct inasmuch as these practices became a source of community, commons, and an ethos. Napster represented a particularly prominent technology of a-legal, free, and voluntary file sharing and downloading. What was iTunes and now Spotify if not a successful attempt to absorb and commercialize elements of this counter-conduct? Once Napster and similar platforms had been suppressed and dismantled, one saw a new enclosure of the musical commons.

the world will look very different. After all, they constitute themselves as religious *orders*, not *disorders*! In a similar vein, as Simmel (1906) reminds us, secret societies in earlier times were extremely ordered, disciplined groups. Indeed, as he shows, with ritualized practices of loyalty such as the swearing of oaths, and techniques of cultivating silence and community, they invent modes of being and modes of group maintenance. In all these ways, then, we see that counter-conduct can be constructive and a source of ordering practices, even if their presence is experienced as threatening amongst powerful elites. Put differently, counter-conduct alerts us to the fact that certain forms of resistance are world-making in a dual sense. They are world-making inasmuch as their acts can change the world. But they are world-making in a second sense: they already create microcosms within a wider social order in which they forge new practices and new identities. They are laboratories whose inventions can sometimes diffuse into the wider world.[5]

Counter-Conduct and Ethical Forms

What distinguishes counter-conduct from other forms of resistance? What differentiates it from the forms of 'everyday' resistance that fascinate James Scott (1985)? Part of an answer has to do with what I call ethical forms. Ethical forms are the identities, practices, objects, and institutions by which conflicts over questions of conduct are made visible, practical, and amenable to adjudication. With this focus on ethical forms I seek to develop Davidson's (2011) key point that counter-conduct offers us a way to better understand relationships between politics and ethics. While it might be fruitful to distinguish norms and practices for analytical purposes (see Bernstein and Laurence, Chapter 4), a focus on ethical forms highlights institutionalized modes in which norms and practices are tightly interwoven (see Gadinger, Chapter 5).

Let us compare the social practice of desertion which Scott (1985) describes in *Weapons of the Weak* with the figure of the conscientious objector (an identity perhaps close to Foucault's 'desertion-insubordination' figure). Scott lists desertion as one of the many everyday ways in which peasants resist those who seek to extract food, rent, labour, taxes, interest, and service from their communities. It is one of the

---

[5] An argument can be made for seeing ordering and disordering as closely related. Adler and Faubert (Chapter 3) note: 'On one hand, social action relies on habitual dispositional knowledge and expectations that are embedded in social practices. On the other hand, endogenous and exogenous factors awaken and stir human reflexive creativity, which lead to the transformation of practices and the knowledge bound with them (Joas 1996)'.

'ordinary weapons of relatively powerless groups' and in Scott's (1985: xvi) view desertion stands alongside foot dragging, dissimulation, pilfering, feigned ignorance, arson, sabotage, and so on.

Conscientious objection is, in contrast, not everyday resistance. It is not underground, faceless, or diffuse. With conscientious objection one has a field of power relations in which an ethical agent is given subjective expression and visibly and audibly enunciated as such. Whether in writing, speeches, prayers, protests, or in the way a subject will steadfastly endure chastisement, imprisonment, and even execution, one sees that practices of the self are articulated and fashioned around nonfighting, which now becomes a site of ethical identity. Indeed, with conscientious objection the conscience itself is named, made visible and tangible, as a ground and a vector of resistance.[6]

Let us note that a Foucauldian approach to ethics does not treat the ethical as an expert domain for the deliberative guidance of policymaking, as normative political theorists do. Nor does it regard the ethical as another explanatory variable – a set of normative ideas that, once factored into our models of change, can better explain policy outcomes and actors' behaviour, as constructivists often do. Instead, it takes a material, practical and historical-nominalist approach to ethics. Ethical forms are produced (though not exclusively) in and through counter-conduct. They mark the point at which ethics, understood as the space in which conscience, conduct, and action intersect, gets materialized and governmentalized. We can be quite empirical and nominalist about ethical forms. They are not universals. They take a variety of shapes and contexts.[7] Not all issues are ethicalized equally or evenly. Ethicality comes and goes.

Ethical forms sometimes emerge as ways of resolving or managing conflicts. Hence, when states accept the legitimacy of certain forms of conscientious objection to military service, when they set up tribunals

---

[6] See Osborne's (1994) insightful point that what we call conscience is not given, but the effect of certain practices and operations. Distinguishing consciousness, conduct, and conscience as different 'temporalities of personhood', he speaks of techniques of conscience, such as confession or psychological avowal, as 'means of anchoring and governing particular forms of conduct', and regards conscience as being a particular 'ethical intensification' of conduct (Osborne, 1994: 498).

[7] My thinking on ethical forms borrows from Ong and Collier's (2005) discussion of 'regimes of living' and Barry's (2004) notion of 'ethical capitalism'. Note that the consideration of ethical forms is not confined to the analysis of practices and identities that states have or have not affirmed. Ethical forms can be materialized in and through objects, materials, and commodities, and in non-state as much as state domains. What are ethical mutual funds, fair trade coffee beans, or recycling labels on bottles if not various ways in which the will to ethical behaviour comes to be given effect and value through definite socio-material forms.

and other modes of interrogation to establish the bona fides of those who claim the status of conscientious objectors (Barker, 1982), and when they create alternative modalities of military service – such as non-combatant duty – then we can say that ethical forms have not only been stabilized, but have contributed to a change in the form of the state itself. At the same time, we should also recognize that ethical forms can themselves become sites of contestation. For example, beginning in the 1970s many states created laws, offices, and provisions that accorded a certain legitimacy to the whistleblower in the public sector. However, so weak and ineffective are some of these provisions that they have often themselves been short-circuited by those who feel they must expose political and bureaucratic wrongdoing by speaking directly through the press. Ethical forms can themselves become sites of ethical and political contestation.

Counter-Conduct after Foucault

Foucault offers us not a fully worked out account of counter-conduct but only some rather fragmentary sketches. Had he not died prematurely, he would doubtless have worked up his reflections on counter-conduct into new publications. Be that as it may, his reflections on counter-conduct, like his wider studies of governmentality, were very much a work in progress. I argue that any attempt to utilize this highly suggestive concept for the purpose of advancing the study of contemporary issues in world politics needs to consider at least two points, the first concerning visibility, the second ambiguity.

In/Visibilities

When Foucault discusses the revolts, dissidences, and rebellions of religious groups in the fifteenth and sixteenth centuries, his account of the social relations of these struggles is highly incomplete. As we saw in our discussion of the immanence of counter-conducts, Foucault is very relationalist in his understanding of how dissenting movements struggle with dominant authorities. But he is far less relationalist about how these struggles relate to a broader society. How are counter-conducts received? Do they mobilize allies beyond their own communities, and if so by what means? Contrast this neglect of the question of the social impact of counter-conduct with the research Foucault conducted on *parrhesia*, or, as he sometimes called it, fearless speech (Foucault, 2010, 2011). Perhaps because of its very nature, Foucault is careful to explain how political *parrhesia* requires an audience. No interlocutors, no *parrhesia*. It plays out in specific settings:

before a potentially hostile assembly, or perhaps in the court of a tyrant. It is here that the *parrhesiast* performs their truth. They speak in the knowledge that they risk their livelihood and perhaps their lives in speaking. The reception of the *parrhesiast*'s words is part of this specific game of power. What happens when we turn to his elaboration of counter-conduct? There, the sense that this too requires a milieu, an audience, or even a public – to use terms that are admittedly anachronistic – is largely missing in Foucault.

In our own densely mediated societies, where politics is largely accessed through heterogeneous modes of publicity (Warner, 2002, cited in Hawkins, 2011: 539; Thompson, 2005), we cannot properly understand resistance in general, and certainly not the intensely ethicalized forms of resistance associated with counter-conduct, unless we attend to the ways in which counter-conduct is seen and not seen. Here, I think it is useful to bring the analysis of counter-conduct into conversation with recent debates on the politics of visibility (Austin and Leander, Chapter 10; Rancière, 1999; Thompson, 2005; Brighenti, 2007). Building on this literature, Austin and Leander are right to note that 'Who and what is seen or ... remains unseen' powerfully shapes political hierarchies and their contestation (Chapter 10). Hence we need to attend more closely to the way in which practices of contestation utilize a play of visibility and invisibility. Foucault is clearly aware of the fact that in some situations dissidence would be tolerated by religious and civil authorities, while in others it would be fiercely persecuted and suppressed. He recognizes this point since he mentions that some dissident movements took the form of secret societies (Foucault, 2007: 198–9; see also Simmel, 1906). Yet when discussing counter-conducts, he does not examine the interplay of visibilities and invisibilities at any length.[8]

In this chapter, I want to introduce the concept of *scene*. I propose a very brief phenomenology of scene as a contribution to a fuller account of how counter-conducts utilize and are shaped by practices

---

[8] In Amsterdam's Rijksmuseum you can view a coloured print by the famous engraver Jan Luyken (1649–1712). It shows nine men and women in a rowing boat floating on the River Amstel. In the background, we see the walls and defences of the old city of Amsterdam. The accompanying text informs us the group are Anabaptists conducting a religious service. Two of them, Pieter Pietersze Bekjen and Willem Jansze, would be immolated in 1569 for practising their faith. The boat is often an allegory for salvation in Christianity (Peter the fisherman of souls, Noah's ark, etc.). Here, it becomes a practice of evasion, invisibility, and protection. But the painting is also a scene. It is perhaps no coincidence that the Anabaptists are located in the water, at the edge of the city, or that the means of their invisibility becomes in the print the most visible sign of their community and commitment. It both expresses and memorializes the Anabaptists' struggle for religious independence. See http://rijksmuseumamsterdam .blogspot.com/2011/10/jan-luyken-pieter-pietersz-bekjen.html

of visibility and invisibility.[9] The scene is a potentially rich, multilay-
ered concept. It has a 'proximity to concreteness' (Rabinow, 2003: 3):
one could say that through media, our dominant experience of the
world is as a flow of scenes. There is, therefore, a certain fit between
the concept and the dominant way the political world is accessed and
processed by Western publics.[10]

Three points about this notion of scene. First, scenes are places of
action, or more accurately, they are where the action happened or is
happening. The scene of the crash, the scene of the crime, the music
scene, and so on.[11] There is nothing natural or self-evident about the
scene. Counter-conduct involves a production of scenes. Andrew
Barry (1999) has illustrated this point well in his research on demonstrations. Demonstrators against road-building, oil extraction, or
illegal whaling strive to bring attention to issues. Typically they do
so by intervening in sites and activities using, say, boats to interrupt
whaling practices, or digging tunnels to obstruct road-building. They
practise a form of direct action in ways that draw reporters, cameras,
and tweets to that site. As I see it all these actors and technologies,
if they succeed in attracting a public's attention, turn site, event, or
incident into a scene. The scene gives complex political issues and
controversies a tangible location and focus, a cast of actors, and often
a narrative. But note that the scene is rarely the work of one actor
in isolation. Scenes are nearly always co-produced. Social movement

---

[9] Rancière (1999: 30) writes that 'Political activity is whatever shifts a body from the
place assigned to it or changes a place's destination'. Politics is somewhat rare for
Rancière, involving unpredictable irruptions in the realm of the perceptible. It happens when a 'part with no part' succeeds in constituting itself as an audible subject, a
perceptible being. This entails 'an ability to produce … polemical scenes … paradoxical scenes' (Rancière, 1999: 41).

[10] Within political science, Etienne Balibar offers a theoretical account of the scene. He
builds in turn on Freud's discussion of 'the other scene', reworking a psychological
model in which certain violences and negative forces structuring globalization and
politics are both invisible and visible, rational and irrational. For Balibar, radical
politics thus needs to access the other scene, rather as a distressed subject might seek
to access their own other scene for the purposes of reckoning with it. My use of scene
is not burdened with this psychological dimension. My use is closer to De Genova's
(2013) sense of scene, which he develops through a discussion of the staging of border
spectacles. For De Genova the border spectacle is a scene which dramatizes 'illegal
immigration' in the form of images of people crowded into small boats or crammed
into trucks. Scenes are stages for the performance of power. They are also related to
the *obscene*, which is always excluded.

[11] Obviously there are some parallels between my notion of scene and Goffman's analytics of frontstage and backstage. While the scene has certain resonances with staging
and performance, the fact that my notion of scene can also allude to and link up with
scenes understood as places of activity, places of distinction and worth, and even foren-
sics (scene of the crime, etc.), derestricts the concept from the realm of performance.

groups may try to stage a scene, but they cannot fully control for the way it will be scripted. The scene introduces ambiguity into counter-conduct, a theme I will return to.

Second, we can speak of making a scene. The parent says to the child: don't make a scene in public! Making a scene is a public display of emotions. Hence the scene also allows us to think about the role which the mediation of emotions play in counter-conduct. It opens connections to recent work on affect (Clough, 2009; D'Aoust, 2014). When demonstrators make a scene they infuse everyday activities such as road-building with powerful emotions. They perform care and concern, vigilance and urgency, and outrage. It is important to ask what place affect occupies in experiences of counter-conduct.

Third, there is the world we call 'behind the scenes'. This might refer to all the unseen work that goes into producing a specific scene. It cautions us that the scene is only the visible tip of a much larger iceberg of practices and relations. Yet it also reminds us of the boundary between the scene and its backstage: the visible and the invisible are not fixed. Political struggles may, under precise circumstances, seek to expose what has happened behind the scenes, with such exposure being a political tactic intended to discredit an opponent (Ku, 1998). Alternately, the selective communication of behind the scenes is sometimes a way to convince a public of the authenticity of certain actors and practices. Perhaps we should not be surprised that the entertainment format called reality TV – a format that has transformed the backstage into a ubiquitous cultural form – turned out to be a conduit for one of its most prominent protagonists to move into the most powerful political office of them all.

We will shortly return to the scene, developing this theme through the case of citizen smuggling and its play of in/visibility. But first it is necessary to make a point about the indeterminate nature of counter-conduct.

The Ambiguity of Counter-Conduct

Who arbitrates counter-conduct? How is it determined whether someone who refuses to fight is really a coward, or one who is following their conscience and genuinely refusing to be governed according to *these* principles by *these* people on *these* terms? To adapt a term made famous by William Connolly (1983), counter-conduct can be regarded as an essentially-contested *practice*. Now, following scholars who stress that all practices are 'socially meaningful patterns of action' (Adler and Pouliot, 2011c: 6), we can say there is an element of interpretation concerned with all practices. However, in counter-conduct the question of the meaning of practices of contestation becomes socially and politically salient. The political fate of actors will sometimes depend on the interpretation of their practice. So how do we know counter-conduct when we see it?

To some extent, at least, this was not a problem Foucault faced. Foucault operated a kind of 'self-imposed rule' to avoid direct engagement with contemporary issues in his research (Fassin, 2009: 49). Indeed, with the important exception of his studies of American and German neoliberalism, his research projects rarely strayed into the twentieth century. He worked largely as a historian, albeit a very unorthodox historian. This meant he had the benefit of hindsight: in retrospect he could discern which patterns of practice, subjectivity, and authority happened to crystallize into stable apparatuses of power, and which did not (Rabinow, 2003: 55). It meant that when he analysed counter-conduct he could zoom in on the actions of groups such as the Anabaptists or the Hussites. While they might have been persecuted in their own time, these movements managed to establish their own religious orders, orders that would, with time, be granted religious and civil legitimacy and acceptance. In other words, precisely because the freedoms they struggled for came, however much later, to be accepted as legitimate and, indeed regarded as integral features of liberal democracy (e.g. civil liberty, religious tolerance), then identifying these actors and causes as counter-conduct is relatively straightforward. One might say that history was on their side.

But if we bring this idea of counter-conduct to bear on our actuality, if we use it to make sense of live conflicts and fluid political situations, then what happens? I think this means we have to acknowledge that counter-conduct is always something in the making. As such, scholars need to attend carefully to the work that different actors perform around a given struggle. This work includes the interventions and commentaries of other scholars who, for example, as experts in ethics, often seek to arbitrate a given conflict by professing as to whether it counts as conscientious action or not.[12] The scholar of counter-conduct is never a neutral and impartial observer in such situations. They too participate, however modestly and marginally, in the production of the practices they are studying.

---

[12] See, for example, recent special issues of journals such as *Intelligence and National Security* (2014) and *Philosophy and Social Criticism* (2016), in which a range of eminent experts in domains such as security and ethics pass judgement on the actions of Edward Snowden.

Smuggler Citizens and Migration
Counter-Conduct

On 8 August 2017 at a trial in Aix-en-Provence a French farmer was given a four-month suspended prison sentence (Fekete et al., 2017: 50). Cédric Herrou had been accused of helping to bring migrants into France illegally. Herrou does not deny he has helped scores of migrants cross the border with Italy, offering them shelter at his farm in the Alps, and moving them along the Roya valley where he lives and farms olives. He makes no secret of the assistance that he, along with a small network of friends and neighbours, has provided to these migrants, many of whom have arrived on European shores having crossed the Mediterranean (Fekete et al., 2017: 15). He was arrested for the first time in August 2016 but the prosecutor dropped the charge, finding that Herrou had acted for humanitarian reasons not for profit (*New York Times*, 2016). He did not stop: on the contrary his actions became all the more overt, especially once his activity became the focus of a major feature in the *New York Times*. The newspaper framed the activity of Herrou and his allies in terms that were both sympathetic and provocative. Herrou embodied a new kind of 'French underground railway' a 'quasi-clandestine resistance' to a situation that, in its treatment of young African men, had 'ugly echoes of the French persecution of Jews during World War II'.[13] It seems this kind of coverage inflamed French authorities and influenced their decision to prosecute Herrou a second time (Chiffon Rouge, 2016).

This was no ordinary trial; it attracted widespread public attention in France and internationally. The case quickly turned into a kind of forum in which questions as to the responsibilities of citizens and states towards migrants amidst the crisis of borders were played out, and where ambiguity and unease felt by many at the prospect of harshly treating and re-deporting those fleeing conflict and poverty was given expression. Some of this ambiguity is captured in the term that has often come to be attached to Herrou and his allies in the media: *citoyen-passeur*. His actions are not unique. He is only the very visible face of wider currents and practices of citizen solidarity and citizen smuggling

---

[13] A point can be made here regarding the repetition of acts of protest. Practice theory sees the repetition of practices as a form of ordering, as well as a mode of explaining social change (Adler and Pouliot, 2011b: 7; Shäfer, Chapter 9). They become ingrained, habitual, a background. What of the repetition of practices of refusal and revolt? Intransigence, commitment, resistance are sometimes accomplished by repetition too. 'We won't back down!' Repetition of practices in the face of all attempts to quash them as the way that intransigence, defiance, commitment, and the justice of one's cause is enacted. Sometimes it is not enough to refuse only once.

of migrants, solidarities that are themselves under attack by political authorities (Fekete et al., 2017).

Immanent Struggles

The Herrou case has certain features in common with the practices of counter-conduct that Foucault describes. Most immediately, I argue, it illustrates the theme of the *immanence of struggles*. If Herrou engages in actions which brazenly challenge the French state and its migration and borders policies, he does so not from a position that is radically exterior to the state, its distinctive notion of French citizenship, or its vision of nationhood. Instead, he wages his struggle in a way that mobilizes and invokes the duty of the citizen towards the foreigner. 'We simply help people. Nothing more than that' (*Vice*, 2017). 'Either I close my eyes, or I don't … I don't have a global solution … But the state is not managing this properly. I think it's my duty. And I don't think it's normal that children have to go through this' (*New York Times*, 2016). Sheltering and protecting the migrants 'isn't our job, but we do it because there is no one else' (*Vice*, 2017).

In his legal defence Herrou's lawyer, Zia Oloumi, had framed his client's actions in terms of core values of the French Republic. As he put it to the court: remember the last word in the Republic's motto of *Liberté, Egalité, Fraternité* (*New York Times*, 2017). The assistance which Herrou provides is not a spontaneous act (even if it might have begun in such a fashion). It is deliberate and deliberated. He has been investigated, arrested, monitored, and warned, and yet he persists in his course of action. Furthermore, his practice is not obligatory, but it is a duty, a calling that leads him to break the law. There is no party or peer group that forces him to behave this way. Instead, he formulates his practice of assistance in the form of an ethicalized choice. Either I close my eyes and my door, or I act.

Here it seems we have another of those 'short-circuits' which Foucault describes when analysing the religious movements in conflict with the Church. For example, with their appeal to Scripture, or more accurately their call for a 'return' to Scripture, they were enacting a more direct relationship to God and salvation, one that professed far less need of the vast pastorate that had inserted itself between the spiritual realm and earthly affairs. Herrou is engaged in a not dissimilar form of direct action: the state, indeed the system of states, along with the network of large humanitarian organizations, is supposed to provide protection for populations, both settled and mobile. But the state and its humanitarian partners are failing. It tries to enforce borders but refuses to manage the consequences, while humanitarianism often ends up as a policing exercise. Hence we learn that Herrou would sometimes collect migrants from a Red Cross camp on the Italian border where authorities had herded migrants (*New York Times*, 2016); the hospitality afforded at his farm in the Alps contrasts with the 'bleak no man's land' of the camp (*New York Times*, 2016). But whether the state or the humanitarian NGOs, whatever the precise locus of failure, here citizenship is cast as practical and ethical action: 'Getting involved is a citizen's duty' (*Humanité*, 2017). The state and its humanitarian partners have failed and into the breach step the citizens, fashioning shelter and providing guidance.[14]

Unlike the religious movements who seek to short-circuit the pastorate, Herrou is, of course, not looking to permanently usurp the state's authority or its role in the management of population. While certain social movements protest borders within a neo-anarchist political logic of 'No Borders', Herrou's reasoning is more circumscribed. He portrays his intervention as a moral duty to assist those the state is either abandoning or persecuting. But it does appear a radical act since he claims to be upholding and enacting the very tradition of citizenship which the state, despite its claims, has in questions of migration abandoned. A short-circuit, then: action which performs the very thing the state (read pastorate in former times) is accused of abandoning.

In/Visibilities

If there are ways in which Herrou illustrates Foucault's argument about counter-conduct, there are also ways in which this case complicates it, and pushes us to refine Foucault's necessarily incomplete observations. Here, let me return to the theme of in/visibility which I flagged earlier.

Herrou's case demonstrates how counter-conduct always puts in motion a particular play of the visible and the invisible. These in/visibilities take multiple forms. First, let us note there are certain practices of making things and people invisible which have a tactical purpose. At one point in his trial, Herrou is asked why he has wiped his hard drive of contacts. He explains he is maintaining the secrecy of others who cooperate with him but who, unlike him, do not wish to become public faces (Chiffon Rouge, 2016). Or the fact that Herrou explains in

---

[14] There is the interesting mirror image of border watchers such as the Minutemen in the US. For the latter it is the martial arm of the state that has failed, meaning that citizens must step up to defend the state's borders against invaders.

one short news clip that when he or his allies pick up migrants on the roads or near the border, they have to hide them in their vehicles (*Vice*, 2017). In other words, they use the same practice any smuggler would use. Hiding migrants is an immediate and tactical *sine qua non*: otherwise the migrants would be seized there and then by the police.

Let us note here a point of connection to debates in practice theory. Adler and Pouliot (2011: 7, emphasis in original) argue that 'practice is more or less *competent* in a socially meaningful and recognizable way'. Competence, or perhaps better, skill, is a prerequisite for Herrou's activity. Smuggling people is by no means a straightforward or self-evident activity, especially when it is performed on an ongoing basis. We know from the growing body of ethnographic research on people smuggling that it requires all manner of competences, which range from the emotional management of people under stress to practices of camouflage, negotiation, and navigation. In Herrou's case, he acquires some of these skills by virtue of being a farmer in a difficult, mountainous terrain. Accordingly he has a practical knowledge of routes, movements, places. Consider the fact that as a citizen smuggler he translates these skills, putting them to work in a new context: action that is both dedicated to saving people and to fostering political debate about policy. It is fascinating to note, then, that practices of how to move around a terrain acquired from the life of farming come to be put to a quite different use. Social movement studies frequently observe how practices of protest are inventive creations (Death, 2010). But here resistance stems in part from repurposing skills learnt in one context, farming, into another, smuggling people across borders and around the terrain.

While on the one hand Herrou uses various learned practices to make people less visible for the purposes of moving them, on the other he has become increasingly open about this activity. To understand this openness, this visibility, let us return to the notion of scene which I introduced earlier. The fact that Herrou stands trial – and will no doubt do so again given his stated refusal to acknowledge laws against solidarity and assistance that he deems illegal and inhumane – is not only a sign that the state wishes to suppress his activity. It is also a sign that Herrou and his allies see the trial as an opportunity to create a scene. They bring the trial upon themselves, not least by cooperating with newspapers such as the *New York Times*:

When we decided to mediatize what we were doing, it was knowing that we would get there [a trial]. This trial is a bit of a platform. A means of explaining what happens, of mediatizing the struggle, of democratizing it (Herrou in *l'Humanité*, 2017, my translation).

We should note in passing that the trial is a particularly prominent form of scene throughout political history. From the trial of Socrates to the impeachment of President Trump, a whole genealogy of politics could be written through a focus on the trial. But here let us keep the focus on Herrou. What makes the trial different as a scene from the kinds of scenes activists and migrants often foster, such as protests at detention centres, airports, or immigration offices? All of these give refusal and resistance to the state's border policies a visible, tangible form, and provide a sort of forum for political discussion. All of them provide ways for people to assemble, both physically and virtually, thereby focusing political energies. But trials bring other elements that can be valuable and make them a distinctive scene. For example, the trial allows for the production and mediation of a particular kind of speaking subject. Given the association of the trial as a judicial space with the production of truth, it authorizes a particular practice of avowal (Foucault, 2014). Hence it brings a certain performance of truth into the activity of resistance. The trial also allows the subject to appear as one who steadfastly commits to a course of action in the face of possible punishment. This also contributes to the production of Herrou as a moral subject. It burnishes his image as the visible face of a much wider play of contestation and refusal of French and European migration policy. It becomes an opportunity for him to accumulate 'visibility-capital' (Austin and Leander, Chapter 10; Heinich, 2012). Finally, the trial has a temporality as well as a distinctive spatiality. Trials deliver verdicts. They punctuate ongoing processes of struggle and resistance. They focus moral and political energies around failures and successes.

I have argued that in making a scene Herrou and his allies bring ethical and political force to the contestation of migration policy. But the scene does a second kind of work. Counter-conduct always places its practitioners at risk. Challenging powerful institutions, norms, and laws invites the possibility of reprisal and violence from state actors and other social groups. In such situations visibility can be a double-edged sword. They can expose the practitioners to greater risk. But visibility can also create security:

The media coverage of the case mobilizes a lot of support. It's very reassuring. Even though I [could] do a few weeks in prison, I know there will be thousands of people out there with me. When the first articles appeared in the regional press, at first I was afraid. I thought that the identity groups, the [fascists], would go up the valley to look for me. I was afraid for my professional life. But it's just the opposite (Herrou in *l'Humanité*, 2017, my translation).

Is This Counter-Conduct?

It seems we can only determine counter-conduct after the fact, or in a very tendential way. We find ourselves in a situation not unlike the one Max Weber – another strangely neglected figure in IR practice debates – sketched when he elaborated the idea of charismatic authority.[15] If Herrou is a moral actor, one who breaks the law in the name of a higher law, this is only insofar as others recognize him as such. This does not require that the state in the form of its legal rulings, absolves him (which it more or less did in passing a suspended sentence). On the contrary, many kinds of counter-conduct are only strengthened by the fact of legal repression. But it does require that a broader network of actors recognize his actions as just, valiant, legitimate, and so on. Weber writes that a charismatic leader enjoys authority in a way that is unstable and prone to breaking down. 'His charismatic claim breaks down if his mission is not recognized by those to whom he feels he has been sent' (Weber, 1946: 246). Herrou is not a leader in this exact sense. But the moral authority he brings to the struggle cannot be modelled as an individual attribute. It is instead a relational one. It endures only as long as he is recognized as such.

Conclusion

This chapter has argued that Foucault's work offers a particular form of practice-oriented approach to power. Moving beyond the view of Foucault as a theorist of discourse, or restricting him to the notion of productive power, the chapter has argued for a reading of Foucault as a historical nominalist and genealogist who maps power relations in a relatively open-ended and avowedly empirical fashion. He offers us not a fixed typology of power, but rather a method that begins with steps that are case-focused, localized, and situated; that explores different forms and modalities of power by working upwards from specific contexts. To deepen this point, the chapter has examined how Foucault mapped one particular kind of resistance, namely counter-conduct. Two lessons for practice-theory approaches to world politics can be extracted from this encounter.

First, counter-conduct is a useful concept because it brings questions regarding the practices of the self – what Foucault sometimes calls ethics – into the study of politics and resistance. That the self is sometimes a stake

[15] I owe this point about the uses of Weber's charisma model to Alen Toplišek (n.d.).

in political resistance is a point that has been overlooked in IR. Foucault offers us tools to examine how selves are made and remade in the course of struggles. A particular benefit of counter-conduct is that it allows us to think about the way that individual actors, dissidents, conscientious objectors, and so on can make a difference in contentious politics. IR has what we could call a macroscopic bias; it tends to focus on large social movements and social forces. It tends to consider a focus on individuals as old-style history (e.g. 'great leaders'). Yet as recent cases including Snowden's imply, we need new tools to make sense of situations in which individuals emerge as key figures and nodal points of resistance. This is an area in which future studies of counter-conduct could be fruitful.

In Chapter 1, the editors of this volume identify questions of scale as one fault line within IR practice theorizing. They contrast approaches which insist on grasping practice at the level of large aggregates and those which focus on 'the everyday actions of individuals in concrete settings'. The account of resistance as counter-conduct in this chapter does not bridge this fault line but it does unsettle some of its assumptions. For the case of the French farmer I have presented here does feature everyday practices. To shelter and move migrants Herrou does utilize certain know how and social practices derived from his everyday life as a farmer. Yet this is precisely *not* a case of what Scott calls 'everyday resistance' because of the visibility which these practices gain in the public sphere. Herrou's practices acquire national and international visibility; they become acts of defiance in the face of state orders; they become rallying points for action and identity for whole communities of migrant solidarity. In other words, at least in this case, counter-conduct presents us with a situation in which aspects of the everyday are transformed so that they cease to be 'microscopic' or merely 'local' and become precisely acts and events that can mobilize large aggregates and impact the grand stage of national and international politics.

The second lesson of this chapter for practice-theory follows from this point about visibility and can be stated like this. It would be rather 'un-Foucauldian' to use Foucault's work as though it offered a timeless set of concepts to map power and resistance. If Foucault is a very situated and historicized thinker, then it follows that connecting his thought to very different times and places calls on us to ask: what is new here? To this end, the chapter has identified key ways in which counter-conduct needs to be modified when brought to bear on very contemporary situations. Here a major challenge is to factor in questions of publics and publicity: How are struggles mediated? How do conscientious acts of resistance mobilize a public? To advance our thinking about counter-conduct *after* Foucault, the chapter has also developed a concept of scene. The scene is the event or the incident once it is mediated, publicized, and reiterated; it brings practices of communication into the study of resistance. Of course, a focus on scenes alone is not sufficient. Rather, future studies might embed the notion of scene in the growing literature on the politics of visibility, while also fostering connections to social movement studies of framing. In this way we could better understand how counter-conduct is at the same time a matter of making contentious things visible and invisible, a move with clear connections to the material as well as the practice turn in IR.

For a Practice Approach to Authority
The Emergence of Central Bankers'
International Authority

Joelle Dumouchel

As Hannah Arendt points out, the etymological root of authority is
not Greek but Latin – *auctoritas* (Arendt, 1958). This observation is an
important one as it helps us to understand the singularity of authority vis-à-vis other ways of conceptualizing power. The Greeks handled
domestic affairs through *persuasion* and foreign affairs through *violence* –
both concepts signal for Arendt (1958) a lack of authority rather than
its presence. In ancient Rome, power was exercised differently. The
territory politically controlled by the Romans was much larger than the
one controlled by the Athenian government and thus called for innovative ways of ruling. Roman rulers were actively involved in creating a
distinct Roman tradition and sense of authority (Furedi, 2013: 47–48).
In the Roman public sphere, *auctoritas* was usually distinguished from
potestas, meaning power, or *imperium,* which designates military power
(Furedi, 2013: 59–63). As such, in contrast to other types of power, a
reference to authority implied the will to generate voluntary compliance: '*[a]uctoritas* represented a claim to influence, respect and esteem'
(Furedi, 2013: 62). From its Roman roots, authority retained a close
connection to legitimacy. Authority is a form of power that is perceived
as natural or necessary.

International Relations (IR) scholars have referred to authority to
challenge the realist idea that patterns of domination depend on the
mere distribution of material power. By using the concept of authority,
they have questioned the anarchic assumption around which the IR
discipline is organized. Orders in IR are not the mere result of coer-
cion, but can also emerge from structures of authority. An influential
body of work that deals with authority has opposed the concept of
hierarchy to the one of anarchy. Scholars from this tradition consider
that the international system comprises authoritative relations between
superordinates and subordinates. One group of scholars that draw on
economic theories argue that relations of authority are social contracts
to which both the superordinate and the subordinate consent. A case

in point is the relation of authority between the United States (US) and the Caribbean (Lake, 2009, 2010). Principal–agent theory (PA) argues that authority is deliberately delegated by states to non-state actors. Constructivists, who have also been actively engaged with the concept of authority, oppose this agent-based conception of authority with a conceptualization that focuses on the intersubjective substance of authority. For a majority of constructivists, authority is sourced from legitimate norms that are socially defined. For instance, international organizations (IOs) display authority at the international level owing to their recognized expertise on specific issues.

This chapter demonstrates that the standard conceptualizations of authority in IR fall short of fully acknowledging the dynamic making of authority. Whereas agent-based conceptions of authority acknowledge that authoritative relations can emerge and disappear, they cannot account for change in the intersubjective context that defines the terms under which authoritative relations are considered legitimate: why some types of actors are perceived as legitimate authorities rather than others. By considering that authoritative relations emerge and last through rational decisions, the contractual version of international hierarchies ignores the variety of sources underlying international authority. On the contrary, a majority of constructivists accept that authority depends on an intersubjective context that can vary. Yet, by departing from institutional sources of authority, they fix authority in specific attributes that place the question of how authority emerges or transforms beyond the scope of analysis (Sending, 2015). For instance, IPE scholars have attributed the international authority of central bankers to the institutions they represent and their expertise, but have ignored the process through which such authority began to be recognized. Moreover, by fixing authority to specific sources, they shut the door on the possibility that the authority of central bankers can disappear.

This chapter outlines an alternative conception of authority based on practice theory. It argues that a practice-based conception of authority is better equipped to account for change by combining the dynamic components of the two standard IR conceptions of authority. Practice theory tackles authority as a process that can account for the emergence and disappearance of authoritative relations, in addition to including the dynamic transformations of the substance of authority. As such, practice theory offers a broader ontology than standard IR studies of authority. Accordingly, I argue that practice scholars have taken two research strategies to approach authority: one that focuses on the social dynamics underlying claims and recognition of authority, and another that looks at the production of the object of authority. The chapter argues that the two research strategies are not mutually exclusive and should be integrated to give a full account of authority in practice. By doing so, it becomes possible to take into account the woven effect of the material, epistemic and symbolic dimension on the construction of authority in time. The chapter empirically demonstrates the heuristic value of the integrated practice framework of authority by looking at the case of the emergence of the international authority of central bankers. It thereby also documents how practice theorists can productively revisit power and change, and hence build bridges across the fault lines of stability and change, and power and the communitarian side of practice. By contrast, the chapter is more clearly anchored on the aggregated practices side, the consciousness side and the theory side of the respective fault lines of the everyday and the aggregate, materiality and consciousness, and theory and practice.

Static Authority and the Problem of Change

Most of the research in IR conceptualizes authority by taking either of two distinct points of departure. On the one hand, agent-based theories approach authority by looking at the delegation of authority through PA theories or the structural relations between superordinate and subordinate entities. On the other hand, constructivists focus on the sources of authority in IR. In this section, I argue that both bodies of literature conceptualize some elements of authority as static, which limits their capacity to account for change in two different ways. Agent-based approaches take into account that authority can emerge and disappear but conceptualize the sources of authority as fixed. Constructivist studies, such as Barnett and Finnemore (2004) and Avant et al. (2010), acknowledge that authority can draw on a variety of sources, but anchor the sources to specific institutions. Yet who has authority in IR and under what terms are not immutable characteristics. Authoritative relations that shape world politics have historically emerged, can transform and possibly fade.

Fixing Authority to Its Configuration

In recent years, a growing body of work has approached authority from the perspective of rational choice. Challenging the notion that the international system is organized through the principle of anarchy, this body of work converges around the idea that hierarchies structurally shape the international system. Two trends can be distinguished. Scholars working under PA have highlighted that states delegate authority to various institutions for functional reasons. Specialized agencies such as IOs can fulfil some tasks more effectively than the state (Hawkins et al., 2006). Moreover, David Lake (2009) has developed an approach to international hierarchies that seeks to explain why states get involved in hierarchical structures. By using an ontology derived from economic theories, Lake theorizes authority as a contractual relation between superordinate and subordinate political entities. Authority is 'a form of legitimate power that entails a right to command by the dominant state and an obligation or duty to comply by the subordinate' (Lake, 2013: 74).

An important characteristic that distinguishes Lake's theorization of authority and PA theory from other approaches is that political entities get involved in relations of authority in a voluntary and conscious fashion. Both approaches highlight the importance of contracts. 'The relations between a principle and an agent are always governed by *a contract*, even if this agreement is implicit (never formally acknowledged) or informal (based on an unwritten agreement)' (Hawkins et al., 2006: 7). Similarly, international hierarchies are based on voluntary contracts under which states delegate parts of their authority to another state. The motivating factor is self-interest. States might subordinate themselves to other states in order to ensure their security or pursue their economic growth. Authority relations are created through bargaining. Lake's theorization of international hierarchies follows the path opened up by Keohane and Nye (1977) with their concept of complex interdependence, which states that the globalized order creates conditions wherein mutual interests are possible. As a result, states engage in bargaining processes and conclude stringing agreements. Lake thus goes one step further by arguing that these negotiating patterns lead to authority relations: 'In any authority relationship, B chooses whether to comply with A's commands, but it is bound by the right of A to discipline or punish its noncompliance' (Lake, 2013: 78).

The emphasis on international hierarchies has helped to draw out the complexity of formal authoritative relations. As Bially Mattern and Zarakol (2016: 624 [italics in the original]) put it, 'hierarchy-centered approaches to IR promise to deliver what anarchy-centered approaches have not: a framework for theorizing and empirically analyzing world politics as a *global system* rather than just an international one'. The concept of international hierarchies can encompass authoritative patterns that take place not only between states but also between states and non-state actors. As Cooley (2003) argues, the era of globalization has witnessed a stark growth of public–private partnerships. Negotiations over the delegation of sovereignty occur very frequently between states and non-state actors. States have subcontracted various tasks to large spectrums of non-state actors, such as non-governmental organizations, credit-rating agencies or IOs. Similarly, Hall and Biersteker (2002) point out that various non-state-related actors convey authority in the international arena. Such an argument echoes global governance studies, which, since Rosenau and Czempiel's (1992) seminal book *Governance without Government*, has sought to identify the array of actors that are granted authority in world politics. IR scholars have shown that configurations of authority in a globalized era can be multiple and complex. For instance, Grande and Pauly (2005: 4) point out that the world has evolved in 'a complicated system of multiple and overlapping hierarchies'.

Fixing Authority to Its Substance

Rather than conceiving authority as originating from the conscious decisions of international actors, another body of work approaches authority by looking at the normative context that makes authority legitimate. Deriving mainly from constructivist scholars inspired by Weberian sociology, this theoretical trend assumes that authority is embedded within socially shared subjectivity. According to this approach, a particular political entity is authoritative not because other actors have decided so, but because the entity possesses certain characteristics that are culturally considered to be worthy of respect and diligence. Constructivists share the assumption that authority is inherently social (Reus-Smit, 2007). By assuming that interests are intersubjectively constructed, they focus on social context rather than individual decisions. Authority involves hierarchical relations that go much deeper than a conscious delegation of power based on interest. What makes a certain entity authoritative depends on sets of characteristics and norms that are socially sanctioned. Political entities are not just authoritative, but are also perceived as such.

A common analytical strategy for this approach is to establish a typology of potential sources of authority. In the image of Max Weber (1998), who developed an ideal-type approach to authority, constructivists have sought to identify the various ideational contents that make political authority authoritative in the international sphere. In the context of a globalized world, they recognize the autonomy of action of many types of actors (Coleman and Bernstein, 2009). Autonomy can derive from a variety of sources. For instance, Barnett and Finnemore (2004: 25) identify four types of authority that can make IOs authoritative – rational-legal, delegated, moral and expert – to which Avant et al. (2010: 11–14) add two further categories, namely institutional and capacity-based authority. IR scholars working from this tradition have acknowledged that different types of authority are likely to produce different outcomes; hence, the importance of differentiating between various sources of authority and understanding their respective characteristics. For instance, Barnett and Finnemore (2004) use the rational-legal ideal type developed by Weber to understand how IOs behave. By pointing to their bureaucratic character, they show that IOs do not always take rational decisions and can display pathological behaviours: 'Bureaucracy is a distinctive social form of authority with its own internal logic and behavioral proclivities' (Barnett and Finnemore, 2004: 3).

The Problem of Change

Whereas the two approaches outlined here differ in focus, they both inhibit the analysis of change in patterns of authority. The body of scholarship that links authority to formal configurations assumes that actors engage in relations of authority based on their self-interests. As such, they do not take into account the various ideational or cultural contexts within which authority is embedded. On the other hand, constructivist scholars recognize that authority depends on an intersubjective context that can take various forms. Yet their framework also limits our understanding of change by fixing the substance of authority to a specific institution that cannot change. By focusing on the sources of authority, constructivists working from a Weberian sociology tradition conceptualize authority as attributive. For instance, Barnett and Finnemore (2004) identify the bureaucratic sources of IOs prior to their analysis. As such, one cannot use their framework to understand change in the sources of authority.

Such attributive characterizations of authority lead constructivists to privilege the institutional embodiment of authority at the expense of understanding the relation between dominant and dominated. Authority is relational. It is not enough to identify authoritative actors and the set of characteristics that place such actors in positions of authority; it is equally important to consider what makes positions of subordination acceptable. As the international hierarchies scholarship argues, authority is formalized into a relation between superordinate and subordinate. In that sense, the framework deployed by international hierarchy scholarship includes the possibility that authority can emerge or disappear. Similarly, the defining characteristic of the 'principal' is to 'be able to both grant authority and rescind it' (Hawkins et al., 2006: 7). Yet by focusing on the voluntary and conscious aspects of authority, agent-based approaches are equally limited as Weberian-inspired constructivism. The terms according to which things are considered legitimate might vary. A conceptualization of authority that can account for change must recognize that authority is relational, as well as allow for potential transformation of the sources of authority.

Moreover, actors do not always accept their position within authoritative relations in a conscious fashion. The most integrated relations of authority are in fact seen as natural. As Bourdieu argues, relations of domination are normally deeply ingrained in society. As such, authoritative relations can be established to the disadvantage of actors, yet still be maintained because they seem natural. Bourdieu (2002: 1) calls this contradiction the *paradox of the doxa*: 'surprisingly, [that] the established order, with its relations of domination, its rights and prerogatives, privileges, and injustices, ultimately perpetuates itself so easily, apart from a few historical accidents, and [that] the most intolerable conditions of existence can so often be perceived as acceptable and even natural'. Austin and Leander (Chapter 10) show how regimes of visibility, the ways in which things appear to us, can contribute to the naturalization of such power dynamics. Authoritative relationships involve symbolic power wherein people in positions of subordination consider their position to be the natural order of things. In such situations, actors can consent to authority even though the pattern of authority plays to their disadvantage. Relations of authority go much deeper than structures of interest; they are also structured through cognition and even feelings. Consequently, to account for change in authority, it is necessary to grasp not only the visible but also the invisible, or in other words, to question the making of what appears to us as natural.

A Practice Approach to Authority

In this section, I argue that tackling authority from a practice perspective offers a dynamic conceptualization of authority that can better account for change in the international system. Practice theory draws on a relational ontology that allows an understanding of authority as a process. By adopting a relational ontology, one does not see stability and change as opposed to one another, but rather as being mutually constitutive. Schäfer (Chapter 9) shows for instance that repetitions occur within the dynamic making of practice. Similarly, Pouliot (Chapter 8) shows that the structural evolution of international practice stems from micro-deviation in the daily performance of practice (see Table 7.1).

Table 7.1 *The ontological underpinning of standard approaches of authority*

	Authority	Possible Sources
Agent-based approaches	Relational (dynamic)	Interest (fixed)
Constructivism	Institutional (fixed)	Various (dynamic)

Consequently, the relational ontology underlying practice theory allows us to combine the two dynamic aspects of the standard IR approaches to authority, while avoiding their static characteristics. A procedural conception incorporates the relational aspects of authority while also accounting for the production of the intersubjective context from which authority can originate. With the help of a relational ontology, practice theory allows us to understand where authority came from and how it might disappear. I argue that scholars of the practice turn have operationalized procedural authority by adopting two research strategies: (1) investigating the social dynamics that underlie claims and recognitions of authority and (2) investigating the process of production of what can be the object of authority. These two research strategies have the advantage of capturing the process of construction of authority in time, as well as accounting for the contingent character of history.[1]

From Static Authority to Authority as a Process

In contrast to standard conceptualizations of authority in IR that draw on a substantial ontology, practice theories draw on a relational ontology. A substantial ontology 'claims that substances (things, beings, entities, essences) are the units or "level" of analysis and that they exist prior to the analysis' (Adler-Nissen, 2016: 94). A relational ontology, on the other hand, assumes that relation precedes substance (Jackson and Nexon, 1999; Mitchell, 1991). This should not imply that substance does not matter, but rather that substance is continuously produced or reproduced. A relational perspective does 'not look for boundaries of things but for things of boundaries' (Abbott, 1995: 857). By starting from the actual making of international politics, a relational ontology avoids imposing a specific pre-defined substance on the analysis. For instance, by looking at how sovereignty is practically negotiated between members of the European Union (EU), Adler-Nissen (2013a) avoids taking the substance of what sovereignty is for granted. In the

---

[1] Practice research can also involve the micro-performances of practices (such as the act of authorizing by signing official documents), which I do not include in this chapter because of their lack of attention to historical context.

daily making of European integration, the substance of sovereignty consists of what is negotiated and renegotiated in practice.

With the help of a relational ontology, practice scholars have prioritized dynamic empirical objects over static ones. Rather than looking at international institutions, they engage with the everyday making of international politics. For instance, practice scholars will be more likely to look at European *integration* rather than the European *Union* (Adler-Nissen, 2014b; McNamara, 2015; Mérand, 2008). Similarly, studying authority from the standpoint of practice leads to a conceptualization of authority as a process. Rather than fixing the substance of authority into pre-given categories, practice theory looks at the production and reproduction of authority in time. In a nutshell, the relational conception of authority shifts the focus of empirical analysis from fixed sources and formal expressions of relations of authority, to the processes of its production and performance.

By conceptualizing authority as a process, it becomes possible to combine the two dynamic components of standard theorizations of authority in IR and discard their static elements. By drawing on a relational ontology, one can conceptualize authority as a relation between superordinate and subordinate entities, in line with international hierarchies scholarship. Yet, unlike international hierarchies scholarship, a procedural conception of authority affirms the diversity of types of relations that pertain between superordinate and subordinate, rather than constraining them to contractual relations. Practice theory, like constructivism, problematizes the substance of authority. Yet, unlike constructivism, practice theory approaches the relation between substance and institution as dynamic, rather than fixed.

Research Strategy 1: The Social Construction of Patterns of Domination

One trend of practice scholars' approach is a view of authority as being vested in social relations. Rather than seeing authority as sourced from specific norms, they look at the play of social interactions within which relations of domination are produced. Drawing mostly on Bourdieusian sociology, this group of scholars conceives relations of authority as constructed through the symbolic distribution of social roles. Pierre Bourdieu, unlike Max Weber, developed a sociology that provides a firm basis for the conceptualization of authority as relational. For Bourdieu, it is not enough to identify the set of characteristics that one needs to possess to be in a position of authority; it is equally important to look at what makes positions of subordination acceptable. Relations of authority are hierarchical relations between those in a position to dominate and those that are dominated. Crucial to the construction of such relations are claims to authority and the recognition of authority.

Therefore, in contrast to the contractual version of international hierarchy, relations between superordinate and subordinated can take various forms. Hierarchical relations are not the mere outcome of voluntary and conscious decisions, but stem from the symbolic incorporation of our social roles. Relations of authority depend not only on the legitimacy of domination, but also on the legitimacy of being dominated. Recognitions of authority and claims to authority work in relation with one another, forming a symbolic organization of authority. As Bourdieu (2001) argues, if one fails to play by the rules of an established symbolic order, it is very likely that one would be perceived as socially awkward or crazy. To illustrate the importance of following the symbolic structure of the social game, one can think of Poprishchin, the protagonist of Gogol's (2006) short story 'The Diary of a Madman', who wakes up one morning with the strong belief that he is the King of Spain. As strong as his belief is, and even when he starts to act accordingly, he is not taken seriously. Since there is no social recognition of his self-proclaimed status, he is treated as a madman and put in an asylum.

Consequently, the investigation of claims to authority has allowed practice scholars to understand the logic of social actions in the process of constructions of authority. Relations of authority are based on the symbolic internationalization of a social role that is not fixed but constructed in time. Relations of authority are constructed through the social struggle to control the legitimate perception of how things ought to be done. Since the practice turn posits that the international realm is always open to change, which actors are considered authoritative and under which conditions remain open questions. Since there are no universal relations of authority, social agents involved in the making of world politics are constantly engaged in social struggles to be recognized as authorities or to maintain their recognized authoritative status. In this sense, it is not enough to point to potential sources of authority; one also has to understand why certain actors are able to claim those sources for themselves. For instance, pointing to moral authority as one source of authority in the international realm provides only one side of the story. As Sending (2015: 17) notes, 'the claim to represent or advance the "public interest" is common to all groups that are engaged in global governance, so we are not wiser as to why some groups succeed with such claims and others do not'.

As such, by looking at claims to authority, one can understand why certain groups succeed to claim ownership over sources of authority while others do not. The analysis of authoritative claims can also inform our understanding of why things are shaped the way they are. Whereas the attributive conceptualization of authority draws a link between types of authority and outcomes, a relational conceptualization engages the construction of authority together with the practices underlying the making of world politics. For instance, Sending et al. (2015) look at the competing authoritative claims that underpin the evolving face of diplomacy. Authoritative claims define the mere notion of what diplomats are and what they can do. 'What makes a diplomat is a claim to jurisdictional control over certain tasks that are sanctioned by the state and recognized in international law' (Sending et al., 2015: 5). The jurisdictional control exercised by traditional diplomats has been challenged in the current context where non-state actors have gained authority to influence the outcomes of world politics. Yet unlike the typology approach, which consists of identifying the authoritative sources of these new actors, the practice approach addresses the relations of authority between traditional and new types of diplomacy. By looking at claims to authority, scholars question how social actors define and redefine their role in a changing environment and the extent to which jurisdictional control has changed. New actors have succeeded in being considered as credible participants in the diplomatic process. For instance, Seabrooke (2015) shows how private consultants have engaged in diplomatic activities with the help of economic expertise. Private consultants have claimed authority through what Seabrooke (2015: 196) calls *epistemic arbitrage*, 'whereby they generate symbolic and economic gains by exploiting and combining forms of knowledge from different professional areas'.

The analysis of claims to authority is not only relevant to capturing changing patterns of authority but also stable ones. As Milliken (1999: 242) nicely puts it: 'orderliness needs to be worked for it to be reproduced'. For instance, Adler-Nissen (2014a) looks at the strategies of traditional diplomats to maintain jurisdictional control over their practice. Through the creation of a diplomatic service at the European level, the institutionalization of the EU External Action Service has challenged state monopoly on diplomatic services. The social struggle for authority mainly occurs at the symbolic level since the level of resources mobilized by the new institution is quite insignificant. More specifically, the social claims for authority occur through the struggle regarding what defines 'genuine' diplomats. Traditional diplomats have sought to maintain their position of authority, for instance by questioning the competence of Catherine Ashton who was appointed as head of the EU External Action Service.

Research Strategy 2: The Production Process
of the Object of Authority

Pierre Bourdieu's praxeological approach has helped practice scholars understand the social struggles underlying claims to and recognitions of authority that occur within the boundaries of a specific social configuration. Yet the repertoire of knowledge upon which actors base their actions goes well beyond the boundaries of a specific social field. For instance, international financial markets, which constitute an important object for contemporary authority in IR, have been structurally produced through a myriad of historical outcomes that are for the most part situated outside the social configuration in which the social struggle for authority occurs. Put differently, the various objects over which social agents claim their expertise or jurisdiction have been historically produced, and Bourdieusian sociology does not provide the analytical tools required to understand this historical process of production.

In contrast, scholars of the practice turn in IR, who have developed analyses based on the sociology of knowledge, have recognized the importance of knowledge in ordering reality (Adler and Faubert, Chapter 3; Bueger, 2015; Leander, 2016; Sending, 2015). Political knowledge is understood here not only in terms of positive knowledge but also in relation to how one comprehends reality: '[I]t constitutes the entirety of all social systems of signs, and in so doing, the symbolic order and stocks of knowledge constituted by these systems which mediate between human beings and the world' (Keller, 2011: 48). This trend of scholarship also foregrounds the crucial role of materiality in establishing the conditions of possibility for the enactment of specific relations of authority. As Bueger and Gadinger (2018: 78) put it, 'practices are bodily activities, involve a range of objects and artefacts and are, therefore, always materially anchored'. As such, whereas the study of claims to authority looks at the social struggles underlying how things ought to be done, the study of the object of authority looks at the historical production of what can be done.

Like the social dynamics underpinning patterns of domination, the construction of an object of authority is a process. Objects of authority are what Knorr Cetina (2001: 191–193) calls *epistemic objects*, which are characterized by a 'lack of completeness of being'. In this sense, objects of authority are always open to change and transformation. Scholars who look at the creation of objects share two characteristics: they put knowledge at the centre of their analysis and they draw on an historical ontology. Hacking (2002: 18) reminds us that 'among the thoughts that underlie historical ontology is this: "one cannot speak of anything at any time; it is not easy to say something new; it is not enough for us to open our eyes, to pay attention, or to be aware, for new objects suddenly light up and emerge out of the ground'". As Anna Leander (2010: 65) puts it, 'practices are always contextual', and Pouliot provides (Chapter 8) one very specific model of how that contextuality can look like. A practice-based conception of authority is similarly contextual. Looking at the historical production of objects thus helps us understand why some objects can be mobilized for claims to authority at a particular historical moment, while others cannot. For instance, Bentley B. Allan (2017) argues that the global climate governance regime is built on a scientific conception of climate, rather than of the biosphere as a whole. '[The object] of climate emerged from a dynamic, interactive process between states and scientists' (Allan, 2017: 132).

The creation of an object and its impact on authority is best exemplified in Sending's (2015) study of the United Nations secretariat. As he argues, this authority was established by claims to competence over the international. Yet the very object of the international as an autonomous sphere that can be acted upon was historically produced over time. It was 200 years after the Treaty of Westphalia that the international system began to be conceived as having a reality of its own (Bartelson, 1995: 36). The creation of the object of the international served as a stepping stone for the establishment of a whole new system of expertise and material artefacts, such as international law and peace techniques. By shifting our attention to the historical production of the object of expertise, Sending goes one step further than Barnett and Finnemore (2004). While not denying that this international organization displayed rational-legal authority, he highlights the production process of what rational-legal authority can be based upon. Without representations of the international as an autonomous sphere, international organizations could not claim distinct forms of expertise that other actors lack: 'the claim to represent the *international* as a distinct space where some tasks were to be handled by the secretariat gave the secretariat and the Secretary-General a level of authority *vis à vis* member states' (Sending, 2015: 52 [italics in the original]).

Joining the Two Research Strategies Together

Most practice scholars approach authority via one of these research strategies, not both.[2] Scholars engaging with the social construction of relations of domination focus on the social positioning of actors and the symbolic construction of their roles. In contrast, scholars addressing the production of objects of authority overlook social dynamics in the process of knowledge production, highlighting instead the construction of

---

[2] For an exception, see Sending (2015).

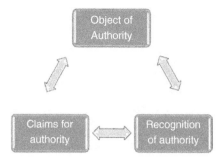

Figure 7.1 Objects, claims and recognition of authority

conditions of possibility – at both epistemic and material levels – for certain relations of authority to take form. I argue that these two research strategies are not mutually exclusive (see Figure 7.1). Both the production of objects and the symbolic construction of social organizations of authority are important in processes of authority making. The study of how things ought to be done and the study of what things can be done are interdependent. By bringing these tasks together, it becomes possible to address the interwoven effects of epistemic, material and symbolic dimensions in the construction processes of patterns of authority through time. In this section, I pursue both research strategies to develop an understanding of the emergence of authority in practice, using the growth of central bankers' authority as an exemplary case.

The Emergence of Central Bankers' International Authority

The authoritative role of central bankers in the international sphere has been widely acknowledged, yet little attention has been focused on how such authority emerged. Central bankers' authority has been analysed from the perspective of standard approaches to authority, which has limited the scope and dynamism of analysis. A first trend of such scholarship has been to fix the authority of central bankers within its configurations. Baker (2006) and Kapstein (1994) have highlighted the positional nature of central bankers' authority. Central bankers' ability 'to influence public policy depends in large measure upon the formal and informal institutional networks that bind them to the central authorities' (Kapstein, 1994: 10–11). Central bankers are involved in a two-level game of governance in which they have to use their international networks to influence domestic opinions, and vice versa. In a similar fashion, Johnson (2016) has shown that by adopting international norms, central bankers from

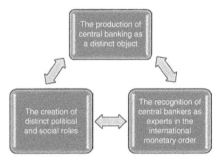

Figure 7.2 Objects, claims and recognition of central bankers' authority

post-communist countries have undermined their own legitimacy within domestic contexts. The second trend, best exemplified by Hall (2008), has been to fix central bankers' authority to a specific form of 'deontic power': a form of power 'that is marked by such terms as rights, duties, obligations, authorizations, permissions, empowerments, requirements, and certifications' (Searle, 2005: 10). In this section, I combine the two aforementioned research strategies to develop a practice-based approach to authority, by showing how the emergence of central bankers' international authority has been an interactive process involving the production of central banking as an independent object of governance, the creation of distinct political and social roles as well as the recognition of central bankers' forms of expertise (see Figure 7.2).

The Production of Central Banking as an Object of Authority

In 1894, Palgrave's *Dictionary of Political Economy* contained no entry for 'central banking' (Singleton, 2011: 11). A reference to the Bank of England can be found under the entry 'banking', but no general term existed to designate the distinctive practices of central banks. It was in 1908, in the context of the US National Inquiry Commission, that the term 'central banking' first emerged. The commission, established in the aftermath of the most severe financial crashes that had hit the US in the last 100 years, sought to undertake a close examination of the country's banking systems. The crisis peaked in the autumn of 1907, when a banking panic led to the bankruptcy of more than 25 banks and 17 trust companies (Bruner and Carr, 2007: 115). The crisis lasted 15 months, during which time 'the value of all listed stock in the United States declined 37 per cent' (Bruner and Carr, 2007: 115). The depth of the crisis came as a shock and revealed the weakness of the American banking system. Even though international markets were strongly integrated, the effect of the crisis was only moderately felt in European capitals. A central issue at play was the role of central banks, which existed in industrialized European countries at that time, but not in the US. The apparent success of European countries in coping with the crisis, compared with their American counterparts, led to the view that the American system of financial governance was inappropriate and inefficient.

Consequently, the fact that 'central banking' was popularized during the commission's inquiry is no coincidence. The commission, also known as the Aldrich Commission, carried out an extensive study of central banks' practices and credit markets in Europe that was published in 24 volumes in 1910. The commission treated the presence of a central bank as a specific way to organize credit and money. As chair of the commission Republican Senator Nelson W. Aldrich (1910: 5) put it, 'I believe that no one can carefully study the experience of the other great commercial nations without being convinced that disastrous results of recurring have been successfully prevented by a proper organization of capital and by the adoption of wise methods of banking and of currency'. The commission's work established the notion that the European system of central banking constituted the modern way to regulate credit and money, while the US National Banking system was considered backward and outdated. In the words of Paul M. Warburg (1910: 513), 'it is now generally acknowledged, even by those who were formerly most unwilling to concede it, that the end of 1907 witnessed one of the most impressive victories of the central banks' system'.

The emergence of the term 'central banking' enabled the rise of a practice of governance that can be separated from the idiosyncratic actions of individual central banks. During the nineteenth-century gold standard, central banks carried out governing functions by ensuring the convertibility of money, yet the rationalization of such functions was anchored in the actions of a few specific central banks. For instance, Bagehot's (1873) book, now perceived as establishing the modern principles of central banking, was solely geared towards the actions of the Bank of England, rather than central banks in general. With the 1908 National Inquiry Commission, central banking came to be considered as a modern way of intervening in monetary and banking systems. Such perceptions persisted even in the aftermath of the 1930s crisis. As Vera Smith (1936: 1) has argued, 'in the present century centralized banking systems have come to be regarded as the usual concomitant, if not one of the conditions of the attainment of an advanced state of economic development. The belief in the desirability of central bank organization is universal'. Consequently, 'central banking' represents the production of a new object of authority, since it established an independent sphere of expert knowledge within which actors could claim authority. The knowledge of central banking principles, such as international monetary policy, established new forms of competence and credibility on the international scene.

Claiming Authority through the Creation of Distinct Political Roles

The rise of central banking as a new object of authority cannot in itself explain the rise of the authority of central bankers. It is also necessary to look at processes of symbolic construction of distinct political roles that enabled some individuals to claim authority over central banking. Such roles also emerged at the turn of the twentieth century. Indeed, until the beginning of the twentieth century, the mere notion of a central banker made no sense. As an historical economist at the Bank of France pointed out, the individual importance that had been attributed to governors during the gold-standard period is mainly a product of historical reinterpretation.[3] The authority of central banks was held collectively rather than individually. Executive bank members were selected on the basis of their capacity to represent shared group values, rather than on their individual merits. Central banks were run as collective enterprises. The Bank of England was managed by a court of directors, the Bank of France by a council of regents. The position of governor existed but did not have specific cultural significance. Rather than showing leadership or powers of initiative, the governor was expected to represent the institution's values. In England, the positions of governor and deputy governor were filled through a two-year rotation system: 'the Deputy-Governor always succeeds the Governor, and usually the oldest director who has not been in office becomes Deputy-Governor' (Bagehot, 1873: 209).

   As such, a first step towards the construction of a distinct political role was to separate the function of central bankers from the institution, a process facilitated by the position's professionalization. The First World War emerged as an important trigger for establishing the governor's function of representing the institution. At the Bank of England, the war weakened the rotary system of governorship that was almost as old as the bank, which was founded in 1694. Instead of serving for two years as tradition dictated, then governor Walter Cunliffe

[3] Interview at the Bank of France, April 2013.

was reappointed for a five-year mandate. By holding their position for an extended period, governors could leave their mark on the institution and had greater scope for defining their own policies. Montagu Norman, who remained governor of the Bank of England for a period of 24 years, became the first to truly endorse the political function of the central banker. Under his leadership, the Bank abolished its old structure of nomination. Hence, the old rotation system for deputy governors was abolished at the end of the 1920s. Staff were also professionalized: '[Norman] was dissatisfied with its concentration of "City men" and wanted a "new breed" of full-time professionals without ties to their own business' (Wood, 2005: 281). In addition, a new position of advisor was created in 1928, which institutionally reinforced the individual importance of the governor (Hennessy, 1992: 2).

Bankers collaborated to reinforce a universal conception of the political role of central bankers. Montagu Norman of the Bank of England and Benjamin Strong of the Federal Reserve Bank of New York (FRBNY) were important vanguards in the establishment of international collaboration between central bankers. Their strong collaboration helped to foster international collaboration between central banks in the early post–First World War period. Their mutual sympathy is often singled out as the main reason for this collaboration.[4] Norman spent some time in his early years as a commercial banker in the US, which gave him a rare familiarity with US commercial culture. The two men maintained regular correspondence and came to share a common vision regarding the role of central banking in the post–First World War economic context. According to Sayers (1976: 155),

By their natures passionately public servants, both of them saw in the institutions they governed instruments for the reconstruction of a broken world economy. They believed especially that they and their opposite numbers in Europe had more chance than any politicians of guiding the peoples of the world, both nationally and internationally, in the adoption and maintenance of policies needing time and patience.

For that purpose, Norman came up with the idea of establishing some sort of 'central banks private club'. In September 1925, he wrote the following to Strong: 'I rather hope that next summer we may be able to inaugurate a private and eclectic Central Banks' "Club", small at first, large in the future' (quoted in Toniolo, 2005: 34). In that spirit, the first international meeting between central bankers took place in July 1927 in Long Island (Cottrell, 1995: 94). Organized by Strong, the meeting

---

[4] See, for example, Ahamed (2009); Cottrell (1995); Sayers (1976).

was attended by the governor of the Reichsbank, Schacht, Norman and Charles Rist, who was in charge of the newly created department of foreign affairs at the Bank of France (Toniolo, 2005: 30–31).

Amid intensified social interactions between central bank officials, the Bank for International Settlements (BIS) was created in 1930. While the immediate cause of the bank's establishment can be found in the Young Plan that addressed Germany's reparation payments, the bank's status provided the institution with a much larger mandate: 'to promote the co-operation of central banks and to provide additional facilities for international financial settlements entrusted to it under agreements with the parties concerned' (Toniolo, 2005: 48). With the establishment of the BIS, social interactions between central bankers became more institutionalized. Monthly meetings in Basel provided a casual context for central bankers to exchange views on various subjects. The BIS thus helped to create a sense of 'we-ness' between central bankers that was maintained over time. Moreover, the BIS provided a forum for central bankers to find some sort of comfort with each other. In the 1960s, for instance, Louis Raminsky, then governor of the Bank of Canada, 'found the meetings were not only "an invariable source of pleasure" but "served a therapeutic purpose" as well' (quoted in Toniolo, 2005: 365). Even when the International Monetary Fund (IMF) was established, the political centres for central bankers remained at the BIS. The BIS had the advantage over the IMF of providing a place where they 'can meet without the benefit of the presence of people from the Department of Finance' (Muirhead, 1999: 236). In fact, the BIS remains a very secretive institution to this day; no minutes of its meetings are recorded. Accordingly, the BIS became an institution where central bankers could create policies in their own way.

Consequently, during the interwar period, central bankers were no longer the mere executors of the institution's policies, but became associated with symbolic baggage that made them authoritative figures in the making of governance. They 'expanded from being "in" authority, which is vested in an office and regulated by rules, to being also "an" authority, which is not regulated by rules and may move beyond it' (Sending, 2015: 44). A distinct sense of what a central banker was began to be recognized by others and endorsed by those holding the position: 'when complimented on his expertise as a banker at a Senate Hearing in 1945, Allan Sproul of the FRBNY responded testily: "I appear here not as a banker ... but as a central banker"' (Singleton, 2011). Or as Einzig (1932: 107–108) put it, the central banker 'should be something between the typical banker and the typical permanent official'.

The Recognition of Central Bankers' Expertise

Central bankers could not have successfully gained authority over central banking without recognition of their new role on the international scene. The economic turmoil that followed the First World War created a structure of opportunities for the authority of central bankers to gain recognition. Two circumstances were particularly significant in this context: first, the re-establishment of the gold standard as an international monetary system; second, the complex issue of war repayments.

The end of the First World War provided an opportunity to rationally conceive of an international monetary order. The nineteenth-century gold standard, normally considered the first international monetary regime, was in fact mainly established in an ad hoc manner. It is only after the First World War that the idea of an international regime with its own set of rules and principles began to be consciously imagined. The Macmillan Committee was created by the British government to determine the cause of the UK's depression. It was during the committee's hearings that the term 'rules of the game' regarding the gold standard appeared for the first time. The term was first used by Sir Robert Kindersley, a director of the Bank of England, then again by Keynes and was included in the committee's reports (Bordo and Schwartz, 1984: 195). The report, published in 1931, emphasized the rules and principles of the international monetary regime: 'Part II contains a review of recent events of economic tendencies, classed under the title "The Main Objectives of the Monetary system"' (Stamp, 1931: 424). The conclusion included an important proposal regarding international monetary policy. More importantly, the report recognized the key role that central bankers must play to make the gold-standard monetary regime work:

Stability of international prices over long and short periods can be maintained only by *co-operation among central banks*. Over long periods stability is largely a question of gold reserves in relation to credit. Stability over a short period in order to mitigate the Credit Cycle is a question of co-operative monetary management (Macmillan Committee, 1931; *emphasis added*).

Recognition of the authority of central bankers also brought issues regarding economic and monetary post-war reconstruction. The international conferences on post-war reconstruction that took place in Brussels in 1920 and Genoa in 1922 were the first occasions that required the specific expertise of central bankers. Initially limited, the presence and influence of central bankers grew over time. In Brussels, central bank representatives were first invited as observers. The governor of the Bank of England was not present. A Bank of England representative accompanied the British delegation and maintained regular contact with the governor to inform him of the conference's outcomes (Sayers, 1976: 153). Soon after the Brussels conference, the Bank of England's governor Montagu Norman was asked by the League of Nations to help sketch a plan for Austrian economic and financial reconstruction (Cottrell, 1995: 87). Reminiscent of the 1922 Genoa conference, the Bank of England proceeded to give an extensive review of its relations between 16 central banks, including the Federal Reserve. The review established the basic principles of central banking that Norman wanted to push on the international agenda, such as collaboration between central banks and institutional autonomy. Moreover, the Genoa conference provided an opportunity for social exchanges between central bankers and experts from the League of Nations' financial committee, an organization that played an important role in developing economic oversight (Pauly, 1997). With the creation of the BIS, the authority of central bankers on the international scene came to be officially recognized. From then on, central bankers have been represented by institutions that have enabled their exercise of autonomous authority on the international scene.

Conclusion

This chapter makes the case of approaching authority in IR from a practice perspective. The relational ontology underlying the practice perspective allows us to account for the contingent nature of history, by addressing the processes through which certain political entities are endowed with authority and under what terms. In contrast with standard IR approaches to authority that identify the terms under which relations of authority take place prior to the analysis, a practice approach begins with the dynamic nature of authority. Patterns of authority are historically produced and reproduced; they can transform and disappear. A practice approach is better equipped to account for change, by treating authority as a dynamic analytical category. To illustrate the heuristic value of a practice approach to authority, the chapter has outlined the process through which central bankers became authoritative figures in global governance. Until the beginning of the twentieth century, central bankers did not have any positions of authority at the international level. It is only during the interwar period that central bankers were recognized as legitimate authorities. The process of construction of their authority was based on: (1) the production of central banking as a distinct object of authority; (2) the institutionalization of the BIS, which provided a forum in which central bankers could claim authority; and (3) recognition of their expertise relating to the complex issues of war repayments and the reconstruction of monetary orders in the aftermath of the First World War.

The chapter has also tested the boundaries of practice theories by highlighting the cross-fertilizing potential of two distinct research strategies pursued by practice scholars. One trend of scholarship inspired by Bourdieusian sociology has tackled the symbolic construction of the social organization of authority through the study of claims to and recognitions of authority. A second trend of scholarship based on the sociology of knowledge has examined the construction of epistemic and material conditions of possibility, by studying the construction of objects of authority. A combination of these strategies makes it possible to account for the woven effects of symbolic, epistemic and material dimensions in the construction of authority. This enables an approach to the making of international authority grounded in social and historical contexts. It offers a clear theoretical framework with which to investigate the various international figures endowed with authority on the international scene, such as financial experts, environmentalists, diplomats and corporate actors. The theoretical framework enables us to interrogate the processes through which such figures became authoritative, as well as highlight the conditions under which their authority is maintained or transformed.

Vincent Pouliot

This chapter jumps through the first 'fault line' identified by the editors in Chapter 1 and examines the problem of change in international practice theory. It starts from the dual – and seemingly contradictory – observation that one may infer from this approach: change is an ever-present condition at the micro-level, while homeostatic tendencies prevail at the macro-level. Indeed, taking a historical perspective, it is easy to observe that practices do change, though mostly around the edges, at a slow pace, and often without a clear sense of (intentional) direction. Diplomacy is an obvious case here, but other international practices – war, commerce, treaty-making, development aid, and so on – display the same evolving nature through time and space. What explains such evolution in the ways in which world politics get performed?

According to some, practice theory is incapable of accounting for the ebb and flow of ways of doing things. Friendly critics such as Duvall and Chowdhury (2011: 337), for instance, find that the framework 'falls short of offering satisfying ways of theorizing change in international politics'. In a recent piece, Hopf (2018: 696) concurs that the play of practice defies theorization: 'There are no scope conditions for practical agency as we are constantly executing practices, and in so doing, changing them, if only marginally'. Central as it may be to the approach, then, the contingency of practice seems largely indeterminate. Hopf's solution to this conundrum is to focus on what he calls 'reflective agency'. Not only is this alternative driver of change easier to theorize but also at the empirical level, he adds, 'reflective awareness ... accompan[ies] significant changes' (Hopf, 2018: 705). As a result, practice scholars would be better off focusing on changes in international practices that hinge on reflectivity, rather than on incremental, non-deliberate transformation, which is analytically intractable and often politically irrelevant.

In this chapter, I take a more sanguine view on the matter. There is no question that accounting for evolution in international practices presents a series of daunting analytical challenges, which I do not claim to resolve in what follows. But this is no reason to give up on the task entirely. While I agree with Hopf that slippages in everyday practices are often inconsequential, I make the case for a more structural take on social transformation. Important as it may be for explaining variation in practices, reflectivity hardly accounts for their differential rate of reproduction – that is, selection. Drawing on the evolutionary metaphor, I focus on the social environment within which variations occur. This 'web of practices' may be more or less supportive of particular deviations, boosting or undermining their chances of spreading through space and time. As such, evolution in international practices is best explained at the structural, not the individual level.

When we shift to a more structural focus, I argue, we become better able to theorize the circumstances under which change in practice appears less a cacophony of agentic performances than a collective orchestra, albeit one devoid of a conductor, to paraphrase Bourdieu (2000 [1972]). The chapter develops this argument in three steps. First, using intentional explanations as a foil, I show the limits of accounting for change in terms of individual choices or reflective agency. Transformations in practices are socially emergent and as such they cannot be traced back to volitions. My second move consists in drawing from evolutionary theory to stand back from agency and introduce a more structural approach to change. I do this very carefully, though, acknowledging the centrality of politics and agency in social evolution. In the third and final section, I gesture toward a typology of supportive practices, which, when present (or actively summoned) in the web of practices within which variations occur, significantly boost their reproductive success. Overall, while the chapter stops short of providing a genuine evolutionary theory of practices,[1] it helps to show how a macro-approach to the problem of change in practices is a necessary complement to the focus on reflective agency currently on display in the literature.

Reflexivity, Intentionality, and Social Emergence

The problem of change is a central one for practice theory. In an important article, Hopf (2018) draws a distinction between two generic modes of transformation: 'change in practice through practice', which occurs as part of the ordinary unfolding of everyday activity, and 'change in practice through reflection', which rests on reflective agency. Hopf

---

[1] For a much more accomplished effort see Adler (2019).

begins by noting the pervasiveness of change through practice, owing to the 'wiggle room' (Adler and Pouliot, 2011b: 7) that is intrinsic to competent performance. Yet he also observes the indeterminacy and insignificance of such social transformations: 'endogenous change in practice through the operation of practices, despite being ubiquitous, does not account for the kind of meaningful and significant change that we mostly care about in the study of world politics' (Hopf, 2018: 688). For that reason, Hopf focuses most of his attention on the second form of transformation, delineating a set of 'scope conditions' for reflective change such as imperfect socialization and 'productive crises' (Hopf, 2018: 696–701). His key conclusion is that practice scholars 'should expect reflective awareness to accompany significant changes under particular circumstances' (Hopf, 2018: 705).

Hopf's insights owe particularly to Dewey's writings, which emphasize the pragmatic search for new solutions when faced with a problem. Starting from the observation that 'habit frees up the reflective mind to consciously deliberate about the world' (Hopf, 2018: 689), this stream of practice theory focuses on the cognitive and social processes through which '[d]isturbances produce intentional states' (Hopf, 2018: 695; see also Adler and Faubert, Chapter 3). From a Deweyian perspective, habits continue more or less axiomatically so long as they work, that is, to the extent that they allow practitioners to go on with their daily activities. When circumstances change dramatically, however, failure follows, prompting actors to pause and question their established ways of doing things. For instance, this is the story that Stein (2011) tells about humanitarians, showing how the community sought to professionalize its practices in the face of mounting challenges. Cornut (2018) proposes a resonating analysis of Western diplomats dealing with regime change during the Arab Spring. Schmidt (2014) makes a similar argument about sovereign basing. In typical Deweyian fashion, he posits stable habits in a first stage; then an environmental stimulus problematizes established practices, prompting reflectivity; followed by 'deliberative innovation' and the selection of innovative practices.

With his theory of 'social learning', Adler (1991) provides the most sophisticated account of international change based on reflective agency. Through a process of 'cognitive evolution', agents become reflective about their practices, enabling both lesson-learning and collective creativity (Adler, 2005). For Adler, such transformation is not a reversing of habit, but the normal course of things. Cognitive evolution happens continuously, not just in times of crisis: 'Practices' innovators, as agents of change, do not make eddies in the stream, but echoing Heraclitus, *are* the stream: they provide it with direction' (Adler, 2019: 196). In a sense, social innovation is all there is because it is the essence of agency. In Adler's account, the 'awakening of consciousness' is dispositional, while creativity is 'human beings' most basic form of action' (Adler 2019: 221–222).

There is no doubt that reflectivity is a key driver of social change. The scope conditions that Hopf lists and the cognitive mechanisms that Adler analyses both capture very important dimensions of how transformation in international practices occurs, and why. The question, though, is whether we can fully explain social change via reflective agency. Here I see three main reasons why the Deweyian approach, illuminating as it may be, faces limitations. First, the concept of crisis, which is the catalyst of reflectivity for Dewey, is problematic because it is generally applied in a post-hoc fashion by the analyst. It seems difficult, both at the level of analysis and practice, to tell a crisis before, or while, it erupts. Must practitioners feel the experience of a crisis for a disruption to count as such? As a category of analysis, the concept bears limited explanatory power over the actual process of practice, which is forward-looking in nature. In any event, it should arguably not be the job of the analyst to determine whether a crisis occurs or not, because this is an eminently political issue: challengers have an interest in upheaval that incumbents do not. As a category of practice, crisis is best left with practitioners, who constantly fight over the applicability of the term precisely in order to justify or oppose change.

Furthermore, the concept of crisis generally implies some form of exogenous shock as the permissive condition for change. Yet the notion of exogenous shock not only amounts to *ex post facto* attributions (as with crises: how to specify a shock *ex ante*?) but it also tends to rely on residual variables by invoking factors left out of the theory. By definition, an exogenous shock is external to the framework; it operates on the outside of the processes accounted for. As a result, shocks often end up covering for gaps in the explanation. While there is little doubt that changing circumstances prompt evolution in practices, it would be more useful to theorize this process from the inside out, that is, endogenously. Environmental changes, in that sense, describe nothing else than shifts in the configuration of practices within which variation occurs (more on this later).

Second, from a practice perspective reflectivity is a background disposition. This is a point that both Adler and Hopf would likely grant, though its implications are worth pondering for a moment. When agents of change think about something, they think from something else (Pouliot, 2008). One can never fully 'get out' of practical knowledge, because it is part of any kind of agency, including the most reflective and strategic ones. In other words, the thinking part of action is nothing but the sea foam atop a deep wave of practicality. Hopf (2018: 699) seems to acknowledge this point when he concedes that '[r]eflection has no direction'. For instance, he argues that 'there is a "sweet spot" for effective difference', which hinges in part on its intelligibility to the audience (Hopf, 2018: 697). And yet, for a practice to be intelligible, it must rest on a set of background dispositions that logically precede any reflection sparked by difference (Taylor, 1993 [1981]).

This leads to my third and most fundamental critique of the Deweyian approach: to equate change with reflective agency is to take a rather short-term and local view on social transformation.[2] It requires identifying specific actors, showing their creativity, and linking their agency to specific changes. Here, explanation requires drawing an arrow from individual intentionality to change in international practices. This takes practice theory very close to choice-theoreticism, which is the dominant view in contemporary social sciences (Jackson and Nexon, 2013). From this perspective, change is intentional and deliberate, not only for its spark but also for its institutionalization and diffusion. People's preferences explain what they want, what they want explains what they do, and what they do explains what obtains collectively. Someone, somewhere, wants the change to happen; others follow suit either because of power differentials or because as a result they collectively pull closer to Pareto optimality. This strikes me as a rather heroic assumption, one that greatly overestimates the extent to which the will of a handful of entrepreneurs can have a direct impact on the form that social transformation takes, at least in the longer run.

In other words, reflectivity may be involved in prompting change, but it says little about the social fate that any given innovation will have. Take, for instance, the rational design model, according to which institutions change when rational agents modify them in order to resolve their coordination and collaboration problems (Martin, 1992). Here the analyst explains change by drawing a direct connection back to the preferences of certain actors: 'the features of international institutions are chosen intentionally, by a conscious or deliberate process of calculation' (Wendt, 2001: 1036). The analyst presumes a link from intentionality to social outcome, often inferring the former from the latter through some kind of backwards inference. Yet this is a problematic move because institutions generally are the by-products of social struggles (Knight, 1994). Far from controlled designs, institutions tend to emerge out of complex interactions in which intentionality dissolves in a set of cooperative and conflictual relations. Institutions,

---

[2] This section builds on Pouliot (2020a).

just like practices, are 'socially emergent' (Sawyer, 2005): they are the result of messy and disorderly generative processes in which a variety of forces (including individual intentional states) bump into each other to produce social machineries that no one owns, to paraphrase Foucault.

This is a point worth making in a discipline primarily concerned with design, preferences, and choices. As Young lamented a long time ago, 'naïve hopes concerning the efficacy of social engineering in the realm of international regimes constitute a common and serious failing among policy makers and students of international relations alike'. Indeed, social emergence is a far more prevalent form of change than design or imposition – even in an increasingly rationalized world:

> Curiously, increases in the complexity of social systems will frequently operate to accentuate the role of spontaneous orders rather than imposed or negotiated orders. [...] it will ordinarily become harder and harder for groups of actors to arrive at meaningful or coherent bargains as the issues at stake become increasingly complex. Accordingly, spontaneous orders arising from interactive behavior loom large in modernized social settings, despite the fact that this runs counter to the widespread propensity to regard such orders as unsophisticated or irrational. (Young, 1982: 287)

If we take Young's point seriously, then emphasizing reflective agency risks overestimating the tightness of the connection between intentionality and change, while underestimating the extent to which social transformation is a collective accomplishment. Through their struggles, intentional agents generate dynamics of change that are generally irreducible to anyone's intentions. Or to use Wendt's (2001: 1037) apt formulation: 'Intentionality at the local or micro-level is fully compatible with no intentionality at the global or macro-level'.

Explaining change in terms of individual processes – whether choices, reflection, or something else – is not the most productive analytical strategy because when it comes to social aggregates, the key issue is not why actor A did the things she did, but rather why the things A did produced the broader social effects they did. Abbott's (2005: 1) example helps drive the point home: 'The real question, for example, is not why it was that Elizabeth Tudor chose not to marry, but rather how it came to be that there was a social structure in which her refusal to marry could have such enduring political consequences'. By implication, instead of looking at people's intentionality to explain social outcomes, we should rather study 'the conditions that make particular individuals particularly important' (Abbott, 2005). While reflective agency may account for the source of novel practices, it does not explain why some innovations stick around while most fall by the wayside.

Put differently, reflectivity may be the proximate factor, but it is insufficient to explain change in international practices. Without a doubt, people deliberate and reflect at different points and to variable degrees, especially when what they do does not seem to work. Yet by equating change with reflective agency, we move far too close to the kind of choice-theoreticism that characterizes the rational design argument (Koremenos et al., 2001). Of course reflective agents play a role in sparking the process, and even in steering it. But to effect change is by nature a deeply social process, full of struggles, relational dynamics, and interactional effects. As such, transformation is generally irreducible to the intentions of any specific player in the game; it is a collective bricolage, so to speak (Pouliot, 2020a; Thérien and Pouliot, 2020). As Wendt (2001: 1036, emphasis original) puts it, 'there will always be *some* intentionality in the process by which institutions are created. However, this does not mean we can automatically conclude that institutions are intended'.

In sum, change in international practices is socially emergent. Social interactions lead to evolving patterns of action that cannot be traced back to the cognitive processes of specific individuals. Transformation often takes place over long periods of time and is slow in coming. What is more, it often results from large-scale social configurations in which agents unknown to each other pull the carpet of history in competing directions. A micro-interactional perspective focused on the conditions of possibility for reflective agency cannot capture these broader dynamics. Explaining changes in international practices rather requires a more structural perspective and one that takes a longer view. This is where the evolutionary metaphor enters the picture.

The Evolutionary Metaphor

What explains that one variation catches fire while most others fall by the wayside of history? This is a particularly thorny question to ask because, at any moment, there are so many concomitant variations going in all kinds of conflicting directions. Instead of resorting to reflective agency, in what follows I want to delve into the social forces that explain evolution in international practices. Micro-deviations do matter, but only when they survive their first occurrence, accumulate through time and space, and form new patterns whose direction and shape generally are not directly owed to a clear, traceable intentionality. To capture these dynamics, we need to stand back from agency. By going macro, we can account not only for variation in practices but also for their spread or disappearance – that is, their selection.

To help resolve the selection puzzle, I draw inspiration from evolutionary thinking.[3] Wary as I am of scientism, I treat evolution strictly as a metaphor; in no way do I want to suggest that the social world is reducible to physical or natural processes. This cautionary note notwithstanding, the fact remains that 'employing evolutionary models explicitly and accurately in the study of world politics is exceptionally difficult' (Gilady and Hoffman, 2013: 308). There is the obvious flashing red light of social Darwinism, which led to eugenics and other flawed schemes of social engineering. There is also the fact that, when we turn to the social world, random genetic mutations and environmental catastrophes have limited analytical purchase. Nonetheless, the evolutionary metaphor helps capture an important dimension of society and politics: the fact that practices vary over time and space, with unequal retention rates. The logic of cultural selection, in other words, bears some resemblance to that of natural evolution: in Wendt's (1999: 321) words, both are 'about differential reproductive success'.

Beyond this general point, I see three other pay-offs in the evolutionary metaphor. First, compared with the more sited, largely interactional take on change that one currently finds in the practice literature, standing back from the level of action helps capture transformations at the macro-level. The evolutionary perspective helps us understand how the transformation of practices hinges not only on reflective agency but also on the structural opportunities afforded, and the constraints posed, by the broader population of practices. The concept of evolution draws attention to the macro-level where selection is driven by the social environment, and more specifically by the web of practices out of which novelty emerges. An evolutionary perspective suggests that, while most micro-deviations never lead to meaningful change, some variations do build up over time.

In order to capture this dynamic, we cannot stay at the granular level of intentional performances and reflective awareness. We have to stand back, and this is precisely what the concept of evolution allows, by introducing a longer view on history and social processes. By comparison, change is an observer-relative concept through and through; that is, change is in the eye of the beholder. Depending on the problem at hand, one's change may be another's continuity, and vice versa. As a perspectival concept, change refers to unusual occurrences and experiences as felt at the level of action. For its part, the concept of evolution

---

[3] The precursor in International Relations is Adler (1991). I am deeply indebted to his views on the matter. See Adler (2005: 29–76, and 2019). Another effort may be found in Thompson (2001). See also Spruyt (1994); and Florini (1996).

hinges on a good measure of detachment or distanciation, which helps objectify structural patterns in the social world. Evolution operates at a macro-level, at which the myriad micro-choices or moves made at the level of action tend to wash out (see the third fault line in Chapter 1). The concept offers a great lens to capture socially emergent dynamics, as it describes the overall effect of countless deviations in a given population.

A second pay-off of the evolutionary metaphor stems from its conceptual apparatus of variation, selection, and inheritance.[4] These are essentially the three stages of evolution. First, there must be divergence from an established pattern, disrupting a seemingly stable process and taking it in a different direction. Second, the divergent pattern needs to survive longer than its initial occurrence and get picked up by others and reproduced, lest it becomes nothing more than a historical idiosyncrasy. And third, a durable pattern must form out of the selected deviation, spreading through time and space to a variable extent. Most variations in practice obviously never go through the three phases, but a full evolutionary process would contain them all.

Third, and finally, the evolutionary approach helps make sense of the fact that many micro slippages do not destabilize macro-patterns – quite the contrary. Remember that to say that practice is competent means that it is adaptive: it morphs around the edges to better deal with changing circumstances. In other words, practice – even slipping performance – has homeostatic qualities at the macro-level. By implication, the study of evolution throws new light on incremental changes *in* (as opposed to *of*) a given practice. Evolution is not necessarily destabilizing for a practice; very often, incremental change instead has reinforcing effects in the broader scheme of things. This critical point is hard to capture from a granular perspective. Of course, small changes in a given practice may lead to the practice's dismay by accumulating over time. Yet increments could also very well reinforce the core practice through minor adaptations. In any event, there is no teleology or grand design at work in the evolutionary approach. Taken individually, variations are indeterminate (though definitely not random as in natural selection): their fate is largely driven by the environment within which they happen to emerge.

---

[4] Gilady and Hoffman (2013: 309). Compare with Adler's three processes of cognitive evolution: innovation, selection, and diffusion; Adler (2005: 73–76; and 2019). I bracket the issue of inheritance in this chapter owing to space limitations. On the 'ratchet effect' in the evolution of practices see Pouliot and Thérien (2015); on the 'grey area' of institutional change see Pouliot (2020b).

Despite its many pay-offs, it is critical to adapt the evolutionary metaphor to the social world. The Darwinian theory of evolution is unashamedly functionalist: the genetic mutations that provide a comparative advantage in a changing environment survive and reproduce preferentially. There is no agency involved, only 'selfish genes' whose fate at the macro level is structurally determined by exogenous transformations in natural habitats. As Zimmer (2006: xxxiv–xxxv) explains, 'on average the survivors will be those variants that, by good fortune, are better adapted to changing local environments'. Random variations that fit with current environmental conditions will tend to survive preferentially. To some extent, this functionalist logic is similar to that of 'historical efficiency' in rational choice institutionalism (March and Olsen, 1998). The institutional forms that survive, in this account, are the ones that are most efficient (or functional) in resolving collaboration and coordination problems (Spruyt, 1994).

I have deep doubts that the survival of the fittest transcribes to the social world, in which survival is most of the time not at stake (Wendt, 1999: 323–324). History is not efficient but contingent. As a rule, the play of practice would seem to trump the logic of functionalism. In addition, the notion of fit implies a stable environment (as well as stable practice) that can hardly obtain in the social world. After all, the social environment is not a given reality operating from the outside, but a 'constellation of practices' (Wenger, 1998a) that are not ontologically distinct from actual ways of doing things. In other words, whether a given variation in practice is fitter than its alternative – and thus more likely to survive and spread – is not an environmental given, but a deeply political process in which the community of practitioners, which forms the social backdrop against which deviations rub, is both party and judge (see Pouliot, 2020a, b).

The simple fact of adding practitioners to the evolutionary equation shifts the logic from Darwin to Lamarck, explain Gilady and Hoffman (2013: 310): 'in Lamarckian evolution, variation arises from a volitional or agentic response to change in the environment and the needs of the organism'. In a famous example, the giraffe's neck lengthens because she wants to eat leaves in the canopy. In this model, selection is explained through the demand for variation: 'whether a specific trait is selected [depends on] whether it provides the individual with an advantage' (Gilady and Hoffman, 2013: 311). By being used (and thus generating the said advantage), the varying trait diffuses and replaces others. The Lamarck alternative takes us back to volition and intentionality in a way similar to the argument based on reflective agency that I criticized earlier. To repeat, there is no doubt that some slippages are intended as such; yet such intentionality can hardly explain the fate of variation in the longer haul.

If selection is primarily driven by the environment, what are the implications in the social world? Essentially, cultural selection tells us that practices best adapted to the circumstances will enjoy better reproductive success than those that are not. This fit is not an objective given, but an intersubjective process, that is, a collective negotiation involving multiple agents and their practices. So what does it mean for a practice to be a better fit than its alternatives? Axelrod (1984: 169) provides a deceptively short answer to this question: 'the evolutionary approach is based on a simple principle: whatever is successful is likely to appear more often in the future'. Being successful, though, is a complicated notion in a shifting social environment full of contradictions. It is of course correct to say that those practices that survive are the ones that work. The analytical problem is that the very definition of 'what works' is itself a matter of practice. Put differently, the retention rate of a variation depends on its social success, which is internally defined by the community of practitioners.

This important point has led several practice theorists to resort to narrative and discourse to explain why certain novel ways of doing things are deemed superior to others by a given collective at a specific point in time. As Neumann (2002: 636) puts it, 'story-telling [...] authorize[s] an unprecedented practice'. The logic of fitting a heterodox practice within the established order of things has a typical form that essentially says 'my performance p is a case of practice P'. The social success of any practice, whether orthodox or deviant, stems from this claim, and as such the fit has to be constructed through political work: 'The politics of practice concern the ways in which agents struggle to endow certain practices with political validity and legitimacy' (Adler and Pouliot, 2011b: 21). In this process, storytelling seeks to fit specific practices into the general model of socially defined competence. Thanks to narrative, heterodox practices push to replace earlier ones under the guise of a new orthodoxy.

Illuminating as it is, the narrative approach does not suffice to explain the evolution of practices. In a way, it is a solution that displaces the problem without fixing it (see the second fault line identified by the editors). While narrative would seem to explain practice selection, it leaves us with a new puzzle: narrative selection. Why do certain discursive forms fly but not others? In other words, what explains successful storytelling? It seems as if the snake is biting its tail here – this is likely what Neumann (2002) had in mind when he suggested that discourse and practice are recursively connected (see also Bernstein and

Laurence, Chapter 4). His point makes sense of course, but it remains very difficult to operationalize. At a minimum, recursivity means that we cannot fully dispense with considering other practices as we explain evolution in practices, because practices explain the differential rate of success of competing narratives, which is taken to explain evolution in international practices.

The implication is that narrative is not enough, in and of itself, to explain the evolution of international practices. As Duvall and Chowdhury (2011: 350) correctly note, 'practices do not just reflect background knowledge; they serve as well to ground or enact a certain linguistic structure'. Simply saying: 'p is a case of P' cannot do the trick entirely on its own, because it does not explain, in and of itself, variation in the success of the different stories being told. We also need to take into account the broader web of practices within which deviations take place.[5]

Webs of Practices

The key argument of this section, drawing on the evolutionary metaphor, is that practices evolve in bunches. Selection is driven by the larger population of practices; in other words, we need to consider that there is something like an ecology of practices.[6] To stick around, a deviating practice needs help to survive its context of emergence and gain some kind of foothold in the world. It is this 'interplay of practices' (Adler and Pouliot, 2011b) that provides the environmental constraints and opportunities for survival and selection.

A key innovation of practice theory rests with its process ontology, by which 'stability is not the opposite of change but an orderly pattern within a process of flux' (Adler and Pouliot, 2011b: 15).[7] Put differently, continuity is not stasis, but the active reproduction of past conditions in the present and future. As such, practices create the conditions for ontological stability as well as for change in everyday life (Adler and Pouliot, 2011b: 18). Practice theory emphasizes both the prevalence of contingency and the reproductive tendency of the social. As such,

---

[5] The web metaphor is meant to draw on Geertz's famous quote, according to which 'man is an animal suspended in webs of significance he himself has spun'. Here I adapt the quote to instead picture agents suspended in webs of practices. For a longer development with a detailed empirical illustration see Pouliot (2020a).

[6] For an (unrelated but similarly structural) argument about organizational ecology in International Relations see Abbott et al. (2016).

[7] On process ontology see also Adler (1991, 2019), Jackson and Nexon (1999), and Pouliot (2016b: 13–16).

the real question is not whether change prevails over stability, or the reverse, but rather this: how is it possible for meaningful social change to be both an ever-present possibility at the level of practice and a relatively rare occurrence in the grand scheme of things?

On the one hand, practice theory predicts much instability in everyday performance. There are two main reasons for this contingency. First, the meaning of practices is inherently ambiguous and unstable. As a rule, collectively held standards are incomplete, unclear, and open to competing interpretations and applications. Here we find Wittgenstein's argument about the indeterminacy of social rules, which allows for different forms of behaviour to possibly fall in line with any given practice (see Sandholtz, 2008). Since competence is not self-interpreting, the same standard typically contains the possibility for orthodox as well as heterodox practices (as latent as the latter possibility may often remain). As a result, 'the same performance is simultaneously different practices', to use Duvall and Chowdhury's (2011: 347) apt formulation. And the reverse is also true: the same practice may simultaneously cover different performances.

Because of the inherent ambiguity of social practices, then, the competence of a performance is subject to conflicting interpretations and varying applications. Hansen (2011) convincingly shows that the political work of practice consists in fitting a specific performance into a general (agreed upon) model of the practice. In a similar spirit, Duvall and Chowdhury (2011: 337) insist on 'the inherent instability of practices' and challenge the 'assumption that practices are to be understood as expressing and conveying a univocal meaning'. Practice may be self-evident to individual practitioners, but that does not preclude contestation at the collective level. As Duvall and Chowdhury (2011: 345) put it, 'the possibility of polysemy is a structural necessity of practices'; all the more so in the international realm, they add, because it 'is not as patterned by shared norms and understandings as a smaller-scale society', and is consequently subject to polysemy and contradiction.

The instability of meanings opens the door to variation in enactments and eventually to change. As I put it with Adler, borrowing Doty's formula, 'new ways of thinking or doing necessarily emerge from the contingent "play of practice," in which meanings are never inherently fixed or stable' (Adler and Pouliot, 2011b: 18). In their critique of my book, Schindler and Wille (2015) show how this politics is at the very root of political clashes between NATO and Russia: does a NATO deployment to the East count as a peaceful move to protect democracies, or is it a new phase of containment against Russia? As they conclude: 'Uncertainty about the meaning of the past destabilizes present practices and thus makes sudden and drastic change possible' (Schindler and Wille, 2015: 330). This analytical point, which owes in part to post-structuralism, is a significant analytical qualification to the experience of self-evidence that practitioners typically have.

The second reason why change is an ever-present possibility at the level of practice stems from the 'principle of indexicality', according to which 'any new situation requires adjusting and re-arranging the practice within it' (Bueger and Gadinger, 2014: 63; see also Schäfer, Chapter 9). This is the basic logic of practice as competent performance. For instance, improvisation and adaptation were at the centre of the young Bourdieu's (2000 [1972]) analysis of the tempo of gift and counter-gift practices, something he called *ars inveniendi* toward the end of his career. The principle of indexicality is the main reason why practices differ from mere habit, in requiring adjustment to the moves performed by others as well as to changing circumstances. Indexicality helps explain why micro-deviation is an ever-present possibility, in and through practice, via the micro-alterations that are a standard part of competent performance: 'there is always wiggle room for agency even in repetition' (Adler and Pouliot 2011b: 7).

To engage in practice is, by nature, to cope with a reactive (social) world. Barnes (2001) gives the example of riding in formation, which cannot be reduced to a set of individual habits. In order to perform competently, each rider must not only perform the practice in a routine or automated way but also constantly adapt to the moves of others, the changing landscape, and other shifting circumstances. As Barnes (2001: 23) concludes: 'The successful execution of routines at the collective level will involve the overriding and modification of routines at the individual level. Practice at the collective level is not a simple summation of practices at the individual level (habits). Shared practice is, as the ethnomethodologists say, a collective accomplishment'. Overall, then, competent practices adjust not only to ambiguous social expectations about competent performance but also to the shifting situation at hand.

My book about multilateral diplomacy in practice contains many illustrations of this process (Pouliot, 2016b). The delegates that climb the pecking order are not simply following the rules or blindly applying their routine day after day. On the contrary, competent diplomats skilfully adapt to a rapidly changing set of circumstances, improvising from established practices as they go. In the thick of the 2011 negotiations over the intervention in Libya, for instance, British delegates made use of accepted ways of doing things (for instance, as 'pen holders') to bend the rules and have the defecting deputy permanent representation speak out against the Gadhafi regime at the Security Council. By moulding practice to a new set of circumstances (a call for regime change under the umbrella of the responsibility to protect), they sowed the grain of incremental transformation (more on this later). Whether the grain fully germinates requires further processes of repetition and institutionalization, but indexicality creates the original condition of possibility.

Interestingly, those scholars who argue against the significance of 'change in practice through practice' do not contest the principle of indexicality as much as they question its significance. Hopf (2018: 694) observes that most micro-slippages are overall inconsequential: 'changes in practice through practice are largely incremental and marginal, not fundamental'. Deviations occur all the time owing to ambiguity and indexicality, yet they generally disappear from sight as quickly. In other words, the debate is not about whether practices vary at a micro-level, but rather about the durability of such ongoing variation. For one Andy Warhol managing to redefine the aesthetics of contemporary art, how many anonymous artists were there who failed to leave their mark on the collective movement?

This, to me, captures the essence of the problem for practice theory. How can we explain that, among countless everyday slippages and deviating performances, only a few rare ones end up catching on and spreading across space and over time? There are many cracks in the social wall, yet relatively few successful jumps through them. Why is that? The evolutionary metaphor, as well as some of the drawbacks of explanations based on intentionality, suggest that the social environment plays a critical role in the selection of some varying practices but not most others.

Admittedly, environmental forces also include material resources and technology, the distribution of power, and so on. More work needs to be done, although the 'new materialism' stream of literature is already throwing much-needed light on the issue. Here I want to focus on the broader population of practices as the key building blocks of the social environment. The main advantage of this conception is that it supplies an endogenous mechanism of selection: what varies and what selects are part of the same ontology. In any event, remember that the ontology of practice includes material artefacts (e.g. the ball in playing football), technological change and invention (e.g. instant replays for referees), and organizational and institutional platforms (e.g. the soccer/football league). The web of practices, in that sense, encompasses patterns of action including their material and organizational bases. This is the social environment within which any given deviation occurs.

While my focus here is on selection, it is important to note that the web of practice also matters for variation. After all, heterodox practices made possible by reflectivity are not new in the sense of coming from nowhere or being the product of imagination: they are instead innovative combinations of existing things and their sedimentation in background knowledge. As Shove et al. (2012: 120) explain, 'practices change when new elements are introduced or when existing elements are combined in new ways'. In other words, creativity does not reinvent the wheel or start from scratch, but rather establishes new connections between specific and general practices. It starts from somewhere – a repertoire of practices – and this starting point is arguably more determinant than the cognitive processes that individuals experience in the form of reflectivity.

For a deviating practice to survive and outlast its context of emergence, there need to be other ways of doing things that back it up. Individuals may fight as hard as they can; they can be the most competent subverters ever; they may reflectively put together the best strategies for change. Yet if they are not in the right social habitat, their efforts are likely to be without effect. Thanks to the configuration within which it is located, a deviating practice may find itself transported by others – carried over, so to speak – or, alternatively, doomed to failure. In the same way that post-structuralists theorize intertextuality, then, we should pay more attention to 'interpracticality'[8] in order to make sense of how practices, orthodox or not, actually hang together. As Figure 8.1 shows, I theorize three main types of practices that help explain micro-deviations' differential rates of success: demonstratory practices, cross-cutting practices, and codification practices. To put it simply, the presence or generation of such practices in the environment of a deviation boosts its chances of success; and reciprocally, their absence means lower odds of selection. Other kinds of practices are likely involved in the selection of varying practices, but these three seem particularly significant.

I define all three types of supportive practices in terms of their effects: the qualifier refers to the allowance of, respectively, public display, relational crossover, and inscription. Whatever their specific form and content, these types of practices should be part of, or brought into, the web within which the deviation occurs; that is, heterodox players must have a way to perform them (obviously with a variable amount of

---

[8] A Google search of 'interpracticality' returned a few dozen references, but I did not find any that refer specifically to the fact that the fate of a single practice owes to the broader population within which it finds itself.

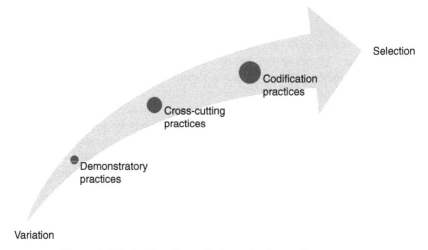

Figure 8.1 Selection through the web of practices

competence). Even though I do not hierarchize the three types (in the sense that one would be more necessary or fundamental than the others), there seems to be some logic to their sequence: cross-cutting practices amplify demonstratory practices (by multiplying audiences), while codification practices prolong the effects of the demonstratory and cross-cutting practices. As mutually reinforcing as the practices may be, however, none seems absolutely necessary for selection to occur. As a social aggregate, evolution is multiply realizable, and as such we should be prepared to observe changing combinations of permissive practices.

To begin with, a demonstratory practice is a practice that extends a claim to competence from an orthodox performance to a heterodox one (see also Walters, Chapter 6, and Austin and Leander, Chapter 10). It boosts the aura of skilfulness of deviance by tying it to established standards of competence in a germane field of action. Take the British move to have a defecting deputy ambassador address the Security Council as the voice of the Libyan people, which Adler-Nissen and I analyse elsewhere (Adler-Nissen and Pouliot 2014). Throughout the negotiations in New York, British and allied diplomats simultaneously enacted various practices, ranging from their control of the Libya sanctions committee through their strong domination on the drafting of resolutions to their close consultation habits with other permanent members of the Council, in order to wrap their deviant performance into an aura of diplomatic competence. As a result, their narrative claim, that 'p' is a case of practice P' (here, giving the floor to a defecting ambassador conforms to the practice of hearing parties to a dispute), was more likely to be successful.

Second, a cross-cutting practice is a practice that generates new social ties between orthodox and heterodox players. It allows heterodox players not only to potentially grow in numbers but also to multiply the audiences to which they may appeal. In the Libya case, British diplomats had prepared the ground for their move by reaching out to practitioners on the outside, including via regional consultations (with Lebanon as intermediary to the Arab League), press conferences given at the United Nations and beyond, and especially by involving the humanitarian community of non-governmental organizations based in New York. This way, the subverters' claim that 'p' is a case of practice 'P' was heard, and often supported, by various quarters that happened to harbour a much more expansive notion of what counts as competent practice than the more conservative elements that sit at the Security Council.

Third and finally, a codification practice is a practice that inscribes heterodox standards of competence as part of the new orthodoxy. It reduces the need for the heterodox claim of competence to be accompanied by demonstratory and cross-cutting practices by prolonging its effect in time and, possibly, extending it across space. Codification works in various ways: the making of text (e.g. law), the inscription in matter (e.g. tools, technology), professionalization (e.g. the development of guidelines and 'best practices'), the creation of organization, and so on. In our Libya example, this is a type of practice that is hard to find, probably because the subverters (essentially the P3: France, the United Kingdom and the United States) figured it was not in their interest to formally inscribe such a precedent in text. Even if they had wanted to do so, such codification would have been rather difficult to obtain given the voting rules of the Council and the amendment procedure of the Charter.

Chances are, though, that even short of full codification, heterodox players figured they could count on the force of precedent should they need to replicate their subversive move in the future. For instance, were the Syrian ambassador to defect from the Assad regime tomorrow, it would not be surprising to hear P3 diplomats refer to 2011 as a precedent, thereby boosting their story ('p' is a case of practice 'P') short of fully fledged codification. While they sacrificed something by not codifying deviation, British and allied diplomats also gained flexibility and opacity – two dynamics that are known to often put the dominant at further advantage. After all, it is doubtful that the Western diplomats were willing to risk other countries similarly pushing for recognizing defecting ambassadors in the future, a political spiral that could easily get out of control.

To conclude this section, it is important to note that the web of practices explains both how certain deviations are selected in, as well as how others are selected out. Absence from the web of practices that reach out to new audiences, demonstrate competence or fix new meanings severely decreases the odds that novelty will stick. And indeed, many cases of evolving practices contain contradictory tendencies, reminding us of the difficulty of macro-social transformation. Take, for example, the case of the selection procedure of the United Nations Secretary-General: on the one hand, new practices such as public hearings have led to significant evolution; on the other hand, the broader institution of the United Nations, especially its public legitimacy, may find itself reinforced by the changes (Pouliot 2020a). In a similar way, the Security Council has been transforming its practices 'on the fly' over the past couple of decades, possibly enhancing its adaptability and longevity (Pouliot, 2020b). Capturing the duality of evolution, especially its adaptive yet contingent logic, remains a daunting challenge and this chapter is but a first attempt at it.

Conclusion

This chapter has made the case for an evolutionary perspective on international practices, joining Adler's long-standing efforts in this vein (Adler, 1991, 2005, 2019). In terms of the first fault line identified by the editors, I sided with those who 'see practice thinking as implying a continuous process of change' (Chapter 1) – although with a structuralist twist. It is certainly correct to argue, as Hopf does (Hopf, 2018), that micro-deviations seldom stick around. Yet most macro-transformations still come out of such processes as they accumulate over time and space. Standing back from individual action helps us see that, most of the time, changes in established practices cannot be traced back to specific instances of reflective agency. The challenge for practice theory, then, is to theorize how the incessant flow of small-scale deviations sometimes accumulates in the form of larger transformations.

At a macro-level, the selection of certain variations in practice is driven by the social environment within which they emerge, and more specifically by the web of practices within which deviant performances find themselves. My argument is meant to complement other practice approaches to change, which tend to emphasize reflective agency as the key engine of significant transformation in world politics. Important as they may be, explanations based on intentionality, reflection, and choice tend to reduce social aggregates to individual volitions, glossing over the socially emergent nature of evolution. Unit-level factors are only indirectly connected to the messy, collectively negotiated process of social transformation. Reflective agency may account for a key source of variation, but not for the selection of new practices as a macro-phenomenon. In any event, reflectivity takes place on background knowledge, which is itself a deposit of practice.

Indeed, it is crucial for practice theorists to continue to problematize the rampant fallacy of choice-theoreticism across the social sciences. In the modern liberal episteme within which we are currently immersed, we are encouraged to imagine self-contained individuals who, through reflection and calculation, stand above the social world in order to volitionally transform it. But as Taylor (1993: 48) reminds us, 'Among the practices which have helped to create this modern sense [of self] are those which discipline our thought to disengagement from embodied agency and social embedding. Each of us is called upon to become a responsible, thinking mind, self-reliant for his or her judgments'. Yet this unquestioned assumption in the social sciences and beyond is just that: a historically constructed, analytically problematic assertion that makes us think that we can somehow stand out of practice. This is perhaps the next frontier in practice theory: showing how even the practice of reflective agency, prevalent as it is today, is itself the result of evolution in our ways of doing things.

Part III

Innovative Concepts

9   The Dynamics of Repetition
Translocal Practice and Transnational Negotiations

Hilmar Schäfer

Repetition is a form of change

Brian Eno

Introduction

In the reception of practice theory, there has been considerable debate regarding its ability to account for social change. While there is basic agreement that social structures need to be enacted in order to persist,[1] there is little reflection on what this actually means in terms of both theory and methodology. Understanding practice theory as a research methodology (Bueger, 2014), I take the theoretical issue of how to address and conceptualize social change as a starting point, and develop a critique of practice theory's tendency to emphasize the stability of the social by centring on the notion of 'routine'. Instead, I propose grounding practice theory in a post-structuralist understanding of repetition and explore the methodological consequences of such a move. I argue that it is essential for practice theorists to reflect on the relationships between recurring practices in order to grasp the dynamics of the social. Practice theory has only fairly recently instigated a thorough reflection on the crucial issues of dynamics and change (Shove et al., 2012). This chapter thus mainly contributes to the fault line of stability and change delineated in Chapter 1. In its analysis, it also addresses the material dimension of social practice that was raised in that chapter as well.

The main theoretical and methodological challenges lie in rendering practice theory both analytically sharp and empirically inclusive. The key is to tune its 'sensitizing concepts' (Blumer, 1986: 148) sufficiently to render social structure visible, while ensuring they remain adaptable to diverse social phenomena. To achieve this, I argue that a

---

[1] For an early formulation of this practice-theoretical idea in IR, albeit under the rubric of constructivism, see Koslowski and Kratochwil (1994).

predominant focus on the notion of routine in practice theory should be replaced by a conception of repetition, which should in turn be informed by post-structuralist insights into the dynamics of the social. While the notion of routine is exclusively tied to bodies, which are able to perform practices skilfully (Reckwitz, 2002: 251), I show that repetition is as much an occurrence as it is a performance and one that encompasses both continuity and change.

Getting an analytical grasp of continuity and change is especially important when analysing the stability of processes in diplomatic institutions, given their logic of rotation. Despite the regular exchange of people who work in such institutions, practices persist. The chapter presents a case study of evaluations and negotiations of world heritage in the UNESCO world heritage programme, one of the most widely ratified international treaties with 193 current member states (and territories). I draw on document analysis and ethnographic data from an ongoing research project, for which I have conducted participant observation at six sessions of the world heritage committee, in Bonn (2015), Istanbul and Paris (2016), Krakow (2017), Manama (2018) and Baku (2019).[2] At these meetings, diplomats negotiate and decide on the creation of world heritage and add proposed sites to the world heritage list. By studying the diplomatic practices that constitute these negotiations, my contribution is also concerned with the broader question of how relations are being made and unmade in international institutions.

The Notion of Routine and the Static Bias of Practice Theory

Practice theory's greatest value lies in decentring common sociological approaches to the social. In what follows I briefly outline how practice theory overcomes the specific theoretical limitations of methodological individualism, structuralism and methodological situationalism. In contrast to individualist or normativist positions, practice theory conceives of the social as bodily practices that are performed in time and space (Schatzki, 1996, 2002). According to this perspective, 'the social is a field of embodied, materially interwoven practices centrally organized around shared practical understandings' (Schatzki, 2001: 3). It is concerned with overcoming traditional dichotomies such as the separation between society and the individual, agency and structure,

---

[2] This study is situated in an ethnographic analysis of global organizations in general (Niezen and Sapignoli, 2017; Riles, 2000) and on world heritage in particular (Brumann and Berliner, 2016).

culture and the material, or thinking and acting. It rejects essentialist beliefs and instead advocates a view of the social world in which contextual relations determine identity. By focusing on practices instead of individuals or structure, practice theory offers a relational perspective on the social that departs from mono-causal explanations of action.

First and foremost, the concept of practice offers an alternative way to think about structure and social order.[3] Practice theorists provide two core arguments to this effect. First, structure is not seen as a solely external constraint on individual action, but rather as 'always both constraining and enabling' (Giddens, 1984: 25). Second, '[t]he relevant social structures and cultural backgrounds are understood dynamically [...] through their continuing reproduction in practice and their transmission to and uptake by new practitioners' (Rouse, 2007a: 645). Practice theorists argue that structure and social order need to be constantly reproduced and maintained by active participants (Bourdieu and Wacquant, 1992: 140). Similar to interpretive approaches, practice theory thus emphasizes the local production of the social, closely relating it to methodological situationalism (Knorr Cetina, 1981a). However, it does not posit situations as self-contained entities, and asserts that analysis cannot be centred on situational interactions alone. This distinguishes practice theory from interactionist approaches, because it views the identity of practices, subjects and material things as determined in contexts. These contexts transcend any given situation and constitute identity in relation to other elements of the social such as other practices, other sites, and history. In this view, practice must be understood as a fundamentally translocal phenomenon.

Pierre Bourdieu's praxeology is fundamentally characterized by this relational view. As he has shown in *Distinction* (1984), the tastes of different social classes, expressed in their choices of preferred objects, create relationships of equality among social groups and relationships of difference between groups. These taste-based class distinctions mean that each class ascribes different values to the appreciated objects. These values are based on dispositions, which are socially constituted and embodied in the habitus. The dispositions are developed over time, with past experiences shaping present judgements and practices. This implies that practices have a temporal dimension, yet they are also characterized by a spatial one. They are connected to specific sites, or – given a broader understanding of 'space' – to different social fields, which shape the habitus of the actors. Thus, practice theory stresses the

---

[3] For an early discussion and an exhaustive contextualization with regard to structuralism see Ortner (1984).

need to explore the temporal and spatial relations that pertain between practices, subjects and materiality.

Anthony Giddens (1984: xxxi) argued that the social has structural properties if and when 'relationships are stabilized across time and space'. Practice is therefore distributed in time and space. In order to account for the stabilization of relations across time and space, practice theory focuses on the tacit knowledge or embodied dispositions that enable active participants to understand a situation and perform actions without conscious reflection. Both Bourdieu (1977) and Giddens (1984) – the two major intellectual sources of practice theory – agree on the central significance of bodily experience. Practice theorists understand human action as non-reflective, guided and upheld by the stability of bodily acquired dispositions that are formed in the course of socialization. Agents' general attitude towards situations is characterized by familiarity: the social appears self-evident to active participants.

This focus on the bodily stabilization of the social, however, has led practice theorists to argue that routinization is central to explanations of social order and should therefore be the theory's central analytical category. As Giddens (1984: 282) has put it, 'Routinized practices are the prime expression of the duality of structure in respect of the continuity of social life'. In his characterization of the practice turn in social theory, Andreas Reckwitz (2002: 255) has also identified practice with routine: 'For practice theory, the nature of social structure consists in routinization. Social practices are routines: routines of moving the body, of understanding and wanting, of using things, interconnected in a practice'.

I argue, however, that the conceptual and methodological problems that stem from centring practice theory on the notion of routine are threefold. After outlining these three sets of issues, I argue that a shift from the notion of routine to that of repetition is able to solve them. First and foremost, centring practice theory on the notion of routine invites an emphasis on reproduction and thus tends to foreground the static aspects of the social. There is a long-standing line of critique of this aspect of practice theory. The critique commonly arises in relation to concerns about Bourdieu's conception of the habitus. Arguably, there is a tendency to emphasize the static elements of society in Bourdieu's work, although this is hardly surprising given that he was interested in explaining the persistence of class differences in 1970s French society. In Bourdieu's view, there are at least two mechanisms that stabilize habitus. One factor is that the embodied dispositions of the habitus tend to be reaffirmed, since 'there is a probability [...] that experiences will confirm habitus, because most people are statistically bound to encounter circumstances that tend to agree with those that originally fashioned their habitus' (Bourdieu and Wacquant, 1992: 133).[4] The second factor is that the embodied dispositions are removed from conscious reflection and are thus difficult to change. These features of the habitus, which is the conceptual core of Bourdieu's approach, have led to widely shared criticism of the 'mechanistic', 'deterministic' and 'static' tendencies of his theory of practice (Garnham and Williams, 1980; Jenkins, 2002; Lash, 1993).

Although practice theory as a movement in social theory (Reckwitz, 2002; Schatzki et al., 2001; Schäfer, 2016b) cannot be identified with Bourdieu's theory of practice alone (Bueger and Gadinger, 2015: 2), the question of stability and change has occupied the theoretical discussion for some time. The reception of practice theory in IR has featured this issue intensively and scholars have developed a critique of the theory's tendency to emphasize routine and stabilization (Duvall and Chowdhury, 2011; Schindler and Wille, 2015). Nevertheless, praxeological approaches regularly emphasize either the stability or instability of the social (Bueger, 2014: 9). But all one-sided approaches to practice theory remain blind when it comes to social dynamics, inherent contradictions and counter-tendencies to order. Taking practice theory as a heuristic, I follow Joseph Rouse's (2007a: 647) assertion 'that different social practices [...] vary in their stability over time, such that the extent to which social practices sustain a relatively stable background for individual action would be a strictly empirical question, admitting of no useful general philosophical treatment apart from characterizing some of the considerations that might generate continuity or change'. Pouliot (Chapter 8) also addresses the issue of how practice theory can account for social change. While I am sceptical about the use of the evolutionary metaphor in general, as it is prone to the association of 'natural selection', I fundamentally agree with two points Pouliot raises: First, what is perceived as macro level change can only be explained in terms of ubiquitous and mundane continued performances of practices. Second, any stabilization of practices always needs to be understood in terms of interrelated practices (and very importantly different kinds of materialities, which Pouliot mentions only briefly in his account) that support each other in a 'web of practices' as Pouliot puts it. In this vein, practice theory needs to be treated as an instrument that accounts for *both* the reproduction *and*

---

[4] It can be shown, however, that there are ambivalent tendencies in Bourdieu's approach and that the static bias of his theory stems from his conception of his theoretical notions as homogeneous entities (Schäfer, 2011). There are proposals to embrace the possible heterogeneity of habitus in social theory (Lahire, 2003, 2004).

the transformation of the social. Thus, in order to describe and analyse diverse social phenomena, we need a conceptual category that does not presuppose either the stability or the instability of the social.

Second, the general focus on routine in practice theory creates a conceptual problem concerning a specific class of practices, namely those that are only seldom performed during the course of a human life. Taking marriage as an example, the practitioners partaking in this social ritual certainly cannot develop a 'routine of marrying', yet they are able to perform 'marriage' in a way that is socially acceptable, so long as certain conventions are being met.[5]

Third, through the notion of 'routine', the extension of practice in time and space and the stability of the social are exclusively attributed to bodies, their incorporated dispositions and tacit knowledge. The same is true of the category of 'habit', which has also been discussed as a central notion for practice theory in IR (Hopf, 2010) (see also the overview on the influence of pragmatism by Adler and Faubert, Chapter 3). Both the notions of routine and habit view the body as the guarantor of social stability and there is a tendency towards a one-sided view that equates habits with the upkeep of stability alone (Hopf, 2010: 555). While bodily dispositions and habits play a vital role in practice theorizing, they cannot be the sole basis for explaining the extension of practice in time and space. Any sole focus on the body inevitably neglects the contribution made by artefacts to the stabilization of the social; the extension of practice in time and space also involves the support of tools, documents and different types of media.

I argue that practice theory can overcome these problems by replacing the focus on routine with the notion of repetition. Repetition is the key to understanding the 'translocal' character of practice, or in other words, its extension in time and space. In order to address both stability and change in the social, greater reflection on the notion of repetition is required.

Practice as Repetition

Only a notion of repetition that has undergone a post-structuralist reworking can provide the basis for understanding the translocal character of practice and addressing the dynamism of the social. There are a number of different ways to conceptualize repetition.[6] The

---

[5] See Austin (1975) for a discussion on the practice of marrying and its conventional requirements.
[6] In the following, I draw on phenomenologist philosopher Bernhard Waldenfels (2001). For a more in-depth discussion see Schäfer (2013).

common understanding is of 'the same thing happening again', which presupposes that the recurring entity is exactly the same in both its occurrences. This understanding emphasizes identity and is centred on a belief in sameness. It can be condensed to the formula $a = a$. This is exactly what the idea of routine conveys: that practices stay the same over the course of time. Yet the philosophical insight that it is not possible to step into the same river twice dates back to antiquity.[7] According to the anti-essentialist perspective of practice theory, the identity of a practice is always imbued with the context it is situated in. Thus, the altered circumstances surrounding a repetition already introduce difference into practice. The revised formula for this would be $a - a'$. Any repetition thus challenges understandings of both plain sameness and pure difference. Things become more complicated when consideration is given to the dimension of time. In order for any repetition to happen, the passing of time is essential. Any recurrence necessarily happens *after* its previous appearance, leaving a temporal gap between both instances. Thus, a diachronic understanding of repetition is required: $a^t - a^{t+1}$. The passing of time is thus an integral aspect of repetition.[8]

A radical understanding of temporality as the foundation of structure has been developed by post-structuralist authors.[9] There has already been some debate concerning the relationship between post-structuralism and practice theory (Giddens, 1987). In my view, the two perspectives converge in some significant ways. Both positions critique the static notion of structure as upheld by structuralism. Consequently, they reject its synchronous analysis of the social. Instead, they argue for a temporalization of structure, understanding the social as a continually unfolding and evolving process, and acknowledging the production of structure in events or practice. While post-structuralism tends to focus on the never-ceasing play of difference, discourse and text (Giddens, 1987: 210–13), thus demanding a complimentary perspective on the (decentred) acting subject,[10] its philosophical discussion of reproduction and change prove useful for practice theory.

Jacques Derrida's (1982, 1988) reflections on repetition are particularly pertinent. In his philosophy of language, Derrida rethinks and extends

[7] This well-known aphorism dates back to Plato's interpretation of Heraclitus' philosophy.

[8] The temporal dimension is vital to Bourdieu's (1977) theory of practice, which draws on Marcel Mauss' (1966) analysis of the gift economy, with its time-lapse between gift and counter-gift, in order to criticize the atemporal perspective of structuralism.

[9] For a dialogue between post-structuralism and practice theory from an IR perspective see Hansen (2011).

[10] As exemplified in the late works of Michel Foucault (1988, 2005) on the technologies of the self.

the structuralist paradigm, which positions meaning as generated by relations of difference between signs. Derrida points to the citational character of signs, arguing that language needs to be repeatable in different contexts in order to be meaningful, and is therefore characterized by a temporal process of meaning production. He arrives at this position by taking the constitutive characteristics of written language (such as the respective absence of sender and recipient of a letter in the situation of reading and writing it) and applying them to signs in general. Derrida temporalizes the process of meaning production and shows that the gap between two instances of the appearance of any sign is constitutive of its meaning, creating the possibility for shifts in meaning to occur. He coins the notion of 'iterability' to describe a sign's ability to be repeatable in different contexts, as well as its susceptibility to change. The logic of iterability thus describes a repetition without any fixed ties to an original, and which encompasses change.

Following post-structuralist insight, repetition can be understood as that which is linked by its reappearance, but which can never be exactly the same. This simple yet consequential insight holds true for every kind of social practice. If we conceive of the social as repetitions in time and space, we are also reminded that at the heart of every repetition of a practice there is difference, because every repetition occurs under already altered circumstances. Adopting an anti-essentialist approach, this means that any contextual difference also has an impact on the identity of a practice. A reworked, post-structuralist understanding of repetition can account for what Bernhard Waldenfels (2001: 7) has called the 'paradox of repetition': the intricate entanglement of identity and difference, of the static and dynamic in repetition. Repetition is a paradoxical association between sameness and difference; it connects and divides at the same time. This perspective stresses the dynamism of repetition and the possibility for change to occur. It is for this reason that I suggest grounding practice theory on the notion of repetition, rather than routine, in order to overcome the tendency towards a static conception of the social. Post-structuralist reflection on the notion of repetition helps to sensitize the analytical gaze to its possible drifts and transformations. Repetition is a heuristically open category that encompasses both continuity and change, thus avoiding any presupposition regarding the nature of practices it describes. Taking 'repetition' as the central analytical category means following a principle of symmetry,[11] which is achieved by employing the same category to account for *both* reproduction *and* change.

---

[11] This is analogous to the principle of symmetry deployed in the strong programme of the sociology of science to explain 'truth' and 'error' (Bloor, 1976).

A practice approach that centres on the notion of repetition can conceive of practice in three interrelated dimensions. First, practices are formations that *repeat themselves*. They are flows of events, moving in time and space and existing before subjects, actually bringing them into being. Practices occur in the social realm and are identifiable and perceivable owing to their recurrence. In this sense, circulating practices are a cultural repertoire that provides subjects with a space of possible citations and re-citations. This dimension of practice is addressed by an analytical perspective, which looks into the distribution, historical trajectory and rhythms of practices. The research questions to be asked here concern the location of practices (where do they occur?), historical events (when did they occur?) and the duration and recurrence of practices. These questions can be pursued by discourse analysis, by looking at texts and documenting the spatiotemporal characteristics and distribution of practices.

Second, practices are formations that are *repeated* by subjects. This dimension refers to the performances of competent bodies that have learned to understand the social and act in comprehensible ways. It highlights the fact that practices need bodies and their performances in order to persist through time and space.[12] Practices exist only as long as they are being repeated in an intelligible way. The social would not exist if it were not continuously performed. This dimension also points to repetition as an important and fundamental means of learning practice, by acquiring embodied knowledge and skills through repeated exercise (see also Adler and Faubert's and Gadinger's discussion of learning and the community of practice approach in Chapters 3 and 5). In order to analyse this dimension of practice, theorists can draw on ethnographic and ethnomethodological traditions of social research, which foreground the bodily performances of competent practitioners.

The distinction between these two dimensions of practice – repeating themselves and being repeated – also figures in work by Elizabeth Shove et al. (Shove and Pantzar, 2007; Shove et al., 2012), who differentiate between 'practices-as-entities' and 'practices-as-performances'. The notion of repetition brings these two aspects of practice together in a single conceptual category. Conceiving of practices as entities, Shove et al. tend to reify practices, such as when they speak of practices 'recruiting' their practitioners or bodies becoming 'carriers' of practice. Although this perspective may provide a fruitful irritation to common sociological thought, it harbours the danger of thinking of practice as a fixed thing with a mind of its own. In contrast, the notion of repetition emphasizes

---

[12] Here, bodies are understood as 'carriers', in an expression coined by Elizabeth Shove and Mika Pantzar (2007).

the point that practice is a fundamentally relational category. In addition, it invokes the third, temporal and dynamic aspect to practice.

Finally, taking Derrida's reflection on iterability into consideration, practices are also *repeatable*. This means that they can always become detached from any given context and linked to new contexts. Any form of stability necessarily encompasses transformation, which opens up the possibility for change. While practices are in principle comprehensible to others, because of shared embodied background knowledge, they are also simultaneously susceptible to divergent interpretations, misunderstandings or changes of meaning. Drawing on post-structuralist theory, Judith Butler (1999: 163–90) has emphasized the political potential of the subversive repetition of practices. Far from being limited to the case of gendered practices, and further developed in her later works (e.g. Butler, 1997), Butler's analysis of linguistic iterability offers useful insights for the praxeological analysis of repetition and transformation in general. Practice theory does not presuppose whether a given phenomenon is stable, but rather analyses the duration, rhythm and scope of practices, and the concrete mechanisms that stabilize their repetition and which might also cause their drift or collapse.

Temporality and sociality are deeply engrained in the process of repetition. The intelligible performance and understanding of a practice depend on past repetitions, while the current repetition confirms its meaning and opens a realm of possibility for future citations by providing a culturally circulating repertoire. It is essential for practice to be shared with others who also understand and perform it. Sociality is not only located at the level of interaction, coordination and collectivity but it also reaches far deeper, already an integral being a part of practice itself.

A practice approach that centres on this conception of repetition avoids the pitfalls of limited sociological explanations and is able to decentre the subject, while avoiding the risk of reifying structure *or* practices as entities in their own right. By developing and employing the concept of repetition, practice theory overcomes not only the opposition between individual and society but also a narrow conception of practices as either fixed routines or situational, singular events. Having outlined this conceptual understanding of practice theory's basic analytical category, I now turn to the perspective's methodological consequences.

Methodological Reflections

Practice theory is centred on a specific methodological perspective, which is focused on generating and directing empirical research (Neumann, 2002). According to Stefan Hirschauer (2008: 172, my translation), practice theories can be understood as types 'of "modest grand theories" as they offer mere frameworks of categories and assumptions for developing substantial theories on specific practices'. Practice theory is thus an open heuristic that limits its theoretical presuppositions in order to grasp and analyse diverse social phenomena. Which categories it takes as the starting point for a particular analysis and how far it takes the exploration of complex and heterogeneous relationships is entirely dependent on the guiding research question.

As practice itself is always translocal, practice theory calls for a translocal methodology.[13] By thinking of practices in terms of repetitions that link different sites and moments in time, the perspective follows the fragile relations that make up the (in)stability of the social, enabling the analyst to grasp the specific contributions of bodies and material artefacts in the process of its stabilization and destabilization. This is a prerequisite for a methodology that opens up sociological theory for analyses of the relationality and heterogeneity of the social. It is not a singular object or an isolated action, but a heterogeneous network of relations connecting different times, places and entities that needs to be taken into account. In other words, the dynamics of repetition are constitutively distributed between bodies and material entities as they extend in time and space.

Depending on the research question, practice theory must constantly shift its focus in order to follow the multiple connections between heterogeneous elements linked in a network of relations. The basic analytical elements of practice theory are subjects, material entities (bodies and artefacts) and practices. No category can be viewed as a safe ground for study, however, although it might be used as a starting point for a given analysis. The category's integrity can always be questioned, thus the analysis must remain flexible and follow relations between very different, heterogeneous entities.

Practice theory takes account of acting subjects, for example, but these subjects are formed in discursive and non-discursive practices; their identity is socially constituted and their agency relies on always already existing and repeating practices. Thus, although practices are performed by practitioners (Duvall and Chowdhury, 2011: 337–43), the practitioners are also performed, in other words enabled to act, by the realm of existing practices and the possibilities for acting that they entail and produce.

The next group of categories is characterized by their material qualities. In the sense established by actor-network theory (Latour, 2005),

---

[13] I have set out this methodology in more detail in Schäfer (2017).

'materialities' need to be understood as relatively durable heterogeneous entities that contribute to a practice, stabilizing it and extending it across time and space. Like bodies, artefacts and media, materialities are responsible for extending practices beyond face-to-face situations of spatiotemporal co-presence. Their specific contribution to this extension differs gradually and needs to be worked out through empirical analysis. Practice theory accounts for bodies as one form of material entities, for example, that provide location for incorporated dispositions and tacit knowledge. But bodies are themselves constituted by practices that shape them in order to modify their surface, their meaning or even their ability to contract and maintain dispositions (Foucault, 1977). It also accounts for artefacts, as another form of material entities that shape practices, but that are shaped in turn by non-discursive and discursive practices.

Finally, practice theory accounts for practices that repeat themselves throughout the social realm and are repeated by participants; these practices are performed, identified and classified according to categories embodied in the subjects' dispositions. But practices need the specific material qualities of artefacts *and* bodies in order to span time and space, both of which also determine their particular repeatability. To describe the characteristics of different kinds of practices, Theodore Schatzki (1996: 91–110) has proposed a useful distinction between 'dispersed' and 'integrative' practices with regard to the circulating aspect of practice. His proposal is to distinguish practices by means of their distribution and extension in social space. Dispersed practices are characterized by their wide extension in social space. Practices such as describing, explaining, ordering and asking questions circulate in the social realm relatively independently of the borders of social fields. They are usually linked to equally dispersed practices such as executing and answering in a temporal manner of succession. In contrast, integrative practices are 'the more complex practices found in and constitutive of particular domains of social life' (Schatzki, 1996: 98). Along Bourdieusian terms, these could be called 'field-specific practices'. As examples of this type Schatzki counts economic, religious and pedagogical practices, recreational and industrial practices, and practices of cooking and farming. Dispersed practices can become part of integrative practices, linking with them and transforming themselves at the same time. While integrative practices, such as questioning members of government in a committee of enquiry, are relatively specific to particular social domains (in this case politics), dispersed practices such as asking and answering questions retain 'more or less the same shape in those different sectors' (Schatzki, 2002: 88). Thinking along these lines and distinguishing between different scopes in the dissemination of practices produces valuable insights into the nexus, or the hanging together of practices (Hui et al., 2017).

The basic categories of analysis, while always debatable, are brought together by practice theory's relational perspective. The theory refrains from localizing the source of action in the intentions of a subject, or even in a singular practice. Instead of mono-causal explanations, it deals with networks of relations between heterogeneous elements linked together in time and space that influence, support and shape a particular practice. In this sense, practice theory is first and foremost an invitation to think outside established conceptual boxes and draw new analytical connections. This requires following relations in time and space, and drawing on historical data, longitudinal observations and participant observations in different localities. This is why multi-sited research, in combination with document analysis, is a particularly important method of practice-theoretical research. In the following section, I turn to the phenomenon of world heritage to illustrate the specific methodology of the praxeological perspective.

Repetition: Continuity and Change in Transnational Negotiations

The Convention Concerning the Protection of the World Cultural and Natural Heritage (1972)[14] is perhaps UNESCO's best-known programme and the most encompassing international treaty on the safeguarding of cultural and natural heritage.[15] The convention revolves around the idea that a site designated 'world heritage' belongs to the heritage of mankind and is therefore of global importance, transcending the boundaries of the nation state it happens to be located in. In order to be designated world heritage, the 'outstanding universal value' (UNESCO Intergovernmental Committee for the Protection of the World Cultural and Natural Heritage, 2015a: § 4) of a site in

---

[14] World Heritage Convention hereafter.

[15] This example is drawn from my current research on cultural heritage, which focuses on UNESCO world heritage. My analytical hypothesis is that the production and understanding of cultural heritage are shaped by a multiplicity of heterogeneous relations: practices of collecting, restoring, renovating and displaying heritage; events occurring in distant places; historical changes; competing principles; embodied competences; documents; the specific material qualities of artefacts; and so on. The study is conducted as multi-sited research (Marcus, 1995, 1998) that links world heritage sites – the actual buildings, cityscapes or landscapes that are being protected under this label – with the multifarious institutional and non-institutional processes involved in their creation, safeguarding, use, contestation and administration.

question must be assigned through a complex valuation process.[16] The institutions governing this process are the World Heritage Committee as the executive organ of the convention and the standing secretariat at the World Heritage Centre in Paris. The committee consists of twenty-one member states to the convention, elected by the General Assembly of States Parties for a four-year term and representing all continents. The committee decides on two world heritage lists. The World Heritage List registers the heritage of mankind, a globally recognized endorsement that accords sites international visibility and attention (these spaces of international visibility form part of an unequal global distribution of power which could be analysed as a regime of visibility in the terms of Austin and Leander, Chapter 10). The List of World Heritage in Danger registers endangered sites, placing them under international scrutiny and raising awareness of the threats they face. The committee draws on the work of three so-called 'advisory bodies': the International Council on Monuments and Sites (ICOMOS), the International Centre for the Study of the Preservation and Restoration of Cultural Property and the International Union for Conservation of Nature (IUCN). ICOMOS and IUCN evaluate the nominated cultural and natural sites respectively.

Sites can be proposed for inclusion in the World Heritage List by any member state of the convention.[17] In the nomination dossier, member states must demonstrate the 'outstanding universal value' of a site in relation to fixed criteria, which are divided into two sets. There are ten criteria of justification for the inclusion of natural and cultural properties. A nominated property should, for example, 'represent a masterpiece of human creative genius', 'bear a unique or at least exceptional testimony to a cultural tradition or to a civilisation which is living or which has disappeared' or 'contain superlative natural phenomena or areas of exceptional natural beauty and aesthetic importance' (UNESCO Intergovernmental Committee for the Protection of the World Cultural and Natural Heritage, 2015a: § 77). In addition, all properties must satisfy the criterion of integrity, which is a 'measure of the wholeness and intactness' of the nominated property (UNESCO Intergovernmental Committee for the Protection of the World Cultural and Natural Heritage, 2015a: § 88). The authenticity of cultural properties must also be demonstrated, and all nominated properties require

---

[16] Research on this specific case is situated within the broader field of valuation studies (Berthoin et al., 2015; Lamont, 2012). For a contextualization see Schäfer (2016a).

[17] For a critical reflection on the tensions between the interests of nation-states in the world heritage programme see Kalaycioglu (2020).

a working protection and management plan. These three requirements form the second set of criteria for inclusion in the World Heritage List.

Evaluations carried out by the advisory bodies produce recommendations to inscribe a nominated site, defer or refer the nomination, or refuse it.[18] These recommendations are turned into draft decisions for the committee, which are then debated at its annual session where the conference method of international diplomacy is employed (Dunn, 1929). In preparation for and during the session, a so-called rapporteur is responsible for collecting amendments to the draft decisions as well as leading the discussion and the amendment process.

All the committee's decisions relating to nominations revolve around the production of documents that are negotiated during its annual session. Here I will focus on one of the committee's specific practices: the technique of drafting decision documents in temporal and spatial co-presence. For this purpose, draft decisions are not only circulated in paper form in the conference hall but also they are also presented on a large computer screen at the head of the room, a detail I return to shortly. The drafting practice is complex; it is neither completely spontaneous nor entirely planned. It is situated in the conference room, but extends beyond it across time and space, linked by repetitions. In the following analysis, I focus on both its translocal extension and the materialities that support this extension.

(1) In order to take a closer look at the drafting practice's translocal extension, we need to understand its specific temporality and spatiality. It is bound to annual meetings with scheduled time slots for debate on predetermined items, and thus kept separate from other diplomatic activities such as speech giving, report reading and social events. The annual repetition and demarcation of the drafting practice make up its specific rhythm. It is also structured by a ritualized opening and closing procedure for each discussion. The chairperson will usually say: 'I now ask our rapporteur if s/he has received any amendments to this draft decision' or 'May I ask the rapporteur to present the amendment to this draft decision'. The rapporteur will answer either: 'We haven't received any amendments' or 'Yes, we have received an amendment from the distinguished delegates of X'. In the second case, she will read out the proposed amendment, which

---

[18] A referral implies that a nomination dossier should be revised for resubmission to the subsequent committee session, while a deferral calls for a more in-depth assessment or study and a substantial revision by the state party, and may be resubmitted at a later point in time (UNESCO Intergovernmental Committee for the Protection of the World Cultural and Natural Heritage, 2015a: §§ 159, 160).

will then be discussed by the delegates before any countering amendments are proposed. The chairperson will repeatedly ask whether there are any further comments or objections, until the amended text is agreed upon by a majority of delegates.[19] The chairperson will then say: 'Then I declare decision X adopted [as amended]'. A stroke of the gavel closes the debate both visually and, more importantly, auditorily. The whole drafting process is thus very ritualized. From time to time, a delegation might try to reopen the discussion concerning a decision already taken, but the ritualistic framework will not allow for it. The chairperson will reply: 'We have already closed this item'.

Although the practice of drafting appears at first glance to be tied to the temporal and spatial co-presence of the delegates, it has fuzzy temporal and spatial boundaries, extending through time and space and interweaving with other social practices. Of course, substantial preparations and negotiation take place before the committee meeting. Most member states maintain specific embassies for UNESCO in Paris in order to facilitate negotiations, and there are meetings at which draft decisions are discussed well before the committee session. Another aspect of the practice's spatiotemporal extension is the manner in which decisions have effects in the future or are re-examined in further debates after the session has closed. The decisions' texts also make concrete reference to other times, such as 'recalling decision no. X, adopted at the 39th session' or 'to be examined at the 42nd session'.

(2) The translocal extension of the drafting practice is supported by different types of linked materialities, all of which can become an entry or focal point for praxeological analysis depending on the guiding research interest. In my view, the analytical focus both on the materiality of the body and the materiality of artefacts is a key feature of practice theory (Schäfer, 2017) and a major contribution to IR scholarship. In the following, I provide a brief overview of some of the diverse materialities involved in the practice of drafting.

First, the practice of drafting relies on the embodied knowledge of diplomats physically co-present at the committee session. Connections

---

[19] Of course, in reality, the process is more complex than this theoretical abstraction suggests. However, during the negotiations that I have witnessed at the world heritage committee, outnumbered parties usually withdraw their proposals once a consensus is emerging and a majority is forming. There are very few occasions when an amendment comes to a vote, the procedure for which is regulated by the Rules of Procedure §35–42 (UNESCO Intergovernmental Committee for the Protection of the World Cultural and Natural Heritage, 2015b).

between different cases are made, for example, on the basis of their diplomatic experience. This is exemplified by the following request, voiced by the head of the Finnish delegation at the 40th session of the committee: 'Since we again have recommendations in this draft decision, I would like to put in the standard paragraph in the end as we did in the case of the rock art site in China'.[20] The competences of the diplomats would be at the centre of an analysis that focuses on the diplomats' bodies, which might ask how policy is being performed and enacted.[21]

A focus on embodied knowledge and routine would be rather limited, however, without considering other materialities involved in the drafting besides the skilled bodies extending the repetition of this practice through time and space. The practice of drafting encompasses PDF documents of proposed draft decisions, for example, which are emailed, printed out and read. During the committee sessions, there are even physically circulating forms, the so-called 'blue drafts', for proposing amendments to draft decisions with short notice. Arguably, the text itself has a specific kind of materiality, relating to the general characteristics of written language as expandable, mutable, annotatable, commentable and so on (Gumbrecht and Pfeiffer, 1988). However, as Annelise Riles (1998: 386) has pointed out, decision documents repeat themselves in terms of 'structure, organisational logic, language, format, typeface, layout and even substantive content'. The wording of the decision texts is thus not entirely unconstrained. It performs implicit standards of wording that may be rendered explicit in the process, such as through comparisons with other situations. In one exemplary case I observed, this is done by the rapporteur explaining a change in wording: 'This is the standard language that the committee adopts when a property is being moved from deferral to inscription, because a draft text that has been agreed on by both the state party and the advisory bodies has not yet been presented'.[22] Here, it is the structure of the text itself, produced by the sedimented formulations of past decisions, that shapes both the discussion and the final decision. The binding power of past wordings needs to be re-enacted by the rapporteur, however, who draws on embodied knowledge to link past and present formulations. Language, knowledge and performance must be aligned in specific ways, therefore, in order to

[20] Discussion pertaining to decision 40COM 8B.20, 15 July 2016.
[21] For ethnographic accounts of diplomatic practices see Neumann (2012) and Niedner-Kalthoff (2015). Niedner-Kalthoff also addresses the affective aspect of politics, with the bodies of diplomats at times showing joy or anger, feeling, thirst or exhaustion, for example.
[22] 15 July 2016.

establish stable relations in time and space and reproduce structures in practice. Repetition is key in maintaining these stable relations.[23]

Finally, in relation of the mediatization of the drafting practice, the computer screen mentioned earlier forms an integral part. Its importance is demonstrated by the diplomats' frequent reference to it: 'We don't have it on the screen', 'Can we have it on the screen?' or 'Can you switch the screen, please?'. The large screen at the head of the conference hall mediates the practice of drafting in specific ways. First, it displays the name of the site discussed for nomination alongside photographic images and the number of the draft decision in question. Second, and more importantly, when the rapporteur takes over and moderates the discussion concerning an amendment, the screen is switched to a Word document prepared by the secretariat that shows the proposed alterations to the original text in 'track changes' format. Third, together with highlighting all the deletions and additions to the text (by showing them crossed out and in red or blue, respectively), the screen displays the conflicting parties as well as the conflicting modifications. The names of countries proposing the alterations appear in square brackets before the altered text. Countries supporting their position and thus co-sponsoring the amendment are added to these brackets as they speak up during the debate. Thus, the majority ratio within the committee is gradually visualized on the screen as the debate progresses. In the process of drafting, visibility and power are thus intricately linked, as discussed also by Austin and Leander, Chapter 10, and Walters, Chapter 6.

As delegates reference the on-screen text and read both modifications and political conflicts it displays, the screen becomes an obligatory passage point (Callon, 1986; Latour, 1992) of the practice of drafting. Alena Drieschova and Rebecca Adler-Nissen (2019) have shown how the use of information and communication technology for 'track-change diplomacy' in international negotiations affects the shareability, visualization and immediacy of information. The incorporation of the technical medium of the screen into the practice of drafting creates a synthetic situation where face-to-face interactions are being augmented by technology (Knorr Cetina, 2009). However, in contrast to the screens used in financial trading, for example, the screen used during negotiations of the World Heritage Committee is a weak scopic system, since its capacity to transgress the situation of co-presence is quite

---

[23] Moreover, there also seems to be a digital infrastructure in the form of a database storing past decisions of the committee, which was mentioned both by delegates and the secretariat during negotiations. On inquiry I was told that the database is available for internal reference only.

limited. The screen does not collect, organize and present data in real time, but only presents information in the form of maps and photos, thus representing and referencing spaces beyond the situation of the conference room. Still, it is not merely a passive tool, since it shapes negotiation practices and is in turn shaped by them.

The tool for the editing work displayed on the screen is simple word processing software, which renders the text visible and modifiable. It is easy to overlook this aspect of the practice, which is usually taken for granted owing to the ubiquity of word processing in daily life. With a word processor, the production and revision of text become fundamentally intertwined. The Word document simultaneously facilitates and *also demonstrates* the amendability of the text to delegates. Once a decision has been finalized, that is, 'adopted', the document is prepared for eventual publication and circulation and its format is changed to PDF, thus rendering it less readily amendable. The document passes through different states that allow different kinds of practices to attach themselves to it. The draft decisions presented to the committee before the session in PDF format become amendable at a certain point in time during the session, by conversion to a Word document format, with practices of reading, discussing, negotiating and editing attaching to this version, and are then 'fixed' once again in PDF format after the final adoption of all committee decisions, with practices of circulating, reading and interpreting attached to this final version.

Conclusion

The discussion began with a critique of the static bias of practice theory, centred on the category of routine. I argued that in order to account for the translocal character of practice, the notion of routine should be replaced with a conception of repetition informed by post-structuralist thought. This category addresses three aspects: that practices repeat themselves, that they are repeated and that they are repeatable. Building on this fundamental understanding of practice, I sketched a methodology that follows relations in time and space and looks at the specific contributions of bodies and other materialities in processes of stabilization and destabilization of a practice. By way of example, I outlined the practice of drafting in international negotiations, drawing on my research on the production of UNESCO world heritage sites. This practice involves heterogeneous elements, including the bodies of diplomats, documents in various forms, texts and the computer screen. It is a distributed practice, extending in time and space well beyond the meeting itself. It persists through time, regardless of changes to committee membership or diplomatic representation.

There is a great deal of rotation in the diplomatic corps. So although the drafting practice relies on certain routines of coping and the embodied 'know how' of diplomats, the notion of routine is not sufficient to grasp the extension of this practice – or any practice for that matter – across time and space. This continuity, as well as impetus for change, transformation and adaptation, also relies on archiving decisions and rendering them accessible online, circulating documents, spending entire days in badly lit and poorly ventilated conference venues, looking at screens, having informal chats in the corridor, as well as formal negotiations and so forth. In short, it relies on repeating practices and heterogeneous materialities. Consequently, employing a practice approach in IR requires reflecting on and ultimately broadening our understanding of the nature of *relations* in the study of international 'relations'.

How can this specific nexus of diplomatic practice be characterized? The interwoven diplomatic practices of negotiating, drafting and decision-making are shaped by reference to past decisions, through the employment of established wording and standardized phraseology. A characteristic trait of diplomatic drafting is the effort to achieve consistency with earlier decisions and wordings. This relies on the memories of physically co-present participants, as well as media such as circulating documents and technical infrastructures (e.g. Word documents, the screen and database). The specificity of drafting lies in its techniques of attaining consistency with former decisions and wording, distinguishing it from other types of writing in academia or artistic text production. The practice of drafting is linked with highly specific integrative practices such as diplomatic negotiations, as well as common and ubiquitous dispersed practices such as editing a Word document in a complex network of practices and materialities. In order to better understand and analyse the practices involved, they can be usefully compared with different social fields, such as other kinds of political deliberations (at the UN or in local parliaments), other kinds of negotiations (such as less formalized haggling), other kinds of valuation processes (such as assessing the quality of food or ascribing marks) or other kinds of media practice (such as the use of screens in private situations or in work settings). Comparisons deliver insights into the specific characteristics of this nexus of practice.

More broadly, drafting decision documents is part and parcel of producing UNESCO world heritage, as are preparing nomination dossiers, visiting sites, engaging local communities, politicians and experts, and so on. There is no clear-cut beginning or end to the creation of world heritage. The whole business is 'messy', as one head of delegation put it in conversation with me. I hope to have shown how practice theory provides the right tools for analysing this mess.

10 Visibility
Practices of Seeing and Overlooking

Jonathan Luke Austin with Anna Leander

Seeing things – *really* seeing them – is difficult. In *On Constructing a Reality*, Heinz von Foerster (2003: 212) provides the neatest physical/physiological example of this (see Figure 10.1) by asking us to

Hold Figure 1 with your right hand, close your left eye and fixate [on the] asterisk of Figure 1 with your right eye. Move the book slowly back and forth along [your] line of vision until at an appropriate distance, from about 12 to 14 inches, [and] the round black spot disappears. Keeping the asterisk well focused, the spot should remain invisible even if the figure is slowly moved parallel to itself.

The blind spot here is produced owing to the absence of photoreceptors at the point on the retina where fibres converge to form the optic nerve. This phenomenon is well known. It is just a mind game, but one with far wider lessons: picking a point of focus, we'll see, always pushes other things to the margins.

Emanuel Adler and Vincent Pouliot (2011a: 3) have led a call within IR that seeks to develop the concept of 'practice' as a conceptual 'focal point' around which empirical and theoretical work of an otherwise eclectic mix can meet. As they suggest, 'the notion of practice ... [makes] interparadigmatic conversations possible' (Adler and Pouliot, 2011a: 3). Already, their claim has been amply proven by the vitality of the ongoing work of the International Practice Theory (IPT) programme within IR.[1] However, and in the older terms of Donna Haraway (1988), any focal point – including focusing on one or another set of social practices – is always partial in the perspectives it brings to

We are grateful to editors and the participants in the two workshops for their comments on earlier versions of this argument.

[1] For theoretical work see, inter alia, Neumann (2002), Pouliot (2008), Adler and Pouliot (2011b), Bigo (2011), Leander (2011), Bueger (2013), Ringmar (2014), Berling (2015), Kustermans (2016), McCourt (2016). For empirical applications see, inter alia, Pouliot (2010, 2016b), Neumann and Pouliot (2011), Bueger (2013, 2015), Bueger and Bethke (2013), Leander (2013, 2016), Acuto (2014), Adler-Nissen (2014b), Adler-Nissen and Pouliot (2014), Autesserre (2014), Sending et al. (2015), Austin (2016, 2017b).

Figure 10.1 An example of the optical illusion used by Heinz von Foerster in his *On Constructing a Reality*

view. It always has blindspots, things it makes invisible. It is thus that in this intervention, we want to introduce and insist on the importance of tending more carefully to the concept of visibility in practice theorizing as a means to ensure that IPT retains the space for (evolving) interparadigmatic conversations. We will argue that tending to visibility, and in doing so locating blindspots centrally in social scientific inquiry, is necessary to ensure that IPT enhances our capacity to look at the world quite differently, sometimes radically so. This we would contend is a matter of no small importance for scholars of IR, particularly if we connect it to (cultivating) the ability to act differently with/in the world (Austin and Leander, 2021; Austin, 2020b).

This insistence on blindspots may perplex when the very introduction of the study of practices to IR and other disciplines has been intended to extend the array of phenomena that scholars pay attention to. IPT seeks to return to the quotidian and every day, the mundane and seemingly simple. It seeks – indeed – to avoid overlooking the lived experience of the world by challenging the dominance of what Cynthia Enloe (2016: 623) terms 'inattentive' scholarship that refuses to notice and take seriously matters that fall outside established scholarly frames. IPT does so by claiming, ultimately, that world politics is about people doing things, performing the world and the political. Politics is practice. Indeed, as the title of Von Foerster's essay indicates, practices are sets of actions that '*construct*' one particular reality. In evoking the non-representational logic of practicality, IPT has made visible – 'opened our eyes' – to how this occurs sociologically: it has expanded our vision. However, Von Foerster introduced his mind game to remind us that 'perceiving' is also a type of 'doing' (a practice) and thus that 'if I don't see' certain practices then 'I am blind' to the fact that there always exist a multitude of other (possible or extant) realities constituted by similar or different types of (world political) practice.[2]

---

[2] Notably, Von Foerster's claims here foreshadow far more contemporary social theory and its focus on the concepts of 'multiplicity' and/or 'performativity' as constitutive of social realities. See, inter alia, Law (1999), Law and Mol (2001), Mol (2002), Deleuze and Guattari (2004), Bryant (2011).

We argue that 'visibility' is a crucial social and social scientific category that can 'forearm' us against the risks of IPT becoming unnecessarily narrow as a research programme. This risk has already been acknowledged, of course. David M. McCourt (2016), for instance, has recently compared the evolution of IPT to that of Constructivism within IR. As he notes, although IPT has sought to avoid becoming an 'ism', it seems quite true that 'a practice theoretic perspective would view IR itself is a practice: a distinct arena of social competition with its own practical logics' (McCourt, 2016: 482). McCourt's point here is not to critique the goals of IPT but, rather, to highlight the danger of overlooking the gradual emergence and standardization of a particular practice theory-driven way of doing social science, itself made up of innumerable little practices, that dictate what the approach can or cannot appreciate about the world around us. The risk, to repeat ourselves, is thus that blindspots are being introduced into IPT; blindspots that, more significantly, are perpetuated and made permanent through the disciplining effects of disciplinary practices that surround all constraining forms of theorizing (Leander 2020; Kratochwil, Chapter 11).

In our argument, the risk of perpetuating blindspots within IPT reflects the fact that our ability to 'see' the world and its realities is enacted in certain inescapably political fields (Brighenti, 2010) or regimes (Van Winkel, 2005; Heinich, 2012) of visibility that focus our vision on some things rather than others. These fields and regimes of visibility generate power and politics in both obvious and less obvious ways. Basic propaganda is implicated in any regime of visibility, for instance, but so are the many 'great divides' of the social sciences (Bourdieu, 1993; Latour, 1993). In world politics, violence, gender, religion, and culture are all intersected by regimes of visibility that establish dichotomies, hierarchies, blockages, and further 'misrecognitions' of the world (Austin, 2017b; Austin et al., 2019). More than this, visibility involves aesthetic sensibilities. It therefore also always implicates affect. It is a 'double' that combines both perception and affect (Deleuze, 1991). As Andrea Brighenti (2010: 44) puts it, visibility is 'an aspect of social life that enables us to introduce thresholds of relevance and selective attention' linked to this double and, so, 'as a property of subjects, sites, events … rhythms' and – indeed – practices, 'visibility is employed as a means of sorting, classifying and ranking…'. Because of this, 'visibility cannot be reduced to traditional sociological categories such as actor, organisation, system, class, gender, race, and so on, although it meaningfully intersects all of them' (Brighenti, 2010: 38). It is a category in its own right.

Thinking in terms of visibility, we thus suggest, sensitizes us to the politics of practice(s) – theoretical and/or otherwise – in a manner that locates perception and aesthetics at the core of world politics. In so doing, the concept of visibility might assist in deepening the work of IPT by quite literally extending its field of vision in a manner ensuring that its blindspots are constantly contested, preventing IPT from becoming a disciplining force and instead turning it into the open space of reflection that Adler and Pouliot wished it to be. To advance this argument, we now proceed in four main parts. First, we explore the ways in which visibility is politically crucial to IR by drawing on long-standing and more recent work in social theory that demonstrates the ways in which *who* or *what* is seen or, inversely, remains unseen is essential for establishing both local and world political hierarchies, ranging from formal political hierarchies to hierarchies in observation. Second, we foreground that while this process and the blindspots entailed are inescapable, a cognizance of its politics provides opportunities for practice theory to broaden its view on what constitutes international relations and so to avoid becoming a sclerotic enterprise, which is both normatively and politically essential for its future as a field of study. Third, we anchor this argument in a real-world example. We focus on the import of visibility for the differing ways in which the use of extraordinary rendition (and torture) by the United States and the Syrian Arab Republic have been made (in)visible to both public and social scientific analysis. Fourthly, we draw on this empirical discussion to argue that practices of making seen or unseen are regimes that predefine the focal point of any (scientific or not) mode of observation or analysis. As a result, we suggest, the study of *any other set of practices* is filtered through regimes of visibility, and hence *practices of visibility filter the way we see all practices*. Tending to visibility, blindspots, and practices of seeing and of overlooking is therefore crucial for the IPT research programme. Finally, we turn to the 'broader' consequences of this deepening of the perceptual and affective lenses of IPT for the discipline of IR and beyond.

Enacting Ambiguous Evolving Regimes of Visibility

Politics is visual. Arguably, it has become increasingly so as we communicate ever more through visual media in a world where 'creativity dispositives' are omnipresent (Weber, 2008; Reckwitz, 2012). Who and what is seen or – inversely – remains unseen can thus be seen as essential for the establishment and maintenance of hierarchies, including formal political hierarchies and, more broadly in the terms of Jacques Rancière (2004) for the division of the 'sensible'. To see this, let's begin by going back a little in time. Ethnomethodology has long studied practices empirically and systematically (Mauss, 1950; Garfinkel, 1967; Liberman, 2013). In one of its classic texts, 'Notes on Police Assessment of Moral Character', Harvey Sacks (1972) describes a problem faced by police officers: inferring the 'goodness' or 'badness' of a person walking down a street or hanging out on a street corner without knowing anything about them. Sacks (1972: 284, emphasis added) describes how police 'treat their beat as a territory of *normal appearances*' based on the idea that 'being noticeable and being deviant seem intimately related'. Spotting criminals thus relies on an 'incongruity procedure' that scans individuals and environments for abnormalities as they are conceived in comparison with the 'normal ecology' of a territory that is 'normative' in the sense of being unnoticeable (Sacks, 1972: 286).

Sacks' description of specialized practices of surveillance are real-world examples of what Rancière (2004) called the 'police order' of society. Rancière's thesis extends Sacks' localized observations and theorizes the presence of a set of largely unconscious or implicit norms and social practices that determine forms of social exclusion and the distribution of power. Norms and practices are repeated and transformed in their repetition (also Schäfer, Chapter 9). Ultimately, these norms and practices are themselves based on the 'distribution of the sensible' which is a means of controlling or ordering what becomes visible or invisible, speakable or unspeakable, and noticeable or not. In this, exclusions and silencings are necessarily implicit. And more than this, if the social order is a police order refusing the possibility of flux and contestation then the social is, to a large degree, an *anti-political* form of order in the sense of both 'translating political controversies into technical objectives' and encouraging a 'non-identification' – a making *in*visible – of certain political issues (Walters, 2009: 116). Anti-political does not here mean *a*political. Quite the contrary: attempting to render certain issues *in*visible (e.g. drone strikes, surveillance data) is often a prompt for their heightened politicization. But the *anti*-political desire seeks to leverage *in*visibility so as to remove certain issues from politics or prevent them from ever arising. It makes them imperceptible and therefore unspeakable. Thus, politics is about vision (however obscured, however partial), and the anti-political is about *attempting* to make-invisible. Following this, a truly politically sensitive IPT must develop a set of methods, practices, and theories that work to make more 'sensible' practices, such as those described by Sacks.

We can begin developing the necessary tools for appreciating the importance of visibility for IPT by turning to two social theorists – Nathalie Heinich (1991, 2001, 2012) and Andrea Mubi Brighenti (2007, 2008, 2010) – who have both worked to re-theorize practices by placing visibility at the core of their thinking. Heinich (2012), to get us started, discusses how a certain 'visibility-capital' (*capital de visibilité*) defines the status of visibility, generally, and plays a specifically central (and historically evolving) role in the morphologies of politics, economics, art, and beyond. It has, for example, taken on a specific contemporary form in the cultivation of celebrities. Celebrity is about 'being known' and being known because one is seen. For Heinich (2012: 66), the mass reproduction of images and the asymmetries in the distribution of who or what is seen in these images has produced a new social category and, in turn, a new social class or 'elite' who gain positive or negative social capital from their relative social (in)visibility.

Importantly, however, Heinich does not connect the (in)visibility of any individual person to their ontological status as a particular kind of person or, that is, to any 'essence' they may possess or to their social status. Instead, she insists that (in)visibility is linked to their place in a visual economy, where it is their image that matters and that comes to take on a place and standing of its own. As she underlines, 'the "star" is not at the origin of the multiplication of their own images (at their base, they are nothing but a person possessing certain talents), but it is instead the images themselves that create the "star"' (Heinich, 2012: 21). Heinich's words here move towards attributing 'worth' or 'value' to (artistic or otherwise) images and objects in and of themselves (c.f. Gielen, 2005). In this regard, she places great importance on the medium of visibility. For her, aesthetic objects must be attributed a certain form of 'agency', a position much work on images and visibility shares (Mitchell, 2005; Latour, 2010; Austin, 2019; Bertram, 2019). The image itself does 'work' in her account: *it is the images themselves that create the 'star'*. To understand how this occurs, Heinich insists that we grapple seriously with issues of perception and affect as they are mediated through objects and aesthetic practices in ways that exceed reason, logic, intention, or interest, or indeed – and as demonstrated by Hansen (1997, 2000) – actually *produce* reason, logic, intention or interests. Heinich's account is particularly pertinent for international practices as she insists on the place of visibility in power and hierarchies. Her focus on visibility as a form of social capital produced both through social inequalities and also the autonomous affects of particular media and objects of representation thus allows us to make quite direct connections to the enactment of practices, power, and politics in realms central to world politics.

Consider images of violence. The fact that such images tend to provoke shock and/or horror to one degree or another – whatever happens afterwards and however much we may become desensitized – reveals these objects not only to be subject merely to a judgement of taste but also to possess an autonomous aesthetic involving both perception and affect. When we observe images of violence they do things to us, whether we want them to or not. However, such objects are unequally distributed in terms of their visibility-capital vis-à-vis distinctly positioned actors (see the example given later). And it is here the political enters. Many societal hierarchies – those based on race, gender, class, and so on – are generated in an affective economy of visibility, constituted by certain practices of making seen or unseen, and affecting how world political practices are perceived. These practices mobilize 'implicit schemata, patterns and selection criteria, [and] culturally acquired competencies' (Reckwitz, 2014: 26). Thus, an execution by the militant group Daesh is seen very differently from an extra-judicial drone strike by the United States. The politics of this are clear. Regimes of visibility are crucially important to making this politics possible: what we see, and how we see it, matters to how we perceive the world.

If Heinich's focus is on visibility as a social category that places the aesthetics of objects at the centre of practice theorizing, then Brighenti's work is especially useful for attending to some specificities of the deployment of visibility in world political practices and specifying the nature of invisibility capital. Brighenti lays out 'three different types of visibility schemes' that allow us to nuance our understanding: a 'social' type, which is an 'enabling resource, linked to recognition', a 'media-type … whereby subjects are isolated from their original context and projected into a different one endowed with its own logic and rules', and, finally, a 'control-type' that 'transforms visibility into a strategic resource for regulation (as in Foucault's surveillance model) or selectivity and stratification (as in Deleuze's society of control model), or both (as in Haggerty and Ericson's surveillant assemblage)' (Brighenti, 2007: 339). Later, Brighenti (2010: 45–50) systematizes these categories in terms of visibility as *recognition*, *control*, and *spectacle*, and conceptualizes an array of practices of making seen (visible) and unseen (invisible) which together form a *field* of visibility. Importantly, Brighenti distinguishes clearly between the 'visual' and the 'visible' by noting how the visible is always *inter-visible*: it is about the crossing of gazes between the observer and the observed (whether these are human or not) and the ways in which the regime of visibility affecting the former interacts with her perception of the latter in order to alter it, positively or negatively (Brighenti, 2010: 44). Taken together, he provides a nuanced toolkit grasping the ambiguous and variable, relationships between politics, power, and the visible, and converting it into a social-scientific category. As he writes:

The relationship between power and visibility is complex: power does not rest univocally either with visibility or with invisibility. In the moral domain, a fundamental tension between recognition and control has emerged. Both practices are connected to visibility. In other words, visibility is not correlated in any straightforward way to recognition and control, or to any specific moral value. As such, it does not constitute anything inherently liberating, nor, conversely, does it necessarily imply oppression. But, in the end, isn't this open range of possibilities what we expect from a sufficiently general descriptive and interpretive social scientific category? (Brighenti, 2007: 340)

Brighenti's final words here are what makes his work particularly useful for IPT, where a set of complex and intersecting practices are often analysed in their chaotic and contradictory deployments, necessitating theoretical and conceptual flexibility in our analysis. Rarely will a single practice or set of practices univocally support or disrupt power relations in one way or another. Instead, the status of practice tends to be both ambiguous and evolving. This is also the case vis-à-vis the visibility of practice. Thinking in terms of visibility is important then to unpack the densely contradictory 'hinterlands' (Law, 2004), 'mangles' (Pickering, 1995) or 'shadows' (Nordstrom, 2004) of practice in a way that nourishes the depth of analysis occurring within IPT.

The Non-Intentional Aesthetic Politics of Visibility and Perception

A few clarifications are now in order. It is important to stress that, of course, when discussing visibility, the use of phrases such as 'making seen' or 'making unseen' can be read in terms of deliberate agency and intentionality; intimating classical understandings of the use of propaganda to purposefully make things seen or unseen. Such manipulations of visibility obviously abound. So do the preparatory efforts to pave way for them, for example by making 'scenes' (Walters, Chapter 6). However, they are far from all we are referring to. Indeed, it is likely that deliberate manipulations of visibility are only a minor part of sustaining a regime of (in)visibility. Consider, for example, the case of racial minorities and – again – their targeting by police. This form of visibility occurs largely because of biases that are firmly held within the minds of police agents and which correlate visibility based on 'looks' – and the deviation of particular 'looks' from a 'normal' standard – as indicating a propensity to carry out crime. There is no intentionality here in the *form* that visibility takes (skin pigment), but, instead, a regime of visibility exists based on dynamics of power and subordination that have evolved over centuries, produced originally through both intentional and non-intentional means. More than this, certain practices work to reproduce regimes of (in)visibility *indirectly*, peripherally, or collaterally to their primary purpose. When wealthy parents dress their children in more expensive clothes than their less-wealthy peers, the goal of these parents is not necessarily to carry out a practice (fashionable dressing) in order to reproduce racial and class hierarchies that feed into a set of regimes of (in)visibility perpetuating political inequality. This process occurs independently of the goal of the originally enacted practice.

For a fuller example, consider the cases described by medical anthropologists who have studied interactions between local and foreign visiting doctors at relatively impoverished hospitals found mostly outside Europe and North America. In one such hospital in Malawi, Wendland (2012: 113) describes how:

One late afternoon I followed sounds of commotion to a bay in the labour ward where a pregnant woman lay convulsing in a prolonged seizure ... It was hot, and the air felt thick with the smells of blood, bleach, and amniotic fluid ... Handwritten notices taped to the walls reminded staff how to resuscitate newborns, clean equipment, and manage haemorrhages. On the hallway floor, cardboard boxes made makeshift containers for 'sharps' – the blades and needles that pose particular dangers in southern African hospitals ... In one of the labour bays, the midwife stood holding the seizing woman's head to one side, ensuring that she could breathe. Two sweating Dutch medical students flanked her, struggling to draw up medication to stop the seizure. The bay was littered with discarded syringes and medicine vials ... Meanwhile labouring women in the other bays cried out: 'Asista, adokotala, thandizani' [sister, doctor, help me]. One of the students looked up, met my eye, and said quietly, 'Welcome to hell'.

What is visible in this case are seemingly chaotic and 'make-do' practices through which doctors at an impoverished hospital treat patients: with cardboard boxes for needles, handwritten notes, and blood disinfected with bleach but not immediately wiped away. These practices are described as 'hell' by foreign doctors. They are the elements of an image of dysfunction, non-professionalism, and essentially a 'lesser' form of medical care. By contrast, local doctors took notice of the foreign doctors' 'white coats [that] bulged with stethoscopes, penlights, pocket medical guides, and other accoutrements' (Wendland, 2012: 112). Those foreign bodies are adorned with material objects that *suggest* the presence of 'better' practices elsewhere, based on an assumption of greater expertise and the fact of greater material capacity: 'the wretchedness of clinical practice in Malawi depended on a contrast with medicine ... elsewhere' (Wendland, 2012: 112).

At the same time, many of the practices that become visible in this example, which seem to be dirty and inadequate, can be 'seen' in quite a different light as representing a remarkable capacity to 'make do' and keep saving lives without the prosthetic aids of advanced technologies. An ability to make do, moreover, that foreign doctors often lacked: visiting doctors 'could rarely feel an enlarged spleen with their hands or confirm profound anemia without a hematocrit by examining a patient's nail beds and mucous membranes. Accustomed to following protocols in which one diagnostic or therapeutic step led to the next, visitors had little capacity to improvise when the required materials were not available'. (Wendland, 2012: 114) The comparative advantage of the practices being carried out by local doctors is made *in*visible through a regime that privileges signs of material cleanliness and abundance (white coats, technologies, etc.) as signals of professionalism. Importantly, however, the emergence of this way of seeing things is not deliberate. Many of the practices that create the impression of 'danger' or 'hell' are entirely necessary and quite effective in this context but they produce aesthetic and affective responses. Likewise, few suggest that doctors in more wealthy states should do away with their advanced medical tools. These are medical practices that those doctors in Malawi themselves would desire. But placed in contrast with their own practices they intensify the perception of the 'wretchedness of clinical practice in Malawi' nonetheless.

This example also captures a second key element of our discussion: the aesthetic aspects of regimes of visibility. The Dutch doctor's remark – 'Welcome to hell' – represents a visceral response to an environment in which dirt and blood pervade. If we were to take a snapshot of this hospital, then the reader would likely feel much the same. We all react to what is visible and sensible through the aesthetic qualities of what is perceived, with aesthetics referring here – and hereafter – to a broad conception of the judgements of sentiments and taste that are evoked whenever we perceive something (Austin, 2019). Necessarily, we are also thus concerned here with thinking visibility in terms of a *political* aesthetics, 'by connecting an idea of ... [the aesthetic] with a cultural diagnosis of, and political commitment to, the historical situation of human practices' (Garcia, 2014: 274). As seen earlier, regimes of visibility alter the affective quality of the aesthetics of particular scenes quite notably. For foreign doctors, this 'hell' could be contrasted to a cleaner, neater, more efficient, and more attractive foreign alternative, while local doctors saw *beyond* this also to the unique efficacy of their own practices of making do. In one case, the aesthetics of the scene led to an overlooking of what else could be seen there and in the other not because – to be sure – regimes of visibility are translated, altered, and adapted based on the social, political, and corporeal positionality of the observer.

Nonetheless, it is worth noting that the aesthetic dimension of visibility does go beyond this: the point here is *not* at all that local doctors in the case cited are not dissatisfied and themselves even disturbed by what they objectively 'see' in their hospital. They are affected by the 'hell' of medical treatment in Malawi to the same – most probably greater – extent as their foreign colleagues, and they desire – as such – the same resources as those colleagues. The aesthetics of visibility, in this sense, cannot be argued with. It may therefore stymie the efforts of certain disenfranchised groups to get their Others to look beyond what they see at first glance and gain a broader optic on the scenes they are coming to encounter. A fundamental tension exists, therefore, in which practitioners or observers have an inherent capacity to 'look at things differently' (i.e. interpret practice differently) but are caught nonetheless in webs of affect, mediated through visibility, that render this process difficult or even undesirable. There is no easy resolution to this tension. Nonetheless, the effects of regimes of (in)visibility must – first and foremost – be considered politically. Once we sensitize ourselves to how our impressions of world political practice are mediated through visibility, aesthetics, and affect, we gain the capacity to think politics differently as well as of reflecting more realistically on the import of sensual perceptions for political agency. The result is that it becomes possible to see a consideration of visibility as holding positive normative capacities, where awareness of its effects can lead to political change at both individual and institutional levels.

As the example given here demonstrates, the concept of visibility can serve a positive (political) role for IPT. Considering visibility forces us to acknowledge how the world becomes 'multiple' in its apprehension in often unintended ways. Practices of making (in)visible, in short, always fashion how other practices are perceived. Employing visibility in our analyses of international practices thus works as a mode of sensitization provoking an awareness of what was taken for granted, went unsaid, and passed unseen in world politics. More than this, we have seen how the concept forces us to acknowledge the place of aesthetics and affect in the political practices we observe and such an acknowledgement will often call radically into question assumptions of the 'reasoned' or 'rational' nature of practices by articulating a less scholastic view of world political practices and therefore perhaps also a more strongly objective one (Crone, 2014; Leander, 2017; Austin, 2020a).

One of the attractions of practice approaches is that they lead us away from the 'hyperintellectualization' of scholars who commit the fallacy of assuming that *their* categories and forms of reasoning are shared by and guide the observed (Reckwitz, 2002: 258). In contrast, the aesthetic and affective dimensions of practice matter actually as much for the classical realms of world politics: diplomacy, military cooperation, international organizations, global governance, European integration, international law, and so on, as it does for the realm of the political world outside the borders of these classical realms and in practices of theorizing. Theorists, statesmen, people, and things are engaged in often non-intentionally producing an aesthetic politics of visibility. Indeed, we want to stress the import of recognizing this fundamental 'symmetry' of practices in IPT and thus of extending the study of practices generally, as well as tending to practices of seeing and overlooking also to more marginalized and disenfranchised actants, whether they are humans such as torturers and terrorists, activists, artists, doctors, and shamans, or things such as digital infrastructures, border fences, and facial recognition software. And while shifting our vision in these ways will often be deeply uncomfortable, it is of fundamental political import. It will help us see the fissures and fractures from which potentials for political change may arise (Austin, 2017b; Leander, 2017).

Seeing and Overlooking Practices of Torture

In order to flesh out this discussion, we now draw on an extended example of the importance of visibility for IPT. To begin, we would like to ask the reader to consider Figures 10.2, 10.3, and 10.4. Each of these depicts the process by which prisoners were 'rendered' from a point of capture to a

Figure 10.2 Post-9/11 rendition of captured prisoners by the United States from Afghanistan to Guantanamo Bay

Figure 10.3 Post-9/11 rendition of captured prisoners by the United States from Afghanistan to Guantanamo Bay

detention facility, where they were typically tortured, by either the United States (post-2001) or the Syrian state (post-2011). You may already be familiar with Figures 10.2 and 10.3, which show the early stages of the (extraordinary) rendition of prisoners from Afghanistan that began in 2002. Prisoners are bound to the floor by mesh cables, wear heavy-duty earmuffs, and in other pictures are seen to be masked with surgical-looking equipment such that they can neither see nor hear. They are then hooded. The goal is total sensory deprivation. An American flag is hung in the background. Soldiers can be seen either standing in the foreground, not interacting with the prisoners, or sitting, with their legs crossed over each other. These men seem – more than anything – quite relaxed with what is going on: nonchalant, calm, unwinding; taking it easy.

Figure 10.4 will be unfamiliar and is quite hard to make out: pixelated lumps and colours splotched with blackness. It comes from a video filmed in Syria, the content being clearer when watched. The lumps making up the picture are bodies, bent over and bowed forward. Their hands are tied behind their backs and their faces are blindfolded. But this means of achieving the state of being blindfolded is entirely improvised: the T-shirt of each prisoner is pulled forward above their eyes. If this is unclear,

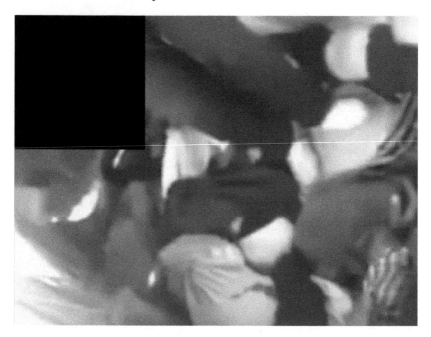

Figure 10.4 Post-2011 'rendition' of prisoners by the Syrian Arab
Republic during the Syrian civil war

try it. If you are wearing one, pull your T-shirt upwards from its seam
at your waist and over your head. You will see that you *can* still see. The
fabric stretches out and becomes porous. It does not possess the capacity
to block sight entirely. Hence, prisoners must also bow down. If you are
wearing a buttoned shirt then this procedure will not work: the buttons
will either not hold or will leave gaps in your vision. In this case, the video
demonstrates an alternative solution: the crafting of a blindfold from a
piece of cloth, probably torn from your shirt itself. In either case, the per-
meable properties of cloth like this means that prisoners need to remain
bowed to be truly blindfolded. Prisoners can still hear, however: there
are no earmuffs in these images. Instead, a soldier can be seen traversing
over the backs of the tightly squeezed together prisoners and whipping
them to enforce their bowed position and prevent them from talking to
each other. He shouts and screams and falls as the aircraft moves from
side to side. This soldier does not seem at all relaxed.

These images depict military practitioners carrying out what seems a
quite different set of activities. In one there is beating and whipping, and
in the other there is mere infrastructure: a process of transporting prisoners. In one set of images, we see brutal human practices and in the other

seated soldiers watching numbly as their 'cargo' is transported from site to site. That is what we can *see*. Nonetheless, many of their *possible* 'intervisibilities' with ourselves as viewers and wider publics, or a host of even more invisible actants, are often overlooked (Brighenti, 2007: 326). When we describe the images, as we have here, we do not express exactly what we see or could be seeing. A certain regime or field of visibility and our position and relation to this regime and field will fashion the tone and tenor of each description and the seeing it renders. So will our sense of aesthetics and our affective sensibilities that are deeply embedded within our corporeality as acting human subjects. These fields and the aesthetic and affective sensibilities associated with them may be somehow ingrained in human practice at its broadest level (Garcia, 2014; Austin, 2017a).

Whether or not they are, the (in)visibilities they engender are ultimately indeterminate. They are modulated also by the personal history, experiences, and sensibilities of each observer. The consequent ambiguous, non-intentional, and aesthetic practices of seeing and overlooking will appear self-evident to us all and are therefore unlikely to provoke much reflection. For the same reason, their enactment cannot be better discerned from an observing individual sitting outside this practice than from someone inside it. Insider informants will not be telling stories about them or translating vernacular visibility to the kinds of visibility outside observers may be more accustomed to. Precisely because of this resistance to observation, regimes of (in)visibility are prone to be re-enacted and reproduced. Precisely for this reason, it matters that IPT attends to them more carefully.

The regimes of (in)visibility through which we understand these images are all the more likely to be reproduced in our practices of seeing and observing because they are closely intertwined not only with 'seeing' but also 'sensing' more broadly. As Laura Marks (2004) argues, it is important to recognize that images are haptic rather than just optic. The separation between the image and the observer that an optic understanding of images rests on breaks down if one begins to think of images as 'grabbing' the observer and in turn being 'grabbed' by the observing gaze. On this account images are also sensuous: you can feel them physically, touch them, smell them. Regimes of (in)visibility are therefore reproduced not only through vision but also through the broader 'bodily unconscious' of us all, the core of our experiential engagement with the world, the point where 'the eye and the body of the observer merge, and in doing so merge with what they observe' (Taussig, 2009: 86).

What, then, are the regimes of (in)visibility these two sets of images are likely to re-enact and reproduce? In what ways are most people, including ourselves, likely to look at them? First, although the practices these images hint at – torture and killing – are subject to great controversy in both cases, we would not expect to find any symmetry in their descriptions; neither within each set of images nor between the two sets but, rather, the re-enactment of dominant points of view. The practices carried out by the United States in the first set of images have variously been defended as justified by the threats of global terror or alternatively been critically related back to a critique of the discourse of sovereign exceptionalism during 'states of emergency' leading to the systemic production of bare life and/or more simply to a condemnation of the leaders of the Bush regime and/or the CIA as having made possible or 'ordered' rendition. In either case, this renders the 'cogs in the machine' – the relaxed-looking soldiers – relatively invisible as violence workers. They are, after all, transporting men for torture. They are, however, visible as professionals without qualifiers. They do not beat or whip. They are simply 'carrying out their duty' while following all the relevant rules and regulations. Inversely, the bodies of the men being transported are transformed beyond seeing into monstrous cyborgs. They are wrapped in hoods and earmuffs. Things to be shunned and feared. Things it's most comfortable not to look at.

In the case of the second set of images, our eyes immediately focus upon the man who (in the video) is jumping and whipping bodies. This figure becomes a perpetrator of war crimes entangled with the leadership of the Syrian state, which is considered, in the end, a 'pro-torture' regime in and of itself, leading to a corruption of all limits of moral restraint. He is not a professional. He is not even a violence worker: he is a criminal seen in his criminality. By contrast, we can see more of the men he is harming: while they appear as lumps, we can still 'see' their screams and moans, and the patterns on their T-shirts: reflective of their personalities or their interests or their favourite football team. We see the tortured as humans, for the moment at least, and the torturer as inhuman: a precise inversion of the first image. Here, the affective power of visibility is brought to bear upon the viewer. And while much of this has to do with the biases and prejudices of world politics against the non-Euro-American world, it is important to recall that when white soldiers come to torture brown bodies in a closer manner to that being depicted in Figure 10.3, the temptation of any Euro-American observer is typically to sever direct links between these figures and their own identity, or that of the nation-state they belonged to. For example, for many, the perpetrators in Abu Ghraib were aberrant figures, non-reflective of the values of the democratic United States. These figures risked puncturing the dominant regime of visibility presenting the 'Civilized West' in one way and the 'Barbaric Arabs/Muslims' in another.

Tending to (in)visibility can help us look at these images differently and reflect on some of their usually overlooked aspects. For example, it may help us draw attention to the socio-material *agencements* that 'French Pragmatists' have made central to practice theoretical toolkits. It may help us see the practical work being undertaken by the mundane 'missing masses' of materiality (Bénatouïl, 1999; Baert and Da Silva, 2010; Bueger and Gadinger, 2015). In Figures 10.2 and 10.3, much of the 'work' undertaken to restrain and ensure the sensory deprivation of the prisoners is achieved by material objects: hoods, cables, earmuffs, and shackles. These objects allow the soldiers to rest and relax on the plane. Their work in ensuring sensory deprivation is the result of decades of 'congealed labour' carried out by the United States, and incorporating scientists, psychologists, and doctors, to discover the most 'effective' way to carry out these practices (McCoy, 2012; Austin, 2016). The political significance of this becomes clear, however, when we apply the same analysis to Figure 10.4, and allow it to reinstate a form of symmetry. Here, the Syrian soldier is attempting to enforce precisely the same practice as his American colleague: sensory deprivation by removing sight and sound from the prisoners transported. But he lacks the 'congealed labour' gifted to these latter violence workers and so must rely on improvised material props as well as be constantly vigilant that the prisoners do not raise their backs: hence the shouting and beating of the prisoners. This is why he is not relaxed, but also why his involvement in rendition would likely be 'judged' more seriously when made visible than that of his American counterparts: it is *he* who is acting to disappear these men, unlike those American soldiers who watch passively as one set of missing masses go about creating another. Nonetheless, stripped of the regimes of (in-)visibility through which they are typically observed and normatively or politically evaluated, the practices depicted in each of these videos are identical.

There are two issues here. First, the difficulty of perceiving the role of those material 'missing masses' in enabling and structuring the visibility of practice. A difficulty – simply – of 'seeing' what is happening. Second, the ways in which we as viewers and the men on screen as actors are distinctly affectively proximate or distant from the reassuringly regulated, legal, and 'clean' system of violence depicted in Figure 10.2. Dramatics of the case aside, not much is different here from our earlier discussion of hospitals. But consider nonetheless Edmund Clark and Crofton Black's (2016) reflections on their own attempts to put together the story of rendition through photographs, redacted documents, and legal documents:

In piecing together evidence of rendition, our account includes *locations where nothing happened and people who never existed.* A flight crew, enjoying a rest and recuperation stop in Palma de Mallorca, travelled under *false names with no addresses* other than anonymous PO boxes. A plane filed a flight plan for Helsinki but *never arrived there,* going instead to Lithuania, then recorded its onward destination as Portugal while travelling to Cairo. A company registered in Panama and Washington DC gave power of attorney to a man whose address turned out to be a student dormitory where *no one of that name was known...* [emphasis added]

As they note, all these little misdirections are 'masks, obscuring by design and revealing by accident' (Clark and Black, 2016). Hiding behind these masks not only lay a torture regime that was arguably as 'brutal' as that ongoing in Syria today – albeit at a smaller scale – but also much 'cleaner' in its visibilities: luxury jets, holding companies, redacted text, and relaxed soldiers. The power to work with visibility in these ways – to engage successfully in the 'management of gazes' (Brighenti, 2010: 51) – is intimately related to our ability to perceive what practices are, how they emerge, and what they mean. This is related to William Walters' description in Chapter 6 of practices of secrecy, and how they are implicated in regimes of (in)visibility, but it also goes further. Our gazes are managed not only by active, intentional efforts to make-invisible, but also by material objects, those missing masses, that we find very difficult to recognize as being crucial to the enactment of practices, and perhaps most importantly by the affective and aesthetic qualities of the field and regimes of visibility shaping our engagement with images of violence. Ultimately, what becomes clear in examples like this is the import of tending to (in)visibility. It stands at the heart of our ability to observe and theorize practices and hence also of our ability to engage them politically.

Contesting and Shifting Focal Points in Practice Theorizing

To conclude, we can now enunciate two key points that are always interconnected when considering visibility. First, there exist *practices of making seen and making unseen which together form a regime of (in-)visibility.* These practices are materially embedded, technologically mediated, and – today – often digitally and algorithmically structured. They work through affect and emotion as much as through language and reflection. (In)visibility as a mode of analysis is thus distinct from 'discourse'. Of course, both speak to conditions of enunciation within a social sphere. But visibility is distinct in ways in which it does not privilege the ideational or the semiotic but integrates materiality, affect, aesthetics, circulation, and beyond. Second, these practices of making seen or unseen form regimes that predefine the focal points of any (academic/scientific or otherwise) mode of observation or analysis. As a result, and for IPT specifically, the study of any other set of practices is filtered through these regimes of visibility, and hence *practices of visibility shape the way we see all practices*. All practices – torture and terrorism, diplomacy and negotiation, kissing and sex, bombing and shooting, writing and reading – are made (in)visible by these ontologically prior practices of making seen and unseen. These practices are, in one sense, ontologically prior to any other practice: they always structure how we see or participate in any other practice. In doing so, regimes of (in)visibility are fundamentally about power, politics, and order. Indeed, appreciating this fact allows us to suggest that many world political hierarchies are produced by practices of making seen and unseen and that IPT therefore needs to be far more attentive to them, lest it contribute to conservatively reproducing the status quo (Austin, 2017b). Combining the ontological sensibilities of IPT with a sensitizing understanding of visibility opens up the possibility of politicizing practice theorizing more thoroughly than has previously been achieved.

This politicization takes place across the five fault lines fracturing IPT according to Alena Drieschova and Christian Bueger in Chapter 1. Enacting ambiguous evolving regimes of (in)visibility is at the same time stabilizing existing power-relations *and* an opportunity for counter-practices transforming them. Similarly, on the one hand regimes of (in)visibility are materially inscribed, embodied, reflecting 'unintentional aesthetic' sensemaking. On the other, they form part of consciousness and rationality. The 'strategies' of the American and Syrian torturers we describe are material *and* conscious. Third, and still along similar lines, in our account the everyday and the aggregate are connected. The interactions we describe between local and visiting doctors in the Malawi hospital are both mundane quotidian interactions *and* enactments of different aggregate regimes of (in)visibility and of the visceral reactions associated with them. Fourth, in our discussion power and communities are not opposed to each other. Rather, the regimes of (in)visibility we discuss are core to upholding both power *and* communities, where power is crucial in the making of communities and communities in the making of power. Along these lines, the images of white torturers in Abu Ghraib disturbed both community and power by 'puncturing' the regime of (in)visibility upholding the distinction between the Civilized West and the Barbaric Muslims and the order within each community. Fifth and finally, we conceive of practice theory as being about practice *and* theory. We have provided an argument that is both about regimes of (in)visibility (theory) and about the doings of US/Syrian tortures and of foreign and local doctors in Malawian hospitals (practice). More generally, the kind of practice theorizing we discuss flattens the distinction between theory and practice, treating theorizing as a specific kind of practice. As we point out, also theorizing is contextual, embodied, affective, aesthetic, and messy in its enactment of regimes of (in)visibility and inescapably dirty as it enacts the politics associated with them.

Beyond that capacity to politicize IPT in a manner transgressing the binaries that keep haunting theoretical work in IR and beyond, thinking the study of practice through the lens of (in)visibility also expands our awareness of the repertoire of practices relevant to practice thinking by 'opening up' previously black-boxed sets of practices concerned with questions of power, its construction, and its projection. Take, for instance, the concept of *soft power*. Generally, this refers to the capacity to gain influence not through blunt power-projection but via the capacity to be 'attractive' to potential allies or adversaries. As Nye argues in his work on this subject, it is the 'attractiveness of a country's culture', the 'friendly and attractive' nature of its 'policing', its dedication to 'attractive causes such as economic aid or peacemaking' or 'attractive' ideology that ensures influence (Nye, 2004: X, 5, 9, 10, 6). In the end: 'soft power is attractive power' (Nye, 2004: 6). Notably, at no point does Nye suggest what actually makes something attractive per se. Seen through the lens of visibility, however, it becomes clear that whatever is deemed globally 'attractive' is not seen as such solely due to a reasoned or logical debate over contents (e.g. a sober look at the advantages of democratic institutions). Instead, attractiveness is fashioned by regimes of (in)visibility in which aesthetic and affective qualities are central. Cultivating such an attractive aesthetics requires a carefully constructed and contingently arrived at regime of (in)visibility that draws focus to that which attracts and distracts from that which does not. Soft power, in this sense, is nothing but the expression of a specific regime of visibility, and a capacity to manipulate it; to make seen and unseen and to shift the quality of the seeing.

Examples like these demonstrate why (in)visibility is something that the state and other centres of power attempt to control to such a high degree. Indeed, and to come to a conclusion, consider Rancière's (1998: 28) reflection on the 'visibility and invisibility of repression' in reference to the 1961 massacre in Paris by police of peaceful Algerian and French-Algerian demonstrators. Rancière notes how the 'police cleared the public space and, thanks to a news blackout, made its own operations invisible':

For us, this meant that something had been done in our country and in our name, and that it was taken away from us ... At the time, it was impossible even to count the victims. A phrase used by Sartre in his preface to *Les Damnes de la terre* helps us to understand, *a contrario*, the meaning of that twofold disappearance: '*The blinding sun of torture* has now reached its zenith, and it is lighting up the whole country'. Now, the truth is that *this blinding sun never lit up anything.* Marked and tortured bodies do not light up anything. We know that now, now that images from Bosnia, Rwanda and elsewhere show us much more than we were shown in those days (Rancière, 1998: 28).

What we perceive in the world is always controlled, both directly and indirectly, intentionally and non-intentionally, through practices of making seen and unseen, filtered through the affective, aesthetic, and material. For France to retain its image as a democratic and – indeed – 'enlightened' state required it blot out the 'blinding sun' of its torture that Sartre hoped would revolutionize society. The United States, we have seen, has sought much the same in its similar machinations. And the same battle is occurring in the summer of 2020. In this regard, the abstraction of the 'police' as a core symbol of state power should never be taken to be represented 'primarily [as] a strong-arm repressive force' but, rather, as a 'form of intervention which prescribes what can be seen and what cannot be seen' (Rancière, 1998: 28). And it is this power that practice theory must reckon with.

Part IV

Conclusion: The Future
of Practice Theorizing

11 Practices and a 'Theory' of Action? Some Conceptual Issues Concerning Ends, Reasons and Happiness

Friedrich Kratochwil

Introduction

This contribution examines several important philosophical and episte-mological issues raised by the practice turn in IR. It provides some crite-ria for appraising its heuristic promise as well as the potential conceptual pitfalls that such a reorientation of theorizing would entail. Given the experience of various previous turns and the often-disappointing discrepancy between expressed hopes and actual results, such a critical assessment is necessary. Only in this way can we hope to avoid the 'fla-vour of the month' syndrome, familiar in much of the field's theorizing, which often limits itself to recasting old problems in a new terminology without providing significant new insights.

To that extent I see my task here not so much in contributing to the interesting conversation among various scholars who have turned from largely structural concerns with systems and codes to the actual way in which decision-makers and new actors try to influence both the political agenda and the making of policy choices. Rather I try to open up what Wendt (2001) once called the *contrast space* to the dominant rationalist and functionalist explanations concerning the constitu-tion and reproduction of the social world. In other words, I attempt to create a new space for thinking about action by subjecting on the one hand the rational choice paradigm as well as the *technique* para-digm (*techne*) derived from the process of producing an object relying on a certain skill or expertise to criticism. On the other hand, I also try to show the shortcomings of the functionalist logic derived from the part/whole distinction in systems theory, and of a teleological mode of thinking about *the end of history*. That such an attempt goes far beyond the normal questions of data, methodology or even of 'theory-building' will become obvious when I discuss issues of acting, which bear little resemblance to choices under uncertainty, the felicific calculus or of retrodicting from a supposedly known *telos* of humanity. I also claim that different from theoretical propositions whose criteria of assessment is 'truth' – established by tests and truth conditions – practical choices need a different, axiological framework, in which the validity of norms and norm application matter. Pressing them into the framework of efficient causes leaves the issue of judgement and of the interaction between the 'is and the ought' unattended.

Finally, I have to admit my scepticism concerning the common tendency to borrow certain concepts from other fields in the hope to find the theoretical hammer to nail everything down, because 'truth' silences every opposition. Such a practice is particularly pernicious for investigations of the social world, which is not natural (mind independent) but artificial, built largely of the concepts that mediate our interactions. For me this search for a view from nowhere, rather than from within this world – as if we were God, or as if philosophers had become the mouthpiece of universal reason – expresses a soteriological longing, not a critical stance.

This recognition has important implications not only for social science but also for philosophy, since it can no longer claim to preside over the attribution of an ultimate warrant on the basis of understanding what truly 'is', or what can be known in accordance with the criteria of universal reason. Rather, philosophy must take its cues from the actions and events of our social and historically contingent world and, subject them to scrutiny. As Hume (1875) once put it, 'true philosophy' must contribute to our world-making by examining the 'commerce and conversations' of actual historical people and societies, instead of relying on abstract or idealized assumptions.

In short, such a reorientation requires a fundamental shift in thinking rather than simply positing a new formal object, focusing now on practices, as opposed to power or systems. Rather this shift calls into question some of our most basic assumptions about the world and how we know it, dispelling the myth that this occurs through the discovery of incontrovertible foundations or through clear and distinct ideas and a particular method, as the epistemological tradition suggested. It is also not surprising that a new sensibility for conceptual issues and a wariness of 'false friends' such as 'habits' and 're-actions' becomes decisive when we think about praxis and engage in analogous reasoning or metaphorical extensions which buttress our assertions.[1]

These initial remarks provide an outline of the argumentative steps of this chapter. In the second section I begin with a brief sketch of some

---

[1] The term 'false friends' originated in applied linguistics to make language learners aware that borrowing words even within the same language family can misfire. 'Burro' in Spanish, for example, does not mean 'butter' as it does in Italian (or the quite similar 'beurre' in French), but 'donkey'.

conceptual issues concerning theory-building in IR and the social sciences in general. The central puzzle that concerns me is that despite considerable controversies regarding particular theories and their episte-mologies, the notion that a good theory is the 'answer' to our practical problems still remains widely accepted. This is surprising since the dis-tinctive nature of the realm of praxis was already recognized in antiquity, suggesting that 'acting' cannot be subject to theoretical criteria. This critique was later reiterated in controversies concerning explaining and understanding, and in the more fundamental criticisms of the American pragmatists. But, except in the field of law, this critique was never able to break the allure of 'theory'. Even Kant, who wrote two further *Critiques* after the first one, and who suggested in the last that different domains require different modes of analysis (Kant, 1998), was still convinced that understanding of practice meant having a 'good theory' (Kant, 1991).

Things are even worse when we consider that 'ideal theory' has of late colonized the old prudential domains of law and ethics, as witnessed in the law and economics movement, as well as the transcendental turn, to which even 'pragmatics' were subjected. Here the early Habermas[2] and Rawls' construction of an 'ideal theory' (Rawls, 1971) – developed behind the veil of ignorance in the 'original position' – are examples. My aim in this section is to demonstrate that the arguments in favour of theory misunderstand the nature of practical judgements. The lat-ter does not represent a logical subsumption under a major premise or an application of abstract principles to a factual pattern, but consists instead of the mutual constitution of facts and principles so that both the major and minor premise must buttress the final judgement. I develop this argument further through a closer reading of Kant's problem of 'stupidity', which suggests that practical judgements cannot be reduced to logical subsumptions since it neglects the role played by judgement. Judgement is an independent capacity that is in a way innate, but that must be cultivated through experience and imagination.

In order to get a preliminary overview of the different ways in which we act, I examine in the third section our 'doings in the world'. I dis-tinguish re-actions from actions and show the similarities that pertain between two types of actions that aim at the production of objects, but which can be distinguished by the products they bring into existence:

---

[2] Although the term 'transcendental pragmatics' was coined by Karl Otto Appel, the early Habermas was close to this way of thinking (see, for example, Habermas, 1968), before he changed his framework after his encounter with speech act theory in the 1970s, which finally resulted in the *Theory of Communicative Action*. This latter work nevertheless retains in its criteria for an 'ideal speech situation' the notion of the pos-sibility of ultimate epistemic justifications for practical matters.

objects brought about by technical know-how (*techne*), or works of art (*poiesis*), such as poetry and drama. Needless to say, certain works such as sculptures or plays cut across these distinctions. Finally, there is also 'acting' in a practical sense (praxis). Praxis takes place in time and has a performative element in the sense that choice concerns an intended end, but seldom concerns only the selection of the means to a given goal, as the modern conception rational action suggests.

To create scope for the development of a more adequate analysis of action (the fourth section), I identify 12 significant differences that arise from acting in time and in an open horizon, where no 'final end' is in sight – even though actors' choices do not occur without purposes – and the situations are not given, but evolve from the choices of actors. I claim that any analysis of practical choices must be attentive to these differences, separating praxis from theory.

This sets the stage for an examination of the supposed final end of all action, to which the classical tradition, and utilitarian action theories, have drawn attention, and for which 'happiness' provides a bridge between classical and modern theories of action. I argue, however, that this bridge is a false friend and should be resisted, since utilitarian action theories are blind to the time-dimension of actions and attempt to circumvent the difficulties that arise when we must choose not only strategies for given ends, but have to select among competing goals. In this context I also show that the final goal, as construed in the narrative of a fulfilled life (cf. Aristotle), is entirely different from the systemic or instrumental reasoning that follows from the final end in utilitarianism or from prophesies relying on a known *telos* of humanity.

In lieu of a summary I provide in the last section some further thoughts on doing research concerning practical matters. When the allure of a theory providing the answers to our dilemmas of choosing has been disappointed and we cannot limit ourselves to routines, or the necessary know-how of making things, then we have to face that praxis also entails existential choices and the responsibilities coming with them.

Taking Stock

The status of theories in IR has been contested, as the history of the field can be told as a succession of theories. There were the initial misgivings regarding the inter-war attempts to subject international political life to new institutions, and its critique concerned the issue whether power and purpose were mystified by liberal ideology, which had made 'peace' (and with it the status quo) the supreme goal of international politics.[3] While this theme of realist criticism remained, things changed dramatically after the Second World War, when IR largely became part of political science and increasingly methodological issues attained priority.[4] Particularly in the United States, methodological rigour – supposedly leading to scientific predictions and explanations – was extolled, only to be challenged by Hedley Bull's plea for a 'classical approach', instigating the Second Debate (Bull, 1966). A period of relative calm followed, before the third (and perhaps fourth) debate occurred, challenging the positivist interpretation of scientific progress. Thomas Kuhn's innovation of distinguishing between normal und revolutionary science raised the issue of commensurability between different theories, and the inter-paradigm debate disturbed the neat picture of 'scientific progress' as a near automatic process of conjecture and refutation. This controversy provided the background for the fourth debate to flourish, despite being regarded by its originator, Yosef Lapid, as the third debate.[5]

In this way the recent 'turn to practice' could represent the newest attempt to revisit some issues, which pragmatists, constructivists and post-modernists have tried to articulate before. But the new controversy harks back not only to earlier epistemological issues concerning particular 'theories' – pitting explanations against understanding – but also to the more general question of what a theory 'is for' (in the sense of both Cox's and Brown's questions) in the social realm. While those questions are obviously important, they strangely circumvent the question – which should be obvious for pragmatists – of why we believe that it has to be a *theory* which provides the answer to our quest. Instead – after some initial bows to the pragmatists – one is apparently ready to engage with theorizing as usual, by passing over the critical potential for creating new insights that a focus on praxis promises. Here the issue of judgement and of learning from experience by participation in civil life come to mind, as Hume suggested. Thus, the space of practical choice is not limited to ends–means rationality or unchangeable laws but has as a defining dimension that it takes place in *historical time* and not only a space/time continuum. It presupposes first that one has identified satisfactorily a situation requiring a decision – and here collective and transgenerational decisions cannot be reduced to individual action – and second that the relevant facts of the matter are hardly all given, since their relevance shifts in the light of (third) a project.

[3] See, for example, Carr (1964).
[4] With the notable exception of the United Kingdom, for a discussion of the differences between different (national) schools of IR in Europe see Friedrichs (2004) and Dunne (1998).
[5] Lapid did not count the inter-paradigm debate in his typology (Lapid, 1989).

But if we accept this three-cornered problem when analysing practical choices, it is clear that the subsumption model of theory, bringing the facts under either a law or a norm or principle, is woefully inadequate. This nomological explanation scheme, commonly identified with theory, marks also a key difference between logical positivism, interested in (objectivist) explaining by relying on efficient causality, and those understandings – taking the Weberian subjectivist point of view – where norms and values provide the reasons for action. The latter function differently from causes in that they neither compel an action, nor do they lose their validity by being refuted in a particular case. These two problems raise tricky issues for explanations of actions. It therefore seems strange that even normative thinking has been invaded by the theoretical ideal, in that in 'ideal theory' a law-like first premise – even if conceived analogously as a normative principle – is supposed to do most of the work in telling us why an action was or has to be undertaken.

However, embracing this theoretical ideal is problematic. First, we soon realize that it is not so much the clarification of the principles contained in the first premise but rather the dilemmas that arise when fact-patterns can be brought under different, competing principles, which are the real challenges. To cite an example from international law: is the Israeli building of a wall in Palestinian territory an issue of principles of general international law, of the laws of war, of humanitarian law or of general human rights (ICJ, 2004)? This is by no means an exceptional situation confined to the field of international law, as any real life case proves. Similarly, the Kantian distinction between higher order principles, characterized by superior deontic force imposing duties on actors and simple (positive) rules for conduct, provides no solution to the issue of conflicting duties, as Kant's own example of the absolute duty to tell the truth demonstrates.[6]

This leads to a further problem: if principles and facts do interact, facts are as important for choosing the right principle, as principles and norms are for selecting the relevant facts. This interaction effect appears circular, so that the trick of good judgement consists in solving the hermeneutic problem of fitting both facts and norms (principles) together. Such a procedure prevents our reasoning from becoming

---

[6] Kant illustrates this point by participating in a debate surrounding a problem posed by Constant. Do I have to tell a stranger who is knocking on my door whether or not I hide a friend who has asked for shelter in my house since he is being pursued by someone who obviously wants to harm him? Kant thinks we have a duty to tell the truth, although by accepting the request of the friend and providing him with shelter, we also make (an implicit) promise to protect him from harm.

logically vicious or committing acts of 'stupidity' – as Kant would have it – by simply applying a general principle to a fact-pattern without further ado. Thus if a judge applied the rule of 'no swimming in the basin' to a man who saved the life of a drowning child, he would act stupidly in this Kantian sense. The *Dummheit* (stupidity), which Kant wistfully describes as a 'flaw, which cannot be cured',[7] has nothing to do with an inability to reason logically, since it is quite common among professionals, even academics, as he points out. Furthermore, this is not an issue of the vagueness of norms since even clearly descriptive concepts (Fuller, 1958; Hart, 1958) create similar problems: no one would doubt that an ambulance or fire-truck should be entitled to enter a park in order to attend to a victim of a heart attack or put out a fire, even if the prohibition 'No vehicles in the park' is posted everywhere. Whether a motor-driven skateboard is a 'vehicle' is an even trickier question.

In short, the interaction of facts with norms (Habermas, 1993) requires the interdependent capacities of imagination and experience to solve such complexities. Simple logical prowess will not suffice, as Hume has pointed out (Livingstone, 1984), and both capacities – experience and imagination – are acquired and exercised through the participation in the practices of social and public life rather than through demonstration or logic. Functioning in the social world has more to do with both knowing how than knowing what, and with performing certain actions competently rather than with explaining them by means of a causal scheme. After all, people learning to ride a bicycle are not helped by knowing that they have to solve a couple of simultaneous equations.

We must, however, be careful also to avoid the opposite error: assuming that habit and tacit knowledge are the keys to an adequate understanding of action *tout court*. Here the often-idiosyncratic use of the philosophical writings of Wittgenstein, Polanyi (1958) and Oakeshott (1962, 1975) might be misleading, if stripped of context. Wittgenstein's (1953) examples in the *Philosophical Investigations,* are taken largely from mathematics and drills, but they are hardly apt for illuminating the complexities of interactions in non-routine (crisis) situations. Here the notion of knowing how to proceed in new situations, instead of just replicating a familiar action sequence, stands in obvious tension with the drill example.

Most importantly for analysing practical choices is the recognition that language is clearly not a representation that mirrors an already existing world. Instead, it is productive of the social world. Similarly mistaken is to conceive of language in terms of individual utterances

---

[7] Kant, *Kritik der Reinen Vernunft* A 134–35; B 173–74.

(and limit oneself to content analysis owing to the bias of methodological individualism), instead of paying attention to the ways in which meaning is created and communicated (syntactic, semiotic, pragmatic, conceptual), as exemplified by ordinary language analysis, by Searle's brand of institutionalism[8], by speech acts (Searle, 1980) or by Grice's inferential pragmatics governing conversations (implicature) (Rolf, 2013). Finally, finding in practices the 'gluon' of society (Adler and Pouliot, 2011b) is possible only if we buy the analogy underlying the old unity of science dream: that understanding the social world must follow the same path as discovering the physical world. Strangely, this notion of 'science'[9] is still popular, despite particle physics having debunked the idea of a 'given world', in which we only need to lift the veil to see what there is (Zeilinger, 2005).[10]

While the turn to practice in IR clearly tries to address some of these issues,[11] there was always the danger of eclectically picking and choosing parts of different vocabularies and conceptualizations, with little awareness of their different semantic and philosophical heritages and implicit incompatibilities.[12] If the excursions into philosophy – a common feature in all turns – are to be useful, we must not forget that our concepts are not free-standing, but acquire their meaning largely through their relations in semantic fields. This explains why unearthing and transplanting concepts comes at a price, as the example of false friends leading to mistaken analogies suggested.

In short, we cannot limit our attention to problems that arise when the sharp edges of one concept rub up against another when we try to fit them together. Indeed, the underlying metaphor might be grossly misleading. For one, we know from experience that hardly any concept in the social science has 'sharp edges', and can be used according to the set-theoretical specifications of traditional taxonomies (clear attribution and exhaustiveness). But this means that friction is not the issue, but rather that ordering them requires from us to examine their family resemblance, instead of searching for a specific property, which all instances share and which justifies our attributions. In this sense, our conceptualizations follow a different logic than traditional epistemology suggests. For thinking through the implications of this realization,

---

[8] See, for example, Searle (1995).
[9] See the criticism of the physicist/philosopher of science Toulmin (2001).
[10] Whether physics, which is no longer materialist but panpsychist, can provide a new paradigm as Alex Wendt (2015) has suggested, remains highly speculative.
[11] For a seminal analysis of this turn see Bueger and Gadinger (2014); see also Adler and Pouliot (2011b).
[12] For a critical assessment see Kratochwil (2011).

the logic of best exemplar and its metaphorical extensions – often with some problematic or even undecidable cases – is probably more helpful.[13] It is here that theories, which rely on a referential approach to meaning, and those modes of analysis – inspired by pragmatism and ordinary language philosophy – differ most markedly. The former search for essential properties and causal patterns, the latter tend towards explication and the analysis of language-games and forms of life that Wittgenstein introduced.

Let us now turn to the false friend of habits, which have recently been foregrounded by the turn to practices.[14] Habits are certainly an important part of social life and clearly relate to debates of the role of institutions (Searle, 1995). Nevertheless, it is rather doubtful whether doing things by rote provides the appropriate template for dealing with reflective choices,[15] or even those choices that involve risk or uncertainty. Taking routine behaviour as a template for a general theory of action appears rather problematic. Instead, what is required is the patient explication of different *cases* and types of actions that do not seem to follow the same logic, even when we can perhaps discern some commonalities. But since commonalities are not obvious or relevant to all cases, only a closer examination of the *tertium comparationis* can provide us with a warrant.

Consider also the converse problems emphasizing updating and learning in choice situations. Here the silent (or not so silent) assumption is that radical uncertainty – as invoked for example in the Keynesian argument regarding un-knowables – can be treated analogously to decisions under risk (except that the latter rely on extremely rare events). But this is another false friend. Risk assessments depend in one way or another on known distributions, whereas radical uncertainty entails that we do not even know what we are looking for. While this has engendered heated debates relating to the financial crisis – and various models of risk have been developed to deal with panics and returns to market stability – it seems that holding on to counterfactually valid norms is probably better than Bayesian updating. But it is also clear that, given the collective action problem, such 'holding on' is hardly possible for someone in the midst of the herd, unless s/he has enough of a buffer to survive a possible crash. Here an institutional fiat decision is clearly required, rather than relying on individual action according to rational standards.

---

[13] Here the work of George Lakoff provides much food for thought (Lakoff, 1987; Lakoff and Johnson, 1999). For a good discussion of those issues and some the contributions of cognitive psychology see Davis (2005).

[14] See, for example, Hopf (2010); the importance of habits has also been stressed by Oakeshott (1962).

[15] Aristotle, *Politics* 1332a38.

Thus neither going with the flow, nor learning by updating, nor falling back on traditional practices does justice to this type of situation. Instead, these situations call into question the normal intentional action model when addressing action in institutional frames. The latter explodes not only the individualistic action model by pointing to aggregation problems and unintended consequences (such as runs on a bank), but also by alerting us to important collective concerns that are badly misrepresented by individual intentional accounts and strategic interaction models.

The collective 'we' is not simply an aggregate of individuals (we all singly). Instead this 'we' (collectively) comes into existence by a speech act – as in the case of 'we, the people' – whose representatives have powers to make choices and prescribe behaviour, which neither individuals nor aggregate groups possess.[16] These problems have been discussed both in the context of corporations and their separate personality, and in terms of representation, but so far they have hardly impressed theorists beholden to the mistaken tenets of methodological individualism. In short, there is not one solution to all action problems. Thus to frame these rather different problems as theoretical issues, or to reduce them to questions of production or expert technique, is unlikely to succeed.[17]

But this does not mean that no solutions are available, even if they are of a practical nature relying more on experience and imagination than on theoretical propositions. Which strategies work in the social realm has then more to do with how things go during the situation which is experienced as a 'crisis',[18] and whether the conventions that endow certain moves with meaning and can serve as signals, rather than with assuming that we know the game and that the problems to be solved are either technical, or can be taken care of by processes which automatically move towards an equilibrium.[19] To that extent any engagement with practice that neglects the contingent historical dimension of choice-situations and that is satisfied with the acquisition of know-how of the agents, who become mere executors of pre-packaged programmes – misses the point, even though many of our doings in the world are habitual. Here the recent intervention by McCourt (2012) should be taken seriously.

[16] For a seminal discussion of those issues see Hans Lindahl (2018).
[17] See, for example, Tetlock (2005).
[18] *Krisis* in Greek means originally the ineluctable moment of choice that cannot be mastered by avoidance or routines but in which the case or situation changes its character. In Aristotle's *Poetics* it occurs usually in the third act, thus providing the criteria for either a tragedy or a comedy.
[19] This is already in games of coordination with several equilibria – which are logically equivalent but differ markedly in distributive consequences – a rather heroic assumption.

These brief remarks have several implications for how to approach problems of praxis. One is that the hopes placed in grand or even ideal theories – starting from abstract models and looking then for their possibilities of application – are essentially mistaken. The second is that relying on ingrained habits and ways of doing things comes at a price.[20] It gives rise to the pathologies of the garbage can model of decision-making (Cohen et al., 1972), where solutions are in search of problems, rather than the other way around (skipping the stage of deliberation and analysing the actual situation requiring action).

Finally, the traditional way of insuring oneself against errors of judgement by appealing to the law of large numbers and by identifying patterns,[21] where individual variations 'wash out', has also its problems. In the name of universal validity a lot of information is thrown away. For practical purposes, however, it might indeed be more useful to know, for example, the etiology of certain types of wars – such as asymmetric war, guerrilla war, punitive war, or wars involving whole nations (as opposed to conflicts fought by mercenaries), rather than looking for a general theory of war and deriving some theorems from the assumptions or engaging in generalizations from large data-sets.

The usual counterargument to those observations is, that only what is generally or universally true can claim to provide warranted knowledge, so that such trade-offs seem justified. But that cannot be right for three reasons: one, because the taxonomies of the social world – as in the case of classifying wars – are not based on natural facts or some common essence, but depend on certain interests. A war fought for balance of power reasons is different from wars fought by a nation for its place in the sun, and a low-intensity warfare has other dynamics than those of mass armies.[22]

Secondly, since an engagement with the realm of praxis has to be attentive to the question of action in its strategic context, it requires a different know-how than just fabricating some object according to certain rules of the trade, or of looking for equilibrium points, that in the absence of complete information cannot be specified. Part of the context is therefore that we are acting in historical time and that because our social world is not natural, we cannot understand it as an analogue to a given world out there.[23] The latter conception is already

---

[20] For a first-hand account by a former practitioner in applying best practices in United Nations missions see Zanotti (2011).

[21] See, for example, the ongoing Correlates of War Project at the University of Michigan.

[22] See, for example, Clausewitz's interest in 'small wars' and their dynamics in Davis and Daase (2015).

[23] For a further development of this point see Kratochwil (2014).

problematic enough for the sciences – as it seems nowadays tenable only if one is a creationist and believes that the world is now 'finished' – but it is hardly compatible with Darwin or modern cosmology.

The third point is that in studying the artifice of the social world we have to pay attention to the concepts by which we build this social world and take their embeddedness in semantic fields, as well as their historical transformations into account. To that extent the issue cannot be one of accurate description of a Cartesian match between the *res cogitans* and the *res extensa*. After all, both the historical developments leading to this particular situation – which again is always a selection of all the things which occurred but are considered (ir)relevant, as well as the choice of the future project we try to realize – remain largely out of sight.

Making, Acting and Responding: A Classification of Our 'Doings'

The upshot of this discussion is a prima facie presumption that a new approach to the problem of practice has to take the problems of acting in temporality and historical contingencies seriously instead of assuming a priori that action can be subjected to theoretical criteria, such as universality and necessity, as considered to be appropriate for all domains. But this assumption cannot be right, since Kant already suggested that aesthetic judgements, for example, are of a different sort than theoretical ones. The former are not true or false without becoming thereby simple indications of idiosyncratic likes or dislikes. Similarly, laws as prescriptions are valid or invalid, and it is irrelevant, that owing to their counterfactual validity, they violate the logical criterion of true/false which governs theoretical assertions.

Consequently, I maintain that practice is a realm with its own logic (without necessarily endorsing the usual aesthetic take). Furthermore, I contend that the traditional way of dealing with this problem has been unsatisfactory since very often the problem was misdiagnosed as one of applying theoretical insights incorrectly. The traditional fall-back was then to counsel prudence, but prudence was not understood as a specific form of knowledge, but was treated as a substitute or second best. This allowed us to continue to 'beat up the cat for not barking' and continue to extol theory, since barking was apparently considered 'higher' than meowing.

Since my task here is to look at some of the philosophical issues involved, I shall not primarily draw on the IR literature in the following. Instead, I want to question the traditional knowledge hierarchy by examining more closely the different forms of our doings in the world and linking them to

different forms of knowing, so as to corroborate my argument why theoretical standards might be problematic for analysing action.

For that purpose I want to delimit the realm of praxis by distinguishing it first from events – largely those of nature – to which we respond,
while being in the world and looking for orientation; and second, by
separating our productive activities which result in objects, from acting, that is, choosing a goal, which finds its end in the act of choice
itself. While such an approach suggests a certain Aristotelian bent, it is
important to realize that it is one which is far from Aristotle's preoccupation with essences and the natural order of 'higher' and 'lower' things
in the *kosmos*, since it owes a considerable debt to ordinary language
philosophy (conceptual analysis) and speech acts.[24] Nevertheless, a
brief recapitulation of the classical action/knowledge debate is in order.

After the sceptic's challenge to our naïve trust in what our senses
disclose, one thing seemed clear already in antiquity: that a reliance on
mere sense perceptions cannot provide the necessary warrants for our
beliefs in many important instances. The oar that seems broken in water
gets miraculously whole again when removed; this realization cautions
us in taking sense perceptions at face value. The separation of belief
(*doxa*) and truth (*aletheia*,), of appearance and true being, become then
the template for deciding knowledge claims, since if something truly
'is',[25] this ontological warrant justifies our assertions.

---

[24] In a way, I want to make a similar argument as Frost and Lechner have developed by
showing the Aristotelian *phronesis* is compatible with the Winchian account of acting;
that is, considering practices from within rather than via an externalist account. While
I do not entirely agree with them on the reasons they provide for criticizing externalist
accounts, I do agree with the first part of their argument (Frost and Lechner, 2016a).

[25] Actually *aletheia* means originally that something is out in the open, is no longer hidden but discloses itself. It relies on a simple visual metaphor but sets up the object/
concept dichotomy that originally privileges the object, which, however, has to be
cleansed from accidental properties so that its true being becomes visible. This leads
on the one hand to reification when the object becomes the measure of all things and
when the principle of the excluded middle (is/is not) is applied, that determines meaning according to this timeless existence criterion. On the other hand, it leads to the
Copernican revolution in that the 'noumenal world' where the things in themselves
exist, but cannot be described or known unless they are brought under concepts and
categories by which we apprehend the (unknown) world, a move which privileges the
subject. However, a third possibility could be that truth reveals itself in time – which
gives rise to cults or personal conversions, sometimes based on surprisingly detailed
observational knowledge (such as of the stars in Egyptian or Mayan calendars) or
personal insights. While this suggests that the universe of meaning is wider than the
set of true sentences (since only meaningful sentences can be true but not vice versa
as juridical and aesthetic judgements show), we usually do not apply the term 'knowledge' to them since we usually cannot give a warrant for our observations (why and
not only that this constellation repeats itself), or for the insight which is only partially
communicable, based on a personal soteriological experience.

Furthermore, being heir to the Socratic and Platonic criticisms of the sophists, who had put the arguments of the sceptics to good use and profit, Aristotle realized, nevertheless, that both the Socratic notion of what could count as knowledge and Plato's ontological ideas were not satisfactory.[26] The Socratic questions inquiring into the specific *arete* of people, what they are good at, be they shoemakers, priests or politicians, relied on a model of knowledge which was derived from the specific skills, emerging with the division of labour in a society. But this model, relying on a 'knowing how', quickly got into trouble when we left the realm of making things (*techne*) and applied it to larger questions, such as steering the ship of state.

While the latter metaphor become ingrained in the Western tradition – and a captain of a ship certainly must possess some knowledge of the stars and the weather – the metaphor breaks down when we attempt to derive from this expertise the claim that a captain also has superior insight as to the destination of the ship, or on what occasion, and for what purpose it was to leave the port. 'Being good at' follows in the latter case a different logic, which cannot be reduced to either the know-how of making things or to the stringency of inferences that Aristotle examines at great length in the *Organon*, for example.[27]

In the realm of praxis where action is at issue, and, in particular, when we want to act well, we are confronted with certain distinct features of that domain which we cannot ignore. A dozen or so important differences come to mind: first, contingency is introduced by the fact that actions take place in time, privileging thereby the particular not the general; and second, that therefore the knowledge necessary for practical questions fits badly the logical model of inference that operates with a general major (universal) premise and a minor (factual) premise insuring the conclusion (explanation).

Third, actors are neither served by logic alone, nor are they helped by the knowledge of what is true in general. Rather, given time pressures, they need a quick diagnostics identifying what best characterizes the present problem. Furthermore, and fourth, since s/he is never confronted with exhaustively defined situations and complete knowledge of

---

[26] See his (lost) treatise *On Ideas* of which we still have some fragments. See the illuminating discussion of Fine (1995). See also Aristotle's remarks in his *Metaphysics* at 990 b 17 and at 1039 a 2ff.

[27] Mainly his book on the *Categories*, *On Interpretation*, the *Prior* and *Posterior Analytics*. Although the *Topica*, which is historically also part of the *Organon*, and references frequently the Analytics, deals together with the Rhetoric with non-necessary truth and runs with the various *Ethics* parallel to the better worked out criteria for 'theory' (*prima philosophia*).

all the strategies available, the search for new information is costly and indeterminate (Conlisk, 1996). Consequently, in such situations the criterion of completeness, that is, of not having overlooked something that might become important down the line, is more important than maximization. But this skill involves, fifth, experience and imagination, guiding the analogical reasoning. Sixth, given this predicament, not only a quick heuristics but also a flexible rather than a purely maximizing or minimax strategy is demanded, since choices often cannot be postponed and windows of opportunity open and close.

This also necessitates, seventh, a sense of timing as an important element,[28] as well as having, eighth, a viable fall-back strategy,[29] if it turns out that one had misjudged the initial situation, or that the dynamic of interaction does not develop along the expected lines. Doing more of the same (much helps much) according to the metaphysical principle of the continuity of nature is hardly then a prudent and defensible strategy.

The ninth important point is that the grammar of acting well not only comprises that we reach our goals, but also in what fashion we do this. Problems arise in this context, since we are likely to interfere in our pursuits with the goals of others and competition can quickly degenerate into conflict. Therefore, tenth, there has to be a general respect for 'the law' which becomes a collective good in the sense of a *bonum*, not a commodity – and which regulates such interferences – and the specific allowances, prohibitions, exceptions and exemptions for which the law provides.[30] These provisions become sedimented in codes or precedents and form a specific tradition (Krygier, 1986), which, in turn, serves as the background for making choices and deciding authoritatively cases in a court.

Eleventh, since many actions we undertake are taken on behalf of others, who are our clients, patients or students, we owe them particular fiduciary duties. The latter are important but cannot be derived from the general obligations we owe to all humans, or even to all fellow citizens.

Twelfth, by experience I obviously do not mean that a person must have performed the very same actions and routines frequently, even if they are of crucial importance in the case of production (*techne*) and in modern 'normal' science. Rather it suggests that the prudent person must have been exposed to a variety of things, that s/he must have

---

[28] Here Aristotle already mentions the importance of the *kairos*.
[29] This point has been particularly made by Clausewitz in his controversy with von Bülow who wanted to formulate a comprehensive strategy for any war (Paret, 1986).
[30] This is the *nomos basileus* argument rehearsed by Aristotle, *Politics*. 1287 a 3–6.

learned to compare situations and to find ways of 'going on', rather than getting stymied by an instance which refutes traditional wisdom, or embarking on normalizing non-conforming cases, in order to expand the data-base and prepare for a scientific test. Similarly, 'imagination' here does not mean that we engage with the hunt for unicorns or with time-travel because we can imagine them; it has to result from practical experience rather than a roaming phantasy.

Time, Action and the Question of 'Happiness'

Let us now explore how our understanding of action gets affected when we try to normalize it and consider it in terms of technical knowledge, or when we conceive of it as a commodity supplied by a theoretical model operating with some idealized conception of rationality. Such an exploration is useful for avoiding at least some of the above twelve errors which have plagued the theorizing of praxis.

The preliminary clarifications given earlier suggested that the term 'acting' is used in different senses, an observation, which seems to fit the distinction of a wider and a narrower meaning. As argued, the former stands for our doings in the world, which include the actions of the *homo faber*, such as producing something, the nearly automatic reactions we have when we want to avoid a tile falling from a roof, or even the activation of some drills which have conditioned us, so that we can effortlessly skate or ski downhill. But our doings also entail activities which are carried out and accomplish their end by the very act by which they are executed. For example, in taking a bus, which transports me from A to B, I reach my goal, and when I arrive nothing remains but a recollection (and perhaps a token, such as a ticket).

The general point is that in all cases an actor does something, or in other words intervenes in the world for some purpose, as in Aristotle's *hou heneka* (one acts *in order to*), which provides him with an organizing principle for his threefold distinction. There is action, which is executed or performed on the one hand, and there is production, which aims at creation of an artefact. Given these divisions, we notice that the notion of production is further subdivided into technical and artistic production, such as creating a chair as opposed to a play or poem. Of course, there are overlaps, since, for example, a play is written in order to be enacted – rather than having as its purpose a written-down version in the form of a book.

As the last example shows, the distinctions are far from exclusive and unequivocal, as would be required by a traditional taxonomy. After all, a drama is more like acting not only for the actors but, in a way, also for the audience, which participates by sympathetic extension and thus experiences the Aristotelian *katharsis*.[31] We should also notice a further inconsistency in our usage of these concepts, such as when we call a performance of a play, a production, emphasizing thereby the many instrumental activities necessary for staging. Consequently, the point of our analysis cannot be a correct labelling, but rather the realization what the use of terms highlights or backgrounds; we must understand the grammar governing the use of our concepts.

Some new complications arise when we analyse acting jointly and our actions are part of a larger undertaking, such as Rousseau's famous stag hunt, or when we play a duo. In that case our being part of a plan pre-supposes that our individual actions have to mesh, particularly when we act in a strategic environment. This then is somewhat different from Weber's cyclists, by which he explicates the concept of social action – in terms of interdependent decision-making – where no joint intention is necessary,[32] but a coordination problem arises in spite of the shared purpose to avoid a collision – and the outcome will depend on the inter-action of the choices both bicyclists make.

Furthermore, the characterization of something as an action or activity emphasizes *time*, since that is the most important frame, which is foregrounded.[33] It distinguishes what is going in acting from what occurs in nature, or what happens *to* us when rocks fall, tsunamis inun-date the terra firma or the sun rises or sets. Finally, there are just mere re-actions to an event, as already mentioned, such as an oncoming car that makes me jump to the side. Although the latter is still not a purely causal event – as what I do is not really unintentional – but this usage strains the notion of an action, as shown by the use of the term 're-action'. On the other hand, the term 're-action' is also used when we just want to indicate that something is done in response rather than an actor remaining passive and doing nothing.

As we have seen, further confusion arises from the fact that many actions are the result of rigorous training, so that they become near

---

[31] But there is an important difference between suffering (syn = together pathos = suffering) with someone else through sympathetic extension and acting. While the extension seems like an action, that is, opening myself to a new experience, I am taken in by the account of what happened to someone else and now to me. Here we are in the thrall of pathos, more victims than actors. Thus, the tragedy might be a less apt example than the stories told about exemplary action in the genre of history as *res ges-tae*, which might strengthen our resolve to act in an equally exemplary fashion, when the opportunities arise (although *hybris* might then just be around the corner).
[32] Rather, the desire to avoid a collision motivates both actors singly.
[33] See the important contribution by Jackson and Nexon (1999).

automatic (as in the case when we skate or play the violin). These activities are neither part of an explicit intention for each single action, which we perform in sequence, nor of a joint enterprise. It requires only one initial explicit intention, or the commencement – such as to perform, for example, by skating or playing Beethoven's Violin Concerto.[34] But since these activities are not natural (but near instinctual *re-actions*) and must have been learned, some form of reflexivity and learning by doing must be presupposed. To what extent the expectation that a stimulus-response model of the conditioned Pavlovian dog – so dear to strict behaviourist action-explanations instantiating the *actio est reactio* of efficient causality – can serve as a general template is, however, rather dubious. Instead of pressing these activities in the Procrustean bed of efficient causality – because of a mistaken notion that only efficient causality can actually explain – we had better modify our conceptualizations in the opposite way. Here three examples shall suffice for buttressing my claim. One is to demonstrate the potential for a new heuristic that follows from a modification of the rigid conceptual framework of efficient causality; the other two suggest what gets lost when the paradigm of instrumental action is extended and used for the analysis of more complicated individual and collective action sequences. Finally, such moves allow us to map out a contrast space that frees us from those myopias.

As to the first: consider in this context the example of wolfs hunting in packs. They must continuously adjust their actions to each other, so that their behaviour satisfies the criteria of a 'joint intentionality', as Bratman (2014) has proposed. But that means that our traditional distinctions of relying on rigid dichotomies of actions and events, nature and culture, need to be modified. 'Nature' is no longer the realm of pure necessity form the moment we include animals in our analysis and study their intentional actions, including cooperative activities and tool-making. Here Hume has provided us in his *Treatise* with one of the first programmatic speculations,[35] and Alexander Wendt has – more daringly – tried his hand at explicating quantum mechanics in a way that requires from us that we no longer hold on to a rigid distinction between mind and matter (Wendt, 2015).[36]

Now consider, second, the consequences *of* narrowing the focus, not by denying intentionality, but by interpreting all action in terms of

---

[34] For an interpretation of habits as an evolutionary response to cognitive overload see Hopf (2010).

[35] Hume, *A Treatise of Human Nature*. Bk. 1, Part III, sec. 16.

[36] For a review of this book see the symposium in *International Theory* (n.p.)

instrumental action. It arises in two contexts: one by trying to interpret the Aristotelian *hou heneka* not only case by case, but relating the different actions of the chains of actions to one last goal – linking thereby also all the different goals together in a scheme of goals and sub-goals. Aristotle's ascription of a *telos* was designed to place all actions within a meaningful horizon and to avoid an infinite regress in the absence of a supreme goal. The solution to the infinite regress is that thereby two decisive characteristics of acting get out of sight: the performative element of actions and the point that they are taking place in irreversible time, which comes to an end, but not by reaching a preordained result (product or historical *telos*).

The result of treating actions as part of a *telos* or a system is that it draws our attention to the selection of means, as every action is not only considered by itself allowing for different actions in time but it considers them only as stepping-stones for some product or final purpose. In this way the illusion arises that all the steps are more or less rationally determined as backward induction shows, since an actor who wants the 'end' must also choose the necessary means. But this conceptualization backgrounds the problem that practical choices in life are episodic and no one single line leads to a predetermined goal. If there is a predetermined end in life, it is death because we are mortal. But death is not an action or a purpose, but rather an event that inevitably happens to us (unless we commit suicide).

To that extent the end of all actions cannot be determined in the same way, even if it seems to be clear that the *hou heneka* of all acting is to realize something. All we have, though, is a chain of actions which – when looked at from the final outcome – show how one thing led to the other, without however allowing for a strict backward induction that would specify these steps *ex ante*. Looking *ex ante* at possible chain(s), certain opportunities can be identified at every decision point, which quickly morph into numerous possible chains so that we quickly lose our orientation. Besides, in going through the different episodes of the train of decisions, the opportunities we identified *ex ante* might turn out to lead to blind alleys, while other things which initially had not even entered our choice horizon, actually provide us with the possibility of going on. While in a narrative recounting how one thing happened after another is transformed – when seen *ex post* – into the necessary steps to an end, a moment's reflection shows that this cannot be a causal path, one that could have been perspicuous to us *ex ante*.

For this reason the overarching goal of praxis, that is, the happy life (*eudaimonia*), can no longer be simply read off a predestined end, since our life is evolving in different situations, rather than moving on one-track only.[37] Consequently, Aristotle's *eudaimonia*, usually translated as happiness, is actually not an ultimate goal in the sense that it dominates all others, but addresses the quality of all the choices taken together rather than their role in an ends/means chain. This qualitative take lends meaning to the execution of actions and even to events, even if they were just chances or had not been intended. Thus, Aristotle's conception of happiness retains – despite some ambiguity – its link to *praxis* rather than to production (*techne*) or prophecy, since he conceives happiness (*eudaimonia*) as a fulfilled life that results from having acted well in various situations and spheres rather than one thing that has finally been reached.[38]

If we fail to notice the differences between a systemic (nearly a-temporal) conceptualization – provided by a systems perspective and its part/whole logic – and the 'fulfilled life' version of 'happiness' – stressing temporality and the plurality of experiences – we remain blissfully unaware of the difference in the conceptions of happiness. In the first instance we treat happiness as a good that, like a resource, can be maximized through instrumental or strategic action. In the second instance, we treat it rather as a sequence of performances that worked out and gave us satisfaction. Closure can in the latter case only be reached through the narrative at the end of a fulfilled life, by showing that one had good reasons to be satisfied, since one had acted well and had been connected to and appreciated by others. Solon's remark to Croesus (who had amassed enormous riches and power), that nobody can be considered happy, rather than just lucky, before his end,[39] might

---

[37] One could now object and point to death as the last certainty that informs our choices. But it seems that even here the concrete guidance is missing. This certainty has given rise to hedonism on the one hand – with all the problems that reappear again in utilitarianism whether there are different kinds of pleasures or only one kind that has to be maximized. The problem was well analysed by Sen's (1977) 'rational fools' argument. On the other hand it occasioned speculations about after-life and leaving the ultimate verdict as to the worthiness of the conduct to some judge in the thereafter as in the Egyptian religion that inspired Plato, and – in different ways – Judaic or Christian eschatology. In both, however, it is not the individual who is the ultimate master of his destiny, as deliverance comes from the messiah or is determined by God's final judgement at the end of times, or as in the radical version of Calvinist Protestantism by predestination, which Weber explored. Another version emphasizes good deeds which are rewarded in the beyond and the restoration of the fallen nature of man through sacraments and the faith in salvation that lets the actors in the here and now conceive of themselves as only pilgrims who are 'on the way'. For an examination of the latter problem see Barbato (2013).

[38] On a modern conception of a fulfilled life see also Wolf (2010).

[39] Herodotus, *The Histories* at Book I, 25–33 (Solon) and 32–96 (Nemesis) at 50–79.

be a bit harsh, even though his larger point of the fragility of a happy life is well taken.[40]

This leads me to my third point, about the contrast space. We can see how a systemic or functional conceptualization of happiness as an over-arching goal pushes the analysis of action in the direction of *techne* and production, and finally towards exchange. Such a move necessitates the invention of a calculus in terms of individual utilities and risks, which, as discussed, is predicated on known distributions and normalized instances. Furthermore, by the extension of this system to the society at large, Bentham's (1789) 'felicific calculus' of the legislator who provides for the 'greatest happiness', or for the greatest happiness of the greatest number (John St Mill), is then just around the corner.

Of course, there remains the problem of the interpersonal comparability of utilities, but that problem can be circumvented if a powerful new convention penetrates social exchanges: money. Then the focus shifts from the performance or the production to the exchange, which serves as the new paradigm for acting. Thereby even the bartering of old – for example, exchanging my freedom for protection through a feudal contract, which created a new social bond – is overcome by the metaphor of a normal trade, as money serves now as a medium of exchange, measure and store of value, and solves thus the difficulties of barter and of the interpersonal utility comparison. This commodification frees trade from the fetters of earlier conventions, making things which seemed solid, melt into thin air, as Marx observed (Marx and Engels, 1976). However, any relation to praxis understood as the setting of goals in specific but problematic situations has then been lost.

These shortcomings explain perhaps the observable popularity of grand narratives which since the Enlightenment have gained acceptance and which form nowadays a counter-paradigm to the reductionism of instrumental action. The narratives, as I have argued elsewhere, draw their strength from a teleology that traditionally had been part of the prophetic tradition (Kratochwil, 2014). Here Kant's teleology of nature in his *Perpetual Peace* and various theories of progress come to mind.[41]

---

[40] Herodotus uses this Solonic message for framing his story of the subsequent nemesis that struck Croesus, in spite of all his efforts to insure himself against various feared disasters, and Herodotus provides thereby a cautionary tale against the temptations of *hybris*.

[41] Kant uses here a line from Lucretius *De rerum natura*. It reads: 'fata volentem ducunt, nolentem trahunt' (nature leads the willing and forces the unwilling); see Kant (2011: 112). Significantly Kant speaks here about the *List der Natur* (Cunning of Reason) although even the materialist Lucretius still speaks of 'fate'. But as Kant's discussion makes it clear nature has now become the stand-in for God's hand (*manus gubernatoris*), which had to be discerned in the fateful events of history and which had already in Adam Smith become the 'unseen hand' of a 'system' (the market).

Nevertheless, such prophetic narratives also take a final end for granted and make out of events and the intermittent choices of the actors signs of the things to come. Here the speculations about the emergence of a world community in international law or of the end of history provide us with further examples.[42]

It is ironic that the 'grand narratives', which rely for their persuasiveness not on the a-temporal notion of a system, but on a prophecy concerning the final destiny of mankind, result in a similar myopia, by utilizing an entirely historical prop. Its Kantian version is also patently incompatible with Kant's own emphasis on individual freedom and responsibility, making instead out of actors the miserable 'cogs of machines' that he so abhorred and against which pragmatists later warned.

Conclusion

The bane of conclusions is that readers might expect to find the argument neatly packaged, or that some catchy phrases will stick in their memory. The laborious steps, designed to disabuse the readers of their reliance on some unexamined 'truths', can then be quickly relegated to oblivion, together with the anxiety which this exercise entailed. I shall resist such a temptation for several reasons, even if this position violates the practice of paper-writing.

First, if I argued that philosophy cannot be the ultimate court standing outside our common world and deriving from it the claim to provide the 'view from nowhere', then I would involve myself in a performative contradiction if I provided now 'new and improved' instructions for getting on with one's research. These choices have to be made by the individual researcher, not by some critic or consultant. They have to be executed with integrity and have to be fought for in the institutions of learning, which usually preach pluralism, but adhere to the notion of truth with a big T. Even if the latter no longer is dispensed by God, the Church, or the king, but by the high priests of 'science', the dangers of such orthodoxies are all the same.

Second, if the reader can take anything home from this discussion then it is the realization that the 'one size fits all' epistemology is of no use and that we have to come to terms with the fact that there is no ultimate foundation. So instead of starting with theoretical propositions – following the standard textbook advices (King et al., 1996) – and then casting around for their application and tests, such a suggestion does

---

[42] For a more extensive discussion see Kratochwil (2011), Chapter 5.

not lead very far. It forgets that we always start in the middle of things and not from a point outside the social world, which would endow tests with meaning beyond doubt. I argued instead that we get to a problem not through abstractions, but through the analysis of how we formulate an issue that startles us. This emplaces a problem in a certain semantic field, and alerts us to the relevant conceptual connections, which have to be examined. Similarly, to start in ethics (when conceived as an ideal theory) with ultimate principles or even with best practices, is likely to engender the pathologies described by the garbage can model of decision-making, despite our good intentions, as Kant's remarks about *Dummheit* become applicable.

Third, if acting is crucially connected to freedom and responsibility then asking at the end of this exercise the question of what one is now to do seems rather odd. Admittedly, neither a new theory was presented, nor was a new research agenda proposed. But reading between the lines reveals that this chapter adumbrates more than a lifetime's work. The road to happiness lies in doing it. Thus, the contrast space has been mapped; now it has to be explored. If it provides food for thought, *sapere aude*!

12 Conclusion
Concepts and the Future of International Practice Theorizing

Alena Drieschova and Christian Bueger

Concepts are the core building blocks of international practice theories (IPT). As Guzzini (2013: 535) notes, 'just as terms are co-constitutive of language, concepts are co-constitutive of theories; they are words in which, but also for which our theorizing is done. Not only are concepts the means to achieve theorizing, but theorizing is also a means to redefine concepts. We constantly rewrite our dictionary'. In this sense, the advancement of concepts of IPT is an attempt to rewrite the dictionary of IR. It implies bringing back established concepts such as 'practice' to the centre of attention, to show the force of novel ones, such as 'repetition' and 'visuality', and to reinterpret classical terms, such as 'knowledge' and 'action'.

If for any theory concepts are central, as they negotiate between the general, the abstract and the concrete, between theory and empirics, in international practice theorizing, concepts gain additional priority. Practice theorists embrace non-essentialist forms of theory. As Bourdieu notes, theory needs to be seen as a 'temporary construct which takes shape for and by empirical work and which gains less by theoretical polemics than by the confrontation with new objects' (Bourdieu, 1985: 11). Theory, in this sense, is better thought of as a collective activity, that is, the practice of theorizing. In the practice of theorizing, concepts are one of the core elements. They are tools for describing, ordering, conceptualizing, understanding and explaining. As tools they transform through their use in actual research situations. They become reformulated by being confronted with new empirical objects. Theorizing implies a conversation between the world and a community of theorizers. It is a translation process of the world drawing on the empirical material that theorizers gather with the assistance of concepts. But theorizing is centrally also a conversation among theorizers. Making visible the major conversations of this volume, both within the community of practice theorizers, but also beyond, is the core objective of this concluding chapter.

Together, the contributors to this volume argue that practice theorizing is best advanced through conversations on and reinterpretations of concepts, such as knowledge, norms, change, visibility or action. Such an emphasis demonstrates the benefits of understanding practice theory as a unique yet heterogeneous intellectual project, while also inviting a dialogue with other theoretical approaches to the international. Communication about concepts allows us to articulate respectful differences among various lines of practice theorizing. It also demonstrates how the diversity of the practice theoretical dictionary provides fertile grounds for the advancement of research. Practice theories hang together through these communicative activities, which form a web of concepts and their use. This web constitutes the space of practice theorizing.

In the following, we first recount some of the benefits of interpreting practice theorizing as conversations on concepts. Arguing to understand practice theorizing as ongoing work in developing a web of terms and concepts in order to interpret, explore, conceptualize, understand and explain international practices, we proceed in recasting the conversations and divergences between the chapters, and between practice scholars and other theoretical approaches. Throughout we aim at providing a sketch of the conceptual structures of practice theorizing and its relations to other lines of theory in IR. We end in an outlook evaluating which concepts and related problems have received substantial treatment, and which ones will require further attention.

Theorizing and Conversations

Practice theories are diverse, as the chapters in this volume have shown. For practice scholars, this diversity is a strength, not a weakness. The unruliness of practice prohibits a unified account and requires pluralist perspectives. This, however, makes it difficult to present or grasp practice thinking in definitive terms. The majority of practice scholars agree on a basic definition of practices as nexuses of doings and sayings organized by practical knowledge. This is, however, often already where consensus stops and disagreements start. There are ongoing conversations over how to think the relation between doings and sayings, and hence the relation between the material and the expressive and linguistic, how practices are organized, and how practical knowledge should be conceptualized. The five fault lines discussed in the introduction are indicative of the preferences and priorities that scholars embrace.

If there is a lack of agreement over these questions and different concepts have been employed to address them, others have argued, however, that there is a notable practical consensus among scholars: they share a range of basic commitments in their work (Adler and Pouliot, 2011b; Bueger and Gadinger, 2018). The debate about the identity of practice theories also concerns the question how broadly we should think about the label and which variants of culturalist theorizing should be included under its umbrella. The narrative approach introduced by Neumann (2002), Pierre Bourdieu's work and Etienne Wenger's Community of Practice approach were the first ones in IR associated with the practice label. How wide we should cast the net and what to include under the term remains controversial. Some authors have argued that, for instance, Actor-Network Theory should be excluded from practice theorizing (Nexon and Pouliot, 2013). Others insist that it is a part of that family (Bueger and Gadinger, 2018). Whether to include this particular set of concepts or not, the point is certainly not to strive for a finite set of 'approaches' which would define the core of practice theory once and for all. Thinking with fault lines and the associated conceptual and methodological challenges provides a different direction. Practice theorizing is then understood as an open and ongoing process. It requires the introduction of new terms and the reformulation of concepts. While one has to be aware of 'false friends', as Kratochwil (Chapter 11) warns us, many of the productive concepts might be formulated initially elsewhere than in IR, whether that is social theory, sociology, anthropology or geography.

Yet, the growing range of debates concerning the core concepts and identity of practice theorizing is not only a side effect of the growth of the field but they are also productive. In so far as scholarly progress is achieved through debate, controversy and dialogue, practice scholars are on the road to leave the 'quiet of certitude' and the preference for the 'monologue of instruction' and focus in its stead on the 'arduous give-and-take of serious engagements' among practice scholars, but also with those who disturb self-assuredness (Kratochwil, 2000: 75). The continued growth of the field makes it possible to go well beyond the mere promotion of the general ideas and promises of practice thinking and 'to start to understand and spell out differences and, in so doing, to promote lines of practice theorizing with a greater internal consistency' (Gherardi, 2016: 23). The first goal of the preceding conversations was hence one of 'articulating respectful differences among various practice theories' (Gherardi, 2016: 23). Secondly, one of the core contributions of the chapters is that they open new lines of conversation between practice scholars and other theories in IR. Rather than merely advocating for the benefits of practice theorizing they aim at engaging in conversations with other advocates of culturalist theorizing that might also draw on notions of practice, or those constructivist and rationalist accounts in the discipline that more fundamentally disagree with the core commitments of practice theorizing.

Concepts, Conversations and the Future of the Practice Agenda

The chapters of this volume are invitations for a dialogue with other perspectives, but they also demonstrate the benefits of understanding practice theory as a unique perspective, and show what it brings to the table that has been hitherto missing. They do so by taking specific concepts, such as power, norms or change as their point of departure. Why are concepts the right entrance into such conversations?

Emphasizing the building blocks of theory first of all challenges any rigid understanding of the borders between theoretical vocabularies. Rather than a conversation among the like-minded or between paradigms, and '-isms', the focus turns to different interpretations of concepts and the conceptual relations that inform them. Practice theorizing is heterogeneous, and so are the border zones. Concepts then enable conversations.

Concepts help us to order the world; they are vital to make sense of empirical phenomena. They are 'generalized statements about whole classes of phenomena rather than specific statements of fact' (Becker, 1998: 109). So, concepts may operate as 'empirical generalizations' (Becker, 1998: 128). But they are not simply summaries of facts. They are rather interpretations of experienced phenomena, and provide those phenomena with meaning. There are always similarities and differences between certain real-life phenomena. By summarizing them under a singular concept we chose to highlight their similarities and discard their differences. As such, concepts are always relative, they depend on a given tempo-spatial context; and they are relational in that they exist in relation to other concepts and broader conceptual spaces. In line with Wittgensteinian thought, the meaning of a concept moreover should not be seen outside its usage. Concepts have a history, they are tied to practices, in our case practices of research.

It is possible to share concepts without agreeing on a particular theory, and it is even possible to not agree on the content of concepts and still have a shared conversation around them. This is particularly the case for sensitizing concepts: 'whereas definitive concepts provide prescriptions of what to see, sensitizing concepts merely suggest directions along which to look. [...] They lack precise reference and have no bench marks which allow a clean-cut identification of a specific instance and of its content. Instead they rest on a general sense of what is relevant' (Blumer, 1954: 7). Indeed, it has been argued that the majority of concepts of international practice theorizing are sensitizing concepts (Bueger and Gadinger, 2018: 135; Mol, 2010: 262). Concepts in this sense make possible the anticipation of new experience. They not only allow us to generate descriptions but also, as Nicolini (2017: 24) notes, '"bring worlds into being" in the texts we compose'.

Concepts can be formed as well as assembled in different ways; they can be normative, classificatory, creative or derived from philosophical, inductive or abductive research (Leiulfsrud and Sohlberg, 2017). Concepts organize and generalize experiences. A discussion on concepts, rather than about theory, allows us to grasp theorizing as an ongoing process which is not separated from empirical work, because concepts entail fewer a priori presumptions than entire theories. This creates room for manoeuvre and establishes more space for creative play. A focus on concepts therefore has the advantage that it allows to preserve one of the key strengths of practice research, which 'is not in its coherence and predictability, but in what at first sight, or in the eyes of those who like their theories to be firm, might seem to be its weakness: its adaptability and sensitivity' (Mol, 2010: 262).

The focus of this volume has then been to investigate concepts that play a crucial role in broader IR scholarship and that have elucidated elements of practice as an ontological phenomenon. As outlined, concepts such as norms, change, power or knowledge are fundamental in practice theory, but they are so in IR more broadly.

These concepts point us to the inherent tensions and controversies within the practice theoretical debate. The concept of change leads us to the question of whether practices are predominantly routines or whether we should conceive of them as repeated actions with the ever-present inherent possibility of change, as Schäfer argues (Chapter 9). The concept of normativity not only raises the question to what extent practices are the execution of norms (as becomes apparent in the debate between Gadinger, Chapter 5, and Bernstein and Laurence, Chapter 4) but also the question of the importance of standards and ethics for evaluating practices, as Walters raises in Chapter 6. Kratochwil's reflections on the absurdity of a practice theory (Chapter 11) allow us to discuss the possibility of a theory of practice, and the inherent tensions, which arise between theory as the universal and practice as the particular, the situated, and enacted phenomenon. On the one hand, theorizing about practice distances us from practice, from the concrete practical enactments in the world. On the other hand, theorizing itself is a practice. Starting out from these concepts hence allows us to see the breadth of practice scholarship, while also appreciating the debates and tensions that are shaping the practice turn discussion in IR.

None of the concepts discussed in this volume is situated in a vacuum; indeed, they form part of the shared vocabulary of IPT. Yet they overlap with one another in significant ways and different scholars relate them to each other differently. For example, the visibility of changes in practices can contribute to the retention of those changes, as Pouliot argues (Chapter 8). Being visible, or sometimes being invisible can be a form of power as Austin and Leander claim (Chapter 10). Investigating the relation between concepts is to scrutinize where many of the most fruitful engagements among practice scholars are taking shape. They are often the places in which scholars who see the practice term from different angles can reach shared understandings, but they are also the areas of productive tension and debate. By way of illustration, the cognitive dimension and the normative dimension of practices overlap in the area of unconscious cognitive processes and the internalization of norms, both of which can form the background from which practices are executed and understood. At the same time a focus on unconscious cognitive processes and internalized norms indicates that change might be a very slow and incremental process, whereas a focus on the performative dimension of practices can lead to a notion of abrupt change, because '"everyone can see" that everyone else has seen that things have changed' (Swidler, 2001: 87). Scholars interested in power tend to downplay the importance of change, while those interested in performativity often overemphasize the contingent character of the international system. A focus on materiality frequently implies a neglect for ethical considerations and a lack of attention to the cognitive dimension of practice. Zooming in on the concepts and their relations to each other thus promises to highlight the full analytical richness of practice theoretical approaches.

Lastly, while these concepts do a lot of work in helping us elucidate practices, they are not exclusive to practice oriented scholarship. They are rather concepts with which the entire IR community has at least some familiarity, and different branches of IR scholarship have used some of these concepts as their core building blocks to construct theory. Normativity and knowledge play a key role in constructivist scholarship, power in poststructuralist and realist work, and repetition in poststructuralist research to name but a few examples. Highlighting the ways in which these key concepts inform the notion of practices then also permits delineating the boundaries, and underline the synergies, convergences and conflicts between IPT and other research programmes. Clarifying these relations is as much about identifying avenues of commensurability and dialogue, maybe even some forms of a division of labour between practice theorizing and other theoretical approaches, as it is about highlighting the distinctiveness of the practice turn.

The Semiotic Web of Concepts Cast in This Volume

Conversations on concepts and empirical, indeed practical, problems will advance the agenda of practice thinking in IR further. Articulating respectful differences, recognizing the inherent tensions and divergences within IR's practice theorizing has been one of the drivers. The dialogue with other forms of IR theorizing, whether it is those on the culturalist spectrum fond of the concept of practice, or those in the discipline that dispute the core assumptions of practice theory, was the second.

The chapters in this volume have cast a semiotic web of concepts for practice theorizing. The concepts the individual chapters explicitly focused on are knowledge, norms, power, authority, change, repetition and visibility. Relationships of these concepts to others, such as emotions, performance and materiality, were established within the individual chapters. Out of the multifaceted conversations between these chapters a semiotic web emerges, which is necessarily open-ended and can be cast in many further ways. Relations to other concepts can be added to it, perhaps ad infinitum. What follows is thus merely an illustrative sketch of this semiotic web of concepts that characterizes practice scholarship.

Various authors in the volume have cast the connections between knowledge and power. For Adler and Faubert (Chapter 3) knowledge emerges through practices of knowledge production in epistemic communities of practice, and power is tied to peer recognition within those communities. For Dumouchel (Chapter 7) knowledge is linked to power when actors manage to develop socially recognized expertise and thus acquire authority over an object of authority that they themselves have constructed. By contrast, Walters (Chapter 6) focuses on the power that actors acquire when they manage to transfer practical knowledge from one context to another to obtain desired outcomes.

All three chapters then also establish a link between knowledge, power and change. For Dumouchel change occurs when actors succeed in getting their authority recognized over an object that they have created. For Adler and Faubert change is linked to epistemic communities of practice, to the innovations that happen within them and transitions between different communities of practice. For Walters changes happen as a result of struggles between an established order and those actors who promote an alternative world view in practices of counter-conduct. According to Walters, counter-conduct is world-making because it can create change in the world, but it also already creates an alternative micro-world. The change that occurs is non-linear and unpredictable; it emerges from the struggles between the established order and actors engaged in counter-conduct, in the process of which the established order might well adopt some of the counter-conduct practices. Change emerges from the interactions between different actors, not on the basis of rational design.

Walters's discussion of counter-conduct includes elements of Schäfer's discussion of repetition (Chapter 9). Repetition highlights sameness and difference all at once. A repeated action is very similar to the action it is repeating, yet it occurs in a different context, and in adaptation to that context changes as well. The farmer Herrou employs practices acquired during farming and puts them to an entirely different purpose, namely smuggling refugees across borders. What is more, for Walters, repetitions of acts of resistance are necessary to develop a certain intransigence in a fight for change, to add a certain force to make change possible in a struggle against established practices. Yet this is how Walters's conception of change differs from Schäfer's conception of change, even as both make use of repetition to explain change. For Schäfer, repetition highlights the ever-present possibility of change, the inherent instability of practices and hence structures, because practices invariably have to be repeated in order to be retained. In that repetition there is sameness, but there is also an inherent variation and difference because any action can never be executed in exactly the same way, and it will certainly always occur in a different context. Change is a possibility in every repetition. Pouliot agrees with Schäfer that these micro-slippages occur, but for him they are epiphenomenal in explaining broader societal change. Moreover, such creativity in performing repetitions as often reproduces the larger prevailing structure as it challenges it because, frequently these new performances actually make the overall structural context more durable, more adaptable to its surroundings. Pouliot argues that in spite of these micro-slippages there is an astonishing degree of macro-stability, which deserves explanation. In order to explain bigger societal changes, he says we have to focus on more structural factors, which allow certain changes in practices to be retained, while others fall by the wayside. In line with Walters, change is for Pouliot often the unintentional outcome that emerges from interactional effects. Specifically, he focuses on the environment, the web of practices that surrounds a given change in practice, and which might promote the retention of that change, or not.

One set of practices that can promote the retention of changes is demonstratory practices, which promote the visibility of the given changes. For Pouliot the public display, the visibility of practices, is one of the structural conditions that can lead to change. Similarly, for Adler and Faubert (Chapter 3), visibility and performance are important for actors to establish societally recognized expertise in their knowledge area. In that sense Pouliot (Chapter 8) and Adler and Faubert agree with Austin and Leander (Chapter 10). Yet for Austin and Leander invisibility can be a form of power too, when they focus, for example, on the invisibility of the crimes of the powerful. For them established elites use visibilities and invisibilities to maintain and support their power. Resistance lies in the need to uncover these regimes of visibility and invisibility. Walters focuses on the same play of visibility and invisibility, but from the perspective of the challengers to established social orders. Making things visible in the form of the scene, can lend power to counter-conduct. At other times power lies in making things invisible, for example when hiding migrants in a truck.

For both Austin and Leander as well as Walters, visibility creates power because it generates emotional effects in the audience. The scene is a public display of emotions, and in more general terms for Austin and Leander the perception of visibility has emotional effects. For many practice scholars, visibility is also tightly connected with public performance, as the notion of the scene demonstrates all too well.

For Walters (Chapter 6), there is an inherent ethical and normative dimension in making things visible and invisible, because actors do so to challenge the established normative order on ethical grounds. Counter-conduct is based on 'practices of the self', on ethical principles, which drive actors to behave in a certain way and contest a given normative order. Gadinger (Chapter 5) similarly establishes links between power and norms. For him, power relations can structure normative orders. Norms create a standard against which practices can be evaluated. The actors whose norms become normalized acquire power through that process of normalization; simultaneously powerful actors are more likely to have their norms normalized. Power operates in norms also through mechanisms of membership and inclusion and exclusion. Norms always create boundaries between norm-followers and those who are considered to be deviant.

With that much at stake, norms tend to be inherently unstable for Gadinger (Chapter 5), and perpetually subject to contestation. For Gadinger, normative change is an ever-present possibility. For him, as for Walters, norms are not independent ontological categories, both rather adopt a material and a practical approach to norms. For Gadinger, as practices are inherently normative and norms always contain a practical dimension, the everyday execution of norms permits to draw attention to the inherent possibilities of change. This perspective differs from Bernstein and Laurence (Chapter 4), who see an avenue of social change emerging from the discrepancies between norms and practices that can sneak into social settings over time. Different from Pouliot (Chapter 8), for them change occurs not just within a broader web of practices, but rather in a broader environment, of which norms invariably form a part.

There is also a link between norms, knowledge and practices of knowledge production. Becoming part of an epistemic community of practice also entails learning the moral standards the community embraces, as both Adler and Faubert (Chapter 3) as well as Gadinger (Chapter 5) argue. In more general terms, Adler and Faubert argue that any background knowledge that is tied to the execution of practices entails a normative dimension. They suggest that this normative dimension does not necessarily have to be tacit, but can well be based on active reflection, because it is linked to making normative judgements.

For Pouliot, reflective agency itself is a practice that is potentially subject to change; it emerged and evolved, and could perhaps even disappear in the future. Seeing reflective agency as a practice is only moving one step further from seeing theory, theorizing and knowledge production as a practice, as both Kratochwil and Adler and Faubert argue. For Kratochwil (Chapter 11), this also entails that the social field of theorizing contains certain socio-practical dynamics that might not serve scholars to get a better grasp of the subject they are studying. For example, if IR scholars were to take the practice turn seriously, they would have to realize that it involves fundamentally changing the practices of conducting research. Primarily it would entail recognizing that concepts are practical and not theoretical categories. Both Kratochwil and Walters argue that concepts and theories cannot have a universal dimension, and be applicable across time, place, historical contingencies and societies. Scholars rather have to acknowledge their historical dimension, how they change over time in different historical settings and how they adapt to concrete circumstances. Concepts are situated practical categories that serve as tools to address a particular situation at hand, and might be entirely useless in a different context. In many ways, Kratochwil thus challenges the very modest effort at developing IPT that this edited volume has engaged in. Yet, as we would argue, even with his critique he directly contributes to the semiotic web of concepts of IPT that this volume has sketched out.

The Conceptual Web and Its Relation with Other Theorizing

The web of concepts stretches out beyond this volume, and even beyond practice theorizing. As Chapter 1 argued, the establishment of IPT has to be seen in the light of several border zones to other approaches to the international, in particular constructivism, poststructuralism and other strands of culturalist theorizing. Many of these have introduced the practice term earlier, without giving it centre stage. The border spaces between practice theories and other IR approaches are not 'dead zones', but lively sites of conversations and, potentially, controversy. This has been vividly demonstrated throughout the chapters.

Several authors extended invitations to non-practice scholars to join the conversation and argue about the meaning of a concept, and hence contribute to expanding the web of concepts. Thus, Gadinger (Chapter 5) highlights the affinities and differences between many practice scholars and constructivist norm research. For many constructivists, norms are the primary unit of analysis, and they are concerned about maintaining the ontological independence of norms. By contrast, many practice scholars object to the isolation of norms, and argue that these are to be analysed as an inherent element of practices. Bernstein and Laurence side in this controversy with the constructivists, eager to maintain the distinction between norms and practices, but they suggest that constructivists should nonetheless direct analytical attention to practices, because in the discrepancies between practices and norms lies the potential for changes to social orders.

Dumouchel (Chapter 7) argues that constructivists in their analysis of authority have a too static approach. They tend to highlight how a particular normative environment creates specific forms of authority, but not how conceptions of desirable expertise emerge and fade in practice and interactions. Adler and Faubert (Chapter 3) extend a hand to the epistemic communities research programme and encourage it to be more ambitious by not just focusing on the areas in which scientific knowledge shapes policies, but by also highlighting how knowledge is a category that is present in any form of social activity and thus shapes social outcomes more generally.

Others reach out to the poststructuralist research agenda. Schäfer (Chapter 9) thus highlights how practices expose similar characteristics as signs in discourse. Both need to be repeatable and repeated, which creates a certain structure, but an inherently instable one. Repetition is never exactly the same, and it certainly always occurs in an at least slightly different context. Change is thus an ever-present possibility. Pouliot (Chapter 8) similarly reaches out to poststructuralist scholarship when he refers to the web of practices that ensures the selective retention of some practices over others as doing the same work that narrative and discourse do in poststructuralist and some versions of constructivist scholarship. Walters (Chapter 6) highlights the key role practices play in Foucault's work, and he also makes a methodological point when emphasizing the importance of description for practice scholarship in particular and the discipline of IR in general.

Scholars in this volume also connect to liberal institutionalist work. Pouliot thus challenges the rational choice model of institutional development by design when highlighting the unpredictable and non-linear trajectory of institutional developments. Dumouchel questions the institutional hierarchy literature by arguing that it considers only one form of authority based on a transactional approach of exchanging public goods, and remains blind to the many different versions of authority that can be and have been historically constructed. Austin and Leander (Chapter 10) relate their work to the concept of soft power and highlight how attraction plays a key role for soft power to emerge. Yet the soft power literature has been largely treating attraction as a black box. It is not quite clear where it comes from. A focus on regimes of visibilities, Austin and Leander argue, allows scholars to theorize attraction.

The purpose of this book has been to open up conversations, not to close them. In this sense, the semiotic webs that we have sketched are purposefully incomplete. They have left many threads hanging in the air. Those threads are there on purpose, for other scholars to pick up and continue weaving the conceptual web. Practice theorizing is an invitation to an open-ended and collective project.

Next Steps in Practice Theorizing

The wealth of practice scholarship that has emerged over recent years has made significant theoretical inroads. Practice scholars have by now spent much time reflecting on some of the conceptually tricky terrain that a focus on practices generates. Around specific nodal points the web is very well spun. Thus, many theoretical reflections have emerged about the relations between practices and norms and normativity (see, for example, Adler, 2019a; Bernstein and Laurence, Chapter 4; Gadinger, Chapter 5; Lechner and Frost, 2018; Wiener, 2018). Similarly, scholars have thought a lot about questions of change and stability (Adler, 2019a; Hopf, 2018; Pouliot, Chapter 8; Schäfer, Chapter 9; Stappert, 2020). This does not mean that everything has been said on these issues. They are grand topics that will certainly continue to come up when scholars will tackle empirical questions, but the semiotic web in these areas has already been well crafted. At this point, this is perhaps where we should leave them – potentially open-ended questions that might have to be addressed if and when the need arises. Whoever has to address them can draw upon a substantive body of work that has gone into reflecting on these issues.

Yet there are other areas that deserve much more attention. The semiotic web remains quite thin, for example, when it comes to connecting technologies, tools and artefacts to practices. Materiality and technology are two concepts that are noticeable by their absence in this edited volume, although a few chapters do draw on them (see, for example, Austin and Leander, Chapter 10; Schäfer, Chapter 9). Whether or not Actor-Network Theory belongs to the family of practice theories, there are fruitful conversations to be had between practice scholarship and Actor-Network Theory and science and technology studies. The embodied, material and functional nature of practices implies that tools, technologies and artefacts are essential for their execution. Yet with a few rare exceptions (see, for example, Adler-Nissen and Drieschova, 2019; Pouliot, 2010) there is not much IR scholarship that theorizes and reflects upon the ways in which practices and artefacts interrelate with one another and mutually condition each other. There is a need for significantly more work in this area, especially at a time of huge and decisive technological changes.

Another area where the semiotic web could be spun significantly more thickly concerns questions of gender in practice theorizing. The absence of gender, queerness, femininity and masculinity as concepts in this edited volume is perhaps telling in this regard. Yet there are potentially highly fruitful conversations and collaborations to be had between gender and queer scholarship and practice scholars. On a more general level, practice scholars could gain significant methodological insights from the wealth of innovative empirical research gender scholars have conducted. Gender and queer scholarship, in turn, could profit conceptually from the sophisticated theoretical discussions that have animated practice scholars in IR. Empirically, concepts of gender could invigorate analyses of the more traditional diplomatic settings, where many practice scholars have directed their attention. How do, for example, gender dynamics impact on inter-state negotiations? Do mutual attractions, possible jealousies or similar sexual orientations among diplomats have an impact on the dynamics of negotiations and possible negotiation outcomes? Which practices have diplomats developed to deal with these issues?

These questions directly relate to another issue area that deserves more attention among practice scholars, namely the connection between practices and affect and emotions. There is a proliferating literature on emotions in IR (see, for example, Hall, 2015; Hutchison and Bleiker, 2014) that links up very well with practices. Some practice scholars have already conducted work on this connection (Adler-Nissen and Tsinovoi, 2019; Austin and Leander, Chapter 10; Bially Mattern, 2011; Walters, Chapter 6), specifically focusing on the link between emotions and the performative dimension of practices. Yet more research could pay attention to the connection between emotions and the embodied dimension of practices. Empirically, there would be fruitful avenues for studying the link between emotions and practices of warfare, or emotions and the very physical dimensions of practices of diplomatic negotiations, such as fatigue, hunger, alcohol consumption and so on.

To some extent this also links up with developing new methodological approaches for the study of practices in IR. Practice scholarship lends itself to the development of highly innovative methodologies, such as using the self as a tool of analysis (Neumann and Neumann, 2015). Other innovative approaches practice scholars have used include reformulations of the ethnographic spectrum of methods, such as participant observation and shadowing, rethinking the use of focus groups or developing forms of action research with international practitioners (Bueger and Gadinger, 2018). A practice lens also creates room for experimentation with practices through deliberately intervening in practitioner settings or exploring the ethnomethodological ideas of experimentation. Indeed, in the conduct of new empirical research with the help of innovative methodologies lies the largest promise of practice scholarship at this stage, and this is where practice scholars should now focus most of their attention.

Finally, practice scholars will also have to devote more substantial energy to the question of how they want to theorize practice. Kratochwil's (Chapter 11) warning about the limits of any generalisations to actually tell us something about situations of action needs to be taken seriously. While the majority of practice theorizers reject any project of building grand theory, the question of if and how generalisations about practices are appropriate and at what level these should operate will need to be addressed. This question will gain in importance the more empirical and detailed descriptions of practices are conducted. These not only face the challenge of how to order the messiness of practices but also how to present results in ways that makes them intelligible to others, including those not familiar with practice theorizing. New ways of tinkering with the purpose of abduction, of building ideal types, forming new concepts or finding other means to make research relevant outside the immediate context of inquiry will be needed.

We do not think that streamlining and unifying the very diverse set of practice theories in IR holds any promise. On the contrary, it would quell and inhibit the highly innovative and creative work that emerges in this branch of scholarship. Instead, we encourage scholars to continue the conversations among practice theorists, with strands of theorizing outside the practice turn for cross fertilization and inspiration, and, above all, with practitioners. Conducting empirical research and venturing beyond armchair theorizing is where the largest promise of practice theorizing lies.

References

Abbott, A. (1995). Things of boundaries, *Social Research*, 62(4), 857–82.
  (2005). The Historicity of Individuals, *Social Science History*, 29(1), 1–13.
Abbott, K., J. F. Green and R. O. Keohane. (2016). Organizational Ecology and Institutional Change in Global Governance, *International Organization*, 70(2), 247–77.
Abrahamsen, R. and M. C. Williams. (2011). *Security beyond the State: Private Security in International Politics*, Cambridge University Press.
Acharya, A. (2004). How Ideas Spread: Whose Norms Matter? Norm Localization and Institutional Change in Asian Regionalism, *International Organization*, 58(2), 239–75.
Acuto, M. (2014). Everyday International Relations: Garbage, Grand Designs, and Mundane Matters, *International Political Sociology*, 8(4), 345–62.
Acuto, M. and S. Curtis, eds. (2013). *Reassembling International Theory: Assemblage Thinking and International Relations*, Palgrave Macmillan.
Adams, M. (2006). Hybridizing Habitus and Reflexivity: Towards an Understanding of Contemporary Identity? *Sociology*, 40(3), 511–28.
Adler, E. (1991). Cognitive Evolution: A Dynamic Approach for the Study of International Relations and Their Progress. In E. Adler and B. Crawford, eds., *Progress in Postwar International Relations*, Columbia University Press, 43–88.
  (1992). The Emergence of Cooperation: National Epistemic Communities and the International Evolution of the Idea of Nuclear Arms Control, *International Organization*, 46(1), 101–45.
  (1997). Seizing the Middle Ground: Constructivism in World Politics, *European Journal of International Relations*, 3(3), 319–63.
  (2005). *Communitarian International Relations: The Epistemic Foundations of International Relations*, Routledge.
  (2008). The Spread of Security Communities: Communities of Practice, Self-Restraint, and NATO's Post-Cold War Transformation, *European Journal of International Relations*, 14(2), 195–230.
  (2019). *World Ordering: A Social Theory of Cognitive Evolution*, Cambridge University Press.
Adler, E. and S. Bernstein. (2005). Knowledge in Power: The Epistemic Construction of Global Governance. In M. Barnet and R. Duvall, eds., *Power in Global Governance*, Cambridge University Press, 294–318.

Adler, E. and B. Crawford, eds. (1991). *Progress in Postwar International Relations*, Columbia University Press.

Adler, E. and A. Drieschova. (2021). The Epistemological Challenge of Truth-Subversion to the Liberal International Order, *International Organization*, 75(2), 359–86.

Adler, E. and P. Greve. (2009). When Security Community Meets Balance of Power: Overlapping Regional Mechanisms of Security Governance, *Review of International Studies*, 35(S1), 59–84.

Adler, E. and P. M. Haas. (1992). Conclusion: Epistemic Communities, World Order, and the Creation of a Reflective Research Program, *International Organization*, 46(1), 367–90.

Adler, E. and V. Pouliot. (2011a). *International Practices*, Cambridge University Press.

(2011b). International Practices, *International Theory*, 3(1), 1–36.

(2011c). International Practices: Introduction and Framework. In E. Adler and V. Pouliot, eds., *International Practices*, Cambridge University Press, 3–35.

(2015). Fulfilling the Promises of Practice Theory in IR, *International Studies Quarterly Online*, www.isanet.org/Publications/ISQ/Posts/ID/4956/Fulfilling-The-Promises-of-Practice-Theory-in-IR.

Adler-Nissen, R., ed. (2012). *Bourdieu in International Relations: Rethinking Key Concepts in IR*, Routledge.

Adler-Nissen, R. (2013a). Sovereignty. In R. Adler-Nissen, ed., *Bourdieu in International Relations: Rethinking Key Concepts in IR*, Routledge, 179–92.

(2013b). *Bourdieu in International Relations: Rethinking Key Concepts in IR*, Routledge.

(2014a). *Opting Out of the European Union: Diplomacy, Sovereignty and European Integration*, Cambridge University Press.

(2014b). Stigma Management in International Relations: Transgressive Identities, Norms and Order in International Society, *International Organization*, 68(1), 143–76.

(2014c). Symbolic Power in European Diplomacy: The Struggle between National Foreign Services and the EU's External Action Service, *Review of International Studies*, 40(4), 657–81.

(2016). Towards a Practice Turn in EU Studies: The Everyday of European Integration, *Journal of Common Market Studies*, 54(1), 87–103.

Adler-Nissen, R. and A. Drieschova. (2019). Track-Change Diplomacy: Technology, Affordances, and the Practice of International Negotiations, *International Studies Quarterly*, 63(3), 531–45.

Adler-Nissen, R. and V. Pouliot. (2014). Power in Practice: Negotiating the International Intervention in Libya, *European Journal of International Relations*, 20(4), 889–911.

Adler-Nissen, R. and A. Tsinovoi. (2019). International Misrecognition: The Politics of Humour and National Identity in Israel's Public Diplomacy, *European Journal of International Relations*, 25(1), 3–29.

Aelst, P. V. et al. (2017). Political Communication in a High-Choice Media Environment: A Challenge for Democracy? *Annals of the International Communication Association*, 41(1), 3–27.

Agamben, G. (1998). *Homo Sacer: Sovereign Power and Bare Life*, Stanford University Press.

Ahamed, L. (2009). *Lords of Finance: The Bankers Who Broke the World*, Penguin.

Akrich, M. (2010). From Communities of Practice to Epistemic Communities: Health Mobilizations on the Internet, *Sociological Research Online*, 15(2), 1–17.

Aldrich, N. W. (1910). An Address by Senator Nelson W. Aldrich before the Economic Club of New York, 29 November 1909, on the Work of the National Monetary Commission. Archives: Library of Congress, Collection Nelson W. Aldrich Papers.

Allan, B. (2017). Producing the Climate: States, Scientists, and the Constitution of Global Governance Objects, *International Organization*, 71(1), 131–62.

   (2018). From Subjects to Objects: Knowledge in International Relations Theory, *European Journal of International Relations*, 24(4), 841–64.

Amin, A. and P. Cohendet. (2004). *Architectures of Knowledge: Firms, Capabilities, and Communities*, Oxford University Press.

Andersen, M. S. and I. B. Neumann. (2012). Practices as Models: A Methodology with an Illustration Concerning Wampum Diplomacy, *Millennium*, 40(3), 457–81.

Antoniades, A. (2003). Epistemic Communities, Epistemes and the Construction of (World) Politics, *Global Society*, 17(1), 21–38.

Arbatov, A. (2016). Saving Nuclear Arms Control, *Bulletin of the Atomic Scientists*, 72(3), 165–70.

Archer, M. (1988). *Culture and Agency: The Place of Culture in Social Theory*, Cambridge University Press.

Arendt, H. (1958). *The Human Condition*, University of Chicago Press.

   (2006). *Between Past and Future*, Penguin.

Aristotle. (1975). *Nicomachean Ethics*, translated by H. Rackham, Harvard University Press.

Ashley, R. (1989). Living on Border Lines: Man, Poststructuralism and War. In J. Der Derian and M. Shapiro, eds., *International/Intertextual Relations*, Lexington Books, 259–323.

Ashley, R. and R. B. J. Walker. (1990). Speaking the Language of Exile: Dissident Thought in International Studies, *International Studies Quarterly*, 34(3), 259–68.

Austin, J. L. (1975). *How to Do Things with Words*, Oxford University Press.

   (2016). Torture and the Material-Semiotic Networks of Violence Across Borders, *International Political Sociology*, 10(1), 3–21.

   (2017a). *Small Worlds of Violence: A Global Grammar for Torture*, Graduate Institute Geneva.

   (2017b). We Have Never Been Civilized: Torture and the Materiality of World Political Binaries, *European Journal of International Relations*, 23(1), 49–73.

   (2019). Security Compositions, *European Journal of International Security*, 4(3), 249–73.

   (2020a). The Departed Militant: A Portrait of Joy, Violence, and Political Evil. *Security Dialogue*, 51(6), 537–56.

   (2020b). The Poetry of Moans and Sighs: Designs for and against Violence, *Frame: Journal of Literary Studies*, 33(2), 13–31.

Austin, J. L., R. Bellanova and M. Kaufmann. (2019). Doing and Mediating Critique: An Invitation to Practice Companionship, *Security Dialogue*, 50(1), 3–19.

Austin, J. L. and A. Leander. (2021). Designing-With/In World Politics: Manifestos for an International Political Design, *Political Anthropological Research on International Social Sciences (PARISS)*, 2(1), 83–154.

Autesserre, S. (2014). *Peaceland: Conflict Resolution and the Everyday Politics of International Intervention*, Cambridge University Press.

Avant, D. D., M. Finnemore and S. K. Sell, eds. (2010). *Who Governs the Globe?* Cambridge University Press.

Axelrod, R. (1984). *The Evolution of Cooperation*, Basic Books.

Baert, P. and F. C. Da Silva. (2010). One Hundred Years of French Social Theory: Form Structuralism to Pragmatism. In P. Baert and F. C. Da Silva, eds., *Social Theory in the Twentieth Century and Beyond*, Polity, 12–51.

Bagehot, W. (1873). *Lombard Street, a Description of the Money Market*, Smith.

Bain, W. (2003). *Between Anarchy and Society: Trusteeship and the Obligations of Power*, Oxford University Press.

Baker, A. (2006). *The Group of Seven: Finance Ministries, Central Banks and Global Financial Governance*, Routledge.

Barbato, M. (2013). *Pilgrimage, Politics and International Relations: Religious Semantics for World Politics*, Palgrave Macmillan.

Barker, R. (1982). *Conscience, Government, and War: Conscientious Objection in Great Britain, 1939–45*, Routledge & Kegan Paul.

Barnes, B. (2001). Practice as Collective Action. In T. R. Schatzki, K. Knorr Cetina and E. von Savigny, eds., *The Practice Turn in Contemporary Theory*, Routledge, 25–36.

Barnett, M. and R. Duvall. (2005). Power in Global Governance. In M. Barnett and R. Duvall, eds., *Power and Global Governance*, Cambridge University Press, 1–32.

Barnett, M. N. and M. Finnemore. (1999). The Politics, Power, and Pathologies of International Organizations, *International Organization*, 53(4), 699–732.

(2004). *Rules for the World: International Organizations in Global Politics*, Cornell University Press.

Barry, A. (1999). Demonstrations: Sites and Sights of Direct Action, *Economy & Society*, 28, 75–94.

(2004). Ethical Capitalism. In W. Larner and W. Walters, eds., *Global Governmentality: Governing International Spaces*, Routledge, 195–211.

Bartelson, J. (1995). *A Genealogy of Sovereignty*, Cambridge University Press.

Barth, K-H. (1998). Science and Political in Early Nuclear Test Ban Negotiations, *Physics Today*, 51(3), 34–9.

(2006). Catalysts of Change: Scientists as Transnational Arms Control Advocates in the 1980s, *Osiris*, 21(1), 182–206.

Becker, H. (1998). *Tricks of the Trade: How to Think about Your Research while You're Doing It*, University of Chicago Press.

Bellamy, A. J., P. Williams and S. Griffin. (2010). *Understanding Peacekeeping*, 2nd ed., Polity Press.

Bénatouïl, T. (1999). A Tale of Two Sociologies: The Critical and Pragmatic Stance in Contemporary French Sociology, *European Journal of Social Theory*, 2(3), 379–96.

Benner, T. and P. Rotmann. (2008). Learning to Learn? UN Peacebuilding and the Challenges of Building a Learning Organization, *Journal of Intervention and Statebuilding*, 2(1), 43–62.

Bentham, J. (1789). *An Introduction to the Principles of Morals and Legislation*, London: Dover Publications.

Berling, T. V. (2015). *The International Political Sociology of Security: Rethinking Theory and Practice*, Routledge.

Bernstein, R. J., ed. (1985). *Habermas and Modernity*, MIT Press.

Bernstein, S. (2000). Ideas, Social Structure, and the Compromise of Liberal Environmentalism, *European Journal of International Relations*, 6(4), 464–512.

 (2013). Global Environmental Norms. In R. Falkner, ed., *The Handbook of Global Climate and Environment Policy*, John Wiley & Sons Ltd., 127–45.

 (2014). The Publicness of Private Global Environmental and Social Governance. In J. Best and A. Gheciu, eds., *The Return of the Public in Global Governance*, Cambridge University Press, 120–48.

Bernstein, S. and H. van der Ven. (2017). Best Practices in Global Governance, *Review of International Studies*, 43(3), 534–56.

Berthoin Antal, A., M. Hutter and D. Stark, eds. (2015). *Moments of Valuation. Exploring Sites of Dissonance*, Oxford University Press.

Bertram, G. W. (2019). *Art as Human Practice: An Aesthetics*, Bloomsbury Academic.

Best, J. and A. Gheciu. (2014a). *The Return of the Public in Global Governance*, Cambridge University Press.

 (2014b). Theorizing the Public as Practices: Transformations of the Public in Historical Context. In J. Best and A. Gheciu, eds., *The Return of the Public in Global Governance*, Cambridge University Press, 15–44.

Betts, A. and P. Orchard. (2014). Conclusions. In A. Betts and P. Orchard, eds., *Implementation and World Politics: How International Norms Change Practice*, Oxford University Press, 270–85.

Bially Mattern, J. (2011). A Practice Theory of Emotion for International Relations. In E. Adler and V. Pouliot, eds., *International Practices*, Cambridge University Press, 63–86.

Bially Mattern, J. and A. Zarakol. (2016). Hierarchies in World Politics, *International Organization*, 70(3), 623–54.

Bigo, D. (2011). Pierre Bourdieu and International Relations: Power of Practices, Practices of Power, *International Political Sociology*, 5(3), 225–58.

Bloor, D. (1976). *Knowledge and Social Imagery*, University of Chicago Press.

 (2001). Wittgenstein and the Priority of Practice. In T. Schatzki, et al., eds., *The Practice Turn in Contemporary Theory*, Routledge, 103–14.

Blumer, H. (1954). What Is Wrong with Social Theory? *American Sociological Review*, 19(1), 3–10.

 (1986). What Is Wrong with Social Theory? In ibid.: *Symbolic Interactionism. Perspective and Method*, University of California Press, 140–52.

Boltanski, L. (2011). *On Critique. A Sociology of Emancipation*, Polity Press.

Boltanski, L. and L. Thévenot. (2006). *On Justification. Economies of Worth*, Princeton University Press.

Bonditti, P., D. Bigo and F. Gros, eds. (2017). *Foucault and the Modern International*, Palgrave Macmillan.

Bordo, M. D. and A. J. Schwartz, eds. (1984). *A Retrospective on the Classical Gold Standard, 1821–1931*, University of Chicago Press.

Bourbeau, P. (2017). The Practice Approach in Global Politics, *Journal of Global Security Studies*, 2(2), 170–82.

Bourdieu, P. (1977). *Outline of a Theory of Practice*, translated by R. Nice, Cambridge University Press.

(1984). *Distinction. A Social Critique of the Judgement of Taste*, Harvard University Press.

(1985). The Genesis of the Concepts of Habitus and of Field, *Sociocriticism*, 2(2), 11–24.

(1990). *The Logic of Practice*, Stanford University Press.

(1993). *The Field of Cultural Production: Essays on Art and Literature*, Polity Press.

(2000 [1972]). *Esquisse d'une théorie de la pratique*, Seuil.

(2001). *Langage et pouvoir symbolique*, Seuil.

(2002). *Masculine Domination*, Stanford University Press.

Bourdieu, P. and L. J. D. Wacquant. (1992). *An Invitation to Reflexive Sociology*, University of Chicago Press.

Bratman, M. (2014). *Shared Agency*, Oxford University Press.

Brighenti, A. M. (2007). Visibility: A Category for the Social Sciences, *Current Sociology*, 55(3), 323–42.

(2008). Visual, Visible, Ethnographic, *Etnografia e ricerca qualitativa*, 1(1), 91–114.

(2010). *Visibility in Social Theory and Social Research*, Palgrave Macmillan.

Brown, C. (2012). The 'Practice Turn', Phronesis and Classical Realism: Towards a Phronetic International Political Theory? *Millennium: Journal of International Studies*, 40(3), 439–56.

Brown, J. S. and P. Duguid. (1991). Organizational Learning and Communities-of-Practice: Toward a Unified View of Working, Learning, and Innovation, *Organization Science*, 2(1), 40–57.

Brumann, C. and D. Berliner, eds. (2016). *World Heritage On The Ground. Ethnographic Perspectives*, Berghahn.

Bruner, R. F. and S. D. Carr. (2007). Lessons from the Financial Crisis of 1907, *Journal of Applied Corporate Finance*, 19(4), 115–24.

Brunnée, J. and S. J. Toope. (2010). *Legitimacy and Legality in International Law: An Interactional Account*, Cambridge University Press.

(2011). Interactional International Law and the Practice of Legality. In E. Adler and V. Pouliot, eds., *International Practices*, Cambridge University Press, 108–35.

(2019). Norm Robustness and Contestation in International Law: Self-Defence against Non-State Actors, *Journal of Global Security Studies*, 4(1), 73–87.

Bryant, L. R. (2011). A Logic of Multiplicities: Deleuze, Immanence, and Onticology, *Analecta Hermeneutica*, 3, 1–20.

Bucher, B. (2014). Acting Abstractions: Metaphors, Narrative Structures, and the Eclipse of Agency, *European Journal of International Relations*, 20(3), 742–65.

Bueger, C. (2011). Communities of Practice in World Politics – Theory or Technology? *52nd Annual International Studies Association conference*, 16–19 March.

(2013). Pathways to Practice: Praxiography and International Politics, *European Political Science Review*, 6(3), 383–406.

(2014). From Expert Communities to Epistemic Arrangements: Situating Expertise in International Relations. In M. Mayer, M. Carpes and R. Knoblich, eds., *The Global Politics of Science and Technology*, Vol. I, Springer-Verlag, 40–54.

(2015). Making Things Known: Epistemic Practice, the United Nations and the Translation of Piracy, *International Political Sociology*, 9(1), 1–19.

(2017a). Let's Count Beyond Three: Understanding the Conceptual and Methodological Terrain of International Practice Theory, *International Studies Quarterly*, 2. Available at: www.isanet.org/Publications/ISQ/Posts/ID/5478/Lets-count-beyond-three-Understanding-the-conceptual- and-methodological-terrain-of-international-practice-theories. (Accessed 13 November 2021).

(2017b). Practices, Norms and the Theory of Contestation, *Polity*, 49(1), 126–31.

Bueger, C. and F. Bethke. (2013). Actor-Networking the 'Failed State' – An Enquiry into the Life of Concepts, *Journal of International Relations and Development*, 17(1), 30–60.

Bueger, C. and F. Gadinger. (2007). Reassembling and Dissecting: International Relations Practice from a Science Studies Perspective, *International Studies Perspectives*, 8(1), 90–110.

(2014). *International Practice Theory: New Perspectives*, Palgrave Macmillan.

(2015). The Play of International Practice, *International Studies Quarterly*, 59(3), 449–60.

(2018). *International Practice Theory*, Palgrave Macmillan.

Bull, H. (1966). International Theory: The Case of a Classical Approach, *World Politics*, 15(3), 361–77.

(2012). *The Anarchical Society: A Study of Order in World Politics*, Palgrave.

Butler, J. (1997). *Excitable Speech. A Politics of the Performative*, Routledge.

(1999). *Gender Trouble. Feminism and the Subversion of Identity*, Routledge.

Buzan, B. and O. Waever. (2003). *Regions and Powers: The Structure of International Security*, Cambridge University Press.

Byrne, A. (2017). Hungary's Orban Vows to Defend Poland from EU Sanctions. *Financial Times*, 22 July. Available from: www.ft.com/content/b1bd2424-6ed7-11e7-93ff-99f383b09ff9.

Cadman, L. (2010). How (not) to Be Governed: Foucault, Critique, and the Political, *Environment and Planning D*, 28(3), 539–56.

Callon, M. (1986). Elements of a Sociology of Translation: Domestication of the Scallops and the Fishermen of St Brieuc Bay. In J. Law, ed., *Power, Action and Belief: A New Sociology of Knowledge?* Routledge, 196–233.

Carlsnaes, W. (1992). The Agency-Structure Problem in Foreign Policy Analysis, *International Studies Quarterly*, 36(3), 245–70.

Carr, E. H. (1964). *The Twenty Years Crisis*, Harper Torchbooks.

Castells, M. (1996). *The Rise of the Network Society*, Blackwell.

Clark, E. and C. Black. (2016). The appearance of disappearance: The CIA's secret black sites, *The Financial Times*, 17 March.

Clough, P. (2009). The New Empiricism: Affect and Sociological Method. *European Journal of Social Theory*, 12(1), 43–61.

Coe, N. M. and T. G. Brunell. (2003). Spatializing Knowledge Communities: Towards a Conceptualization of Transnational Innovation Networks, *Global Networks*, 3(4), 437–56.

Cohen, M., J. March and J. Olsen. (1972). A Garbage Can Model of Organizational Choice, *Administrative Science Quarterly*, 17(1), 1–25.

Cohendet, P., F. Creplet and O. Dupouët. (2001). Communities of Practice and Epistemic Communities: A Renewed Approach of Organisational Learning within the Firm. Retrieved from ResearchGate: www.researchgate.net/publication/228587324_Communities_of_Practice_and_Epistemic_Communities_A_Renewed_Approach_of_Organizational_Learning_within_the_Firm.

Coleman, W. D. and S. F. Bernstein. (2009). *Unsettled Legitimacy, Political Community, Power, and Authority in a Global Era, Globalization and Autonomy*, University of British Colombia Press.

Collier, S. (2009). Topologies of Power: Foucault's Analysis of Political Government beyond "Governmentality", *Theory, Culture & Society*, 26(6), 78–108.

Conlisk, J. (1996). Why Bounded Rationality? *Journal of Economic Literature*, 34(2), 669–90.

Connolly, W. (1983). *The Terms of Political Discourse*, Princeton University Press.

Cooley, A. (2003). Thinking Rationally about Hierarchy and Global Governance, *Review of International Political Economy*, 10(4), 627–84.

Cornut, J. (2018). Diplomacy, Agency, and the Logic of Improvisation and Virtuosity in Practice, *European Journal of International Relations*, 24(3), 712–36.

Cortell, A. P. and J. W. Davis. (1996). How Do International Institutions Matter? The Domestic Impact of International Rules and Norms, *International Studies Quarterly*, 40(4), 451–78.

Cottrell, P. (1995). The Bank of England in Its International Setting, 1918–1972. In R. Roberts and D. Kynaston, eds., *The Bank of England: Money, Power, and Influence 1694–1994*, Clarendon Press, 83–139.

Créplet, F., O. Dupouët and E. Vaast. (2003). Episteme or Practice? Differentiated Communitarian Structures in a Biology Laboratory. Retrieved from Research Gate: www.researchgate.net/publication/228720203_Episteme_or_practice_Differentiated_Communitarian_Structures_in_a_Biology_Laboratory.

Crone, M. (2014). Religion and Violence: Governing Muslim Militancy through Aesthetic Assemblages, *Millennium: Journal of International Studies*, 43(1), 291–307.

Cruikshank, B. (1996). Revolutions within: Self-Government and Self-Esteem. In B. Andrew, O. Thomas and R. Nikolas, eds., *Foucault and Political Reason: Liberalism, Neo-Liberalism and Rationalities of Government*, University of Chicago Press, 231–52.

D'Aoust, A.-M. (2014). Ties that Bind? Engaging Emotions, Governmentality and Neoliberalism: Introduction to the Special Issue, *Global Society*, 28(3), 267–76.

Davidson, A. (2011). In Praise of Counter-Conduct, *History of the Human Sciences*, 24(4), 25–41.

Davis Cross, M. K. (2013). Rethinking Epistemic Communities Twenty Years Later, *Review of International Studies*, 39(1), 137–60.

Davis, J. (2005). *Terms of Inquiry: On the Theory and Practice of Political Science*, Johns Hopkins University Press.

Davis, J. and C. Daase, eds. (2015). *Clausewitz on Small Wars*, Oxford University Press.

De Genova, N. (2013). Spectacles of Migrant "Illegality": The Scene of Exclusion, the Obscene of Inclusion, *Ethnic and Racial Studies*, 36(7), 1180–98.

Dean, M. (1994). *Critical and Effective Histories*, Routledge.

(2010). *Governmentality: Power and Rule in Modern Society*, 2nd ed., Sage Publications.

Death, C. (2010). Counter-Conducts: A Foucauldian Analytics of Protest, *Social Movement Studies*, 9(3), 235–51.

Deleuze, G. (1988). *Foucault*, University of Minnesota Press.

(1991). *Qu'est-ce que la philosophie?* Éditions de minuit.

Deleuze, G. and F. Guattari. (1987). *A Thousand Plateaus: Capitalism and Schizophrenia*, Athlone Press.

(2004). *A Thousand Plateaus*, Continuum.

Derrida, J. (1982). *Margins of Philosophy*, University of Chicago Press.

(1988). *Limited Inc.*, Northwestern University Press.

Dessler, D. (1989). What's at Stake in the Agent-Structure Debate? *International Organization*, 43(3), 441–73.

Dewey, J. (1916). *Democracy and Education*, The Macmillan Company.

(1922). *Human Nature and Conduct*, Henry Holt and Company.

(1984). *The Early Works of John Dewey, 1882–1953*, Vol. IV of The Quest for Certainty, J. A. Boydston, ed. Southern Illinois University Press.

(1988). *The Middle Works of John Dewey, 1899–1924*, Vol. XII of Reconstruction in Philosophy and Essays, J. A. Boydston, ed., Southern Illinois University Press.

Doty, R. L. (1993). Foreign Policy as Social Construction: A Post-Positivist Analysis of U.S. Counterinsurgency Policy in the Philippines, *International Studies Quarterly*, 37(3), 297–320.

(1996). *Imperial Encounters*, University of Minnesota Press.

(1997). Aporia: A Critical Exploration of the Agent–Structure Problematique in International Relations Theory, *European Journal of International Relations*, 3(3), 365–92.

Douglas, M. (1986). *How Institutions Think*, Syracuse University Press.

Dunlop, C. A. (2009). Policy Transfer as Learning: Capturing Variation in What Decision-Makers Learn From Epistemic Communities, *Policy Studies*, 30(3), 289–311.

Dunn, F. S. (1929). *The Practice and Procedure of International Conferences*, Literary Licensing.

Dunne, T. (1998). *Inventing International Society: A History of the English School*, St. Martin's Press.

Duvall, R. D. and A. Chowdhury. (2011). Practices of Theory. In E. Adler and V. Pouliot, eds., *International Practices*, Cambridge University Press, 335–54.

Eagleton-Pierce, M. (2013). *Symbolic Power in the World Trade Organization*, Oxford University Press.

Eikeland, O. and D. Nicolini. (2011). Turning Practically: Broadening the Horizon, *Journal of Organizational Change Management*, 24(2), 164–74.

Einzig, P. (1932). *Montagu Norman: A Study in Financial Statesmanship*, K. Paul, Trench, Trubner & co., ltd.

Enderlein, H., S. Wälti and M. Zürn, eds. (2010). *Handbook on Multi-Level Governance*, Edward Elgar.

Engelkamp, S. and K. Glaab. (2015). Writing Norms. Constructivist Norm Research and the Politics of Ambiguity, *Alternatives: Global, Local, Political*, 40(3–4), 201–18.

Enloe, C. (2000). *Maneuvers: The International Politics of Militarizing Women's Lives*, University of California Press.

(2016). Flick of the Skirt: A Feminist Challenge to IR's Coherent Narrative, *International Political Sociology*, 10(4), 320–31.

Epstein, C. (2011). Who Speaks? Discourse, the Subject and the Study of Identity in International Politics, *European Journal of International Relations*, 17(2), 327–50.

(2012). Stop Telling Us How to Behave, *Socialization or Infantilization? International Studies Perspectives*, 13(2), 135–45.

(2013). Norms. In R. Adler-Nissen, ed., *Bourdieu in International Relations*, Routledge, 165–78.

Ezrahi, Y. (2012). *Imagined Democracies: Necessary Political Fictions*, Cambridge University Press.

Fassin, D. (2009). Another politics of life is possible, *Theory, Culture & Society*, 26(5), 44–60.

Fekete, L., F. Webber and A. Edmond-Petit. (2017). *Humanitarianism: The Unacceptable Face of Solidarity*, Institute of Race Relations.

Fierke, K. (2002). Links Across the Abyss: Language and Logic in International Relations, *International Studies Quarterly*, 46(3), 331–54.

(2010). Constructivism. In T. Dunne, M. Kurki and S. Smith, eds., *International Relations Theories: Discipline and Diversity*, Oxford University Press, 161–78.

Fine, G. (1995). *On Ideas Aristotle's Criticism of Plato's Theory of Forms*, Oxford University Press.

Finnemore, M. (1996). Constructing Norms of Humanitarian Intervention. In P. Katzenstein, ed., *The Culture of National Security*, Columbia University Press, 153–85.

Finnemore, M. and K. Sikkink. (1998). International Norm Dynamics and Political Change, *International Organization*, 52(4), 887–917.

Fischer, D. (1997). *History of the International Atomic Energy Agency: The First Forty Years*, International Atomic Energy Agency.

Fligstein, N. and D. McAdam. (2011). Toward a General Theory of Strategic Action Fields, *Sociological Theory*, 29(1), 1–26.

Florini, A. (1996). The Evolution of International Norms, *International Studies Quarterly*, 40(3), 363–89.

Forsberg, T. (2012). Vincent Pouliot, International Security in Practice: The Politics of NATO-Russia Diplomacy, *Europe-Asia Studies*, 64(1), 169–71.

Foucault, M. (1971). *The Order of Things: An Archeology of the Human Sciences*, Pantheon.

  (1977). *Discipline and Punish. The Birth of the Prison*, Routledge.

  (1988). Technologies of the Self. In L. H. Martin, L. H. Gutman and P. H. Hutton, eds., *Technologies of the Self: A Seminar with Michel Foucault*, University of Massachusetts Press, 16–49.

  (1990). *The History of Sexuality, Volume One*, Vintage.

  (2000). The Subject and Power. In F. James, ed., *Michel Foucault: Power*, The New Press, 326–48.

  (2003). *Society Must be Defended: Lectures at the Collège de France 1975–1976*, Palgrave Macmillan.

  (2005). *The Hermeneutics of the Subject. Lectures at the College de France 1981–1982*, Picador.

  (2007). *Security, Territory, Population: Lectures at the Collège de France 1977–78*, Palgrave Macmillan.

  (2008). *The Birth of Biopolitics: Lectures at the Collège de France 1978–1979*, Palgrave Macmillan.

  (2010). *The Government of Self and Others: Lectures at the Collège de France, 1982–1983*, Palgrave Macmillan.

  (2011). *The Courage of Truth (The Government of Self and Others II): Lectures at the Collège de France, 1983–1984*, Palgrave Macmillan.

  (2014). *Wrong-Doing and Truth-Telling: The Function of Avowal in Justice*, University of Chicago Press.

Franck, T. (1990). *The Power of Legitimacy Among Nations*, Oxford University Press.

Freeman, R., S. Griggs and A. Boaz. (2011). The Practice of Policy Making, *Evidence & Policy*, 7(2), 127–36.

Frega, R. (2014). The Normative Creature: Toward a Practice-Based Account of Normativity, *Social Theory and Practice*, 40(1), 1–27.

Friedrichs, J. (2004). *European Approaches to International Relations Theory*, Routledge.

Friedrichs, J. and F. Kratochwil. (2009). On Acting and Knowing: How Pragmatism Can Advance International Relations Research and Methodology, *International Organization*, 63(4), 701–31.

Frost, M. and S. Lechner. (2016a). Two Conceptions of International Practice: Aristotelian Praxis or Wittgensteinian Language Games? *Review of International Studies*, 42(2), 334–50.

  (2016b). Understanding International Practices from the Internal Point of View, *Journal of International Political Theory*, 12(3), 299–319.

Fuller, L. (1958). Positivism and Fidelity to the Law – A Reply to Prof. Hart, *Harvard Law Review*, 71(4), 630–72.

  (1969). *The Morality of Law*, revised edition, Yale University Press.

Furedi, F. (2013). *Authority: A Sociological History*, Cambridge University Press.

Gadinger, F. (2016). On Justification and Critique: Luc Boltanski's Pragmatic Sociology and International Relations, *International Political Sociology*, 10(3), 187–205.

Garcia, T. (2014). *Form and Object: A Treatise on Things*, translated by M. A. Ohm and J. Cogburn, Edinburgh University Press.

Garfinkel, H. (1967). *Studies in Ethnomethodology*, Prentice Hall.

Garnham, N. and R. Williams. (1980). Pierre Bourdieu and the Sociology of Culture: An Introduction, *Media, Culture and Society*, 2(3), 209–23.

Gherardi, S. (2016). To Start Practice Theorizing Anew: The Contribution of the Concepts of Agencement and Formativeness, *Organization*, 23(5), 680–98.

Giddens, A. (1984). *The Constitution of Society. Outline of the Theory of Structuration*, University of California Press.

   (1987). Structuralism, Post-Structuralism and the Production of Culture. In A. Giddens and J. H. Turner, eds., *Social Theory Today*, Stanford University Press, 195–223.

Gielen, P. (2005). Art and Social Value Regimes, *Current Sociology*, 53(5), 789–806.

Gieryn, T. F. (1999). *Cultural Boundaries of Science: Credibility on the Lin*, University of Chicago Press.

Gilady, L. and M. J. Hoffman. (2013). Darwin's Finches or Lamarck's Giraffe, Does International Relations Get Evolution Wrong? *International Studies Review*, 15, 307–27.

Go, J. (2008). Global Fields and Imperial Forms: Field Theory and the British and American Empires, *Sociological Theory*, 26(3), 201–29.

Gogol, N. V. (2006). *Diary of a Madman and other Stories*, Dover Publications.

Goldstein, J. (2001). *War and Gender: How Gender Shapes the War System and Vice Versa*, Cambridge University Press.

Golsorkhi, S., L. Rouleau, D. Seidl and E. Vaara, eds. (2010). *Cambridge Handbook of Strategy as Practice*, Cambridge University Press.

Gordon, C. (1991). Governmental rationality: An introduction. In G. Burchell, C. Gordon and P. Miller, eds., *The Foucault Effect: Studies in Governmentality*, University of Chicago Press, 1–52.

Grande, E. and L. W. Pauly, eds. (2005). *Complex Sovereignty: Reconstituting Political Authority in the Twenty-First Century*, University of Toronto Press.

Grimmel, A. and G. Hellmann. (2019). Theory Must Not Go on Holiday. Wittgenstein, the Pragmatists, and the Idea of Social Science, *International Political Sociology*, 13(2), 198–214.

Gronow, A. (2011). *From Habits to Social Structures: Pragmatism and Contemporary Social Theory*, Peter Lang.

Gross Stein, J. (2011). Background Knowledge in the Foreground: Conversations about Competent Practice in "Sacred Space". In E. Adler and V. Pouliot, eds., *International Practices*, Cambridge University Press, 87–107.

Gumbrecht, H. U. and K. L. Pfeiffer, eds. (1988). *Materialities of Communication*, Stanford University Press.

Guzman, G. (2013). The Grey Textures of Practice and Knowledge: Review and Framework, *European Business Review*, 25(5), 429–52.

Guzzini, S. (2000). A Reconstruction of Constructivism in International Relations, *European Journal of International Relations*, 6(2), 147–82.

(2005). The Concept of Power: A Constructivist Analysis, *Millennium*, 33(3), 495–521.

(2013). The Ends of International Relations Theory: Stages of Reflexivity and Modes of Theorizing, *European Journal of International Relations*, 19(3), 521–41.

Haak, S. (2006). *Pragmatism, Old and New: Selected Writings*, Prometheus Books.

Haas, E. B. (1997). *Nationalism, Liberalism, and Progress: The Rise and Decline of Nationalism*, Vol. 1, Cornell University Press.

(2000). *Nationalism, Liberalism, and Progress: The Dismal Fate of New Nations*, Vol. II, Cornell University Press.

Haas, P. M. (1992). Introduction: Epistemic Communities and International Policy Coordination, *International Organization*, 46(1), 1–35.

(2004). Addressing the Global Governance Deficit, *Global Environmental Politics*, 4(4), 1–15.

Habermas, J. (1968). *Erkenntnis und Interesse*, Suhrkamp.

(1993). *Faktizitaet und Geltung*, Suhrkamp.

Hacking, I. (2002). *Historical Ontology*, Harvard University Press.

Hafemeister, D. (2016). *Nuclear Proliferation and Terrorism in the Post-9/11 World*, Springer.

Hagstrom, W. O. (1965). *The Scientific Community*, Basic Books.

Hajer, M. (2003). Policy without Polity? Policy Analysis and the Institutional Void, *Policy Sciences*, 36(2), 175–95.

Håkanson, L. (2010). The Firm as an Epistemic Community: The Knowledge-Based View Revisited, *Industrial and Corporate Change*, 19(6), 1801–28.

Hall, R. B. (2008). *Central Banking as Global Governance: Constructing Financial Credibility*, Cambridge University Press.

Hall, R. B. and T. J. Biersteker, eds. (2002). *The Emergence of Private Authority in Global Governance*, Cambridge University Press.

Hall, T. (2015). *Emotional Diplomacy: Official Emotion on the International Stage*, Cornell University Press.

Hamburg, D. A. (2015). *A Model of Prevention: Life Lessons*, Routledge.

Hammarskjöld, D. (1957). *Regulations for the United Nations Emergency Force*, United Nations.

Hanrieder, T. (2016). Orders of Worth and the Moral Conceptions of Health in Global Politics, *International Theory*, 8(3), 390–421.

Hansen, L. (2006). *Security as Practice: Discourse Analysis and the Bosnian War*, Routledge.

(2011). Performing Practices: A Poststructuralist Analysis of the Muhammad Cartoon Crisis. In E. Adler and V. Pouliot, eds., *International practices*, Cambridge University Press, 280–309.

Hansen, M. (1997). Not Thus, after All, Would Life Be Given: Technesis, Technology, and the Parody of Romantic Poetics in Frankenstein, *Studies in Romanticism*, 36(4), 575–609.

(2000). *Embodying Technesis: Technology Beyond Writing*, The University of Michigan Press.

Hansen, T. A. (2015). Scientific Communities of Practice for Learning – Lessons From Ethnographic Fieldwork. Retrieved from Research Gate: www.researchgate.net/publication/281625987_Scientific_communities_ of_practice_for_learning_-_lessons_from_ethnographic_fieldwork.

Haraway, D. (1988). Situated Knowledges: The Science Question in Feminism and the Privilege of Partial Perspective, *Feminist Studies*, 14(3), 575–99.

Hardt, M. and A. Negri. (2000). *Empire*, Harvard University Press.

Hart, H. L. A. (1958). Positivism and the Separation of Law and Morals, *Harvard Law Review*, 71(4), 593–629.

Hausman, C. R. (1993). *Charles S. Peirce's Evolutionary Philosophy*, Cambridge University Press.

Hawkins, D., D. A. Lake, D. L. Nielson and M. J. Tierney. (2006). *Delegation and Agency in International Organizations*, Cambridge University Press.

Hawkins, G. (2011). Packaging Water: Plastic Bottles as Market and Public Devices, *Economy & Society*, 40, 534–52.

Hecker, S. S., ed. (2016). *Doomed to Cooperate: How American and Russian Scientists Joined Forces to Avert Some of the Greatest Post-Cold War Nuclear Dangers*, Vol. I, Bathtub Row Press.

Heinich, N. (1991). *La Gloire de Van Gogh. Essai d'anthropologie de l'admiration*, Éditions de Minuit.

(2001). *La sociologie de l'art*, La Découverte.

(2012). *De la visibilité*, Gallimard.

Hellmann, G. (2009). Beliefs as Rules for Action: Pragmatism as a Theory of Thought and Action, *International Studies Review*, 11(3), 638–62.

(2017). Interpreting International Relations. In G. Hellmann and M. Valbjorn, eds., *The Forum: Problematizing Global Challenges: Recalibrating the "Inter" in IR-Theory*, *International Studies Review*, 19, 296–300.

Hennessy, E. (1992). *A Domestic History of the Bank of England, 1930–1960*, Cambridge University Press.

Hillebrandt, F. (2014). *Soziologische Praxistheorien. Eine Einführung*, Springer VS.

Hirschauer, St. (2008). Die Empiriegeladenheit von Theorien und der Erfindungsreichtum der Praxis. In H. Kalthoff, St. Hirschauer and G. Lindemann, eds., *Theoretische Empirie. Zur Relevanz qualitativer Forschung*, Suhrkamp, 165–87.

Hofius, M. (2016). Community at the Border or the Boundaries of Community? The Case of EU Field Diplomats. *Review of International Studies*, 42(5), 939–67.

Holmes, M. and D. Traven. (2015). Acting Rationally without Really Thinking: The Logic of Rational Intuitionism for International Relations Theory, *International Studies Review*, 17(3), 414–40.

Hooper, C. (2001). *Manly States: Masculinities, International Relations, and Gender Politics*, Columbia University Press.

Hopf, T. (1998). The Promise of Constructivism in International Relations Theory, *International Security*, 23(1), 171–200.

(2010). The Logic of Habit in International Relations, *European Journal of International Relations*, 16(4), 539–61.

(2011). International Security in Practice: The Politics of NATO–Russia Diplomacy. By Vincent Pouliot. New York: Cambridge University Press, 2010, *Perspectives on Politics*, 9(3), 772–3.

(2018). Change in International Practices, *European Journal of International Relations*, 24(3), 687–711.

Hui, A., Th. R. Schatzki and E. Shove, eds. (2017). *The Nexus of Practices. Connections, Constellations, Practitioners*, Routledge.

Hume, D. (1875). On *Essay Writing in Essays, Literary, Moral and Political*, In T. H. Green and T. H. Grose, eds., Longmans, Green and Co, 367–71.

Hurrell, A. (2007). *On Global Order: Power, Values, and the Constitution of International Society: Power, Values, and the Constitution of International Society*, Oxford University Press.

Hutchison, E. and R. Bleiker. (2014). Theorizing Emotions in World Politics, *International Theory*, 6(3), 491–514.

ICJ. (2004). Advisory Opinion on the 'Legal Consequences of the Construction of a Wall in the Occupied Territory of Palestine, ICJ, 9 July 2004.

International Commission on Intervention and State Sovereignty. (2001). *The Responsibility to Protect*, International Commission on Intervention and State Sovereignty.

Jabri, V. (2014). Disarming Norms. Postcolonial Agency and the Constitution of the International, *International Theory*, 6(2), 372–90.

Jackson, P. (2011). H-Diplo/ISSF Roundtable Review of Vincent Pouliot. *International Security in Practice: The Politics of NATO-Russia Diplomacy*, 14–21. Available at: https://issforum.org/ISSF/PDF/ISSF-Roundtable-2-5 .pdf. (Accessed March 2018).

Jackson, P. and D. H. Nexon. (1999). Relations before States: Substance, Process and the Study of World Politics, *European Journal of International Relations*, 5(3), 291–332.

(2013). International Theory in a Post-paradigmatic Era: From Substantive Wagers to Scientific Ontologies, *European Journal of International Relations*, 19(3), 543–65.

Jackson, R. (2000). *The Global Covenant*, Oxford University Press.

Jenkins, R. (2002). *Pierre Bourdieu*, Psychology Press.

Jervis, R. (2011). H-Diplo/ISSF Roundtable Review of Vincent Pouliot. *International Security in Practice: The Politics of NATO-Russia Diplomacy*, 22–9. Available at: https://issforum.org/ISSF/PDF/ISSF-Roundtable-2-5.pdf. (Accessed March 2018).

Jessop, B. (2011). Constituting another Foucault Effect: Foucault on States and Statecraft. In U. Bröckling, S. Krassmann and T. Lemke, eds., *Governmentality: Current Issues and Future Challenges*, Routledge, 56–73.

Joas, H. (1996). *The Creativity of Action*, Polity Press.

Johnson, J. (2016). *Priests of Prosperity: How Central Bankers Transformed the Postcommunist World*, Cornell University Press.

Joseph, J. (2010). The Limits of Governmentality: Social Theory and the International, *European Journal of International Relations*, 16, 223–46.

Joseph, J. and M. Kurki. (2018). The Limits of Practice: Why Realism Can Complement IR's Practice Turn, *International Theory*, 10(1), 71–97.

Joshi, M., S. Y. Lee and R. Mac Ginty. (2014). Just How Liberal Is the Liberal Peace? *International Peacekeeping*, 21(3), 364–89.

Joyce, P. (1994), *Democratic Subjects: The Self and the Social in Nineteenth-century England*, Cambridge University Press.

Kalaycioglu, E. (2020). Governing Culture 'Credibly': Contestation in the World Heritage Regime. In A. Phillips and C. Reus-Smit, eds., *Culture and Order in World Politics*, Cambridge University Press, 294–316.

Kant, I. (1991). *Kant: Political Writings*, H. S. Reiss, ed., 2nd ed., Cambridge University Press, 61–92.

(1998). *Critique of the Power of Judgment*, translated and edited by Paul Guyer and A. W. Wood, Cambridge University Press.

(2011). *Perpetual Peace in Kant: Political Writings*, H. S. Reiss, ed., 2nd ed., Cambridge University Press.

Kapstein, E. B. (1994). *Governing the Global Economy: International Finance and the State*, Harvard University Press.

Karlsrud, J. (2013). Special Representatives of the Secretary-General as Norm Arbitrators? Understanding Bottom-up Authority in UN Peacekeeping, *Global Governance*, 19(4), 525–44.

(2015). The UN at War: Examining the Consequences of Peace-Enforcement Mandates for the UN Peacekeeping Operations in the CAR, the DRC and Mali, *Third World Quarterly*, 36(1), 40–54.

Kassianova, A. (2016). U.S.-Russia Nuclear Lab-to-Lab Cooperation: Looking Back On a Quarter Century of Constructive Relations, *PONARS Eurasia Policy Memo*, (425), 1–6.

Katzenstein, P. (1996). Introduction: Alternative Perspectives on National Security. In P. Katzenstein, ed., *The Culture of National Security: Norms and Identity in World Politics*, Columbia University Press, 1–32.

Keller, R. (2011). The Sociology of Knowledge Approach to Discourse (SKAD), *Human Studies*, 34(1), 43–65.

Kemp, S. R. (2014). The Nonproliferation Emperor Has no Clothes: The Gas Centrifuge, Supply-Side Controls, and the Future of Nuclear Proliferation, *International Security*, 38(4), 39–78.

Keohane, R. (1984). *After Hegemony: Cooperation and Discord in the World Political Economy*, Princeton University Press.

Keohane, R. and J. S. Nye. (1977). *Power and Interdependence: World Politics in Transition*, Little.

Kersbergen, K. and B. Verbeek. (2007). The Politics of International Norms: Subsidiarity and the Imperfect Competence Regime of the European Union, *European Journal of International Relations*, 13(2), 217–38.

Kessler, O. (2016). The Contingency of Constructivism: On Norms, the Social, and the Third, *Millennium – Journal of International Studies*, 45(1), 43–63.

Kilminster, R. (1982). Theory and Practice in Marx and Marxism, *Royal Institute of Philosophy Lecture Series*, 14, 157–76.

King, G., R. Keohane and S. Verba. (1996). *Designing Social Inquiry*, Princeton University Press.

Knight, J. (1994). *Institutions and Social Conflict*, Cambridge University Press.

Knorr Cetina, K. (1981a). Introduction: The Microsociological Challenge of Macro-Sociology: Towards a Reconstruction of Social Theory and Methodology. In K. Knorr Cetina and A. V. Cicourel, eds., *Advances in Social Theory and Methodology. Toward an Integration of Micro and Macro Sociologies*, Routledge, 1–47.

(1981b). *The Manufacture of Knowledge: An Essay on the Constructivist and Contextual Nature of Science*, Pergamon Press.

(2001). Objectual Practice. In T. R. Schatzki, K. Knorr-Cetina and E. Von Savigny, eds., *The Practice Turn in Contemporary Theory*, Routledge, 184–97.

(2009). The Synthetic Situation: Interactionism for a Global World, *Symbolic Interaction*, 32(1), 61–87.

Koremenos, B., C. Lipson and D. Snidal. (2001). The Rational Design of International Institutions, *International Organization*, 55(4), 761–99.

Koslowski, R. and F. V. Kratochwil. (1994). Understanding Change in International Politics: The Soviet Empire's Demise and the International System, *International Organization*, 48(2), 215–47.

Krämer, B. (2017). Populist Online Practices: The Function of the Internet in Right-Wing Populism, *Information, Communication & Society*, 20(9), 1293–1309.

Krasner, S. (1999). *Sovereignty: Organized Hypocrisy*, Princeton University Press.

Kratochwil, F. (1989). *Rules, Norms and Decisions. On the Conditions of Practical and Legal Reasoning in International Relations and Domestic Affairs*, Cambridge University Press.

(2000). Constructing a New Orthodoxy? Wendt's 'Social Theory of International Politics' and the Constructivist Challenge, *Millennium – Journal of International Studies*, 29(1), 73–101.

(2011). Making Sense of "International Practices". In E. Adler and V. Pouliot, eds., *International Practices*, Cambridge University Press, 36–60.

(2014). *The Status of Law in World Society: Meditations on the Role and Rule of Law*, Cambridge University Press.

Krook, M. L. and J. True. (2010). Rethinking the Life Cycles of International Norms: The United Nations and the Global Promotion of Gender Equality, *European Journal of International Relations*, 18(1), 103–27.

Krygier, M. (1986). Law as Tradition, *Law and Philosophy*, 5(2), 237–62.

Ku, A. (1998). Boundary Politics in the Public Sphere: Openness, Secrecy, and Leak, *Sociological Theory*, 16(2), 172–92.

Kuhn, T. S. (1962). *The Structure of Scientific Revolutions*, Chicago University Press.

Kustermans, J. (2016). Parsing the Practice Turn: Practice, Practical Knowledge, Practices, *Millennium: Journal of International Studies*, 44(2), 175–96.

Lahire, B. (2003). From the Habitus to an Individual Heritage of Dispositions. Towards a Sociology at the Level of the Individual, *Poetics*, 31(5–6), 329–55.

(2004). *La culture des individus. Dissonances culturelles et distinction de soi*, La Découverte.

Lake, D. A. (2009). *Hierarchy in International Relations*, Cornell University Press.

(2010). Rightful Rules: Authority, Order, and the Foundations of Global Governance, *International Studies Quarterly*, 54(3), 587–613.

(2013). Legitimating Power: The Domestic Politics of U.S. International Hierarchy, *International Security*, 28(2), 74–111.

Lakoff, G. (1987). *Women, Fire and Dangerous Things*, University of Chicago Press.

Lakoff, G. and M. Johnson. (1999). *Philosophy in the Flesh*, University of Chicago Press.

Lamont, C. and E. Skeppström. (2013). *The United Nations at War in the DRC? Legal Aspects of the Intervention Brigade*, Swedish Ministry of Defence.

Lamont, M. (2012). Toward a Comparative Sociology of Valuation and Evaluation, *Annual Review of Sociology*, 38(1), 201–21.

Lapid, Y. (1989). The Third Debate: On the Prospects of International Relations Theory in a Post-Positivist Era, *International Studies Quarterly*, 33(3), 235–54.

Lapid, Y. and F. Kratochwil, eds. (1996). *The Return of Culture and Identity in IR Theory*, Lynne Rienner.

Lash, S. (1993). Pierre Bourdieu: Cultural Economy and Social Change. In C. Calhoun, E. LiPuma and M. Postone, eds., *Bourdieu: Critical Perspectives*, University of Chicago Press, 193–211.

Latour, B. (1987). *Science in Action: How to Follow Scientists and Engineers Through Society*, Harvard University Press.

(1992). Where Are the Missing Masses? The Sociology of a Few Mundane Artifacts. In W. Bijker and J. Law, eds., *Shaping Technology/Building Society. Studies in Sociotechnical Change*, MIT Press, 225–58.

(1993). *We Have Never Been Modern*, Harvard University Press.

(2005). *Reassembling the Social. An Introduction to Actor-Network-Theory*, Oxford University Press.

(2010). An Attempt at a "Compositionist Manifesto", *New Literary History*, 41, 471–90.

Laurence, M. (2019). An 'Impartial' Force? Normative Ambiguity and Practice Change in UN Peace Operations, *International Peacekeeping*, 26(3), 256–80.

Lave, J. and E. Wenger. (1991). *Situated Learning: Legitimate Peripheral Participation*, Cambridge University Press.

Law, J. (1999). After ANT: Complexity, Naming and Topology, *The Sociological Review*, 47, 1.

(2004). And if the Global were Small and Noncoherent? Method, Complexity, and the Baroque, *Environment and Planning D: Society and Space*, 22, 13–27.

Law, J. and A. Mol. (2001). Situating Technoscience: An Inquiry into Spatialities, *Environment and Planning D: Society and Space*, 19(5), 601–21.

Le Chiffon Rouge. (2016). "Mon inaction me rendrait complice", s'est défendu Cédric Herrou à son procès. 5 January. www.le-chiffon-rouge-morlaix .fr/2017/01/mon-inaction-me-rendrait-complice-s-est-defendu-cedric-herrou-a-son-proces-mediapart-5-janvier-2016.html.

Leander, A. (2010). Practices (Re)producing Orders Understanding the Role of Business in Global Security Governance. In A. Leander and M. Ougaard, eds., *Business and Global Governance*, Routledge, 57–78.

(2011). The Promises, Problems, and Potentials of a Bourdieu-Inspired Staging of International Relations, *International Political Sociology*, 5(3), 294–313.

(2013). Technological Agency in the Co-Constitution of Legal Expertise and the US Drone Program, *Leiden Journal of International Law*, 26(4), 811–31.

(2016). The Politics of Whitelisting: Regulatory Work and Topologies in Commercial Security, *Environment and Planning D: Society and Space*, 34(1), 48–66.

(2017). Digital/Commercial (in)visibility: The Politics of DAESH Recruitment Videos, *European Journal of Social Theory*, 20(3), 348–72.

(2020). Composing Collaborationist Collages about Commercial Security, *Political Anthropological Research on International Social Sciences*, 1(1), 73–109.

Lechner, S. and M. Frost. (2018). *Practice Theory and International Relations*, Cambridge University Press.

Leiulfsrud, H. and P. Sohlberg, eds. (2017). *Concepts in Action. Conceptual Constructionism*, Haymarket Books.

Lemke, T. (2007). An Indigestible Meal? Foucault, Governmentality and State Theory, *Distinktion: Scandinavian Journal of Social Theory*, 15, 43–65.

Lesch, M. (2017a). Norms, Law and Deviance. Doubts About Doubts About the Prohibition of Torture. Paper presented at the conference of the German Political Science Association (International Relations), October 2017, Bremen.

(2017b). Praxistheorien und Normenforschung: Zum Beitrag der pragmatischen Soziologie, *Zeitschrift Diskurs*, 2, 1–23.

L'Humanité. (2017). C'est l'état qui est dans l'illégalité, pas moi. 4 January. Available at: www.humanite.fr/cedric-herrou-cest-letat-qui-est-dans-lille-galite-pas-moi-629732. (Accessed 13 November 2021).

Liberman, K. (2013). *More Studies in Ethnomethodology*, State University of New York.

Liese, A. (2009). Exceptional Necessity: How Liberal Democracies Contest the Prohibition of Torture and Ill-Treatment When Countering Terrorism, *Journal of International Law and International Relations*, 5(1), 17–47.

Lindahl, H. (2018). *Authority and the Globalization of Inclusion and Exclusion*, Cambridge University Press.

Linklater, A. (2011). *The Problem of Harm in International Politics*, Cambridge University Press.

Lipson, M. (2007). Peacekeeping: Organized Hypocrisy? *European Journal of International Relations*, 13(1), 5–34.

Livingstone, D. (1984). *Hume's Philosophy of Common Life*, University of Chicago Press.

Lukes, S. (2005). Power and the Battle for Hearts and Minds, *Millennium*, 33(3), 477–93.

Macmillan Committee. (1931). Report of Committee on Finance and Industry. The National Archives: [On line]. Available at: http://discovery .nationalarchives.gov.uk/details/r/C1851842. (Accessed December 2017).

March, J. G. and J. P. Olsen. (1989). *Rediscovering Institutions: The Organizational Basis of Politics*, The Free Press.

(1998). The Institutional Dynamics of International Political Orders, *International Organization*, 52(4), 943–69.

Marcus, G. E. (1995). Ethnography in/of the World System: The Emergence of Multi-Sited Ethnography, *Annual Review of Anthropology*, 24, 95–117.

(1998). *Ethnography through Thick and Thin*, Princeton University Press.

Marks, L. (2004). Haptic Visuality: Touching with the Eyes, *Framework: The Finish Art Review*, 2, 79–82.

Marx, K. and F. Engels. (1976). *Collected Works*, Vol. 6, Lawrence & Wishart, 487.

Marshall, A. (2010). International Security in Practice: The politics of NATO–Russia Diplomacy, *International Affairs*, 86(6), 1417–18.

Martin-Mazé, M. (2017). Returning Struggles to the Practice Turn: How Were Bourdieu and Boltanski Lost in (Some) Translations and What to Do about It? *International Political Sociology*, 11(2), 203–20.

Martin, L. (1992). Interests, Power, and Multilateralism, *International Organization*, 46(4), 765–92.

Mauss, M. (1950). Les techniques du corps. In P. Gurvitch, ed., *Marcel Mauss: Sociologie et Anthropologie*, Quadriage PUF, 365–86.

(1966). *The Gift. Forms and Functions of Exchange in Archaic Societies*, Routledge.

McCourt, D. (2012). What is at Stake in the Historical Turn: Theory, Practice and Phronesis in International Relations, *Millennium*, 41(1), 23–41.

(2016). Practice Theory and Relationalism as the New Constructivism, *International Studies Quarterly*, 60(3), 475–85.

McCoy, A. (2012). *Torture and Impunity*, University of Wisconsin Press.

McKeown, R. (2009). Norm Regress: U.S. Revisionism and the Slow Death of the Torture Norm, *International Relations*, 23(1), 5–25.

McNamara, K. (2015). *The Politics of Everyday Europe: Constructing Authority in the European Union*, Oxford University Press.

Menand, L. (1997). *Pragmatism: A Reader*, Vintage Books.

(2001). *The Metaphysical Club*, Macmillan.

Merlingen, M. (2006). Foucault and World Politics: Promises and Challenges of Extending Governmentality Theory to the European and Beyond, *Millennium*, 35(1), 181–96.

Mérand, F. (2008). *European Defence Policy beyond the Nation State*, Oxford University Press.

(2010). Pierre Bourdieu and the Birth of European Defense, *Security Studies*, 19(2), 342–74.

Meyer, M. (2010). Caring for Weak Ties – the Natural History Museum as a Place of Encounter Between Amateur and Professional Science, *Sociological Research Online*, 15(2), 1–14.

Meyer, M. and S. Molyneux-Hodgson. (2010). Introduction: The Dynamics of Epistemic Communities, *Sociological Research Online*, 15(2), 1–7.

Miettinen, R., D. Samra-Fredericks and D. Yanow. (2009). Re-Turn to Practice: An Introductory Essay, *Organization Studies*, 30(12), 1309–27.

Miettinen, R. and J. Virkkunen. (2005). Epistemic Objects, Artefacts and Organizational Change, *Organization*, 12(3), 437–56.

Milbank, D. (2018). Trump's 'Fake News' Mantra Becomes an Effective Weapon – against America, *The Washington Post*, 16 April. Available at: www.washingtonpost.com/opinions/trump-bulldozed-truth--and-not-just-in-washington/2018/04/16/0f65718c-41b2-11e8-8569-26fda6b404c7_story.html?utm_term=.24b3a2eedc01.

Miller, C. A. (2006). 'An Effective Instrument of Peace': Scientific Cooperation as an Instrument of U.S. Foreign Policy, 1938–1950, *Osiris*, 21(1), 133–60.

Milliken, J. (1999). The Study of Discourse in International Relations: A Critique of Research and Methods, *European Journal of International Relations*, 5(2), 225–54.

Misak, C. J. (1999). *Pragmatism*, University of Calgary Press.

Mitchell, T. (1991). The Limits of the State: Beyond Statist Approaches and Their Critics, *The American Political Science Review*, 85(1), 77–96.

Mitchell, W. J. T. (2005). *What Do Pictures Want?: The Lives and Loves of Images*, University of Chicago Press.

Moffitt, B. (2016). *The Global Rise of Populism: Performance, Political style, and Representation*, Stanford University Press.

Mol, A. (2002). *The Body Multiple: Ontology in Medical Practice*, Duke University Press.

(2010). Actor-Network Theory: Sensitive Terms and Enduring Tensions, *Kölner Zeitschrift für Soziologie und Sozialpsychologie*, 50(1), 253–69.

Moon, K. (1997). *Sex Among Allies: Military Prostitution in U.S.-Korea Relations*, Columbia University Press.

Mudde, C. (2004). The Populist Zeitgeist, *Government and Opposition*, 39(4), 541–63.

Muirhead, B. (1999). *Against the Odds: The Public Life and Times of Louis Rasminsky*, University of Toronto Press.

Nair, D. (2019). Sociability in International Politics: Golf and ASEAN's Cold War Diplomacy, *International Political Sociology*, 14(2), 196–214.

(2020). Emotional Labor and the Power of International Bureaucrats, *International Studies Quarterly*, 64(3), 573–87.

Navari, C. (2011). The Concept of Practice in the English School, *European Journal of International Relations*, 17(4), 611–30.

Neumann, I. (2002). Returning Practice to the Linguistic Turn: The Case of Diplomacy, *Millennium: Journal of International Studies*, 31(3), 627–51.

(2012). *At Home with the Diplomats. Inside a European Foreign Ministry*, Cornell University Press.

Neumann, I. and V. Pouliot. (2011). Untimely Russia: Hysteresis in Russian-Western Relations over the Past Millennium, *Security Studies*, 20(1), 105–37.

Neumann, I. and O. J. Sending. (2010). *Governing the Global Polity. Practice, Mentality, Rationality,* University of Michigan Press.

Neumann Basberg, C. and I. Neumann. (2015). Uses of the Self: Two Ways of Thinking about Scholarly Situatedness and Method, *Millennium,* 43(3), 798–819.

New York Times. (2016). A French underground railroad, moving African migrants', 4 October.

(2017). Farmer on trial defends smuggling migrants: "I am a Frenchman." 5 January. www.nytimes.com/2017/01/.../cedric-herrou-migrant-smuggler-trial-france.html.

Nexon, D. H. and I. Neumann. (2018). Hegemonic Order Theory: A Field Theoretic Account, *European Journal of International Relations,* 24(3), 662–86.

Nexon, D. H. and V. Pouliot. (2013). 'Things of Networks': Situating ANT in International Relations, *International Political Sociology,* 7(3), 342–5.

Nicolini, D. (2013). *Practice Theory, Work & Organization,* Oxford University Press.

(2017). Practice Theory as a Package of Theory, Method and Vocabulary: Affordances and Limitations. In M. Jonas, B. Littig and A. Wroblewski, eds., *Methodological Reflections on Practice Oriented Theories,* Springer, 19–34.

Niedner-Kalthoff, U. (2015). *Producing Cultural Diversity. Hegemonic Knowledge in Global Governance Projects,* Campus Verlag.

Niemann, H. and H. Schillinger. (2016). Contestation 'all the way down'? The Grammar of Contestation in Norm Research, *Review of International Studies,* 43(1), 29–49.

Niezen, R. and M. Sapignoli, eds. (2017). *Palaces of Hope. The Anthropology of Global Organizations,* Cambridge University Press.

Nordstrom, C. (2004). *Shadows of War: Violence, Power, and International Profiteering in the 21st Century,* University of California Press.

Nye, J. (2004). *Soft Power: The Means To Success in World Politics,* Public Affairs.

Oakeshott, M. (1962). *Rationalism in Politics,* Basic Books.

(1975). *On Human Conduct,* Clarendon Press.

Odysseos, L., C. Death and H. Malmvig. (2016). Interrogating Michel Foucault's Counter-Conduct: Theorising the Subjects and Practices of Resistance in Global Politics, *Global Society,* 30(2), 151–6.

Oliver, J. E. and W. M. Rahn. (2016). Rise of the Trumpenvolk: Populism in the 2016 Election, *Annals of the American Academy of Political and Social Science,* 667(1), 189–206.

Ong, A. and S. Collier. (2005). Global Assemblages, Anthropological Problems. In A. Ong and S. Collier, eds., *Global Assemblages,* Blackwell, 3–21.

Onuf, N. (1989). *World of Our Making. Rules and Rule in Social Theory and International Relations,* University of South Carolina Press.

(1997). *How Things Get Normative,* Hebrew University of Jerusalem.

(2002). Institutions, Intentions and International Relations, *Review of International Studies,* 28(2), 211–28.

(2010). Rules in Practice. In O. Kessler, et al., eds., *On Rules, Politics and Knowledge: Friedrich Kratochwil, International Relations and Domestic Affairs,* Palgrave Macmillan, 115–26.

Orford, A. (2012). In Praise of Description, *Leiden Journal of International Law*, 25(3), 609–25.

Ortner, Sh. B. (1984). Theory in Anthropology since the Sixties, *Comparative Studies in Society and History*, 26(1), 126–66.

Osborne, T. (1994). Sociology, Liberalism and the Historicity of Conduct, *Economy & Society*, 23, 484–501.

Paddon Rhoads, E. (2016). *Taking Sides in Peacekeeping: Impartiality and the Future of the United Nations*, Oxford University Press.

Panel on United Nations Peace Operations. (2000). *Report of the Panel on United Nations Peace Operations*, United Nations.

Panke, D. and U. Petersohn. (2012). Why Some International Norms Disappear, *European Journal of International Relations*, 18(4), 719–42.

Paret, P. (1986). Clausewitz. In P. Paret, ed., *Makers of Modern Strategy*, Princeton University Press, 186–216.

Paris, R. (2004). *At War's End: Building Peace After Civil Conflict*, Cambridge University Press.

Parsons, C. (2015). Before Eclecticism: Competing Alternatives in Constructivist Research, *International Theory*, 7(3), 501–38.

Pauly, L. (1997). *Who Elected the Bankers?: Surveillance and Control in the World Economy*, Cornell University Press.

Pauwelyn, J., R. A. Wessel and J. Wouters. (2014). When Structures Become Shackles: Stagnation and Dynamics in International Lawmaking, *European Journal of International Law*, 25(3), 733–63.

Pech, L. and K. L. Scheppele. (2017). Illiberalism Within: Rule of Law Back-sliding in the EU, *Cambridge Yearbook of European Legal Studies*, 19, 3–47.

Peter, M. (2015). Between Doctrine and Practice: The UN Peacekeeping Dilemma, *Global Governance*, 21(3), 351–70.

Pickering, A. (1995). *The Mangle of Practice: Time, Agency, and Science*, The University of Chicago Press.

Pifre, S. (2017). The Future of U.S.-Russia Nuclear Arms Control, *AIP Conference Proceedings*, 1898(020001), 1–11.

Polanyi, M. (1958). *Personal Knowledge*, University of Chicago Press.

Pouliot, V. (2008). The Logic of Practicality: A Theory of Practice of Security Communities, *International Organization*, 62(02), 257–88.

  (2010). *International Security in Practice: The Politics of NATO-Russia Diplomacy*, Cambridge University Press.

  (2016a). Hierarchy in Practice: Multilateral Diplomacy and the Governance of International Security, *European Journal of International Security*, 1(1), 5–26.

  (2016b). *International Pecking Orders: The Politics and Practice of Multilateral Diplomacy*, Cambridge University Press.

  (2020a). Historical Institutionalism Meets Practice Theory: Renewing the Selection Process of the United Nations Secretary-General, *International Organization*, 74(4), 742–72.

  (2020b). The Gray Area of Institutional Change: How the Security Council Transforms Its Practices on the Fly, *Journal of Global Security Studies*, 6(3), 1–18.

Pouliot, V. and F. Mérand. (2013). Bourdieu's Concepts: Political Sociology in International Relations. In R. Adler-Nissen, ed., *Bourdieu in International Relations: Rethinking Key Concepts in IR*, Routledge, 24–44.

Pouliot, V. and J.-P. Thérien. (2015). The Politics of Inclusion: Changing Patterns in the Global Governance of International Security, *Review of International Studies*, 41(2), 211–37.

Pratt, S. F. (2020). From Norms to Normative Configurations: A Pragmatist and Relational Approach to Theorizing Normativity in IR, *International Theory*, 12(1), 59–82.

Putnam, H. (1995). *Pragmatism: An Open Question*, Blackwell.

Rabinow, P. (2003). *Anthropos Today: Reflections on Modern Equipment*, Princeton University Press.

Ralph, J. and J. Gifkins. (2017). The Purpose of the United Nations Security Council Practice: Contesting Competence Claims in the Normative Context Created by the Responsibility to Protect, *European Journal of International Relations*, 23(3), 630–53.

Rancière, J. (1998). The Cause of the Other, *Parallax*, 4(2), 25–33.

(1999). *Disagreement: Politics and Philosophy*, University of Minnesota Press.

(2004). *The Politics of Aesthetics: The Distribution of the Sensible*, Continuum.

Rawls, J. (1971). *A Theory of Justice*, Harvard University Press.

Raymond, M. and L. DeNardis. (2015). Multistakeholderism: Anatomy of an Inchoate Global Institution, *International Theory*, 7(3), 572–616.

Reckwitz, A. (2002). Toward a Theory of Social Practices: A Development in Culturalist Theorizing, *European Journal of Social Theory*, 5(2), 243–63.

(2012). Affective Spaces. A Praxeological Outlook, *Rethinking History*, 16(2), 241–58.

(2014). *Die Materialisierung der Kultur, Praxeologie*, De Gruyter.

Reus-Smit, C. (2007). International Crises of Legitimacy, *International Politics*, 44(2–3), 157–74.

Richards, R. (1987). *Darwin and the Emergence of Evolutionary Theories of Mind and Behavior*, University of Chicago Press.

Riles, A. (1998). Infinity within the Brackets, *American Ethnologist*, 25(3), 378–98.

(2000). *The Network Inside Out*, University of Michigan Press.

Ringmar, E. (2014). The Search for Dialogue as a Hindrance to Understanding: Practices as Inter-paradigmatic Research Program, *International Theory*, 6(1), 1–27.

Rolf, E. (2013). *Inferentielle Pragmatik*, Erich Schmidt Verlag.

Rosenau, J. N. and E. O. Czempiel, eds. (1992). *Governance Without Government: Order and Change in World Politics*, Cambridge University Press.

Rosenthal, G. (2013). *Statement of Ambassador Gert Rosenthal, Permanent Representative of Guatemala to the United Nations, Wrap-up Session of the Work of the Security Council During the Current Month*. Available at: www.guatema-laun.org/bin/documents/SCUN-wrap-upsession-30april2013.pdf.

Ross, A. (2013). *Mixed Emotions: Beyond Fear and Hatred in International Conflict*, University of Chicago Press.

Rotblat, J. (1967). *Pugwash: A History of the Conferences on Science and World Affairs*, Czechoslovak Academy of Sciences.

Rouse, J. (1993). What Are Cultural Studies of Scientific Knowledge? *Configurations*, 1(1), 1–22.

(1996). *Engaging Science: How to Understand Its Practices Philosophically*, Cornell University Press.

(2001). Two Concepts of Practices. In T. R. Schatzki, K. K. Cetina and E. von Savigny, eds., *The Practice Turn in Contemporary Theory*, Routledge, 198–208.

(2003). *How Scientific Practices Matter: Reclaiming Philosophical Naturalism*, University of Chicago Press.

(2007a). Practice Theory. In St P. Turner and M. W. Risjord, eds., *Handbook of the Philosophy of Science. Philosophy of Anthropology and Sociology*, North Holland, 639–81.

(2007b). Social Practices and Normativity, *Philosophy of the Social Sciences*, 37(1), 46–56.

Ruggie, J. G. (1975). International Responses to Technology: *Concepts and Trends, International Organization*, 29(3), 557–83.

(1998). *Constructing the World Polity: Essays on International Institutionalisation*, Routledge.

Sacks, H. (1972). Notes on Police Assessment of Moral Character. In D. Sudnow, ed., *Studies in Social Interaction*, The Free Press, 280–93.

Sandal, N. A. (2011). Religious Actors as epistemic communities in conflict transformation: The cases of South Africa and Northern Ireland, *Review of International Studies*, 37, 929–49.

Sandholtz, W. (2008). Dynamics of International Norm Change: Rules Against Wartime Plunder, *European Journal of International Relations*, 14(1), 101–31.

Sandholtz, W. and K. W. Stiles. (2009). *International Norms and Cycles of Change*, Oxford University Press.

Sassen, S. (2000). New Frontiers Facing Urban Sociology at the Millennium, *British Journal of Sociology*, 51(1), 143–60.

Saurette, P. and S. Gunster. (2011). Ears Wide Shut: Epistemological Populism, Agritainment and Canadian Conservative Talk Radio, *Canadian Journal of Political Science*, 44(1), 195–218.

Sawyer, R. K. (2005). *Social Emergence: Societies as Complex Systems*, Cambridge University Press.

Sayers, R. S. (1976). *The Bank of England, 1891–1944*, Cambridge University Press.

Schäfer, H. (2011). Bourdieu gegen den Strich lesen. Eine poststruktural-istische Perspektive. In D. Šuber, H. Schäfer and S. Prinz, eds., *Pierre Bourdieu und die Kulturwissenschaften. Zur Aktualität eines undisziplinierten Denkens*, UVK Verlagsgesellschaft, 63–85.

(2013). *Die Instabilität der Praxis. Reproduktion und Transformation des Sozialen in der Praxistheorie*, Velbrück.

(2016a). "Outstanding universal value". Die Arbeit an der Universalisierung des Wertvollen im UNESCO-Welterbe, *Berliner Journal für Soziologie*, 26(3–4), 353–75.

(2016b). *Praxistheorie. Ein soziologisches Forschungsprogramm*, Transcript Verlag.

(2017). Relationality and Heterogeneity: Transitive Methodology in Practice Theory and Actor-Network Theory. In M. Jonas, B. Littig and A. Wroblewski, eds., *Methodological Reflections on Practice Oriented Theories*, Springer, 35–46.

Schatzki, T. (1996). *Social Practices: A Wittgensteinian Approach to Human Activity and the Social*, Cambridge University Press.

(2001). Introduction: Practice Theory. In T. R. Schatzki, K. K. Cetina and E. von Savigny, eds., *The Practice Turn in Contemporary Theory*, Routledge, 1–14.

(2002). *The Site of the Social. A Philosophical Exploration of the Constitution of Social Life and Change*, Pennsylvania State University Press.

Schatzki, T. R., K. Knorr Cetina and E. Von Savigny, eds. (2001). *The Practice Turn in Contemporary Theory*, Routledge.

Scheppele, K. L. (2014). Constitutional Coups and Judicial Review, *Transnational Law & Contemporary Problems*, 23, 51–117.

(2016). *Worst Practices and the Transnational Legal Order (Or How to Build a Constitutional "Democratorship" in Plain Sight)*, Lecture at the University of Toronto, November 2016. www.law.utoronto.ca/utfl_file/count/documents/events/wright-scheppele2016.pdf.

Schindler, S. and T. Wille. (2015). Change in and Through Practice: Pierre Bourdieu, Vincent Pouliot, and the End of the Cold War, *International Theory*, 7(2), 330–59.

(2017). Two ways of criticizing international practices. Paper presented at the EISA conference, Barcelona 2017.

Schmidt, R. (2017). Sociology of Social Practices: Theory or Modus Operandi of Empirical Research? In M. Jonas, B. Littig and A. Wroblewski, eds., *Methodological Reflections on Practice Oriented Theories*, Springer, 3–17.

Schmidt, S. (2014). Foreign Military Presence and the Changing Practice of Sovereignty: A Pragmatist Explanation of Norm Change, *American Political Science Review*, 108(04), 817–29.

Scott, J. (1985). *Weapons of the Weak: Everyday Forms of Peasant Resistance*, Yale University Press.

Seabrooke, L. (2012). The Everyday Politics of Homespun Capital: Economic Patriotism in Housing Credit Systems, *Journal of European Public Policy*, 19(3), 358–72.

(2015). Diplomacy as Economic Consultancy. In O. J. Sending, V. Pouliot and I. B. Neumann, eds., *Diplomacy and the Making of World Politics*, Cambridge University Press, 195–219.

Searle, J. (1980). *Speech Acts*, Cambridge University Press.

(1995). *The Construction of Social Reality*, Penguin.

(2005). What Is an Institution? *Journal of Institutional Economics*, 1(1), 1–22.

Security Council Report. (2014). *In Hindsight: Changes to UN Peacekeeping in 2013*. Available at: www.securitycouncilreport.org/monthly-forecast/2014-02/in_hindsight_changes_to_un_peacekeeping_in_2013.php.

Selby, J. (2007). Engaging Foucault: Discourse, Liberal Governance and the Limits of Foucauldian IR, *International Relations*, 21(3), 324–45.

Sen, A. K. (1977). Rational Fools: A Critique of the Behavioral Foundations of Economic Theory, *Philosophy & Public Affairs*, 6(4): 317–344.

Sending, O. J. (2002). Constitution, Choice and Change: Problems with the 'Logic of Appropriateness' and Its Use in Constructivist Theory, *European Journal of International Relations*, 8(4), 443–70.

(2015). *The Politics of Expertise: Competing for Authority in Global Governance*, University of Michigan Press.

Sending, O. J. and I. B. Neumann. (2011). Banking on Power: How Some Practices in an International Organization Anchor Others. In E. Adler and V. Pouliot, eds., *International Practices*, Cambridge University Press, 231–54.

Sending, O. J., V. Pouliot and I. B. Neumann. (2015). *Diplomacy and the Making of World Politics*, Cambridge University Press.

Shapiro, M. J., G. M. Bonham and D. Heradstveit. (1988). A Discursive Practices Approach to Collective Decision-Making, *International Studies Quarterly*, 32(4), 397–419.

Shove, E. and M. Pantzar. (2007). Recruitment and Reproduction: The Careers and Carriers of Digital Photography and Floorball, *Human Affairs*, 17(2), 154–67.

Shove, E., M. Pantzar and M. Watson. (2012). *The Dynamics of Social Practice. Everyday Life and How It Changes*, Sage Publications.

Simmel, G. (1906). The Sociology of Secrecy and of Secret Societies, *American Journal of Sociology*, 11(4), 441–98.

Singleton, J. (2011). *Central Banking in the Twentieth Century*, Cambridge University Press.

Sismondo, S. (2010). *An Introduction to Science and Technology*, 2nd ed., Wiley-Blackwell.

(2017). Casting a Wider Net: A Reply to Collins, Evans and Weinel, *Social Studies of Science*, 47(4), 587–92.

Smith, V. C. (1936). *The Rationale of Central Banking*, King.

Spruyt, H. (1994). *The Sovereign State and Its Competitors*, Princeton University Press.

Stamp, J. C. (1931). The Report of the Macmillan Committee, *The Economic Journal*, 41(163), 424–35.

Stappert, N. (2020). Practice Theory and Change in International Law: Theorizing the Development of Legal Meaning Through the Interpretive Practices of International Criminal Courts, *International Theory*, 12(1), 33–58.

Stein, J. (2011). Background Knowledge in the Foreground: Conversations About Competent Practice in 'Sacred Space'. In E. Adler and V. Pouliot, eds., *International Practices*, Cambridge University Press, 87–107.

Stern, D. G. (2003). The Practical Turn. In S. P. Turner and P. A. Roth, eds., *The Blackwell Guide to the Philosophy of the Social Sciences*, Blackwell Publishing, 185–206.

Stimmer, A. and L. Wisken. (2019). The Dynamics of Dissent: When Actions Are Louder Than Words, *International Affairs*, 95(3), 515–33.

Sunstein, C. R. (2008). Democracy and the Internet. In J. Van Den Hoven and J. Weckert, eds., *Information Technology and Moral Philosophy*, Cambridge University Press, 93–110.

Svendsen, Ø. (2020). 'Practice Time!' Doxic Futures in Security and Defence Diplomacy After Brexit, *Review of International Studies*, 46(1), 3–19.

Swidler, A. (2001). What Anchors Cultural Practices. In K. Knorr Cetina, T. R. Schatzki and E. von Savigny, eds., *The Practice Turn in Contemporary Theory*, Routledge, 74–94.

Sylvester, C. (2012). War Experiences/War Practices/War Theory, *Millennium: Journal of International Studies*, 40(3), 483–503.

Taussig, M. (2009). *What Color Is the Sacred?* The University of Chicago Press.

Taylor, C. (1993 [1981]). To Follow a Rule.... In C. Calhoun, E. LiPuma and M. Postone, eds., *Bourdieu: Critical Perspectives*, Polity Press, 29–44.

Tazzioli, M. (2016). Revisiting the Omnes et Singulatim Bond: The Production of Irregular Conducts and the Biopolitics of the Governed. *Foucault Studies*, 21, 98–116.

Tetlock, P. (2005). *Expert Political Judgment*, Princeton University Press.

Thérien, J.-P. and V. Pouliot. (2020). Global Governance as Patchwork: The Making of the Sustainable Development Goals, *Review of International Political Economy*, 27(3), 612–36.

Thompson, J. B. (2005). The New Visibility, *Theory, Culture & Society*, 22, 31–51.

Thompson, W. R., ed. (2001). *Evolutionary Interpretations of World Politics*, Routledge.

Tickner, A. (1997). You Just Don't Understand: Troubled Engagements between Feminists and IR Theorists, *International Studies Quarterly*, 41(4), 611–32.

    (2005). What Is Your Research Program? Some Feminist Answers to International Methodological Questions? *International Studies Quarterly*, 49(1), 1–21.

    (2014). *A Feminist Voyage Through International Relations*, Oxford University Press, 1–1.

Toniolo, G. (2005). *Central Bank Cooperation at the Bank for International Settlements, 1930–1973*, Cambridge University Press.

Toplišek, A. (n.d.). *Reading Foucault's 'Counter-Conduct' through Arendt, Weber and Derrida: Politics and Resistance as Power.*

Tóth, C. (2014). Full Text of Viktor Orbán's Speech at Băile Tuşnad (Tusnádfürdő) of 26 July 2014. *The Budapest Beacon*, 29 July. Available at: https://budapestbeacon.com/full-text-of-viktor-orbans-speech-at-baile-tusnad-tusnadfurdo-of-26-july-2014/.

Toulmin, S. (2001). *Return to Reason*, Harvard University Press.

True, J. (2003). Mainstreaming Gender in Global Public Policy, *International Feminist Journal of Politics*, 5(3), 368–96.

    (2008). The Ethics of Feminism. In C. Reus-Smit and D. Snidal, eds., *The Oxford Handbook of International Relations*, Oxford University Press, 1.

UNESCO Intergovernmental Committee for the Protection of the World Cultural and Natural Heritage. (2015a). *Operational Guidelines for the Implementation of the World Heritage Convention*. Available at: https://whc.unesco.org/en/guidelines/. (Accessed 13 November 2021).

    (2015b). *Rules of Procedure*. Available at: http://whc.unesco.org/document/137812.

United Nations. (n.d.-a). *Background – MINUSMA – United Nations Stabilization Mission in Mali*. Available at: www.un.org/en/peacekeeping/missions/minusma/background.shtml.

(n.d.-b). Treaty on Principles Governing the Activities of States in the Exploration and Use of Outer Space, including the Moon and Other Celestial Bodies. Available at: www.unoosa.org/oosa/en/ourwork/spacelaw/treaties/introouterspacetreaty.html.

United Nations Department of Peacekeeping Operations. (2008). *United Nations Peacekeeping Operations: Principles and Guidelines*, United Nations Department of Peacekeeping Operations.

United Nations Security Council. (2013). *Resolution 2098 S/RES/2098 (2013)*. Available at: www.un.org/en/ga/search/view_doc.asp?symbol=S/RES/2098(2013).

Urry, J. (2004). Small Worlds and the New 'Social Physics', *Global Networks*, 4(2), 109–30.

Valverde, M. (2007). Genealogies of European States: Foucauldian Reflections, *Economy and Society*, 36(1), 159–78.

Van Winkel, C. (2005). *The Regime of Visibility*, Nai Publishers.

Veyne, P. (1997). Foucault Revolutionizes History. In A. Davidson, ed., *Foucault and His Interlocutors*, University of Chicago Press, 146–82.

(2010). *Foucault, His Thought, His character*, Wiley.

Vice News. (2017). Passeur citoyen: Rencontre avec Cédric Herrou, l'agriculteur qui aide les migrants. 18 January. Available at: https://news.vice.com/fr/video/passeur-citoyen-rencontre-avec-cedric-herrou-lagriculteur-qui-aide-les-migrants.

Villumsen, T. (2015). *The International Political Sociology of Security. Rethinking Theory and Practice*, Routledge.

Von Foerster, H. (2003). On Constructing a Reality. In H. Von Foerster, ed., *Understanding: Essays on Cybernetics and Cognition*, Springer, 211–27.

Waever, O. (1995). Securitization and Desecuritization. In R. Lipschutz, ed., *On Security*, Columbia University Press, 46–86.

Wallace, T., et al. (2017). Trump's Inauguration vs. Obama's: Comparing the Crowds. The New York Times, 20 January. Available at: www.nytimes.com/interactive/2017/01/20/us/politics/trump-inauguration-crowd.html. (Accessed November 2021)

Waldenfels, B. (2001). Die verändernde Kraft der Wiederholung. *Zeitschrift für Ästhetik und Allgemeine Kunstwissenschaft*, 46(1), 5–17.

Wallmeier, P. (2018). Is Contemporary Practice Theory a Critical Theory? Paper presented at 2018 ISA in San Francisco.

Walters, W. (2002). The Power of Inscription: Beyond Social Construction and Deconstruction in European Integration Studies, *Millennium*, 31(1), 83–108.

(2009). Anti-Political Economy: Cartographies of "Illegal Immigration" and the Displacement of the Economy. In J. Best and M. Paterson, eds., *Cultural Political Economy*, Routledge, 113–38.

(2012). *Governmentality. Critical Encounters*, Routledge.

Waltz, K. N. (1979). *Theory of International Politics*, Addison-Wesley Publishing Company.

Warburg, P. M. (1910). *The Discount System in Europe*, National Monetary Commission, Government Printing Office.

Warner, M. (2002). *Publics and Counterpublics*, Zone Books.

Watson, A. (1982). *Diplomacy: The Dialogue Between States*, Methuen.

Watson, S. (2011). Securing the Practical Turn in Constructivist Theory, *International Studies Review*, 13(3), 532–4.

Weber, C. (1998). Performative States. *Millennium: Journal of International Studies*, 27(1), 77–95.

(2008). Designing Safe Citizens, *Citizenship Studies*, 12(2), 125–42.

Weber, M. (1946). The Sociology of Charismatic Authority. In H. Gerth and C. W. Mills, eds., *From Max Weber: Essays in Sociology*, Oxford University Press, 245–52.

(1978). *Economy and Society*, University of California Press.

Welsh, J. M. (2013). Norm Contestation and the Responsibility to Protect, *Global Responsibility to Protect*, 5(4), 365–96.

Wendland, C. L. (2012). Moral Maps and Medical Imaginaries: Clinical Tourism at Malawi's College of Medicine, *American Anthropologist*, 114(1), 108–22.

Wendt, A. (1987). The Agent-Structure Problem in International Relations Theory, *International Organization*, 41(3), 335–70.

(1999). *Social Theory of International Politics*, Cambridge University Press.

(2001). Driving with the Rearview Mirror: On the Rational Science of Institutional Design, *International Organization*, 55(4), 1019–49.

(2015). *Quantum Mind and Social Science*, Cambridge University Press.

Wenger, E. (1998a). Communities of Practice: Learning as a Social System, *Systems Thinker*, 9(5):2.

(1998b). *Communities of Practice: Learning, Meaning, and Identity*, Cambridge University Press.

(2010). Communities of Practice and Social Learning Systems: The Career of a Concept. In C. Blackmore, ed., *Social Learning Systems and Communities of Practice*, Springer, 179–98.

Wenger, E., R. McDermott and W. M. Snyder. (2002). *Cultivating Communities of Practice: A Guide to Managing Knowledge*, Harvard Business School Press.

Wiener, A. (2004). Contested Compliance: Interventions on the Normative Structure of World Politics, *European Journal of International Relations*, 10(2), 189–234.

(2007). Contested Meanings of Norms: A Research Framework, *Comparative European Politics*, 5(1), 1–17.

(2008). *The Invisible Constitution of Politics. Contested Norms and International Encounters*, Cambridge University Press.

(2009). Enacting meaning-in-use. Qualitative Research on Norms and International Relations, *Review of International Studies*, 35(1), 175–93.

(2014). *A Theory of Contestation*, Springer.

(2018). *Contestation and Constitution of Norms in Global International Relations*, Cambridge University Press.

Wight, M. (1966). Western values in international relations. In H. Butterfield and M. Wight, eds., *Diplomatic Investigations*, George Allen & Unwin, 89–131.

Wille, T. and S. Schindler. (2019). How Can We Criticize International Practices? *International Studies Quarterly*, 63(4), 1014–24.

Winch, P. (1958). *The Idea of Social Science and Its Relation to Philosophy*, Routledge and Kegan Paul.

Winston, C. (2017). Norm Structure, Diffusion, and Evolution: A Conceptual Approach, *European Journal of International Relations*, Online First.

Wittgenstein, L. (1953). *Philosophical Investigations*, translated by Elizabeth Anscombe, Macmillan.

(2009 [1957]). *Philosophical Investigations*, Wiley-Blackwell.

Wolf, S. (2010). *Meaning in Life and Why It Matters*, Princeton University Press.

Wood, J. H. (2005). *A History of Central Banking in Great Britain and the United States*, Cambridge University Press.

Woodward, S. L. (2007). Do the Root Causes of Civil War Matter? On Using Knowledge to Improve Peacebuilding Interventions, *Journal of Intervention and Statebuilding*, 1(2), 143–70.

"Word of the Year 2016 is…" English Oxford Living Dictionaries. Available at: https://en.oxforddictionaries.com/word-of-the-year/word-of-the-year-2016.

"Word of the Year: Frequently Asked Questions." English Oxford Living Dictionaries. Available at: https://en.oxforddictionaries.com/word-of-the-year/word-of-the-year-faqs.

Young, O. (1982). Regime Dynamics: The Rise and Fall of International Regimes. *International Organization*, 36(2), 277–97.

Zalewski, M. (2000). *Feminism after Postmodernism: Theorizing through Practice*, Routledge.

Zanotti, L. (2011). *Governing Disorder: UN Peace Operations, International Security and Democratization in the Post Cold War Era*, University of Pennsylvania Press.

Zeilinger, A. (2005). *Einsteins Schleier: Die neue Welt der Quantenphysik*, C. H. Beck.

Zimmer, C. (2006 [2001]). *Evolution: The Triumph of an Idea*, Harper Perennial.

Zimmermann, L. (2016). Same Same or Different? Norm Diffusion Between Resistance, Compliance, and Localization in Post-Conflict States, *International Studies Perspectives*, 17(1), 98–115.

Zimmermann, L., N. Deitelhoff and M. Lesch. (2018). Unlocking the Agency of the Governed: Contestation and Norm Dynamics, *Third World Thematics: A TWQ Journal*, Online First.

Index

For EU product safety concerns, contact us at Calle de José Abascal, 56–1°, 28003 Madrid, Spain or eugpsr@cambridge.org.

www.ingramcontent.com/pod-product-compliance
Ingram Content Group UK Ltd.
Pitfield, Milton Keynes, MK11 3LW, UK
UKHW020359140625
459647UK00020B/2552